OECD Reviews of Digital Transformation

Going Digital in Brazil

OECD
BETTER POLICIES FOR BETTER LIVES

Please cite this publication as:
OECD (2020), *Going Digital in Brazil*, OECD Reviews of Digital Transformation, OECD Publishing, Paris, *https://doi.org/10.1787/e9bf7f8a-en*.

ISBN 978-92-64-71078-8 (print)
ISBN 978-92-64-93859-5 (pdf)

OECD Reviews of Digital Transformation
ISSN 2708-9150 (print)
ISSN 2708-9169 (online)

Photo credits: Cover © Adobe Stock/Image design © Taï Marc Le Than.

Corrigenda to publications may be found on line at: *www.oecd.org/about/publishing/corrigenda.htm*.

Foreword

OECD Reviews of Digital Transformation: Going Digital in Brazil is part of a new series of OECD country reviews. The OECD Reviews of Digital Transformation analyse recent developments of the digital economy in countries, review policies related to digitalisation and make recommendations to increase policy coherence in this area.

Going Digital in Brazil examines recent developments in infrastructures for the digital economy, telecom markets, and related regulations and policies in Brazil. It reviews trends in the use of digital technologies by individuals, businesses and the government, and examines policies to foster diffusion. The Review also examines opportunities and challenges raised by digitalisation in key areas and analyses policy responses to these changes. The areas covered range from innovation and skills to digital security and data governance.

The Review considers these policies in relation to their coherence among different domains in order to foster synergies across government ministries and institutions, based on the OECD Going Digital Integrated Policy Framework.

Going Digital in Brazil was undertaken following an invitation by the Ministry of Science, Technology, Innovations and Communications of Brazil (MCTIC),[1] which also provided financial support. The Review was carried out by the OECD Directorate for Science, Technology and Innovation under the auspices of the OECD Committee on Digital Economy Policy.

The Review was prepared by a team led by Vincenzo Spiezia and including Laurent Bernat, Elettra Ronchi, Lucia Russo, Jan Tscheke, Verena Weber and Akira Yoshida, under the supervision of Anne Carblanc and Audrey Plonk, respectively former and current Head of the Digital Economy Division. Chapter 2 is based on the findings of the *OECD Telecommunication and Broadcasting Review of Brazil*, prepared by a team led by Verena Weber. The Review has also benefitted from comments by Andrea Andrenelli, Francesca Casalini, Javier Lopez Gonzales, Federico Guanais, Béatrice Guerard, Gernot Hutschenreiter, Mariane Piccinin Barbieri, Dirk Pilat, Sebastian Schich, Barbara Ubaldi, Reyer Van der Vlies and Joao Vasconcelos.

The authors owe much to the support and co-operation of the Ministry of Science, Technology, Innovations and Communications of Brazil, in particular Julio Semeghini Neto, Executive Secretary; Vitor Menezes, Secretary of Telecommunications; Miriam Wimmer, Director, Department of Telecommunications Services; Daniel B. Cavalcanti, Coordinator, Digital Agenda and Regulatory Affairs; and Pedro G. Menezes, Public Policy Specialist.

The Review draws on the results of a series of interviews with a wide range of stakeholders during three missions to Brazil in December 2018, March 2019 and January 2020, including: Abraao Silva (Anatel), Achilles Zaluar Neto (MRE), Alberto Paradisi (CPqD), Alcimar Rangel (GSI), Alexandre Barbosa (CETIC.br), Alexandre Pedro (MEC), Alexsander Moreira (MEC), Ana C. Murahovschi (MS), André Rauen (IPEA), Andriei Gutierrez (IBM), Anna C. de Carvalho (MEC), Artur Coimbra de Oliveira (MCTIC), Breno S. Lobo (BCB), Caio Megale (ME), Carlos A. da Costa (ME), Carlos A. Souza (ITS), Carlos da Fonseca (MRE), Ciro Avelino (MPDG), Cristiane Rauen (MEC), Cristine Hoepers (CERT.br), Daniela Schetino (MCTIC), Demi Getschko (CGI.br), Edson L. Bolfe (Embrapa), Eduardo Magrani (ITS), Fabricio Juntolli (MA), Fernanda De Negri (IPEA), Fernando B. Meneguin (MJ), George Marques (MRE), Guido Amin

1. At the time this report was finalised, provisional measure 980/2020 of 10 June 2020 separated the MCTIC into two ministries: the Ministry of Communications and the Ministry of Science, Technology and Innovations.

Naves (MD), Guilherme Almeida (ENAP), Igor Nazareth (ME), Ingrid Barth (ABFintechs), Irecê Kauss (BNDES), Jeferson Nacif (Anatel), José A. C. Vasco (CVM), José G.S. Gontijo (MCTIC), José L. Gordon (EMBRAPII), José S. Aranha (Anprotec), José V. Santini (PR), Karla A. Cavalcanti (MCTIC), Karla Crosara Rezende (Anatel) , Leonardo A. F. Palhares (E-NET), Lisandro Z. Granville (SBC), Lorena B.C. Passos (TCU), Luca Belli (FGV), Lucia Dellagnelo (CIEB), Luciana Mancini (MRE), Luciano B. Timm (MJ), Luis C. R. França (MA), Luis Felipe S. Monteiro (ME), Marcelo A. Righi (GSI), Marcelo Buz (ITI), Marcelo de L. Souza (PR), Marcelo M. Ramos (ME), Marcelo P. dos Guaranys (ME), Marcelo P. Fontenele (GSI), Marcia Lins e Silva (ME), Márcio G. Barroso (FINEP), Marcos Allemand (SERPRO), Marcos Carvalho (ABFinTechs), Marcos Pinto (PR), Nelson Simões (RNP), Nilo Pasquali (Anatel), Nilton Hamatsu (FINEP), Otavio V. Caixeta (MCTIC), Paula F. Leitão (BCB), Paulo Alvim (MCTIC), Paulo S. Pagliusi (KPMG), Rafael Ansaloni (FINEP), Raquel R. Abdala (ME), Renata Carvalho (ME), Renato A. Oliveira (MCTIC), Ricardo Rivera (BNDES), Ruy Ramos (ITI), Sabrina Passos (GSI), Samir Nobre Maia (MCTIC), Sérgio Alves Jr. (MCTIC) , Sergio P. Gallindo (Brasscom), Sergio Sgobbi (Brasscom), Sheila Pires (Anprotec), Silvia Massruhá (Embrapa), Sylvio Koury (PR), Tatiana Ribeiro (MBC), Vinicius Lages (SEBRAE), Walter L.A. Cunha (CGU), Wilson D. Wellisch (MCTIC) and Ysrael Rodrigues (PR).

On 15 May 2020, the OECD Council invited Costa Rica to become a Member. At the time of preparation of this publication, the deposit of Costa Rica's instrument of accession to the OECD Convention was pending and therefore Costa Rica does not appear in the list of OECD Members and is not included in the OECD zone aggregates.

Table of Contents

Acronyms, abbreviations and units of measure

ABDI	Industrial Development Agency *Agência para o Desenvolvimento da Indústria*
AI	Artificial intelligence
Anatel	National Telecommunications Agency *Agência Nacional de Telecomunicações*
Ancine	National Film Agency *Agência Nacional do Cinema*
ANPD	National Data Protection Authority *Autoridade Nacional de Proteção de Dados*
AUD	Australian dollar
BCB	Central Bank of Brazil *Banco Central do Brasil*
BERD	Business expenditure on research and development
BNCC	National Common Curricular Base for Basic Education *Base Nacional Comum Curricular*
BNDES	Brazilian Development Bank *Banco Nacional de Desenvolvimento Econômico e Social*
BRICS	Brazil, Russian Federation, India, China and South Africa
BRIICS	Brazil, Russian Federation, India, Indonesia, China and South Africa
BRL	Brazilian real
CAD	Canadian dollar
CADE	Administrative Council for Economic Defence *Conselho Administrativo de Defesa Econômica*
CAPES	Foundation for the Coordination for the Improvement of Higher Education Personnel *Coordenação de Aperfeiçoamento de Pessoal de Nível Superior*
CBAP	Brazilian Commission of Precision Agriculture *Comissão Brasileiro de Aquapaisagismo*
CDC	Consumer Defence Code
CERT	Computer emergency response team *Centro de Estudos, Resposta e Tratamento de Incidentes de Segurança*
CERTI	Centres of Reference in Innovative Technologies *Centros de Referência em Tecnologias Inovadoras*
CESAR	Centre for Studies and Advanced Systems of Recife *Centro de Estudos Avançados do Recife*
CETIC.br	Regional Centre for Studies on the Development of the Information Society *Centro Regional de Estudos para o Desenvolvimento da Sociedade da Informação*
CFM	Federal Medical Council *Conselho Federal de Medicina*
CGI.br	Brazilian Internet Steering Committee *Comitê Gestor da Internet no Brasil*
CGSI	Information Security Management Committee *Comitê Gestor da Segurança da Informação*
CIDE	Contribution for Intervention in the Economic Domain *Contribuição de Intervenção no Domínio Econômico*

CMN	National Monetary Council *Conselho Monetário Nacional*
CNI	National Confederation of Industry *Confederação Nacional da Indústria*
CNPDP	National Council for the Protection of Personal Data and Privacy *Conselho Nacional de Proteção de Dados e Privacidade*
CNPq	National Council for Scientific and Technological Development *Conselho Nacional de Desenvolvimento Científico e Tecnológico*
CPA	Applied research centre *Centro de pesquisa aplicada*
CRM	Customer Relationship Management
CSIRT	Computer security incident response team
CTIR	Government Response Team for Computer Security Incidents *Centro de Tratamento e Resposta a Incidentes Cibernéticos de Governo*
CVM	Securities and Exchange Commission *Comissão de Valores Mobiliários*
Decon	State Consumer Protection and Defense Programme *Programa Estadual de Proteção e Defesa do Consumidor*
DIFAL	Difference between the ICMS rate of the destination state and the interstate rate *Diferencial de Aliquotas do ICMS*
DIP	Digital inclusion point
DNI	National Identification Document *Documento Nacional de Identificação*
DPDC	Department of Protection and Defence of Consumers *Departamento de Proteção e Defesa do Consumidor*
DSIC	Department of Information and Communications Security *Departamento de Segurança da Informação e Comunicações*
ECT	Brazilian Post and Telegraph Company *Empresa Brasileira de Correios e Telégrafos*
Embrapa	Brazilian Agricultural Research Corporation *Empresa Brasileira de Pesquisa Agropecuária*
EMBRAPII	Brazilian Company for Research and Industrial Innovation *Empresa Brasileira de Pesquisa e Inovação Industrial*
ENAP	National School of Public Administration *Escola Nacional de Administração Pública*
ENCTI	National Strategy for Science, Technology and Innovation *Estratégia Nacional de Ciência, Tecnologia e Inovação*
ERP	Enterprise Resource Planning
ESALQ	Luiz de Queiroz College of Agriculture *Escola Superior de Agricultura Luiz de Queiroz*
EU	European Union
EUR	Euro
FAP	State research foundation
FAPESP	State Research Foundation of the State of São Paulo
FDI	Foreign direct investment
FINEP	Brazilian Agency for Innovation and Research *Financiadora de Estudos e Projetos*
FIRST	Forum of Incident Response and Security Team
FISTEL	Telecommunications Oversight Fund *Fundo de Fiscalização das Telecomunicações*

FNDCT	National Fund for Scientific and Technological Development *Fundo Nacional de Desenvolvimento Científico e Tecnológico*
FTA	Free-to-air
GaaP	Government as a platform
GB	Gigabyte
GDP	Gross domestic product
GDPL	General Data Protection Law
GDPR	General Data Protection Regulation
GESAC	Electronic Government Citizen Services programme *Governo Eletrônico - Serviço de Atendimento ao Cidadão*
GHG	Greenhouse gas
GSI/PR	Institutional Security Cabinet of the Presidency of the Republic *Gabinete de Segurança Institucional/Presidência da República*
GST	Goods and services tax
HEI	Higher education institution
ICIO	Inter-Country Input-Output
ICLF	Integrated Crop-Livestock-Forest
ICMS	Tax on the movement of goods, transport services and telecommunication services *Imposto sobre Circulação de Mercadorias e Serviços*
ICT	Information and communication technology
IDP	Industry digital plan
IIA	Israel Innovation Authority
IMDA	Infocomm Media Development Authority
INPI	National Institute for Patents *Instituto Nacional da Propriedade Industrial*
IoT	Internet of Things
IPI	Tax for industrialised products *Imposto sobre Produtos Industrializados*
ISP	Internet service provider
ITI	National Institute of Information Security *Instituto Nacional de Tecnologia da Informação*
IXP	Internet exchange point
JEI	Young innovative enterprise *Jeune entreprise innovante*
JEU	Young innovative university *Jeune entreprise universitaire*
kbps	Kilobits per second
km	Kilometre
km^2	Square kilometre
LAB	Laboratory of Financial Innovations
LGPD	General Data Protection Law *Lei Geral de Proteção de Dados*
M2M	Machine to machine
MAPA	Ministry of Agriculture, Livestock and Supply *Ministério da Agricultura, Pecuária e Abastecimento*
Mbps	Megatibs per second
MCTIC	Ministry of Science, Technology, Innovations and Communications *Ministério da Ciência, Tecnologia, Inovações e Comunicações*
MEC	Ministry of Education *Ministério da Educação*

MNE	Multinational enterprise
MNO	Mobile network operator
MPDFT	Public Ministry of Federal Districts and Territories *Ministério Público do Distrito Federal e Territórios*
ms	Millisecond
MVNO	Mobile virtual network operator
NCDS	National Consumer's Defence System
NIC.br	Brazilian Network Information Centre *Núcleo de Informação e Coordenação*
NIT	Technological innovation hub *Núcleo de inovação tecnológica*
NSCP	National School of Consumer Protection
OGP	Open Government Partnership
OTT	Over-the-top
P2P	Peer-to-peer
PADIS	Semiconductor Technological Development Support Program *Programa de Apoio ao Desenvolvimento Tecnológico da Indústria de Semicondutores*
PEA	Privacy enforcement authority
PISA	Programme for International Student Assessment
PKI	Public Key Infrastructure
PL	Law Project *Projeto de Lei*
PMP	Privacy management programme
PNE	National Education Plan *Plano Nacional de Educação*
PNSI	National Information Security Policy *Política de Segurança da Informação*
PPB	Basic production process *Processo produtivo básico*
PPH	Patent prosecution highway
PPIs	Programmes and Projects of National Interest in the Areas of Information and Communication Technologies *Programa e Projeto de Interesse Nacional nas Áreas de Tecnologias da Informação e Comunicação*
PPP	Purchasing power parity
Procon	Consumer's Protection and Defence Authority
PSG	Productivity Solutions Grant
R&D	Research and development
RIA	Regulatory impact assessment
SEBRAE	Brazilian Micro and Small Business Support Service *Serviço Brasileiro de Apoio às Micro e Pequenas Empresas*
Senacon	National Consumer Secretariat *Secretaria Nacional do Consumidor*
SENAI	National Service for Industrial Training *Serviço Nacional de Aprendizagem Industrial*
SENAR	National Rural Apprenticeship Service *Serviço Nacional de Aprendizagem Rural*
SGD	Secretariat of Digital Government *Secretaria de Governo Digital*
SINDEC	National Information System for Consumer Protection *Sistema Nacional de Informações de Defesa do Consumidor*

SISP	Information Technology Resource Management System *Sistema de Administração dos Recursos de Tecnologia da Informação*
SMEs	Small and medium-sized enterprises
SSO	Single sign-on
STEM	Science, technology, engineering and mathematics
STI	Science, technology and innovation
SUS	Universal healthcare system *Sistema Único de Saúde*
SUSEP	Private Insurance Regulator *Superintendência de Seguros Privados*
SVOD	Subscription video on demand
Tbps	Terabits per second
TCU	Federal Court of Accounts *Tribunal de Contas da União*
TRAINS	Trade Analysis Information System
TTO	Technology transfer office
TVOD	Transactional video on demand
USD	United States dollar
VAT	Value-added tax
VC	Venture capital
VoD	Video on demand

Executive Summary

Going Digital in Brazil examines opportunities and challenges raised by digitalisation in Brazil, looks at current policies and makes recommendations to improve them, based on the OECD Going Digital Integrated Policy Framework. The Review focuses on selected components of the framework according to the priorities expressed by Brazil.

Enhancing connectivity

High-quality communication services at competitive prices are crucial for Brazil to go digital. Fixed and mobile broadband penetration is similar to countries in the region, but well below the OECD average. Fixed broadband prices tend to be higher. Expanding quality broadband to rural and remote areas remains a main challenge.

Brazil should take further action to enhance connectivity:

- create a converged and independent regulator for the communication and broadcasting sectors
- reform the legal framework to introduce a simple class-licensing regime for communication and broadcasting services
- enhance co-ordination among federal, state and municipal levels to promote broadband deployment
- merge sectoral funds into a single fund to support further development of the digital economy
- foster the Internet of Things (IoT) by abolishing fees and establishing a separate IoT numbering plan
- carefully design the upcoming 5G auction so as to ensure competition in the market
- implement the recommendations of the 2019 *OECD Peer Review of Competition Law and Policy*.

Increasing adoption and use of digital technologies

Brazil has made significant progress in improving access to the Internet in recent years. Yet, 23% of the adult population had never used the Internet in 2018. Brazilian firms, particularly micro-enterprises, lag behind those in OECD countries in their use of digital technologies.

Brazil should put in place a wider set of policies to upgrade digital skills and address the digital divide:

- raise awareness on the benefits of digital technologies, targeting individuals with low digital uptake and micro-enterprises
- introduce tax incentives for technological upgrade, training and ICT investments for all firms
- remove regulatory barriers to the development of e-commerce; harmonise the rate of the tax on goods and services (ICMS) across states
- facilitate the formal recognition of skills acquired in online courses and vocational training
- increase funding for students in science, technology, engineering, and mathematics
- push forward with the recommendations of the *OECD Digital Government Review of Brazil: Towards the Digital Transformation of the Public Sector*.

Enhancing trust

Brazil has taken significant steps to enhance trust in the digital environment by strengthening digital security, personal data and consumer protection.

To further enhance trust, Brazil should:

- implement the National Cybersecurity Strategy by establishing a wide community of digital security leaders from the public and private sectors
- foster a decentralised approach to digital security governance, with ministries and agencies leading in their area of competence and the GSI/PR as co-ordinator
- strengthen multi-stakeholder dialogue on digital security, building on the Brazilian Internet governance model
- re-evaluate and amend the conditions establishing the National Data Protection Authority (ANPD) in Article 55-A of Law 13.709 to ensure that the Authority operates with full independence from the date of its establishment
- ensure that the rules for appointing the ANPD's Board of Directors and the National Council for the Protection of Personal Data are transparent, fair and based on technical expertise
- guarantee an adequate and predictable budget to the ANPD through a transparent process
- further the implementation of the OECD *Recommendation of the Council on Consumer Protection in E-Commerce*.

Unleashing digital innovation

Brazil's R&D expenditures relative to GDP are above Latin American and Caribbean countries, but still behind the OECD countries. Furthermore, business expenditures account for a smaller share of total R&D in Brazil, particularly in the ICT sector.

To strengthen digital innovation, Brazil should:

- orient public support to digital innovation towards mission-oriented research, building on the model of the National IoT Plan
- ensure adequate, stable and predictable public resources for research in ICTs
- develop clear roadmaps for advancement in key digital technologies, e.g. artificial intelligence and data analytics, in co-operation with all stakeholders
- reform the Informatics Law so as to strengthen its support to innovation
- make the Good Law more suitable for young innovative firms through cash-refund or carry-forward provisions
- increase knowledge transfer between businesses and academia
- strengthen innovation hubs for small and medium-sized enterprises; open e-procurement to innovative solutions from start-ups.

Fostering the digital transformation of the economy

Brazil has developed an encompassing strategy for digital transformation, with a focus on new, data-driven business models in agriculture, industry and services. Further policy actions should be taken in the following sectors:

Agribusiness

- Foster a national innovation network and testbed environment for agribusiness.
- Develop an inclusive framework for agricultural data governance.
- Align the National IoT Plan and the Strategic Agenda for Precision Agriculture.

Manufacturing

- Enhance adoption of foreign technology.
- Reduce taxation uncertainty for new, digitally enabled business models.
- Strengthen governance and co-ordination mechanisms for Industry 4.0 policies.

Fintech

- Create a level playing field for new payment institutions.
- Foster competition in the credit market .
- Enhance co-ordination among financial regulators and promote regulatory sandboxes.

e-Health

- Validate and scale up Brazil's e-Health programme, Connect SUS, across all regions.
- Enhance interoperability and co-ordination between public and private health systems.
- Update the regulatory framework for healthcare data protection and information security.

Building a whole-of-government approach

In 2018, Brazil issued its Digital Transformation Strategy (E-Digital) for the period 2018-21. The strategy aims to co-ordinate different governmental initiatives on digital issues.

In order to develop a whole-of-government approach to digital transformation policies, Brazil should:

- clarify the rules for decision making in the Inter-ministerial Committee for Digital Transformation (CITDigital)
- integrate CITDigital's decisions into the regular policy-making process, for instance though a bill by the Presidency of the Republic
- establish clear appropriations for the implementation of E-Digital in the budgetary law.

Chapter 1

BRAZIL IN THE DIGITAL TRANSFORMATION: OPPORTUNITIES AND CHALLENGES

This chapter sets the scene for the Review. It begins with an overview of the recent economic and social trends in Brazil and the opportunities the digital transformation could provide in improving the life and well-being of citizens. It then presents the current government response, focusing on Brazil's E-Digital Strategy. Next, it introduces the OECD Going Digital Integrated Policy Framework. The final section presents an outline of the Review.

Recent economic and social trends in Brazil

From the turn of the century until the recession in 2014-16, Brazil combined fast economic growth and remarkable social progress. Between 2001 and 2013, real gross domestic product (GDP) grew by 3.5% a year on average, a rate much higher than in the OECD (1.9%), though lower than in Chile (4.5%) and the other BRIICS (Brazil, the Russian Federation, India, Indonesia, China and South Africa) countries (6.2%). The number of poor – defined as people with less than USD PPP 5.50 per day – was cut in half between 2001 and 2014, falling to 18% of the population. The unemployment rate also fell, from 9.8% in 2003 to 6.5% in 2014.

The severe recession from 2014 to 2016 seems to have put a halt on this virtuous cycle. Following the contraction in GDP (-2.1% a year) over this period, the Brazilian economy grew at a much lower annual rate (1.4%) in the following three years (2017-19). The unemployment rate jumped to 12% in 2018 while the number of poor increased by 7.4 million. Inequality remains high by comparison to the OECD, with the richest 10% of the population receiving 42% of total income. Following the Covid-19 crisis, the economy is projected to contract by 7.4-9.1% in 2020 while unemployment is predicted to reach historic highs (OECD, 2020a).

More fundamentally, the favourable constellation that fuelled growth until the 2014 recession – an increasing labour force coupled with rising commodity prices – now seems to be exhausted. Brazil's population is ageing rapidly and public expenditure is proving increasingly difficult to finance (OECD, 2018a), resulting in the government launching structural reforms, such as the recent reform of the pension system.

Tackling these issues requires a variety of complementary measures. Among them, policies to enhance digital transformation have a key role to play. Digital technologies are an enabler for innovation and productivity in firms. High-speed broadband networks provide individuals and firms with access to government services and international markets, and can help to reduce inequalities. Digitalisation may help to reduce regulatory burdens and informality. It can also increase the efficiency of public spending, therefore providing more resources for policies. Online educational resources offer new tools for teaching and provide individuals and workers with new opportunities for training and skills upgrading.

At the same time, the digital transformation may exacerbate existing inequalities, in particular between high- and low-skilled individuals, large and small firms, as well as urban and rural regions. Policies are key to ensure that the potential benefits from the digital transformation are shared across the economy and society.

Digital transformation can fuel productivity growth

Between 2001 and 2013, yearly labour productivity growth in Brazil was slightly above the OECD average (1.5% versus 1.2%), but well below that in the other BRIICS countries (5.1%) (Figure 1.1). Brazil's productivity decreased during the 2014-16 recession (-1.3% a year) but started growing again in 2017-19 (0.4%), albeit at a much slower rate than in the OECD and the other BRIICS countries (0.9% and 3.4%, respectively). By 2019, labour productivity in Brazil was only one-fourth the level it was in the United States. The productivity gap was large also relative to Chile (-34%), Mexico (-30%) and Argentina (-26%).

Digital technologies have the potential to increase productivity in firms across all economic sectors. Big data and data analytics can help firms better understand their production processes, the needs of their clients and partners, and the overall business environment. Digital technologies can also improve firms' access to skills and talent, such as through better job recruitment sites and in the outsourcing of key business functions, all of which can help improve their performance. New technologies can also facilitate access to a range of financing instruments. Finally, online platforms can support the productivity of lower tech service firms, for example by providing them with booking facilities and efficient matching algorithms based on consumer review and rating systems (OECD, 2019a).

Figure 1.1. Labour productivity growth in selected countries, 2001-19

Output per employed person, average yearly growth rates

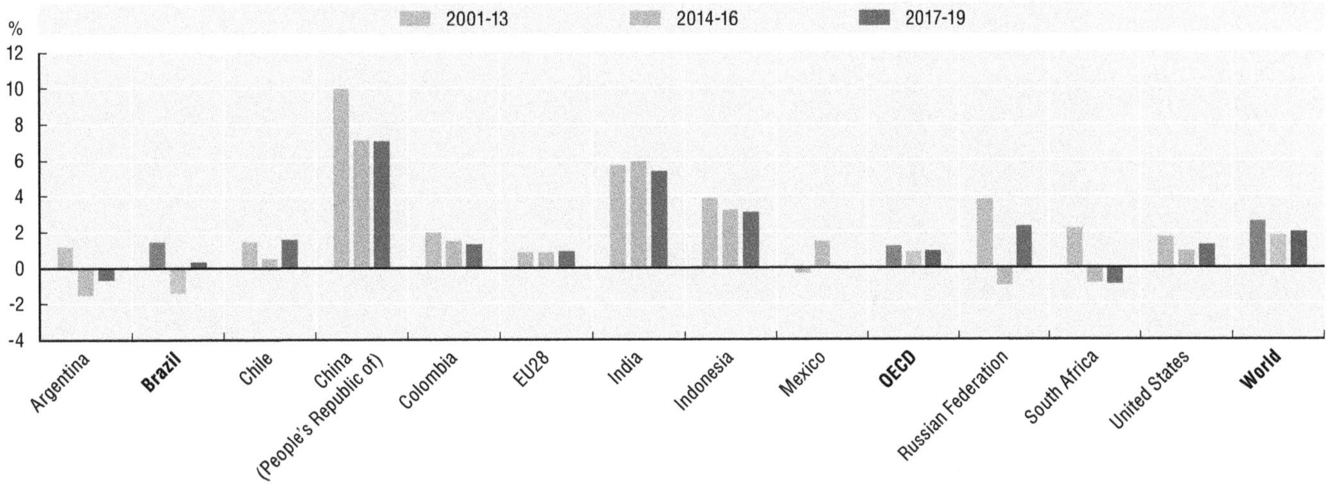

Source: The Conference Board (2019), "Output, labor and labor productivity, 1950-2019 (adjusted version)", *https://www.conference-board.org/data/economydatabase/index.cfm?id=27762* (accessed on 6 May 2020).

The Internet of Things (IoT), in particular, has significant potential for process innovations and efficiency gains. Modern sensors make it possible to collect vast amounts of data, which can be processed by smart devices and fed into production decisions. The resulting big data sets can create further benefits, including the integration of new services and service providers into the value chain (OECD, 2017a).

Despite widespread access to the Internet, Brazilian enterprises lag behind those in OECD countries in the use of the Internet and digital technologies, largely as a result of low uptake by small and medium-sized enterprises (SMEs). Advanced manufacturing – the combination of digital technologies, robotics, IoT and data analytics to improve production processes and product quality – is still at an early stage (see Chapter 3).

In June 2019, Brazil launched a National IoT Plan aiming to "foster the implementation of IoT as a sustainable development instrument for the Brazilian society, capable of increasing competitiveness, strengthen national production chains and promote higher quality of life" (Decree 9.854 of 25 June 2019). The plan specifies 75 initiatives, organised along 4 transversal thematic axes. Agribusiness and manufacturing are among the plan's priority sectors (see Chapter 6).

Improving skills for a digital world

Brazil has made substantial progress over the last decades in facilitating access to education. However, despite the increase in education expenditures and the widespread access to free-of-charge primary and secondary education, educational attainment remains low (Figure 1.2). More than 50% of Brazilians have not attained a secondary education, and 17% did not complete primary education. This is well above the OECD average of 2%. Enrolment in professional training and technical degrees is low, with only 3.8% of secondary students choosing technical courses. Low performance on the OECD's Programme for International Student Assessment (PISA) suggests a low quality of education as well as large disparities in outcomes depending on the socio-economic background of students.

Low skills prevent Internet users and workers from using digital technologies effectively and from benefiting from them, thus creating a second-level digital divide (OECD, 2019c). A lack of skills is also a significant reason for Brazil's low productivity levels (OECD, 2018a). Brazilian employers report having difficulties in recruiting technicians, skilled trades and engineers. ICT professionals represent the second largest shortage (OECD, 2018b).

Figure 1.2. Adult population with a tertiary education, 2018

As a percentage of population aged 25-64

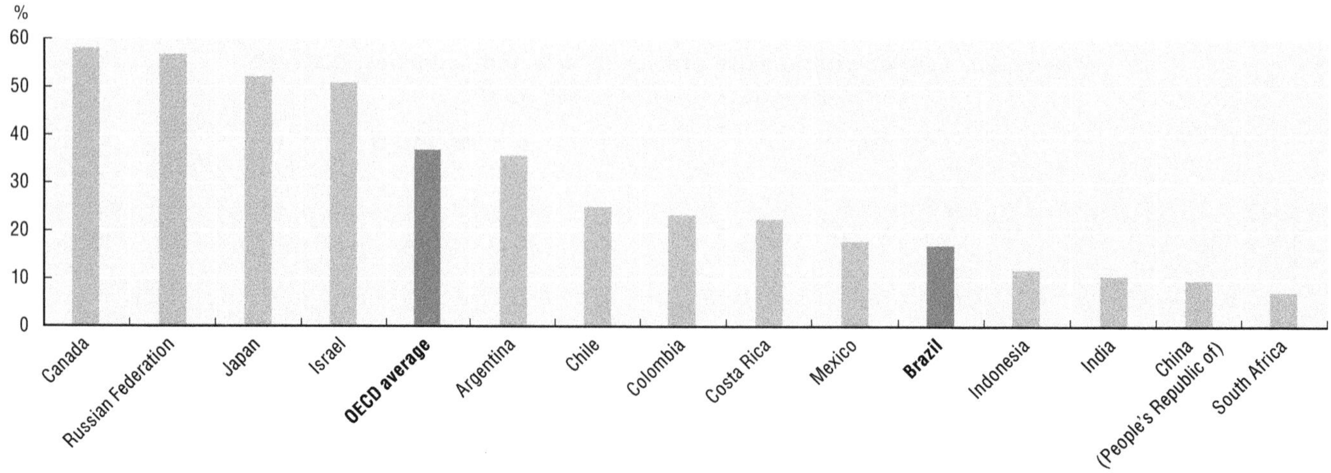

Source: OECD (2019b), *OECD Education at a Glance* (database), *http://dotstat.oecd.org/index.aspx?queryid=93189* (accessed on 6 May 2020).

Brazil has put in place an online education programme for capacity building in the IT sector – the Brazil More Digital (Brasil Mais Digital) – directed at young people aged 16-25. It has also created new vocational training opportunities under the umbrella of the Pronatec programme. While progress has been made, high dropout rates suggest that these programmes could be improved so as to better serve training needs and match skills demand. There is also scope for better aligning university curricula to the job profiles in demand in the labour market (OECD, 2017b).

While creating demand for new skills, digital technologies and big data can also help increase the effectiveness of education and training programmes. Analysis of online vacancies provides more timely information on skills demand across small geographic areas. Big data allows tracking and evaluating the labour market outcomes of participants in vocational education and training, thus providing information on how to improve vocational education and training. Collecting and disseminating timely information on line on the performance of higher education institutions, e.g. universities, helps prospective students take informed decisions.

Online courses and other open educational resources can be used to improve the digital skills across a broader share of the population, in particular among elderly people, low-income and low-skilled individuals as well as those living in remote areas. Several countries have taken initiatives to develop digital skills either for the whole population or for targeted groups that Brazil could learn from (see Chapter 3).

Digital transformation offers opportunities for more competitive markets

Competition is key for creating incentives to invest in the most efficient production technologies, to introduce new innovative products and to reach global best practice (Pinheiro, 2013; IEDI, 2014). However, entry barriers, low integration into the global economy and targeted industrial policies have led to low competition in the Brazilian economy (OECD, 2018a).

According to The World Bank Doing Business indicators, Brazil scores 137th out of 190 economies surveyed for the ease of doing business (Figure 1.3). For instance, starting a business requires 11 procedures in Brazil and takes 18.5 days, while Chile, Colombia and Mexico require fewer procedures that can be accomplished in no more than 11 days. Brazil's regulatory requirements on product markets have long been significantly more cumbersome and restrictive than in OECD countries, and lack transparency and simplicity (OECD, forthcoming). A complex tax system and limited access to credit further restrict internal competition, keeping the relatively large number of small firms in the sector from growing into mid-sized competitors.

Digital tools can help simplify regulatory procedures for market entry and licensing, which are not only more cumbersome and restrictive in Brazil than in OECD countries, they also lack transparency and simplicity. They can also reduce compliance costs with the tax system. New business models in the financial sector, e.g. so-called Fintech, could significantly enhance competition in the market and improve access to credit.

The length and uncertainty of judicial procedures further hamper competition, potentially leading to high costs to firms. Enforcing a standard debt contract takes 731 days in São Paulo, compared to 290 in Seoul, 341 in Mexico City, 426 in Lima or 480 in Santiago (The World Bank, 2019a). Implementing digital judicial files would improve the efficiency of the judicial system. Online platforms can also support the development of out-of-court solutions to conflicts.

Figure 1.3. Ease of Doing Business ranking, 2019

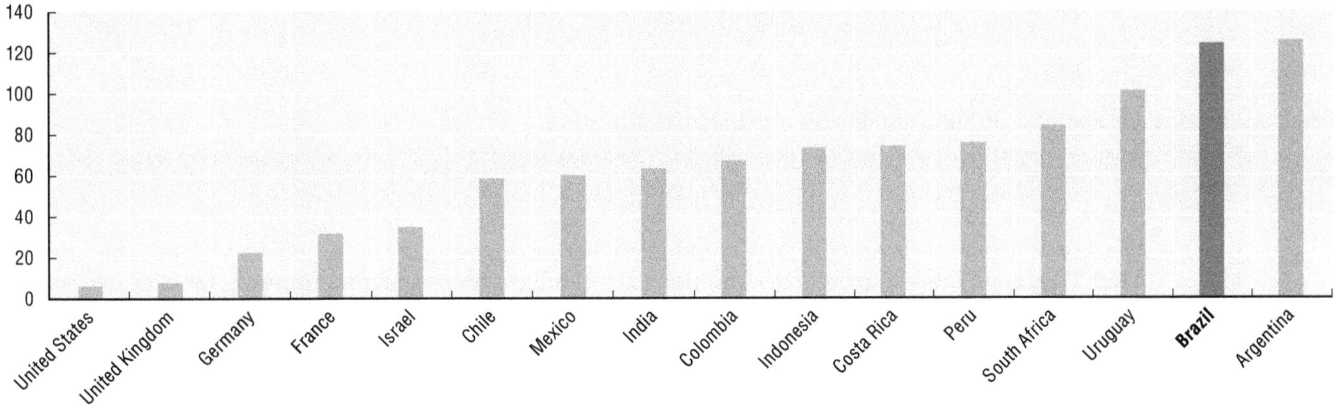

Source: The World Bank (2019a), *Doing Business* (database), *https://www.doingbusiness.org/en/doingbusiness* (accessed on 6 May 2020).

E-commerce has the potential to increase firms' access to larger markets, especially for SMEs. However, e-commerce in Brazil has not reached the full potential of a market of 107.5 million adult Internet users. Only 21% of enterprises sold on line in 2019. In 2017, e -commerce represented just 6% of total retail sales, compared to 20% in the People's Republic of China (hereafter China), 19% in Korea and 12% in the United States (McKinsey, 2019). Nonetheless, e-commerce sales in Brazil grew at an annual rate of 16% in 2019, far exceeding growth in the economy as a whole (Ebit Nielsen, 2020). Privacy concerns (64%) and the inability to pay on line (38%) are among the main reasons reported by consumers for not ordering on line (see Chapter 3).

To address some of the regulatory obstacles mentioned above, the National Congress recently approved a law establishing the "Declaration of the Rights of Economic Freedom" (Law 13.874 of 20 September 2019). The law sets four principles: 1) freedom in doing business; 2) the good faith of individuals; 3) subsidiary, minimal and exceptional intervention of the state on doing business; and 4) recognition of the vulnerability of the individual before the state.

A proposal for a Legal Framework for Start-ups and Innovative Entrepreneurship (Marco Legal de Startups e Empreendedorismo Inovador) was open for public consultation at the time of writing. The objective of the framework is to improve the business environment for start-ups by facilitating investment in small firms and addressing issues arising from labour regulations and public procurement laws.

Digital tools can make growth more inclusive

Brazil spent over 15% of GDP on social benefits in 2016, corresponding to 35% of total public sector expenditure. Social benefits are responsible for more than half of the increase in primary expenditures and continue to outpace GDP growth. While these programmes are crucial for more inclusive growth, a large share of social benefits is paid to households that are not poor, with a limited impact on inequality and poverty (The World Bank, 2019b) (Figure 1.4).

Figure 1.4. Income share held by the richest 10% of the population, 2017

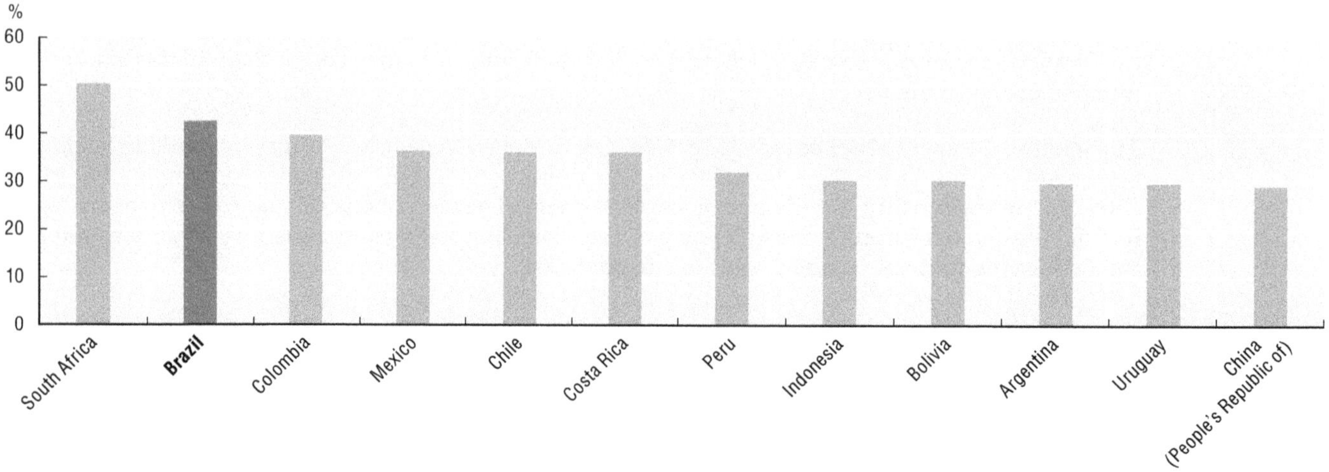

Note: Data for China, Mexico and South Africa refer to 2015, 2016 and 2014, respectively.

Source: The World Bank (2019b), *Poverty and Equity* (database), *https://databank.worldbank.org/reports.aspx?source=poverty-and-equity-database* (accessed on 6 May 2020).

The use of digital tools and big data could allow better targeting social spending to those the most in need. They could also help enforce conditions attached to some social programmes, for example school attendance or medical check-ups for Bolsa Família, thus increasing their effectiveness.

Public health expenditures reached 4.4% of Brazil's GDP in 2018. However, the efficiency of health expenditure appears low compared other countries (OECD, 2015). Digital technologies, such as electronic health records, e-prescriptions and telehealth, can help Brazil improve access to and the quality of healthcare services, particularly in remote areas (see Chapter 5).

Mobile applications could also improve technical assistance to small family farmers, which accounted for 40% of Brazil's total income in 2018, by providing access to digital extension services, technical information (e.g. on plant diseases), as well as to digital services (e.g. accounting and planning software) (see Chapter 6).

Further efforts to reduce informality will be key for more inclusive growth in Brazil, as jobs in the informal economy are lower quality and less productive (OECD, 2018c). By simplifying labour market regulations, the labour market reform in 2017 has strengthened incentives for formal job creation. Brazil can seize the potential of digital tools to reduce informality by simplifying the complex procedures for registering companies and affiliating workers to social security. Digital job platforms could help boost labour market formality by giving tax authorities access to data on such transactions, provided that appropriate regulations are in place (OECD, 2018d).

Cash payments are at the core of informality. Promoting the uptake of digital payment tools would reduce the scope for cash transactions and help unveil informal economic activities. In particular, diffusion of instant payments and other innovative methods could reduce the use of cash even for small transactions and at a negligible cost for users (see Chapter 3).

The Brazilian Digital Transformation Strategy

Recognising the opportunities and challenges raised by the digital transformation, in 2018 the government issued the Brazilian Digital Transformation Strategy (E-Digital), covering a period of four years (2018-21). The strategy co-ordinates different governmental initiatives on digital issues within a coherent framework, to further the digitalisation process of production, promote education and training for the digital environment, and enable economic growth (MCTIC, 2018).

E-Digital is an initiative of the federal government, co-ordinated by the Ministry of Science, Technology, Innovations and Communications (MCTIC). The policy, developed by an Inter-Ministerial Working Group composed of nine government bodies, is the fruit of seven months of meetings, evaluations and public consultations. Representatives of over 30 federal government entities interacted with the core group throughout the process. The strategy also reflects the broad engagement of the private sector, the scientific and academic community, and civil society through many stages of the drafting process.

E-Digital comprises two thematic axes: enablers of the digital transformation and those of the digital transformation *per se* (Figure 1.5).

The enablers include initiatives to create an environment conducive to the digital transformation of the Brazilian economy. Such initiatives include infrastructure and access to information and communication technologies; activities in research, development and innovation; the creation of an appropriate regulatory environment; rules and norms that promote trust in the digital environment; educational and professional skills for the digital economy; and international presence of Brazil.

This enabling environment provides the setting for a number of digital transformation initiatives, both in government and in the private sector. Specific actions relate directly to the process of digital transformation:

- digital transformation of the economy (data-driven economy, connected devices, new business models)
- digital transformation of government (citizenship in the digital world and efficiency in the provision of government services).

Figure 1.5. Axes of the digital transformation in Brazil's Digital Transformation Strategy

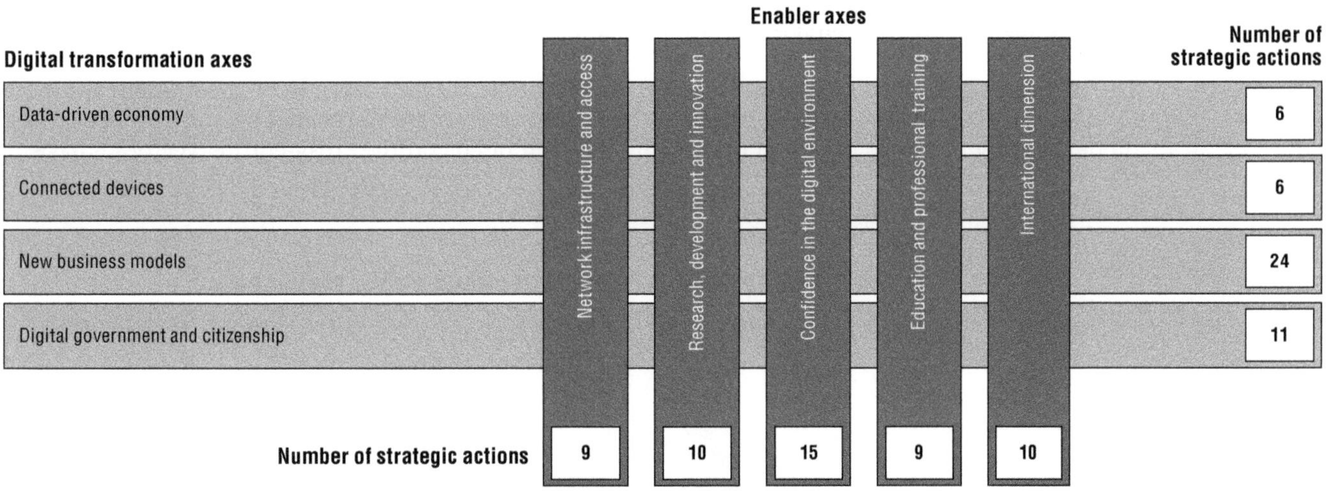

Source: MCTIC (2018), *Brazilian Digital Transformation Strategy: E-Digital, www.mctic.gov.br/mctic/export/sites/institucional/sessaoPublica/arquivos/digitalstrategy.pdf.*

Implementation of the strategy is supported by a steering committee, the Inter-ministerial Committee for Digital Transformation (CITDigital), created by Decree 9.319/2018. CITDigital is chaired by the Government Secretariat of the Presidency of the Republic and is composed of representatives (up to three) of: the Ministry of Foreign Affairs; the Ministry of the Economy; the Ministry of Education; the Ministry of Science, Technology, Innovations and Communications; and the Institutional Security Office of the Presidency of the Republic (Decree 9.804/2019).

E-Digital's strategic actions are assigned to different ministries and agencies with legal mandates for their respective thematic areas; not all of them are directly represented on CITDigital. Nevertheless, such ministries and agencies report on the implementation of such actions to CITDigital and may be invited to participate in specific meetings or thematic groups within the committee.

CITDigital is a federal level committee for horizontal co-ordination, i.e. between ministries. There is also a multi-stakeholder advisory body, with representatives from the private sector, civil society and academia, to provide a cross-cutting approach to CITDigital's mandate. In addition, CITDigital may create thematic sub-committees to discuss specific subjects covered by E-Digital which demand closer attention; such sub-committees may invite experts from government of all levels (federal, state and municipal), the private sector, academia or civil society, to contribute to the debate. The results of thematic sub-committees' work is reported to CITDigital as policy recommendations.

In July 2018, CITDigital established a 2018-19 Action Plan with 34 priority actions out of a total of 100. The action plan details the ministry or institution responsible for each action, whether the action is part of a broader public policy, how it relates to the strategy as a whole, its implementation status, monitoring indicators (or necessary steps to develop and adopt appropriate indicators), among other information. The 2018 Partial Report of the Action Plan was presented and approved by the committee in December 2018.

The budgetary law does not provide any specific appropriation for E-Digital. The strategic actions are projects within the field of responsibility of the different ministries and government agencies, which already have specific budget allocations. Due to the cross-cutting nature of most of E-Digital's initiatives, the funds required for the implementation of one strategic action may correspond to the budget assigned to more than one project or ministry in the executive branch. The MCTIC has a mandate to articulate government institutions and co-ordinate meetings in order to implement and monitor the strategy.

The OECD Going Digital Integrated Policy Framework

As pointed out in E-Digital, digital transformation affects different parts of the economy and society in complex and interrelated ways, making trade-offs between public policy objectives difficult to navigate. *Going Digital in Brazil* aims to help Brazil ensure a coherent and cohesive whole-of-government approach to better respond to the digital transformation and make it work for growth and well-being.

The OECD has developed an Integrated Policy Framework to support a whole-of-government approach to coherent policy making in the digital age. The framework recognises technologies, data and business models as driving forces of digital transformation, and builds on the cross-cutting vector analysis of the transformation across many different policy areas. The framework itself includes seven integrated building blocks (Figure 1.6).

Figure 1.6. OECD Going Digital Integrated Policy Framework

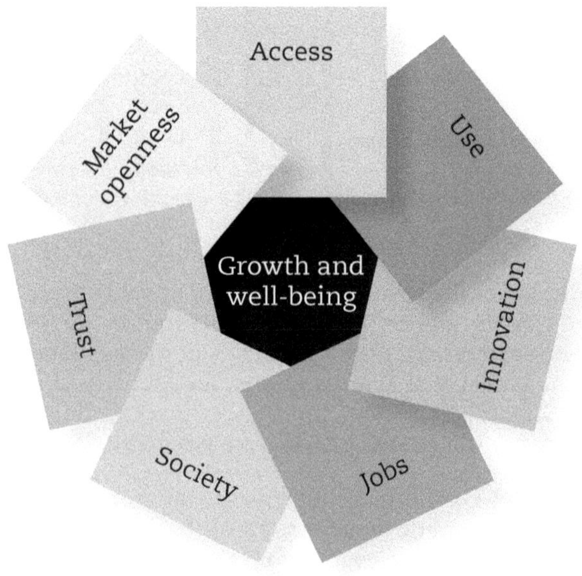

Source: OECD (2019a), *Going Digital: Shaping Policies, Improving Lives*, *https://doi.org/10.1787/9789264312012-en*.

These integrated building blocks do not represent discrete policy domains; rather, each of them brings together multiple policy areas (see more details on each building block below). They also do not stand in isolation, but are related to one another. This configuration underscores that leveraging the benefits and addressing the challenges of digital transformation requires identifying policy areas that are jointly affected and that need to be co-ordinated. It also underscores that all building blocks are needed to make digital transformation work for growth and well-being.

Access

Reliable communications infrastructures and services underpin the use of all digital technologies, and facilitate interactions between connected people, organisations and machines. Similarly, the data that flow through networks have emerged as a source of value in the digital era, but their productive use is predicated on their availability.

As reliable communications infrastructures and services are essential to digital transformation, the first integrated building block concerns access to data, communications infrastructures and services (e.g. fibre optic backhaul, towers, spectrum, international cables), encompassing efficient, reliable and widely accessible broadband communication networks and services and key complementary enablers (e.g. a co-ordinated system of international domain names, increasing uptake of IPv6 Internet addresses, Internet exchange points), data, software, and hardware. These act as the technical foundations for an open, interconnected and distributed Internet that enables both the global free flow of information and, more generally, digital transformation (OECD, 2011). Multiple policy domains need to be considered to ensure access, including: communications infrastructures and services, competition, investment, and regional development.

Use

Access to digital networks provides the technical foundation for the digital transformation of the economy and society, but does not necessarily ensure widespread diffusion of digital tools and their effective usage, which are needed for individuals, governments and firms to reap the benefits of digital transformation through increased participation, innovation, productivity and well-being. Diffusion and effective use crucially depend on investments in ICTs complemented by investments in knowledge-based capital, including data and organisational change; on a favourable business environment, e.g. one that fosters business dynamism; on the availability and allocation of skills; and on trust. Therefore, multiple policy domains need to be considered under use: digital government, investment, business dynamism and SMEs, education and skills, and digital security and privacy.

Innovation

Innovation – another integrated building block – pushes out the frontier of what is possible, driving job creation, productivity growth, and sustainable growth and development. Digital innovation, in particular, has driven radical changes in the ways people interact, create, produce and consume. Digital innovation not only gives rise to new and novel products and services, it also creates opportunities for new business models and markets, and can drive efficiencies in the public sector and beyond. In addition, digital technologies and data drive innovation in a wide range of sectors, including education, health, finance, insurance, transportation, energy, agriculture and fisheries, as well as the ICT sector itself. Multiple policy domains need to be considered to foster innovation, including entrepreneurship and SMEs; science and technology; competition; digital government; and sectoral policies such as energy, finance, education, transport, health and education, among others.

Jobs

Digital transformation has already begun to change the nature and structure of organisations and markets, raising important questions about which jobs might disappear and where new ones will come from, what they will they look like and which skills will be required. At the same time, issues have emerged around who might be most affected, and what can be done to foster new job creation and to align skills development with the changing skills requirements of jobs. Technological advances and the introduction of new business models have given rise to the "platform economy" and have led to the emergence of new forms of work such as "crowd work", "gig work" and other forms of on-demand labour. Making sure that digital transformation leads to more and better jobs will depend on the kind of policies that accompany it, including in the areas of: labour markets, education and skills, and social protection; since the impacts may be concentrated in some industries and regions, sectoral and regional policies will be important, too.

Society

Digital transformation affects society and culture in complex and interrelated ways, as digital technologies change the ways in which individuals, firms and governments interact among and with one another. For digital transformation to work for growth and well-being, it is essential that public policies support a positive and inclusive digital society. To do so, multiple policy domains need to be considered: social policies (e.g. housing and welfare), education and skills, tax and benefit policies, environment, health, and digital government. Digital transformation changes the distribution of benefits, raising the question of where life is getting better, and for whom, making social policies an important part of the policy toolbox. In particular, social policies can help address a range of digital divides.

Trust

Trust is fundamental to the digital transformation; without it, individuals, firms and governments will not fully use digital technologies, leaving an important source of potential growth and social progress unexploited. Countries may benefit from greater cross-border co-operation if they develop comprehensive and coherent national strategies for digital security and privacy to address issues such as the protection of personal data, resilience of essential services (e.g. water, energy, finance, public health and safety), creation of incentives (e.g. cyber insurance, public procurement), support to SMEs, and related skills development, in consultation with all of the relevant stakeholders. At the same time, it is important to continue promoting effective protection to consumers engaged in e-commerce and other online activities, as this will help the digital economy flourish as well as be inclusive.

Market openness

Digital technologies are transforming the environment in which firms compete, trade and invest. Market openness policies related to trade, investment, financial markets, competition and taxation play an important role in ensuring that favourable conditions exist for the digital transformation to flourish. Digital transformation also affects market openness policy domains, raising opportunities and posing challenges. Governments could benefit from periodically reviewing market openness policies and, where appropriate, update them to ensure that they are well suited to making digital transformation work for growth and well-being.

Going Digital in Brazil

The Review is organised as follows:

- Chapter 2 reviews recent developments in the Brazilian communication market, examines the availability and quality of communication networks and services, as well as communication policies and regulation, and provides policy recommendations, based on the findings of the *OECD Telecommunication and Broadcasting Review of Brazil* (OECD, 2020b).
- Chapter 3 reviews recent trends in the use of digital technologies by individuals, businesses and government; obstacles to digital uptake and policies to overcome them; skills for using digital technologies; and provides policy recommendations to spur digital uptake and skills.
- Chapter 4 discusses policies to enhance trust in the digital economy, including how digital security policies can help foster economic and social resilience in Brazil, assesses government initiatives to ensure that personal data are managed in a confidential manner and that privacy is respected, and examines the Brazilian framework for protecting and empowering digital consumers.
- Chapter 5 analyses the science, technology and innovation landscape in Brazil; reviews the main policy instruments to support research and innovation in the digital field; and provides policy recommendations to promote digital innovation.
- Chapter 6 reviews recent transformations in some of Brazil's key sectors – agribusiness, manufacturing and health – as well as the emergence of new business models, such as Fintech, and examines their policy implications.
- Chapter 7 puts into perspective the policies analysed in the other chapters in relation to their coherence across different domains and provides recommendations to foster synergies across government ministries, levels and institutions, based on the OECD Going Digital Integrated Policy Framework.

References

Ebit Nielsen (2020), *Webshoppers 41ª Edição* [Webshoppers 41st Edition], *www.ebit.com.br/webshoppers*.

IEDI (2014), *A Reorientação do Desenvolvimento Industrial* [A Reorientation of Industrial Development], Instituto de Estudos para o Desenvolvimento Industrial, São Paulo.

McKinsey (2019), *Brazil Digital Report*, McKinsey & Company.

MCTIC (2018), *Brazilian Digital Transformation Strategy: E-Digital*, Ministério da Ciência, Tecnologia, Inovações e Comunicações, Brasilia, *www.mctic.gov.br/mctic/export/sites/institucional/sessaoPublica/arquivos/digitalstrategy.pdf*.

OECD (forthcoming), *OECD Economic Surveys: Brazil 2020*, OECD Publishing, Paris.

OECD (2020a), "Evaluating the initial impact of COVID-19 containment measures on economic activity", OECD, Paris, *https://www.oecd.org/coronavirus/policy-responses/evaluating-the-initial-impact-of-covid-19-containment-measures-on-economic-activity*.

OECD (2020b), *OECD Telecommunication and Broadcasting Review of Brazil*, OECD Publishing, Paris.

OECD (2019a), *Going Digital: Shaping Policies, Improving Lives*, OECD Publishing, Paris, *https://doi.org/10.1787/9789264312012-en*.

OECD (2019b), *OECD Education at a Glance* (database), OECD, Paris, *http://dotstat.oecd.org/index.aspx?queryid=93189* (accessed on 8 October 2019).

OECD (2019c), *OECD Skills Outlook 2019: Thriving in a Digital World*, OECD Publishing, Paris, *https://doi.org/10.1787/df80bc12-en*.

OECD (2018a), *OECD Economic Surveys: Brazil 2018*, OECD Publishing, Paris, *http://dx.doi.org/10.1787/eco_surveys-bra-2018-en*.

OECD (2018b), *Getting Skills Right: Brazil*, Getting Skills Right, OECD Publishing, Paris, *https://doi.org/10.1787/9789264309838-en*.

OECD (2018c), *The Productivity-Inclusiveness Nexus*, OECD Publishing, Paris, *https://doi.org/10.1787/9789264292932-en*.

OECD (2018d), *Tax Challenges Arising from Digitalisation – Interim Report 2018: Inclusive Framework on BEPS*, OECD/G20 Base Erosion and Profit Shifting Project, OECD Publishing, Paris, *http://dx.doi.org/10.1787/9789264293083-en*.

OECD (2017a), *The Next Production Revolution: Implications for Governments and Business*, OECD Publishing, Paris, *https://doi.org/10.1787/9789264271036-en*.

OECD (2017b), *Education at a Glance 2017: OECD Indicators*, OECD Publishing, Paris, *https://doi.org/10.1787/eag-2017-en*.

OECD (2015), *OECD Economic Surveys: Brazil 2015*, OECD Publishing, Paris, *https://doi.org/10.1787/eco_surveys-bra-2015-en*.

OECD (2011), *Recommendation of the Council on Principles for Internet Policy Making*, OECD, Paris, *https://legalinstruments.oecd.org/en/instruments/OECD-LEGAL-0387*.

Pinheiro, M.C. (2013), "Inovação no Brasil: Panorama geral, diagnóstico e sugestões de política" [Innovation in Brazil: Overview, diagnostic and policy suggestions], in Veloso, F.A.A., L.V. Pereira and Z. Bingwen (org.), *Armadilha da renda média: Visões do Brasil e da China* [Middle income trap: Perspectives from Brazil and China], Vol. 1, Fundação Getulio Vargas, Rio de Janeiro, pp. 81-106.

The Conference Board (2019), "Output, labor and labor productivity, 1950-2019 (adjusted version)", *Total Economy Database*, April, *https://www.conference-board.org/data/economydatabase/index.cfm?id=27762* (accessed on 6 May 2020).

The World Bank (2019a), *Doing Business* (database), The World Bank, Washington, DC, *https://www.doingbusiness.org/en/doingbusiness* (accessed on 6 May 2020).

The World Bank (2019b), *Poverty and Equity* (database), The World Bank, Washington, DC, *https://databank.worldbank.org/reports.aspx?source=poverty-and-equity-database* (accessed on 6 May 2020).

Note

Israel

The statistical data for Israel are supplied by and under the responsibility of the relevant Israeli authorities. The use of such data by the OECD is without prejudice to the status of the Golan Heights, East Jerusalem and Israeli settlements in the West Bank under the terms of international law.

Chapter 2

INFRASTRUCTURES FOR BRAZIL'S DIGITAL ECONOMY

Recent developments in the Brazilian communication market

The availability of high-quality and fixed and mobile communication services at competitive prices are crucial to go digital. In Brazil, one of the most important challenges in this domain concerns expanding quality broadband to rural and remote areas. With a geographical size of 8.5 million square kilometres (km^2), the country has an area approximately eight times the size of France and Spain combined, while comprising 60% of the Amazon forest within its borders. In addition, a large percentage of the population is sparsely distributed, which exacerbates the issue. This geographical feature creates important challenges for Brazil to expand communication networks in rural and remote areas.

Overview of the Brazilian communication market

A range of indicators can be examined to assess recent developments in communication markets in Brazil. A key starting point is the size of the communication sector, both in terms of revenues and investments, as well as the overall growth in access paths (i.e. subscriptions to communication services).

By 2018, total revenue and investment in the communication sector in Brazil amounted to USD 30 billion (BRL 108.8 billion) and USD 7 billion (BRL 25.8 billion), respectively.[1] From 2015 to 2018, when Brazil's gross domestic product (GDP) contracted by 1.2% (The World Bank, 2020), communication revenues in Brazil contracted by 3.4%, while investments grew by 49% (equivalent to an annual compound growth rate [CAGR] of 14%) during the same period (Figure 2.1).

Figure 2.1. Total communication revenue and investment in Brazil, 2015-18

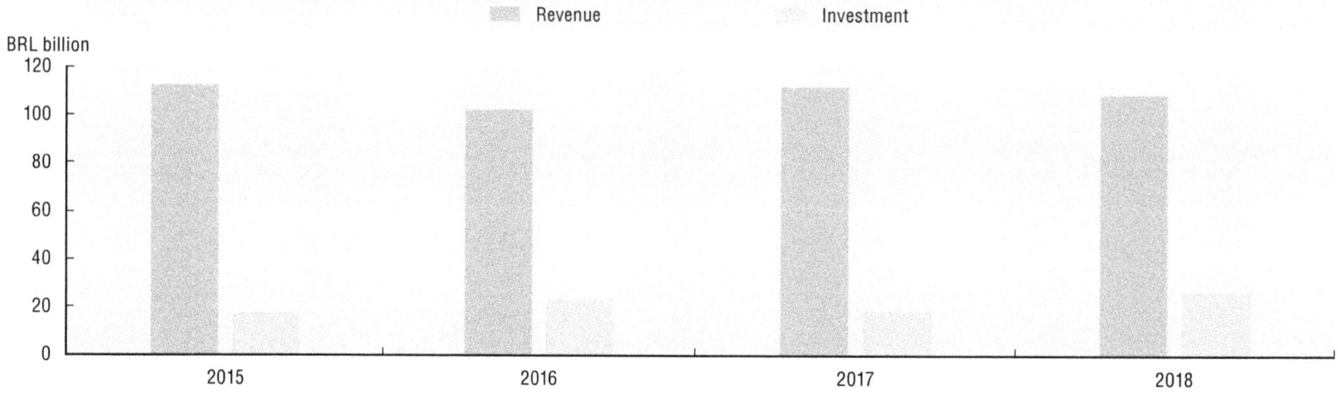

Source: Anatel's response to the questionnaire of OECD (2020a), *OECD Telecommunication and Broadcasting Review of Brazil.*

The percentage of investment as a proportion of revenues in Brazil in 2018 was around 23.8%. This compares to 15.7% in the OECD area for the same year. In 2017, most investment (76%) in the communication sector in Brazil targeted wireless infrastructure (i.e. mobile networks and other wireless infrastructure). Only 24% was used for fixed infrastructure deployment.

In 2015, communication investment per access path in Brazil was around USD 16, which was much lower than the OECD average of around USD 82. This number rose slightly to USD 19.2 by the end of 2018, still below the 2018 OECD average of USD 84, and well below that of Switzerland, which was the leading OECD country at USD 179 per access path at the end of 2018 (Figure 2.2). However, these figures may be a lower bound of the actual investment and revenues in the Brazilian telecommunication sector given the surge of regional small Internet service providers (ISPs). As they lack reporting obligations (e.g. on investments and revenues), small ISPs are only partially accounted for in the statistics of the National Telecommunications Agency (Agência Nacional de Telecomunicações, Anatel).

Total foreign direct investment (FDI) inflows in the Brazilian communication sector amounted to USD 4.9 billion in 2014 (representing 8.72% of the total FDI that year). It decreased to USD 404 million in 2018, or 1% of the total FDI that year. This decrease could reflect movements in mergers and acquisitions, as well as the nature of FDI, which is sensitive to a country's economic cycle, reflecting a degree of volatility, such as the one experienced after investments related to the World Cup and Olympic Games in 2014 and 2015.

Figure 2.2. Communication investment per access path in Brazil and the OECD

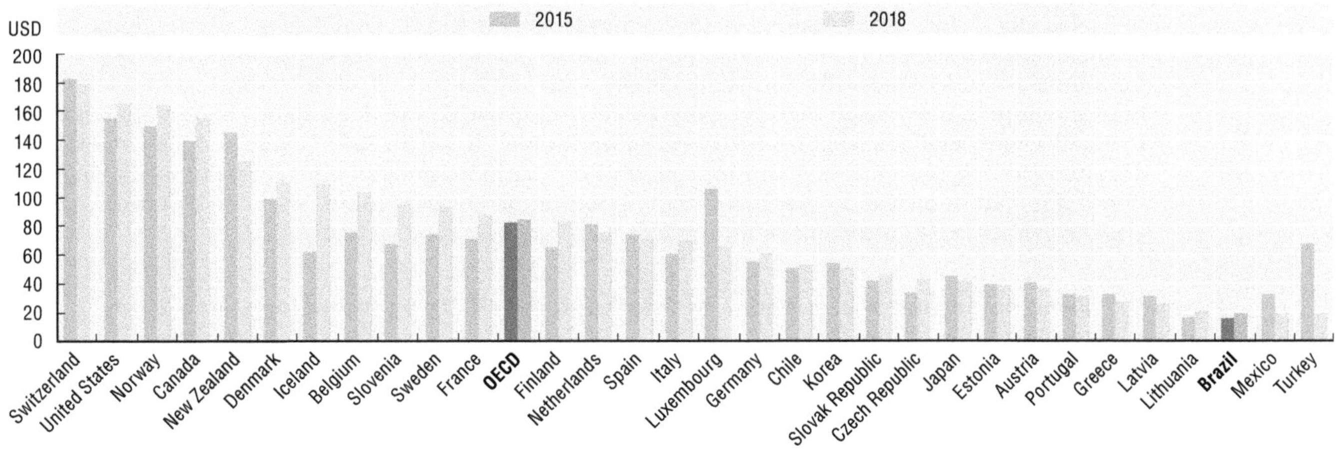

Note: Data for Japan are for 2017 instead of 2018.

Source: OECD (2019d), *OECD Telecommunication and Internet Statistics* (database), *http://dx.doi.org/10.1787/tel_int-data-en* (accessed in May 2020).

There are no FDI restrictions for communication services in Brazil. Communication service providers are required to be incorporated under Brazilian law or controlled by a Brazilian company, but these can, in turn, be controlled by a foreign company or individual. In the broadcasting sector, however, foreign companies or individuals cannot hold more than 30% of the total and voting capital of TV broadcasting companies, as established in Article 222 of the Constitution. Removing barriers to FDI could further help meet policy objectives in broadcasting, such as increased investment, employment, competition and media plurality in the sector.

Subscriptions to communication services (i.e. total access paths)[2] in Brazil have continued to increase. By 2019, there were 315 million access paths, compared to 202 million in 2008. The growth in access paths has mainly been driven by the growth in mobile broadband subscriptions, which more than tripled between 2012 and 2019, from 59.2 million subscriptions to 196.6 million. In contrast, fixed telephony lines have begun to decrease slightly in Brazil since 2014, as they were being replaced by mobile telephony. Fixed broadband subscriptions have also grown in Brazil, passing from 19.8 million access lines in 2012 to 32.9 million in 2019 (Figure 2.3). Brazil, however, lags behind in fixed broadband penetration compared to OECD countries.

Figure 2.3. Evolution of communication access paths in Brazil, 1996-2019

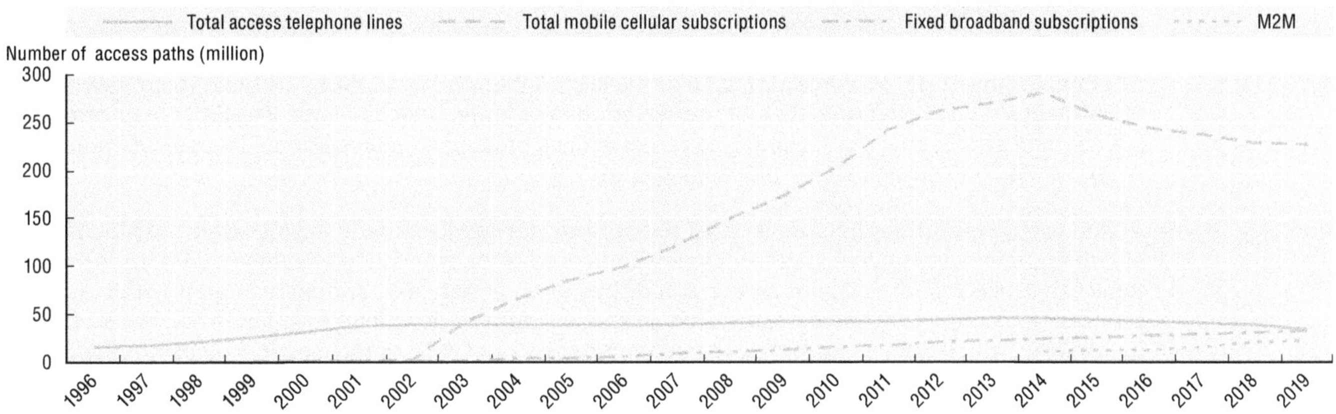

Notes: M2M = machine to machine. Data is for December 2019. M2M data corresponds to Q2 2019.

Source: Anatel (2020a), *Painéis de Dados: Acessos*, *https://www.anatel.gov.br/paineis/acessos* (accessed on 28 May 2020).

Availability and quality of communication services

Fixed broadband services

In June 2019, fixed broadband penetration in Brazil (15.5%) was similar to countries in the region such as Chile (18%), Mexico (15%) and Colombia (13.8%). This represented about half of the OECD average of 31.4%, and is well below leading OECD countries with levels above 40% (Figure 2.4). The indicator of subscriptions per 100 inhabitants may not entirely reflect the actual use of broadband services by households or individuals. The number of people using the Internet is considerably higher, as Brazilian households tend to be larger than the average OECD household, and there seems to be a phenomenon in Brazil where neighbours share broadband subscriptions. In fact, in 2018, 20% of Brazilian households declared sharing their Internet connection with one or more neighbours according to the Regional Centre for Studies on the Development of the Information Society (Centro Regional de Estudos para o Desenvolvimento da Sociedade da Informação, CETIC.br/NIC.br) (CGI.br, 2019).

Figure 2.4. Fixed broadband subscriptions in Brazil and the OECD, by technology, June 2019

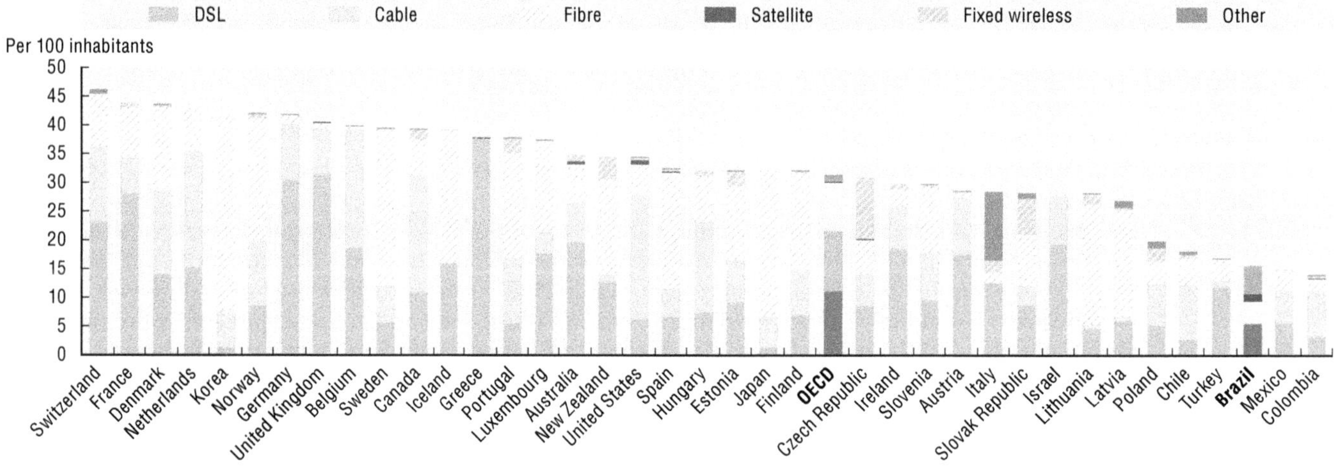

Note: DSL = digital subscriber line.

Sources: OECD (2020b), *Broadband Portal* (database), *www.oecd.org/sti/broadband/broadband-statistics/* (accessed on 20 May 2020); data for Brazil are from Anatel (2020a), *Painéis de Dados: Acessos, https://www.anatel.gov.br/paineis/acessos/* (accessed on 28 May 2020).

At the end of June 2019, most fixed broadband subscriptions in Brazil were digital subscriber line (DSL) subscriptions (34% of total broadband subscriptions), followed by fibre subscriptions (24%). While the share of high-speed fibre in Brazil is higher than in Mexico (22%) and Colombia (14%), Brazil still lags behind the OECD average (27%). The gap in terms of fibre is even larger when compared to leading OECD countries, such as Korea, Japan and Lithuania (above 70%) (Figure 2.4).

Another useful indicator to assess the quality of communication services is the penetration rate by speed tiers. In Brazil, more than half of fixed broadband subscriptions (58%) exhibited speeds above 12 Mbps in June 2019. In particular, 25% of fixed broadband subscriptions in Brazil belonged to the "12-34 Mbps" speed- tier, and 33% of subscriptions exhibited speeds above 34 Mbps. In contrast, in Switzerland, the leading OECD country in terms of fixed broadband penetration, 52% of fixed broadband subscriptions had speeds above 100 Mbps (Figure 2.5).

Actual speeds may differ from advertised speeds and can be measured using different methodologies. M-Lab and Ookla compile results from voluntary speed tests by users, while Steam data, for example, reflect the speeds of online gaming users and thus often a more demanding user group of broadband services.[3] According to M-Lab data, the average fixed broadband download speed in Brazil was 4.84 Mbps in July 2019, which points to a large gap in comparison to an OECD average of 26.8 Mbps. On the Steam platform, the average download speed for fixed broadband in Brazil was 22.7 Mbps, whereas the OECD average was 36.1 Mbps (Figure 2.6).

Figure 2.5. Fixed broadband subscriptions in Brazil and the OECD, per speed tiers, June 2019

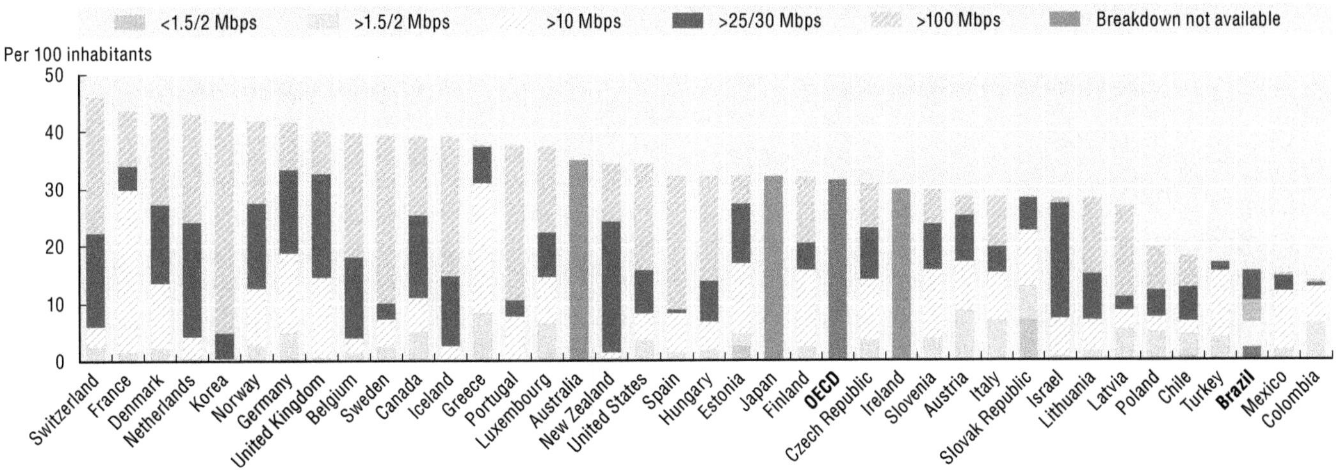

Notes: Mbps = megabits per second. The speed tiers are for end 2018; data on fixed broadband subscriptions per 100 inhabitants are for June 2019. Data for Brazil on speed tiers and fixed broadband subscriptions correspond to June 2019. Brazil uses different speed tiers, which are: <2Mbps, >2 Mbps, >12 Mbps and >34 Mbps.

Sources: OECD (2020b), *Broadband Portal* (database), *www.oecd.org/sti/broadband/broadband-statistics/* (accessed on 20 May 2020); data for Brazil are from Anatel (2020a), *Painéis de Dados: Acessos, https://www.anatel.gov.br/paineis/acessos/* (accessed on 28 May 2020).

Figure 2.6. Average experienced download speed of fixed broadband connections in Brazil and the OECD, 2019

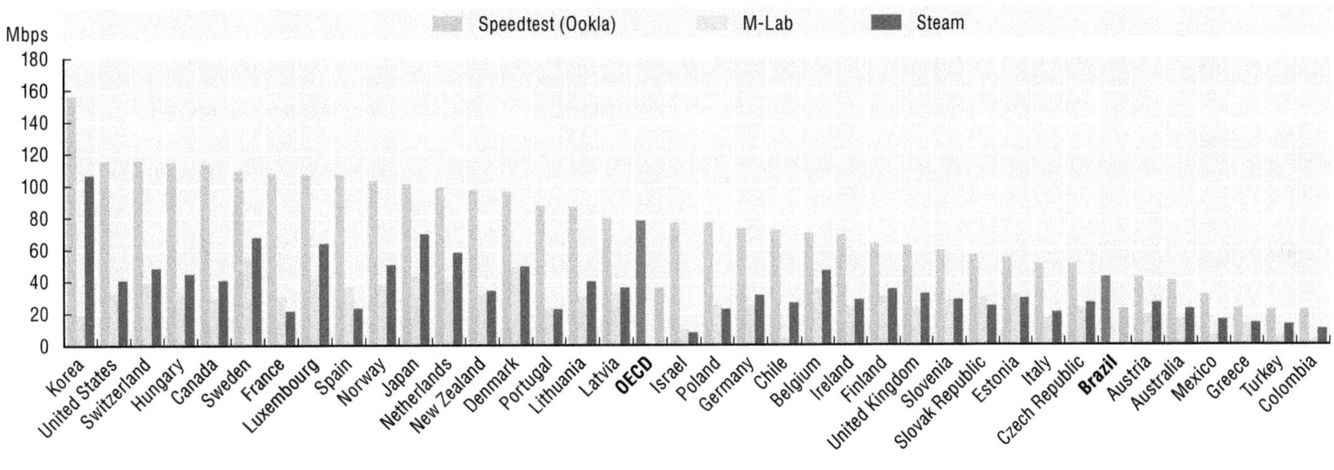

Notes: Mbps = megabits per second. Sorted using Ookla data. Speedtest (Ookla) data are for July 2019, M-Lab (worldwide broadband speed league) speeds were measured in the period from 9 May 2018 to 8 May 2019, Steam data are for July 2019.

Sources: Ookla (2019), "Speedtest", *https://www.speedtest.net/* (accessed on 10 July 2019); M-Lab (2019), "Worldwide broadband speed league", *https://www.cable.co.uk/broadband/speed/worldwide-speed-league/* (accessed on 9 May 2019); Steam (2019), "Steam Download Stats", *https://store.steampowered.com/stats/content* (accessed on 10 July 2019).

Quality measures may also differ across regions in a country and evolve with time. CETIC.br/NIC.br's initiative SIMET measures the quality of Brazilian broadband connections by collecting indicators of broadband connections for the different regions in Brazil based on download speeds, latency and jitter upload (stability of the connection) (NIC.br, 2018). In 2016, the median download speeds among regions ranged from 8.4 Mbps (Northern region) to 10.1 Mbps (Southeast region), while the national median was 9.6 Mbps. There are more accentuated regional differences in terms of latency, with the Northern region exhibiting latency of 57.5 milliseconds (ms), while the Southeast region had 15.8 ms; the national median was 20 ms. In comparison to 2014, download speeds have increased in all Brazilian regions, with the exception of the Southeast region. Meanwhile, latency has also increased in all Brazilian regions, with the largest increase measured in the North region (Figure 2.7).

Figure 2.7. Quality of broadband connections in Brazil

Median download speeds and latency per trimester and per region, 2014 and 2016

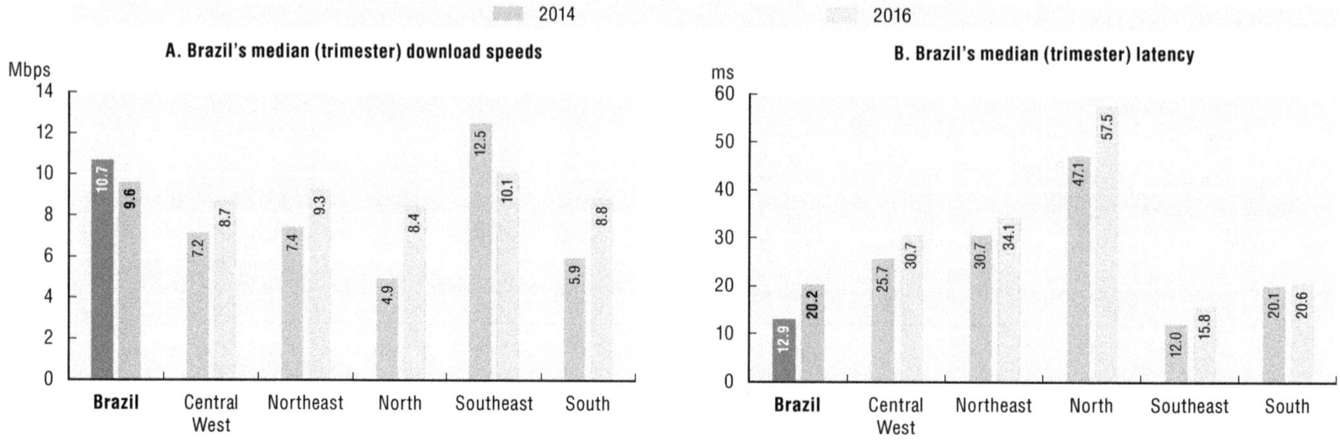

Note: Mbps = megabits per second ; ms = millisecond.

Source: NIC.br (2018), *Banda Larga no Brasil: Um Estudo Sobre a Evolução do Acesso e da Qualidade das Conexões à Internet*, *https://cetic.br/media/docs/publicacoes/1/Estudo%20Banda%20Larga%20no%20Brasil.pdf* (accessed on 20 February 2020).

Mobile broadband services

At the end of June 2019, Brazil had 89.5 mobile broadband subscriptions per 100 inhabitants, compared to 94 per 100 subscriptions in Chile, 74 in Mexico and 53 in Colombia, which is still below the OECD average of 112.8 subscriptions per 100 inhabitants (Figure 2.8).

Figure 2.8. Mobile broadband subscriptions in Brazil and the OECD, by technology, June 2019

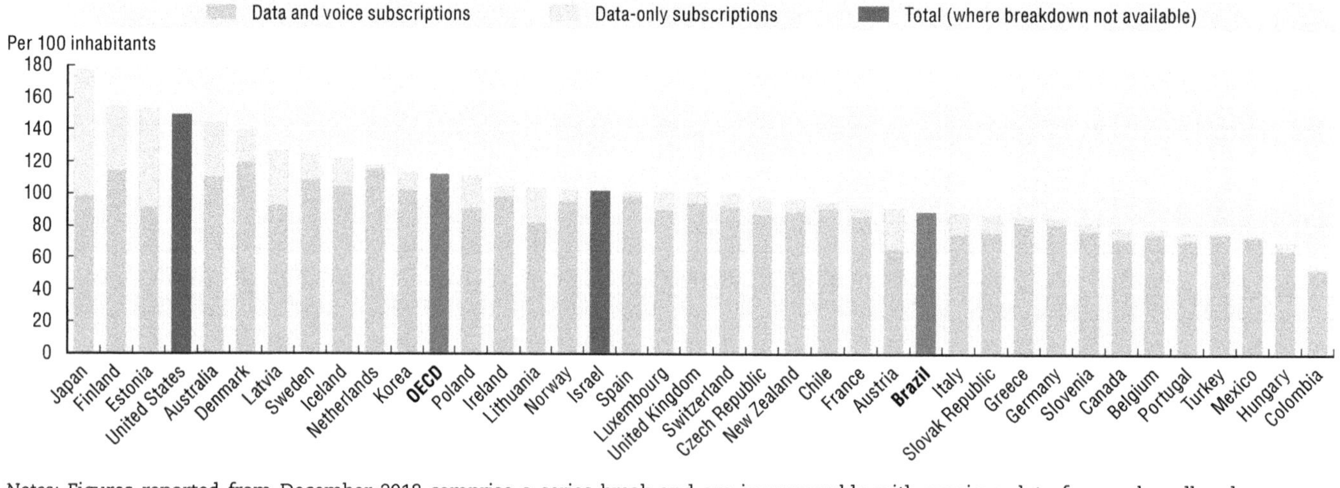

Notes: Figures reported from December 2018 comprise a series break and are incomparable with previous data for any broadband measures Australia reports to the OECD. Data for Canada, Switzerland and the United States are preliminary. Canada: Fixed wireless includes satellite. France: Cable data include VDSL2 and fixed 4G solutions. Italy: Terrestrial fixed wireless data include WiMax lines; other includes vDSL services.

Sources: OECD (2020b), *Broadband Portal* (database), *www.oecd.org/sti/broadband/broadband-statistics/* (accessed on 20 May 2020); data for Brazil are from Anatel (2020a), *Painéis de Dados: Acessos*, *https://www.anatel.gov.br/paineis/acessos/* (accessed on 28 May 2020).

Although mobile broadband networks are more pervasive in Brazil than fixed broadband networks, they do not yet reach all corners of the country. In 2018, 4G was present in 4 676 Brazilian municipalities, covering 96.7% of the population. 3G had an equivalent "coverage" of 99.8% (Figure 2.9). Some municipalities have a large geographic span with many rural and remote areas. As not all inhabitants of a municipality with 3G or 4G signal necessarily live within the covered area, actual population coverage is likely to be lower. Therefore, this indicator (i.e. existence of a network signal within a municipality) does not provide an estimate of the actual percentage of the population covered. Nor does it provide a precise measurement of the geographical span of mobile network coverage.

While the number of municipalities with a presence of mobile networks seems high, many have only been covered by a single operator. In the first half of 2018, 3 071 municipalities with less than 30 000 inhabitants were almost entirely served by a single provider, and lacked roaming agreements. The National Telecommunications Agency (Agência Nacional de Telecomunicações, Anatel) has indicated that 4 747 roaming agreements would need to be established to ensure full mobile coverage of these municipalities across all major mobile service providers (Tele.síntese, 2019).

Figure 2.9. Presence of 3G and 4G signals within municipalities, estimated as a percentage of the population[1] in Brazil, 2015-18

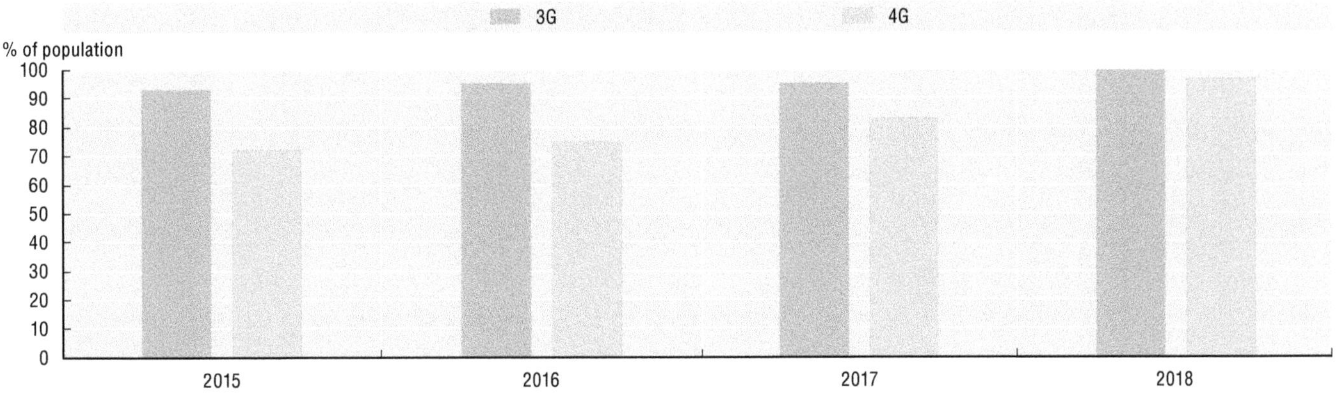

1. The indicator represents the existence of a network signal in a given municipality. Population coverage is estimated by the number of inhabitants in the municipality which has the presence of a mobile network signal. Although it may provide an approximation of the percentage of the population covered by mobile networks, it does not provide a precise measurement of the geographical span of mobile network coverage.

Source: Anatel (2020b), *Telefonia Móvel – Municípios atendidos, https://www.anatel.gov.br/setorregulado/component/content/article/115-universalizacao-e-ampliacao-do-acesso/telefonia-movel/423-telefonia-movel-municipios-atendidos* (accessed on 20 February 2020).

In terms of the quality of mobile broadband, indicators collected by OpenSignal and Ookla, using different methodologies, can be useful to compare the average mobile network performance between Brazil and OECD countries. For 3G and 4G networks, OpenSignal measured average download mobile broadband connection speeds of 13 Mbps for Brazil in May 2019. This was roughly in line with speeds in Chile (12 Mbps) and Colombia (10 Mbps), but considerably below the OECD average (27 Mbps) and leading OECD countries such as Korea (52 Mbps). Similarly, Ookla speed tests for mobile networks in July 2019 show Brazil with download speeds for mobile broadband of 23 Mbps, close to its regional peers, but below the OECD average of 40.89 Mbps (Figure 2.10).

Figure 2.10. Mobile broadband download speeds in Brazil and the OECD, 2019

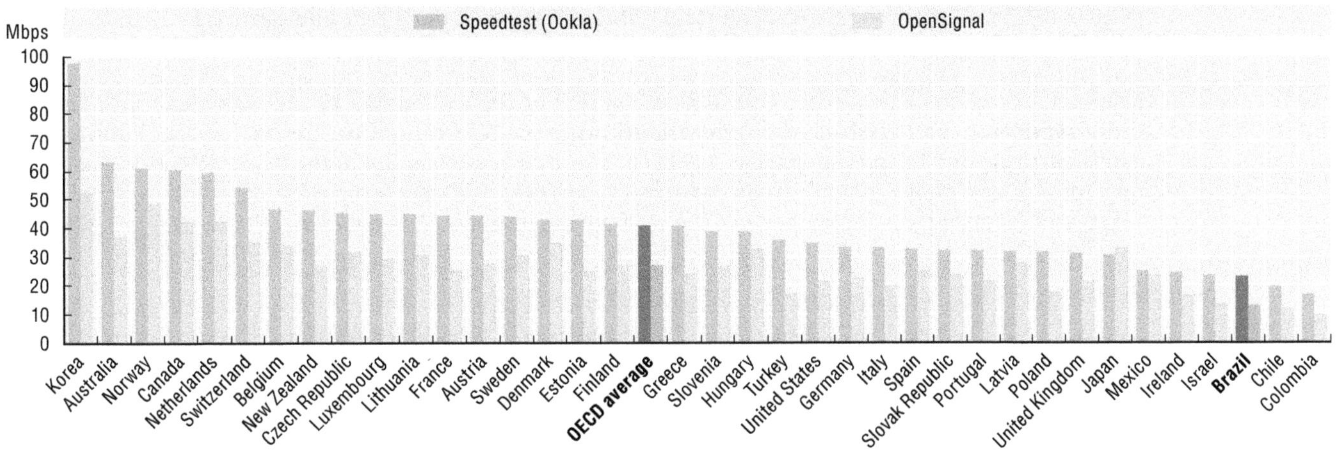

Notes: Mbps = megabits per second. Speedtest (Ookla) data are for July 2019, OpenSignal data are for the average download connection speed on long-term evolution networks, May 2019. OpenSignal data for Estonia, Latvia, Lithuania, Luxembourg, Mexico and Slovenia are for February 2018 instead of May 2019. The definition of download speeds for Opensignal is "...average download speed experienced by Opensignal users across an operator's 3G and 4G networks".

Sources: Ookla (2019), "Speedtest", *https://www.speedtest.net/* (accessed on 10 July 2019); Opensignal (2019), *The State of Mobile Experience*, May 2019, *http://dx.doi.org/www.opensignal.com/sites/opensignal-com/files/data/reports/global/data-2019-05/the_state_of_mobile_experience_may_2019_0.pdf.*

Another indicator linked to the service experience of mobile subscribers is the amount of data used. The OECD average mobile data usage per month was 4.65 GB in 2018, up from 2.42 in 2016 (out of 34 OECD countries for which data were available). The top OECD countries for data usage in 2018 were Finland (19.4 GB) and Austria (16.4 GB). In comparison, Brazil's average monthly mobile data consumption was 1.25 GB in 2018, up from 0.47 GB in 2016. Brazil also lags behind its regional peers of Colombia (1.62 GB) and Mexico (2.11 GB) (Figure 2.11).

Figure 2.11. Mobile data usage per mobile broadband subscription in Brazil and the OECD, 2016-18

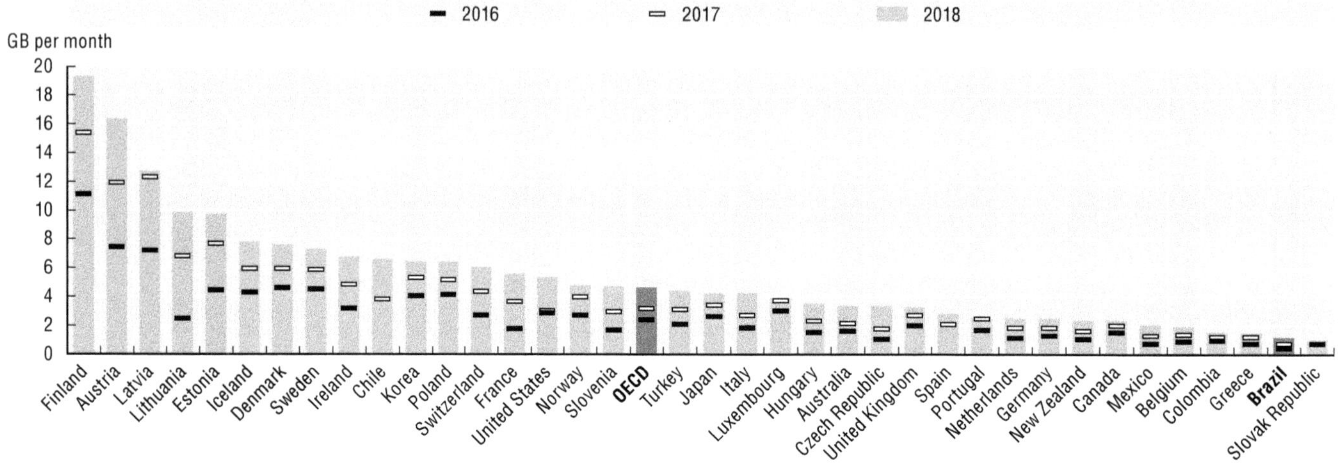

Notes: GB = gigabyte. Methodology: The multiplier 1 024 is used to convert terabyte into gigabyte; the total amount of gigabytes is divided by the yearly average number of mobile broadband subscriptions. For Australia, data reported for December 2018 and onwards are being collected by a new entity using a different methodology. Figures reported from December 2018 comprise a series break and are incomparable with previous data for any broadband measures Australia reports to the OECD.

Sources: OECD (2020b), *Broadband Portal* (database), *www.oecd.org/sti/broadband/broadband-statistics/* (accessed on 20 May 2020); data for Brazil are from Anatel's response to the questionnaire of OECD (2020a), *OECD Telecommunication and Broadcasting Review of Brazil.*

Internet of Things

The OECD has been collecting data on machine-to-machine (M2M) embedded mobile cellular subscriptions, a subset of the Internet of Things (IoT), since 2012.[4] The OECD has also developed a framework to measure different IoT categories according to their network requirements (OECD, 2018a). By June 2019, there were 298 million M2M subscriptions in the OECD, up from 108 million at the end of 2014. In Brazil, the number of M2M connections has also increased since 2014, passing from 10 million in 2014 to 22 million in June 2019. The level of M2M SIM cards per 100 inhabitants was 22 in the OECD and 10.6 in Brazil in June 2019 (Figure 2.12).

In Brazil, one of the key barriers to the development of the IoT relates to the high taxes and fees for these services. In particular, charging contributions to the Telecommunications Oversight Fund (Fundo de Fiscalização das Telecomunicações, FISTEL) over IoT devices results in those services being partially unprofitable or simply unviable in the country. Beyond taxation issues, establishing separate numbering plans and fostering the deployment of the numbering protocol IPv6 could also foster the IoT in Brazil.

Backhaul and backbone connectivity

Fibre backhaul and backbone connectivity are important to bring fibre closer to the end-user to support projected capacity demands, including those raised by 5G networks (OECD, 2019e). According to Anatel, by 2015, only 48.2% of municipalities in Brazil were served by fibre backhaul. By 2019, this indicator had risen to 70% (Figure 2.13); that is, 3 882 municipalities connected to fibre backhaul. While a municipality may have the presence of backhaul, given the heterogeneity in the size of municipalities, the presence of backhaul is not a measure of full geographic coverage of this wholesale input. Moreover, the presence of fibre backhaul does not imply that the wholesale operator is under any open access obligations (Anatel, 2019b).

Figure 2.12. M2M embedded mobile cellular subscriptions in Brazil and the OECD, June 2019

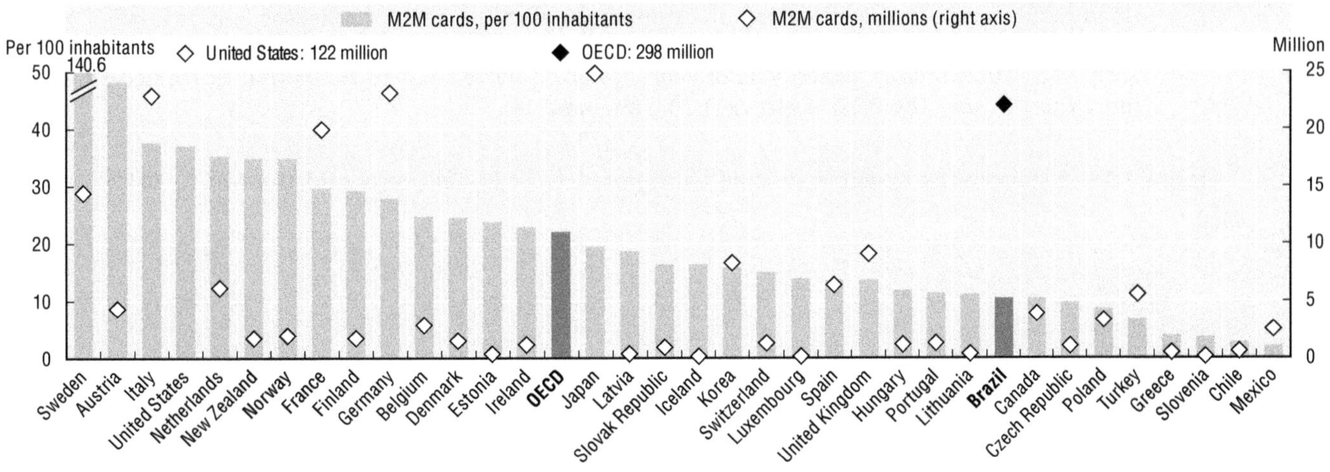

Notes: M2M = machine to machine. Data for Australia reported for December 2018 and onwards are being collected by a new entity using a different methodology. Data for Switzerland are preliminary.

Source: OECD (2020b), *Broadband Portal* (database), *www.oecd.org/sti/broadband/broadband-statistics/* (accessed on 20 May 2020).

Figure 2.13. Number of municipalities with fibre backhaul connectivity in Brazil, 2015-19

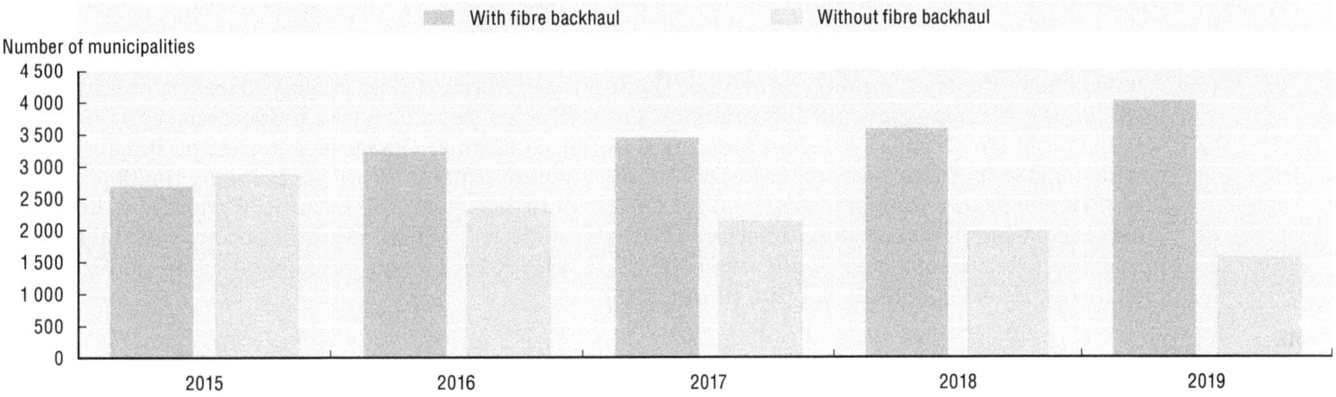

Source: Anatel (2019b), *Mapeamento de Redes de Transporte*, *https://www.anatel.gov.br/dados/mapeamento-de-redes* (accessed on 13 September 2019).

Challenges persist for achieving full coverage of backhaul connectivity, as 51% of the municipalities without fibre are located in the North and Northeast. This can be a serious obstacle for affordable broadband given that in Brazil, 24.2% of municipalities only have one fibre backhaul provider (Table 2.1).

Table 2.1. Number of fibre backhaul providers present in municipalities in Brazil, 2019

Backhaul providers (fibre)	Number of municipalities	Share of municipalities (%)
0	1 558	28.0
1	1 350	24.2
2	1 031	18.5
3	593	10.6
4	406	7.3
5 or more	632	11.3

Source: Anatel (2020c), *Plano Estrutural de Redes de Telecomunicações (PERT) 2019-2024, Atualizaçao 2020*, *https://sei.anatel.gov.br/sei/modulos/pesquisa/md_pesq_documento_consulta_externa.php?eEP-wqk1skrd8hSlk5Z3rN4EVg9uLJqrLYJw_9INcO4m2N1jXIPEu1rXnv7UHJFGKd-jO_xz5ZYqyuXgvKFPZe9U7a4FRauel0Ej_GJ3pzD2sKi_sQQhtHNHQk_javEK* (accessed on 15 March 2020).

Autonomous systems and IPv6

Good performance in the allocation of autonomous systems and IP addresses is indicative of a well-functioning Internet ecosystem. In terms of the allocation of autonomous systems, Brazil ranks high, with 7 451 autonomous systems as of February 2020, more than 16 times that of Mexico (450), and more than 4 times the OECD average (1 703) (Figure 2.14).

Figure 2.14. Autonomous systems in Brazil compared to regional peers and the OECD, 2019

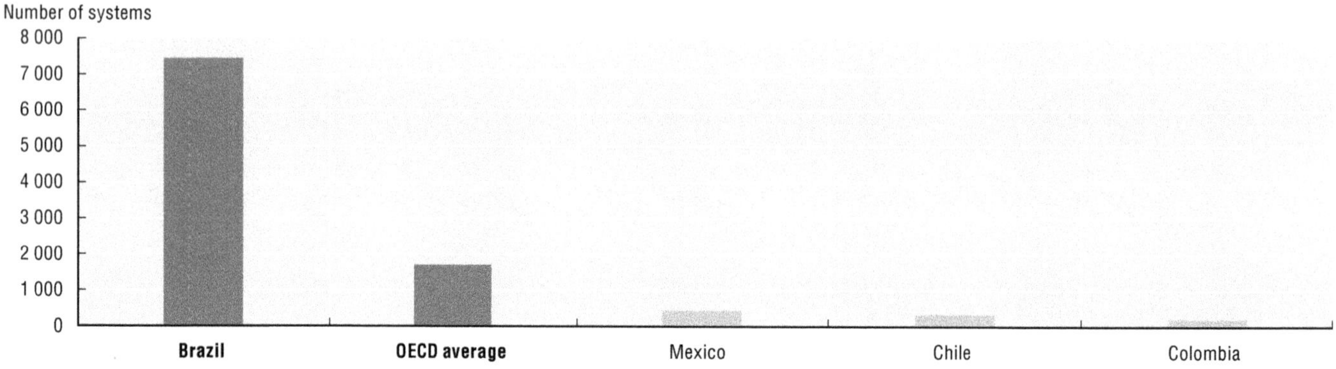

Notes: Autonomous systems are the networks that form the Internet. They range from Internet service providers (ISPs) to small local ISPs; academic, military or government networks; or firms with a particular need for network independence.

Source: Maigron (2020), *Regional Internet Registries Statistics* (database), *https://www-public.imtbs-tsp.eu/~maigron/RIR_Stats/* (accessed on 19 February 2020).

The large increase in autonomous systems in Brazil starting in 2008 coincides with the initiation of measures to deploy the newer version of the Internet Protocol (IPv6), mainly driven by initiatives of NIC.br, the Brazilian Network Information Centre (Núcleo de Informação e Coordenação), under the mandate of the Brazilian Internet Steering Committee (Comitê Gestor da Internet no Brasil, CGI.br), which added to Anatel's efforts to foster IPv6 deployment (Anatel, 2014). Encouraging the deployment of IPv6 has been a long-standing goal for OECD countries, given the current IP address exhaustion and increasing demands for connected devices such as IoT, which require not only scalability of IP addresses, but also secure applications (OECD, 2014c; 2018c). Brazil ranks well compared to OECD countries in terms of IPv6 adoption (Figure 2.15).

Figure 2.15. Registered IPv6 addresses in Brazil and the OECD, 2020

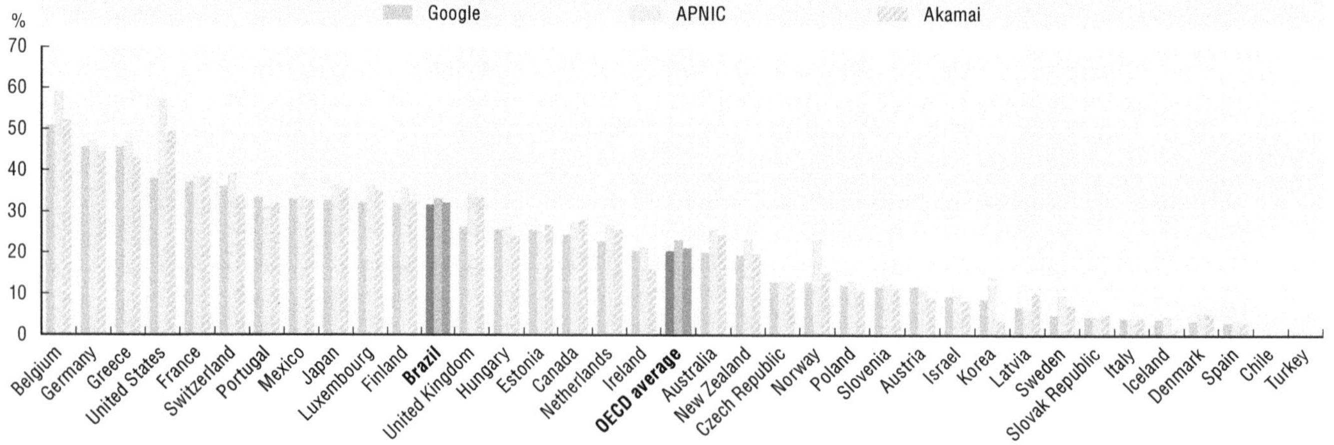

Note: Registered IPv6 addresses ranked by Google statistics.

Sources: Google (2020), "Per-country IPv6 adoption", *https://www.google.com/intl/en/ipv6/statistics.html#tab=per-country-ipv6-adoption* (accessed in February 2020); APNIC (2020), "IPv6 measurement maps", *http://stats.labs.apnic.net/ipv6* (accessed in February 2020); Akamai (2020), *State of the Internet: IPv6 Adoption Visualization*, *https://www.akamai.com/uk/en/our-thinking/state-of-the-internet-report/state-of-the-internet-ipv6-adoption-visualization.jsp* (accessed in February 2020).

Internet exchange points

Internet exchange points (IXPs) play a crucial role in IP interconnection, as they keep the exchange of traffic local rather than routing data via other countries, which increases latency and may be more costly (Weller and Woodcock, 2013). Also thanks to initiatives from NIC.br, Brazil has built-up a substantial number of IXPs, the Brazilian IXP System (Ponto de Troca de Tráfego, PTT Metro), and is the leading country in the region when it comes to the overall number of IXPs.

Brazil currently has 34 active IXPs with more than 3 500 participants that exchange traffic at the national level. While the number of IXPs depends on a range of factors, including the size of the economy and the geographical situation of a country, Brazil ranks higher in terms of the number of IXPs than most OECD countries (Figure 2.16). With more than 1 700 participants and an average traffic of around 4.8 Tbps (Packet Clearing House, 2020), the Ponto de Troca de Tráfego Metro São Paulo constitutes one of the largest IXPs in the world in terms of participants. It also constitutes the third-largest IXP in terms of average traffic, just after the Deutsche Commercial Exchange Frankfurt, Germany (DE-CIX) with 5.8 Tbps (terabytes per second), and the Amsterdam Internet Exchange, Netherlands (AMS-IX) with 5.6 Tbps (Packet Clearing House, 2020). A number of foreign South American providers also rely on the Ponto de Troca de Tráfego Metro São Paulo, which functions as a continental hub.

Figure 2.16. Number of Internet exchange points in Brazil and the OECD, 2019

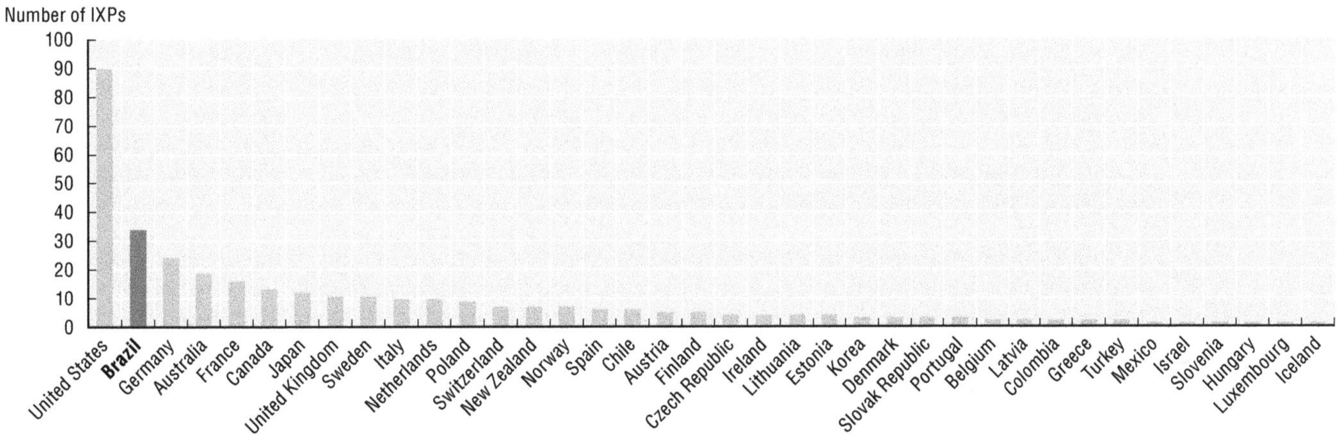

Notes: IXP = Internet exchange point. Only Internet exchange points listed with at least three participants are included.

Source: Packet Clearing House (2020), *Internet Exchange Directory* (database), *https://www.pch.net/ixp/dir* (accessed on 18 February 2020).

Latency is the lowest in the Southeast Region of Brazil, where most IXPs and the two largest ones (São Paulo and Rio de Janeiro) are situated. The median latency in the Southeast (15.9 ms) is almost four times less than in the North (57.4 ms) (NIC.br, 2018). The elevated latency in the North Region further demonstrates the low availability of backhaul in the region and confirms quality of service differences found. Moreover, the low availability of backhaul also results in differences with respect to the amount of traffic interchanged (Packet Clearing House, 2020).

The .br domain

An interesting feature of Brazilian Internet infrastructure is that the revenues from the domain name registration, the Brazilian country code top-level domain (ccTLD), managed by NIC.br/CGI.br, are used to fund improvements in Internet management and infrastructure. Among others, NIC.br/CGI.br used the revenues from the ccTLD.br to promote programmes to enhance traffic management, measure the quality of broadband connections, and the above-mentioned support for IPv6 adoption and operation of IXPs. NIC.br also invests its revenues in the implementation and operation of IXPs.

As of April 2019, .br was the seventh most popular domain in the world. With the creation of new subdomains, it now provides for more than 120 different options. Among others, there are subdomains to identify specific interests (such as "ong.br", "art.br", "eco.br"), or cities (for example, "rio.br", "manaus.br", "cuiaba.br", "floripa.br", "foz.br") (Convergência Digital, 2019).

To date, around 89% of Brazilian companies use the .br domain and 3% use one of the various Brazilian subdomains (CGI.br, 2018). Nevertheless, high usage of .br does not necessarily indicate that the respective content is also hosted in Brazil. In fact, data collected in 2013 showed that only 54% of Brazilian websites using the ccTLD.br are hosted in the country (OECD, 2014a), which could indicate that certain website owners do not consider it to be cost-effective to host their content locally.

Submarine fibre cables

Another crucial infrastructure for connectivity are submarine cables. In this regard, Brazil is well-served, with a total of 19 cables, giving the country access to a network of cables amounting to almost 180 000 km (TeleGeography, 2020). Many of the landing stations are located in Fortaleza (Northeast), the closest point to Africa and Europe, and in Santos and Rio de Janeiro (Southeast), the most populated region. Seven cables were added between 2017 and 2018, and five new ones are planned to be ready for service in 2020 or 2021, reflecting the growth of submarine fibre connectivity. The largest cables, South America-1 (SAm-1) and GlobeNet, with 25 000 km and 23 800 km respectively, were deployed in 2000 and 2001.

Data centres

Data centres have become a critical infrastructure for connectivity as cloud computing becomes key to enable on-demand access to digital services. In absolute terms, Brazil has a considerable number of data centres (111) (Cloudscene, 2019) when compared to OECD countries (Figure 2.17). Nevertheless, given the size of the market, the number of data centre deployments could indicate a non-competitive environment or higher costs in comparison to other countries, which does not make local data centres attractive to companies relying on cloud services. For example, energy is a major input for data centres. Energy prices in Brazil are comparatively high, with Brazilian companies paying almost twice as much (USD PPP 269, purchasing power parity) per MWh as the OECD average (USD PPP 143) as of 2017 (IEA, 2019). This may also be partially explained by high taxes at the state level (i.e. Imposto sobre Circulação de Mercadorias e Serviços [ICMS], as explained below).

In addition, communication network quality, capacity and prices may hold investors back from deploying data centres. Bureaucracy related to land acquisition and municipal approval of construction projects, as well as high tariffs for importing capital goods necessary for establishing a data centre are also cited as a common hindrance.

Figure 2.17. Data centres in Brazil and the OECD, 2019

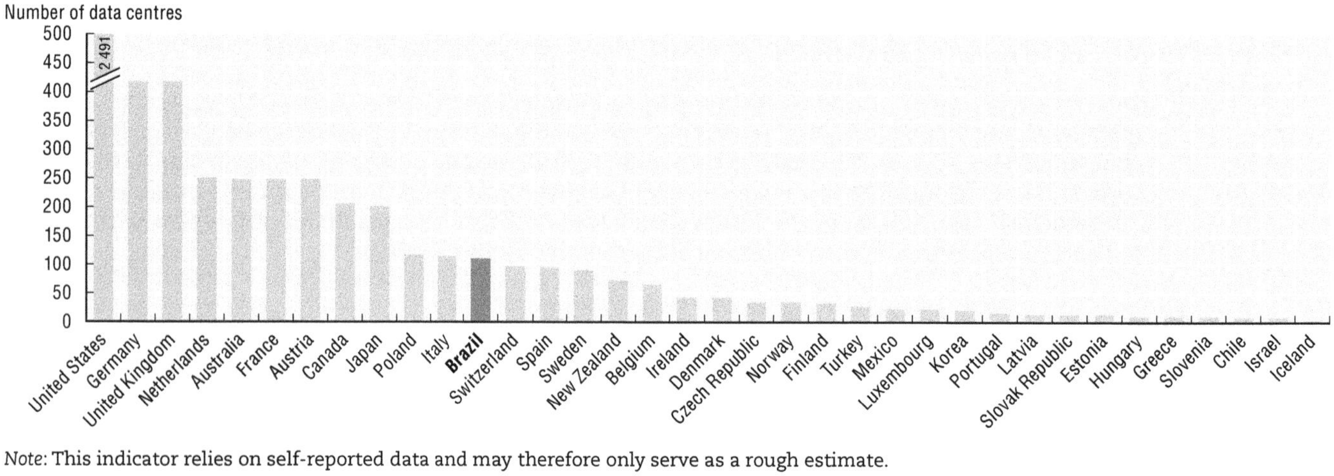

Note: This indicator relies on self-reported data and may therefore only serve as a rough estimate.

Source: Cloudscene (2019), *Markets: Brazil, https://cloudscene.com/market/data-centers-in-brazil/all.*

Prices for fixed and mobile broadband services

Communication prices are one indicator of the level of competition in a market and can influence the take up of services, especially in countries where there is unmet demand by low-income groups. According to a survey conducted in 2018 by CETIC.br/NIC.br, affordability was the main reason for the lack of Internet adoption by households in Brazil, reported by 61% of respondents (CGI.br, 2019).

The OECD's telecommunication baskets provide detailed information on Brazil's prices for fixed and mobile communication services compared to OECD countries and its regional peers. The OECD uses a pricing methodology that designs usage baskets (i.e. low, medium and high usage) for different consumption patterns. It collects the data twice a year, using prices on websites that are shown for consumers at a certain date. This assumes that rational consumers can make decisions based on the information available to them.

In terms of mobile broadband services (i.e. mobile voice and data plans for smartphones), for a low-usage type of basket (i.e. 0.5-5 GB of data volume consumed per month), data from November 2019 show that Brazil has quite affordable plans compared to OECD average prices (Figure 2.18). For the basket of 300 calls and 1 GB of data, Brazilian consumers paid USD PPP 12.9, compared to the OECD average of USD PPP 24.9. For a high-usage basket, Brazil exhibited low prices, with the exception of mobile broadband plans with unlimited voice and 20 GB, where plans in Brazil were twice as expensive as OECD average plans (USD PPP 105.3 vs. USD PPP 46.4). Although prices of mobile broadband service plans seem affordable, it should be noted that price baskets do not take into consideration the actual speeds enjoyed by consumers (Figure 2.10). Therefore, although mobile broadband prices in Brazil may be lower, it may be because the quality experienced by users is also lower than in OECD countries.

Figure 2.18. Mobile broadband prices in Brazil compared to its regional peers and the OECD, November 2019

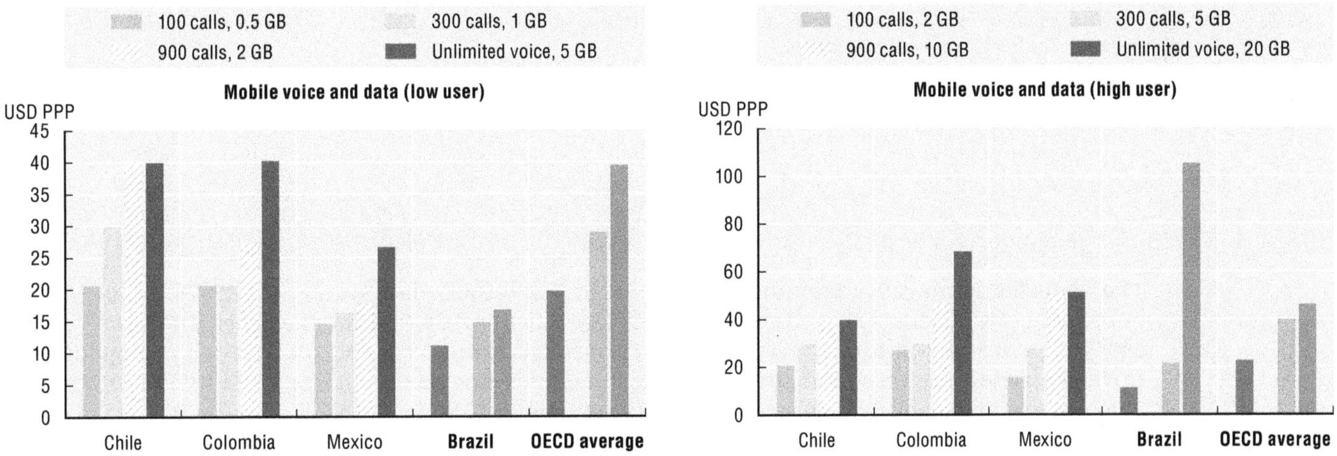

Notes: PPP = purchasing power parity; GB = gigabyte. Mobile voice and data baskets range in terms of number of voice calls, SMS included and data allowance (gigabytes per month). For more details on the OECD price basket methodology, please refer to OECD (2017b), "Revised OECD Telecommunication Price Baskets", *www.oecd.org/sti/broadband/DSTI-CDEP-CISP(2017)4FINAL.pdf*.

Source: OECD calculations based on Strategy Analytics (2019), "Teligen tariff & benchmarking market data using the OECD methodology", *https://www.strategyanalytics.com/access-services/service-providers/tariffs---mobile-and-fixed/*.

The affordability of fixed broadband services is less evident, which may be a result of the lack of transparency in Brazilian advertised offers for fixed broadband services. As of December 2019, with the exception of the baskets with very low download speeds (i.e. 256 kbps), Brazil displayed higher prices for fixed broadband for all other usage profiles (i.e. low, medium and high), compared to the OECD average and its regional peers such as Chile, Colombia and Mexico (Figure 2.19). The gap is more evident for plans with download speeds higher than 10 Mbps. A medium-usage basket of 30 GB data volume with these speeds in the OECD has an average price of USD PPP 31.6, while it is USD PPP 56.1 in Brazil. The same usage basket in Chile, Colombia and Mexico is USD PPP 30.6, USD PPP 44.7 and USD PPP 32.4, respectively. It should also be noted that these national averages may not reflect disparities in prices among regions, especially in rural and remote areas, which are likely to have higher prices due to the lack of consumer choice.

Both the quality and prices of communication services are important dimensions of the competitive dynamics of the market. In the case of Brazil, the high level of taxes (e.g. ICMS) in the sector may be an important factor influencing the affordability of communication services.

Figure 2.19. Fixed broadband prices (medium-usage basket) in Brazil compared to its regional peers and the OECD average, December 2019

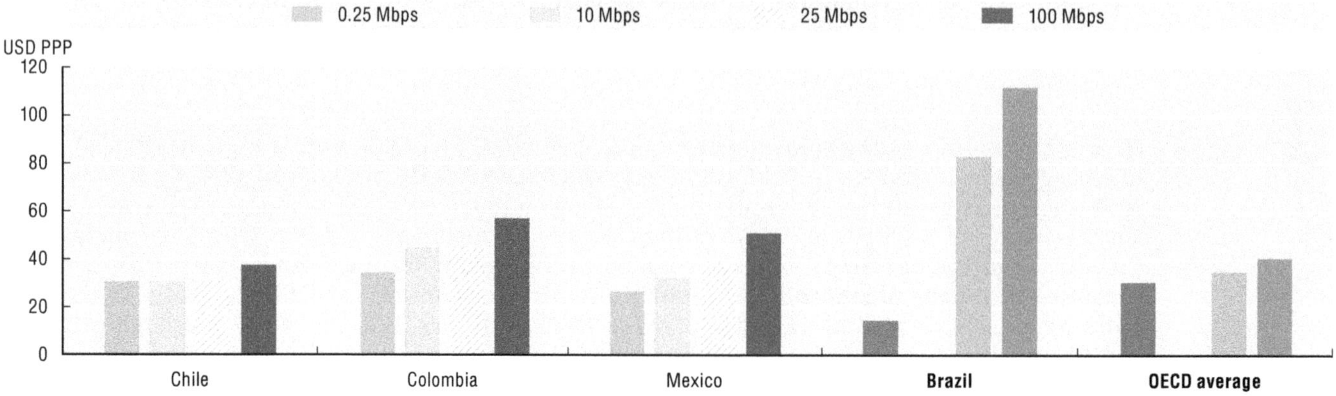

Notes: PPP = purchasing power parity; Mbps = megabits per second. In the low-usage alternative, data allowances of plans range from 5 GB to 100 GB/month; in the medium-usage alternative, the data allowance ranges from 15 GB to 300 GB/month; in the high-usage alternative it ranges from 45 GB to 900 GB/month following the OECD methodology approved by all member countries. Price baskets take into account data volumes per month (measured in GB) as well as download speeds (measured in Mbps). Since 2014, Anatel has banned data caps in the commercial offers from the largest players; the leading feature of the fixed broadband baskets in Brazil is download speeds. For more details on the OECD price basket methodology, please refer to OECD (2017b), "Revised OECD telecommunication price baskets", *http://www.oecd.org/sti/broadband/DSTI-CDEP-CISP(2017)4FINAL.pdf*. The prices taken into account in Brazil for the OECD baskets consider promotional prices for the valid period of the offers (e.g. 12 months), and revert to the price-cap tariff afterwards.

Source: OECD calculations based on Strategy Analytics (2019), "Teligen tariff & benchmarking market data using the OECD methodology", *https://www.strategyanalytics.com/access-services/networks/tariffs---mobile-and-fixed*.

Developments in market structure

Communication market participants

The liberalisation of the communication sector in Brazil took place during the 1990s. Following the enactment of the General Telecommunications Law (Lei Geral de Telecomunicações [LGT], No. 9 472 of 1997), the state-owned company Telebrás was privatised in July 1998 and split-up into a long-distance privately owned operator (Embratel), three regional fixed line companies and eight wireless carriers. Telebrás was re-established as a state-owned company in 2010.

Currently, the largest players in the communication market in Brazil are Telefônica, under the brand Vivo (owned by Telefónica Spain); Telecom Americas, under the brand Claro (owned by America Móvil); Oi; and TIM Brasil, owned by Telecom Italia. For fixed broadband players, the operators with the largest market shares are Claro, Vivo and Oi. For mobile voice and mobile broadband, the main players by market share are Vivo, Claro, TIM and Oi. The evolution of the market shares in the last eight to ten years regarding these services are analysed further below, as they are useful to comprehend the competitive environment in Brazil.

In terms of broadcasting services, in December 2018, Brazil had 862 commercial free-to-air (FTA) nationwide television channels, 131 public nationwide channels (generating own content), 20 874 commercial regional channels and 75 public regional channels (as relay stations). According to audience rankings from Kantar Ibope Media, Globo is the most-watched channel. It is part of the Globo Group, which is owned by the Marinho family. Among all TV channels, the three most-watched have been Globo, SBT (owned by Silvio Santos Group) and Record (Record Group), which are all FTA channels.

Pay TV service providers have a particular standing in Brazil. Although they provide audio-visual services similar to those of FTA broadcasting, pay TV is categorised in the country as a telecommunication service and regulated according to each activity within its value chain. Two main economic groups dominated the Brazilian pay TV market in 2019, with a combined market share of 78.9%. Claro (also owning Embratel and Net) had 49.2% of the market followed by Sky/DirecTV at 29.7%. Two other large groups – Oi, Vivo (also owning GVT)– together shared 18.1% of the market. Algar, which in December 2018 had 0.5% of the pay TV market, exited the market in February 2020.

In terms of content production and content packaging, the market is also concentrated. From the total subscriptions in terms of individual pay TV channels registered by the National Film Agency (Agência Nacional do Cinema, Ancine) in December 2018, 50.4% were divided between only two economic groups, Globo and Warner Media (Ancine, 2019).

As in OECD countries, there are various over-the-top (OTT) media services offers in Brazil. Under the current Brazilian legislation, OTT services and applications are classified as value-added services (serviço de valor adicionado, SVA) and are neither considered telecommunication nor broadcasting services. In terms of audio-visual services, several commercial offers exist in terms of video-on-demand subscriptions (SVoD) (e.g. Netflix and Globoplay) and transactional video on demand (TVoD) (e.g. Telecine On and Sky Play App). Estimates for 2018 indicate that the number of unique OTT audio-visual service subscriptions in Brazil was around 21.3 million, a subscription base which has been constantly growing since 2011 (Katz, 2019).

Fixed and mobile broadband market dynamics

The number of fixed broadband subscribers has tripled, from approximately 11 million subscriptions in 2008 to 32.9 million in 2019. The three largest providers of fixed broadband in 2019 covering 66% of the market were Claro Brasil with a 29.1% market share, Vivo (21.3%) and Oi (16%) (Figure 2.20). In the last 11 years, Claro's market share grew from 11.2% in 2008 to 29.1% in 2019. This is likely related to Claro's ownership of Embratel, the fixed incumbent of wholesale access services in Brazil, and Net, one of the largest pay TV (cable) operators in the country.

Figure 2.20. Fixed broadband market shares in Brazil, 2008 and 2019

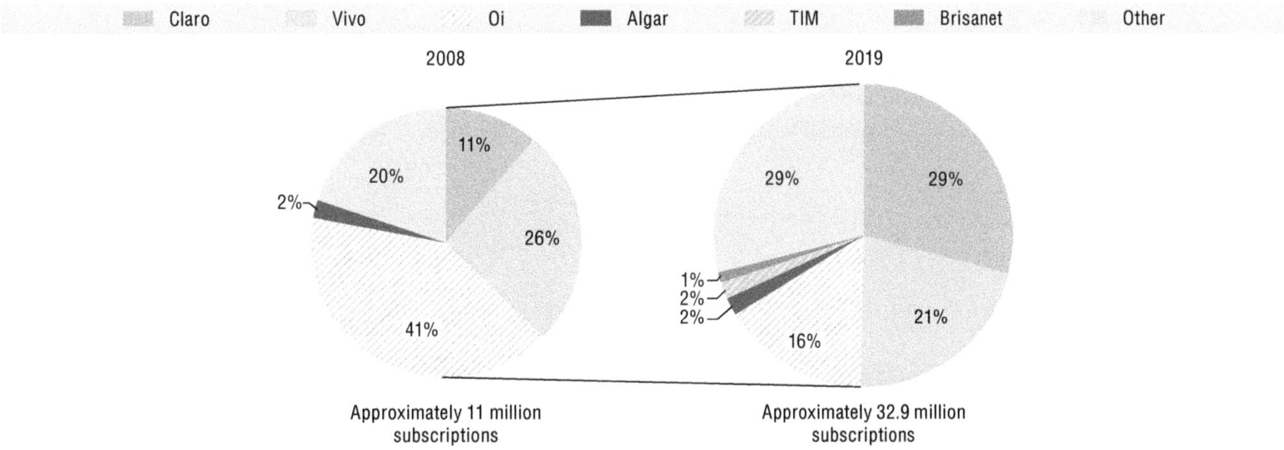

Source: Anatel (2020a), *Painéis de Dados: Acessos*, *https://www.anatel.gov.br/paineis/acessos* (accessed on 28 May 2020).

The fixed broadband market in Brazil is characterised by a large heterogeneity among players. There are currently more than 13 000 ISPs in Brazil, which includes large operators offering bundles of communication services as well as small providers operating in remote areas not yet commercially attractive to larger ISPs. There has been noteworthy growth in recent years of "small providers" of broadband access (*prestador de pequeno porte*, or "Other" in Figure 2.21), defined by Anatel as ISPs with a national market share of less than 5%. These providers have a fibre presence in 2 451 municipalities, and 783 of these cities rely solely on small providers for fibre access, which corresponds to 14% of the cities in Brazil (Anatel, 2019a). According to Anatel, small ISPs accounted for 18.4% of Brazil's fixed broadband subscriptions in 2018, and more than 20% in 2019.

The mobile broadband market has undergone considerable changes in the last nine years, growing from approximately 174 million to 196.6 million mobile broadband subscriptions. In 2008, the leading mobile network operator (MNO) was Claro, with a market share of 42.6%, followed by Vivo (20.2%). In 2019, Vivo became the leading MNO with a market share of roughly 31%, followed by Claro (28.8%) and TIM (24.1%) (Figure 2.22). In 2019, other smaller MNOs amounted to 1.1% of the market share (i.e. Nextel, Algar and Sercomtel) and mobile virtual network operators (MVNOs) accounted for less than 0.01%

of the market (Teleco, 2019). These data do not take into account the acquisition of Nextel by Claro in March 2019 (approved by Anatel in September 2019).

There are 8 authorised MVNOs in Brazil and 14 certified MVNOs (branded resellers that do not require prior authorisation by Anatel), bringing the total to 22 MVNOs. The main licensed MVNO is Datora Mobile Telecomunicações with 533 000 users in 2019. The MVNO market witnessed the exit of one MVNO, Porto Seguro Telecomunicações, in 2019.

Figure 2.21. Share of fixed broadband subscriptions per Internet service provider in Brazil, 2015-18

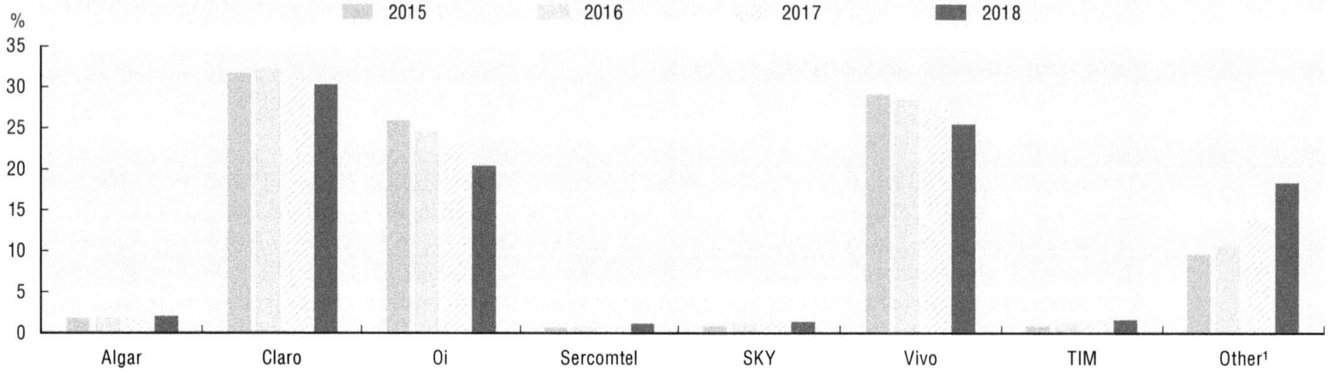

1. Small Internet service providers.

Source: Anatel (2019a), *Plano Estrutural de Redes de Telecomunicações – PERT*, *www.anatel.gov.br/dados/pert* (accessed on 20 September 2019).

Figure 2.22. Mobile broadband market shares in Brazil, 2010 and 2019

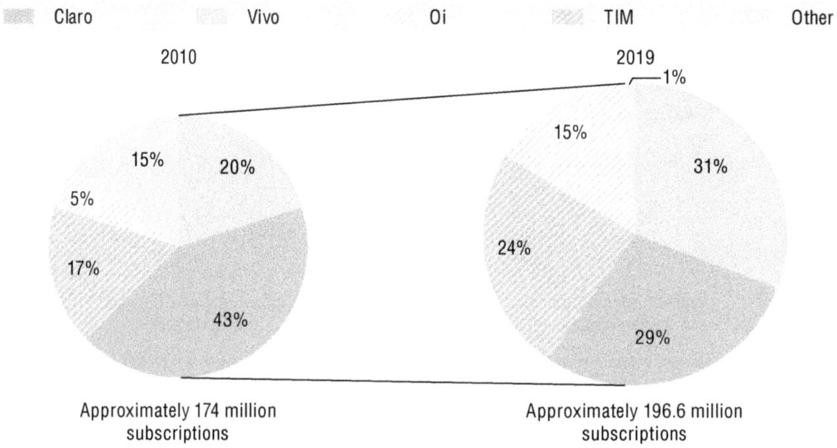

Source: Anatel (2020a), *Painéis de Dados: Acessos*, *https://www.anatel.gov.br/paineis/acessos* (accessed on 28 May 2020).

Main regulatory and policy developments

Institutional framework

A number of bodies or agencies in Brazil have direct or indirect responsibilities over the communication sector. The National Telecommunications Agency, Anatel, is the telecommunication regulator. The Ministry of Science, Technology, Innovations and Communications (Ministério da Ciência, Tecnologia, Inovações e Comunicações, MCTIC) is responsible for public policy related to the sector. The competition authority in Brazil, the Administrative Council for Economic Defence (Conselho Administrativo de Defesa Econômica, CADE), has the mandate to promote competition, approve mergers and acquisitions, and investigate antitrust violations.

For broadcasting, and specifically for FTA, the MCTIC acts as a public policy maker and a *quasi*-regulator (i.e. responsible for the monitoring and control of the broadcasting sector, directly and indirectly). Concerning pay TV, which is defined as a telecommunication service within the legal framework in Brazil, the role of regulating this service is shared by Anatel and Ancine, as established by the 2011 SeAC Law which defines production, programming, packaging and distribution activities in the pay TV value chain. Anatel is responsible for regulating the pay TV distribution, and Ancine for programming and packaging of pay TV. Ancine also has the mandate to foster competition and regulate issues related to the development of the Brazilian film industry, including content-related issues.

Within the executive power, the Ministry of Economy, particularly through the Secretariat of Competition Advocacy and Competitiveness (Secretaria de Advocacia da Concorrência e Competitividade, SEAE), has an important mandate on competition advocacy. The Ministry of Justice carries out its consumer protection role through the National Consumer Secretariat (Secretaria Nacional do Consumidor, Senacon), as well as a general audio-visual content classification role.

Senacon is in charge of formulating, promoting, co-ordinating and implementing the national consumer protection policy. There are also more than 800 state and local departments for consumer protection, Procons, linked to the executive power, which also oversee communication companies. Anatel also has some consumer protection functions.

Moreover, judicial institutions such as the Federal Supreme Court (Supremo Tribunal Federal) and the independent bodies that do not belong to the executive, legislative or judiciary branches, such as the Federal Court of Accounts (Tribunal de Contas da União, TCU) and the Public Prosecutor's Office (Ministério Público), have important roles related to constitutional, legal and budgetary external controls.

Finally, non-governmental organisations such as the CGI.br and the Self-Regulatory Advertising Council (Conselho Nacional de Autorregulamentação Publicitária, CONAR), play key roles in integrating Internet service initiatives and promoting ethical advertising, respectively.

Main recommendations from the *OECD Telecommunication and Broadcasting Review of Brazil*

Improving the institutional and regulatory framework

Creating a converged regulator and separating policy from regulatory functions

Particularly in the area of broadcasting (including pay TV services), regulatory and policy roles are not clearly defined. Multiple authorities are tasked with developing and implementing policy and regulation (e.g. the MCTIC, Ancine and Anatel). Contrary to international best practices, there is no clear distinction between general policy formulation and the issuance of *ex ante* regulation to tackle market failures, promote competition and protect consumers. This poses considerable challenges for the coherence of regulation and policies.

In addition, multi-purpose IP-based networks have enabled the provision of different services over the same network. The increase of convergence that blurs the contours of previously distinct sectors rises the complexity of how these institutions interact.

To address the convergence of communication and broadcasting services, a number of OECD countries such as Australia, Hungary and the United Kingdom have merged their broadcasting and communication regulators, while others have taken concrete actions to increase the flexibility of the regulators to limit the overlapping of functions and facilitate the implementation of converged regulation (OECD, 2008; 2017a).

In order to strengthen the institutional framework and following good international practice, it is recommended to create an independent convergent authority responsible for communication and broadcasting markets (including pay TV) and for monitoring evolving OTT services, while ensuring that an arm's-length principle be kept between regulation and policy making.

Increasing the independence of the regulator and creating an independent oversight for regulatory impact assessments

The existence of a strong sectoral regulator is key for the effective implementation of the objectives set by the government and reducing market uncertainty and promoting a well-functioning sector (OECD, 2014b). It is paramount for the communication sector to ensure the adequate funding of the regulator and its financial independence, through a multiannual, clearly defined budget, ring-fenced from the rest of the government budget.

Despite improvements in Anatel's budget setting and stability since 2018, its financial autonomy is not secured due to the lack of budgetary control Anatel has over sector fees to fund the regulator (Fundo de Fiscalização das Telecomunicações, FISTEL).

In addition, the control exercised by the TCU is potentially undermining Anatel's independence, limiting its capacity to properly carry out its functions. As previously acknowledged by the OECD in 2008, performance assessment by national audit offices can serve to protect the public interest. However, the extent to which *ex ante* assessment and advice from the TCU is applied to the regulatory agencies in Brazil is an unusual practice (OECD, 2008). A clear accountability framework needs to be balanced with effective autonomy of the regulator, as the maintenance of certain prerogatives is essential to ensure the technicality, impartiality and predictability of the regulatory function (Moreira, 2004). Moreover, the personal liability of public servants should be limited.

Finally, despite improvements in the regulatory impact assessment (RIA) framework, and the fact that Anatel being the most active regulator in Brazil to promote RIAs, Anatel has limited experience with the implementation of quantitative RIAs (Aquila et al, 2019). Brazil should implement an independent body to systematically review RIA reports of different institutions with regulatory roles, ensuring oversight and quality, through a "whole-of-government" approach and with permanent co-ordination mechanisms and bodies that address the need for policy coherence and strategic commitment in the long term (OECD, 2016).

Establishing a converged regulatory and policy framework

Establishing regulatory and policy regimes that are attuned to convergence and emerging market trends requires that regulators and policy makers rethink existing frameworks to ensure that they are still applicable and coherent. The first step is ensuring that the rules are clear and consistent for operators across the communication sector. The second is eliminating any double windows and overlap of functions that may cause confusion and legal uncertainty.

Licensing of communication services in Brazil is still considerably fragmented. Different authorisations are required for each type of communication service provided. Anatel has gradually simplified its classification of communication services and licensing framework over the years. There are currently four main service categories in Brazil that require an authorisation: 1) fixed telephony; 2) mobile telephony; 3) "multimedia services" such as fixed broadband; and 4) pay TV. In addition, under the current licensing framework, some services are classified as value-added services, which are neither considered telecommunication nor broadcasting services. Value-added services can include OTT, but also layers of the Internet service provision excluding "last-mile" access. The most prominent example of a value-added service is the Internet connection service (i.e. authentication of the user in the network that originated in the past due to dial-up Internet services).

For broadcasting services, the licensing regime applies different requirements to FTA broadcasting and equivalent pay TV services. In addition, it is also cumbersome and may enable political influence in the granting of FTA licences.

All service categories are subject to a number of different regulations, fees and taxes, which are not only burdensome for companies, but also pose barriers to entry in a convergent ecosystem. Moreover, the plurality of definitions, even for the same service (i.e. broadband service provision), leads to arbitrage opportunities of both regulatory measures and taxation.

A good practice to be applied to all communication services would be to abandon all individual authorisations required for communication service providers and to replace them with a single class-licensing regime, valid for all services, except for where there is resource scarcity, such as spectrum.

Enhancing the co-ordination of policies and regulation at all levels of government

In order to ensure that norms are applied coherently, roles must be well-defined, double windows eliminated and overlap of functions reduced. From a general level, it is paramount that federal, state and municipal levels co-ordinate efficiently, particularly on broadband expansion in the country. Co-ordination among the three levels of government is particularly important for streamlining rights of way, easing antenna deployment and harmonising power density regulations. It is also vital for ensuring pluralism related to broadcasting services.

More specifically, other institutions that should improve co-ordination and reduce overlap are the competition authority, CADE and sector regulators, particularly concerning the audio-visual sector and pay TV services, as well as those regarding institutions responsible for consumer protection, such as Senacon, Procons and Anatel. For competition issues concerning the audio-visual sector, in the absence of a converged regulator, it is important to clarify the role of each sector regulator and to anticipate dispute resolution procedures in the event of divergent opinions. For consumer issues, it is important that already existing co-operation mechanisms are further formalised to improve transparency and enhance the exchange of information.

Ensuring effective regulatory enforcement

An important aspect of a well-functioning regulator is the efficacy of its regulatory enforcement measures, extending to how the regulator's decisions are reviewed through administrative or judiciary processes. Despite its sanctioning powers, Anatel has imposed far more fines than it has been able to collect. Between 2010 and 2017, Anatel imposed 60 000 fines; only 66% of them were fully paid by operators, representing 13% of the monetary value of the total fines imposed (Anatel, 2017). To improve enforcement of applied fines and increase collection, Anatel should carefully substantiate the sanctions, which should fit the nature of the offence. Fines should be high enough to deter behaviour, but at the same time follow the principle of proportionality to deter appeals.

Moreover, as Anatel reflects on a variety of alternatives beyond purely monetary sanctions, such as warnings, Conduct Adjustment Agreements (Termos de Compromisso de Ajustamento de Conduta, TAC) and future obligations (*obrigação de fazer*), whereby operators can trade the fines for investment obligations, it is important that they be based on granular data and on the establishment of a coherent sanctioning framework. A thorough analysis *ex ante* to establish where such obligations should be imposed, and *ex post* monitoring of their implementation are warranted.

Overhauling the taxation, fees and tariff framework

The high level of fees and special taxes severely impacts the communication sector in Brazil. The high fees likely contribute to the total cost of communication services, compromise the sector's potential for innovation and investment, thus hindering the adoption and affordability of communication services.

In light of the extensive positive spill-over effects of communication services on the Brazilian economy and society, the high taxes and fees should be reconsidered and ways identified to reduce them. Brazilian states levy the ICMS, which applies to the movement of goods and transport and telecommunication services. The ICMS burden is of particular concern as it potentially effects the cost of communication services and consequently their use. Brazilian states should therefore consider harmonising the ICMS across states and reducing the applicable ICMS rate to communication services to the extent possible.

In the long run, it is recommended to pursue the efforts for a fundamental reform of the indirect tax framework to reduce the distortions caused by the current indirect tax treatment of the communication sector. In line with former OECD work on taxation issues in Brazil, it is suggested to consolidate consumption taxes at the state and federal levels into one value-added tax with a broad base and full refunds for input VAT paid (OECD, 2018b; 2019a).

Another important aspect regarding the simplification of the fees framework in Brazil concerns sectoral funds. Fees paid to FISTEL have been integrated into the Contribution for the Development of the National Film Industry (Contribuição para o Desenvolvimento da Indústria Cinematográfica Nacional, CONDECINE) and the Contribution to Foster Public Broadcasting (Contribuição para o Fomento da Radiodifusão pública, CFRP). However, the Universal Service Fund (Fundo de Universalização dos

Serviços de Telecomunicações, FUST) and the Telecommunications Technological Development Fund (Fundo para o Desenvolvimento Tecnológico das Telecomunicações, FUNTTEL) are still accounted for separately, which results in three different funds in Brazil (FISTEL, FUST, FUNTTEL). In line with streamlining and convergence, Brazil should consider integrating all contributions into one, as was done, for example, recently in Colombia (OECD, 2019c). Integrating all fund contributions into one single contribution may furthermore reduce administrative costs and increase efficiency.

Improving market conditions

Lowering barriers to entry and easing infrastructure deployment

The deployment of communication infrastructure, especially concerning access to rights of way and the installation of cellular sites, continues to be a rather cumbersome process in Brazil. Operators must comply with federal as well as local regulations, which may vary by municipality and state. To reduce the costs of infrastructure deployment, Brazil should further establish dig-once policies, including for the construction of highways, energy transmission lines, etc. The federal government should harmonise the application of the Antennas Law by issuing norms that promote the deployment of infrastructure under the principle of positive silence.

Streamlining rights of way will also be key to increase backhaul and backbone connectivity. Fibre backhaul, if accompanied by an effective open access regime and continued monitoring of competition dynamics, should also help decrease the costs of deploying 4G and 5G mobile networks, which will be important for reaching end users in rural and remote areas of Brazil.

Ensuring efficient spectrum management

One prerequisite for mobile communication services in Brazil is the availability of spectrum, which is assigned through spectrum auctions. In general, the design of such an auction should take into account policy objectives of increasing the coverage of communication networks while enhancing competition in mobile markets. The converged regulator should balance public policy objectives and avoid coverage obligations from becoming an impediment for certain actors to bid, as well as eliminating any industrial policy obligations that may distort auction results or raise deployment costs.

As the upcoming 5G auction in Brazil has been hailed as being the largest auction for 5G spectrum ever, stakeholders are observing the auction's design very closely. The design of spectrum auctions depends on three main elements: reserve prices, coverage obligations and spectrum caps. In Brazil, auctions have, in general, followed good practices. With the approval of Law 13.879 on 3 October 2019, spectrum licences in Brazil can now be successively renewed, without limit, after the first 20-year term. Each renewal is accompanied by a payment, determined by Anatel, which operators may exchange for investment commitments. As spectrum auctions are one of the main tools countries use to foster competition in mobile markets, Anatel should closely observe and analyse the effects of this new arrangement on the market entry of new mobile operators.

Fostering competition in communication and broadcasting markets

The competitive dynamics of the communication sector in Brazil, at a national level, have been relatively stable over time when measured by market shares. Particularly in the mobile telephony market, the level of concentration, measured by the number of operators and the Herfindahl-Hirschman Index, is relatively low, but this continues to evolve dynamically with the vertical integration among network operators and service providers. In Brazil, challenges to competition in the communication sector relate to access to essential infrastructure and potential anticompetitive conduct tending to foreclose the market. As the availability of services and number of service providers is not homogenous across the country, barriers to competition vary considerably, and are determined by the specific circumstances in each municipality.

Competition is a serious concern for broadcasting. There has been no effective enforcement of competition principles in the case of FTA broadcasting services, with content production being concentrated among a few major FTA broadcasters and insufficient development of independent domestic content production (Mendel and Salomon, 2011). For pay TV, despite the recent contraction in the number of subscribers, the market is also rather concentrated, varying across the pay TV value chain, with higher concentration in the market of content distribution and significant concentration in the programming and packaging of content (Ancine, 2019).

Competition in the communication sector in Brazil is protected and promoted via *ex ante* sectoral regulation and *ex post* antitrust regulation. In this regard, CADE, the Brazilian competition authority, has *ex post* independent jurisdiction over investigations of anticompetitive practices and *ex ante* jurisdiction for mergers in the telecommunication sector. Anatel also has specific *ex ante* competition attributions in the sector. The Secretariat of Competition Advocacy and Competitiveness conducts competition advocacy in general towards government agencies and society.

In order to improve Brazil's Competition Law and policy framework, it is crucial to refer to recommendations provided by the OECD Competition Committee in its 2019 Peer Review of Brazil (OECD, 2019b), which lists a number of recommendations to CADE in terms of its institutional governance, prioritisation of cases, settlement policies and merger notification thresholds. These recommendations also apply for the review of the communications and broadcasting sectors, particularly in the case of removing the 20% threshold for market share. For communication services, it is important that market power determinations be based on a rigorous assessment of all the factors affecting competitive conditions in the market under investigation, rather than market shares alone (OECD, 2019b). The low threshold established in the Brazilian jurisdiction means that the likelihood of false positive is high, that the inference can be easily contested by defendants, and should therefore be removed.

Strengthening national policies and evidence-based policy making

Expanding broadband networks and services

E-Digital is an important step towards establishing a coherent governance model for digital initiatives. However, with the exception of the number of public schools to be connected, no quantitative targets have been defined, and rely on aggregate global comparison indexes. Moreover, while high-speed broadband is mentioned in both the decree and background document, no minimum desired speed for broadband is indicated (as is done in most OECD countries, with concrete targets measured in terms of percentage of population, households or business connected with 30 Mbps, 50 Mbps or even 100 Mbps).

To ensure effective evaluation of policy programmes (such as Connected Brazil), clear milestones and specific targets must be defined from the start regarding coverage, speed, population, number of schools and health centres connected, etc. (by geographic market), with complete measurements taken at the beginning to serve as baseline values. Broadband connectivity initiatives supported by the government should seek to be sustainable and involve local stakeholders, privileging infrastructure sharing (such as ditches, ducts and poles), and implementing reasonable, cost-based and objective access rates for such infrastructure.

Promoting inclusive and forward-looking audio-visual public policies

Contrary to the national policy strategies that exist in the communication sector (e.g. E-Digital 2018-2020, Connected Brazil Programme), there is currently no overarching public policy for broadcasting, pay TV and emerging OTT services/VoD, which is necessary in an increasingly convergent environment. FTA broadcasting, in particular, has not received much attention in sector regulation and public policy making. In a country like Brazil, where FTA is the predominant means for consumers to access information, this is a particular concern with respect to inclusion, media pluralism and diversity.

In an increasingly converged landscape, it is important to define a holistic technology-neutral policy vision for the broadcasting, pay TV and VoD markets, once the regulatory and institutional reform is carried out and clear roles are assigned between the sector or converged regulator and the policy-making institutions (ministerial or as a separate audio-visual authority).

Improving data collection for evidence-based policy making

Well-functioning institutions that develop evidence-based regulations and policies should continue to improve the collection and analysis of sector information. The lack of consistency of the overall institutional and regulatory framework of the broadcasting sector in Brazil has led to a profound scarcity of data on broadcasting services, for both the most basic and the more advanced indicators. There is a deficiency of systematically collecting and reporting data which are needed to analyse market performance, the state of competition in the sector and the effectiveness of broadcasting policies.

For communication services, data collection and reporting is done by Anatel, the MCTIC and CETIC.br. In 2019, Anatel launched an ambitious data portal that compiles data on access, product certification, consumers, spectrum, concessions and licensing, quality, and regulation (Anatel, 2020a). The portal continues to be enhanced, but users can already access the original data, broken down by service and region, and use the system to conduct their own analysis. Moreover, CETIC.br, a department of NIC.br, also produces and monitors indicators through household and enterprise surveys (as well as educational, health and cultural organisations) on access, use and adoption of ICT. Improvements are still needed regarding connectivity coverage maps.

To allow consistent communication public policy and regulatory design, detailed and updated data must be available on deployment, adoption and usage of communication and broadcasting services, including emerging trends.

Box 2.1. Key recommendations to improve communication infrastructure and services in Brazil

Improving the institutional and regulatory framework

Creating a converged regulator and separating policy from regulatory functions

- Create a converged independent regulator overseeing the Brazilian communication and broadcasting sectors by merging the regulatory functions of Anatel, Ancine and the Ministry of Science, Technology, Innovations and Communications.
- Introduce a clear separation between policy making and regulation in the areas of broadcasting, pay TV and emerging OTT/VoD.

Increasing the independence of the regulator and creating an independent oversight for regulatory impact assessments

- Increase the independence of the sector – or converged – regulator.
- Promote an independent decision-making process on the part of the regulator. Focus the important role of the Federal Court of Accounts on *ex post* assessments. Limit the personal liability of public servants.
- Establish an independent oversight body to review the regulatory impact assessments of different institutions with regulatory roles.

Establishing a converged regulatory and policy framework

- To adapt the legal framework to a converging communication and broadcasting market, reform the legal framework to introduce a simple class-licensing regime for communication and broadcasting services.
- Remove legal restrictions on the integration of the pay TV value chain and cross-ownership between telecommunication and pay TV services on both foreign and domestic service providers.

Enhancing the co-ordination of policies and regulation at all levels of government

- Enhance the co-ordination of the federal, state and municipal levels on issues such as streamlining rights of way and easing antenna deployment to promote broadband deployment, particularly in underserved areas.
- Promote co-operation arrangements between the Administrative Council for Economic Defence and sector regulators to eliminate multiple and possibly competing decisions ("double windows"), particularly on broadcasting issues (including pay TV).

Box 2.1. Key recommendations to improve communication infrastructure and services in Brazil *(cont.)*

- Improve co-operation and reduce overlapping functions in the regulatory design and enforcement of consumer protection regulations by upscaling co-operation instruments among Senacon, Procons and Anatel.

Ensuring effective regulatory enforcement

- Anatel should strengthen its enforcement framework, seeking to establish proportionate sanctions (monetary or non-monetary) based on quantitative evidence and targets, considering the severity of the violation and the resulting harm.
- If Anatel wishes to continue promoting Conduct Adjustment Agreement (TAC) as a regulatory compliance tool that allows operators to commit to investment obligations instead of paying fines, it should carefully set and monitor these obligations.

Overhauling the taxation, fees and tariff framework

- Harmonise the ICMS across states, as also recommended in Chapter 3 of this Review. Reduce the high ICMS rates for communication services to the extent possible because of their negative effects on adoption. In the long run, pursue the fundamental reform of the indirect tax framework to reduce the distortions caused by the current indirect tax treatment of the communication and broadcasting sector.
- Merge sectoral funds into one single fund to reduce costs and increase efficiency. Ensure that the contributions to the funds are used for the further development of the digital economy in Brazil, including broadband deployment. In the long term, consider abolishing all sectoral contributions.
- Actively promote the entry of Mercosur countries into the WTO Information Technology Agreement, which creates a credible schedule for the reduction of tariffs on an increasing number of ICT goods, as also recommended in Chapter 6 of this Review.

Improving market conditions

Lowering barriers to entry and easing infrastructure deployment

- Reduce barriers to entry as much as possible.
- Further increase backhaul and backbone connectivity and promote open wholesale access models.
- Foster the Internet of Things (IoT) by eliminating taxes such as FISTEL establishing a separate IoT numbering plan, and re-examining outright IoT permanent roaming restrictions.
- Consider removing the legal restrictions on foreign direct investment in broadcasting in which foreign companies or individuals cannot hold more than 30% of the total and voting capital of free-to-air broadcasting companies.

Ensuring efficient spectrum management

- Closely monitor the effects of the changes introduced by Law 13.879 regarding a successive renewal of spectrum licences on market entry and competition in mobile markets.
- Carefully design the upcoming 5G auction as the vast amount of spectrum planned to be placed in the market combined with the possibility of successive renewal of spectrum licenses translates into high stakes of the effects of this auction on the competitive dynamics of the market.

Fostering competition in communication and broadcasting markets

- Follow the recommendations of the 2019 *OECD Peer Review of Competition Law and Policy in Brazil* (OECD, 2019b). Remove the 20% threshold for market share as a proxy for market power from the Competition Law. Issue guidelines for a clear analytical framework to assess market dominance.

Box 2.1. Key recommendations to improve communication infrastructure and services in Brazil *(cont.)*

Strengthening national policies and evidence-based policy making

Expanding broadband networks and services

- Establish targets for the Connected Brazil programme and other programmes aiming to expand networks and monitor their implementation. Improve co-operation among governmental entities and across the different levels of government (national, state and municipal) for the implementation of broadband connectivity initiatives.
- Expand high-quality broadband networks to underserved regions by fostering investment in infrastructure in order to bridge the digital divide.

Promoting inclusive and forward-looking audio-visual public policies

- Design an integrated and overarching public policy vision for broadcasting, pay TV and emerging OTT services/VoD.

Improving data collection for evidence-based policy making

- Substantially improve the data collection of the broadcasting sector and continue to improve the collection and analysis of statistical information with respect to connectivity coverage maps and the use of communication services.

References

Akamai (2020), *State of the Internet: IPv6 Adoption Visualization*, Akamai, *https://www.akamai.com/uk/en/our-thinking/state-of-the-internet-report/state-of-the-internet-ipv6-adoption-visualization.jsp* (accessed on 12 February 2020).

Anatel (2020a), *Painéis de Dados: Acessos* [Data sets: Subscriptions], Agência Nacional de Telecomunicações, Brasilia, *https://www.anatel.gov.br/paineis/acessos* (accessed on 28 May 2020).

Anatel (2020b), *Telefonia Móvel – Municípios Atendidos* [Mobile Telephony: Covered Municipalities], Agência Nacional de Telecomunicações, Brasilia, *https://www.anatel.gov.br/setorregulado/component/content/article/115-universalizacao-e-ampliacao-do-acesso/telefonia-movel/423-telefonia-movel-municipios-atendidos* (accessed on 20 February 2020).

Anatel (2020c), *Plano Estrutural de Redes de Telecomunicações (PERT) 2019-2024, Atualizaçao 2020* [Structural Plan of Telecommunication Networks (PERT) 2019-2024: Update 2020], Agência Nacional de Telecomunicações, Brasilia, *https://sei.anatel.gov.br/sei/modulos/pesquisa/md_pesq_documento_consulta_externa.php?eEP-wqk1skrd8hSlk5Z3rN4EVg9uLJqrLYJw_9INcO4m2N1jXIPEu1rXnv7UHJFGKd-jO_xz5ZYqyuXgvKFPZe9U7a4FRauel0Ej_GJ3pzD2sKi_sQQhtHNHQk_javEK* (accessed on 15 March 2020).

Anatel (2019a), *Plano Estrutural de Redes de Telecomunicações – PERT* [Structural Plan of Telecommunication Networks (PERT)], Agência Nacional de Telecomunicações, Brasilia, *https://www.anatel.gov.br/dados/pert* (accessed on 20 September 2019).

Anatel (2019b), *Mapeamento de Redes de Transporte* [Backhaul Network Maps], Agência Nacional de Telecomunicações, Brasilia, *https://www.anatel.gov.br/dados/mapeamento-de-redes* (accessed on 13 September 2019).

Anatel (2017), *Relatório Anual 2017* [Annual Report 2017], Agência Nacional de Telecomunicações, Brasilia, *https://www.anatel.gov.br/Portal/verificaDocumentos/documentoVersionado.asp?numeroPublicacao=348395&documentoPath=348395.pdf&Pub=&URL=/Portal/verificaDocumentos/documento.asp*.

Anatel (2014), *GT-IPv6 Grupo de Trabalho para Implantação do Protocolo IP-Versão 6 nas Redes das Prestadoras de Serviços de Telecomunicações: Relatório Final de Atividades* [GT-IPv6 Working Group to Implement the Internet Protocol Version 6 (IPv6) on Telecommunication Providers' Networks: Final Report of Activities], Agência Nacional de Telecomunicações, Brasilia, *https://www.anatel.gov.br/Portal/verificaDocumentos/documento.asp?numeroPublicacao=325769* (accessed on 17 March 2020).

Ancine (2019), *Assinantes no Mercado de Programação na TV por Assinatura 2019* [Programming Market Subscribers For Subscribers to Pay TV], Agência Nacional do Cinema, Brasilia,*https://oca.ancine.gov.br/sites/default/files/repositorio/pdf/informe_assinantes_no_mercado_de_programacao_-_versao_diagramada.pdf*.

APNIC (2020), "IPv6 measurement maps", *http://stats.labs.apnic.net/ipv6* (accessed on 20 February 2020).

Aquila, G. et al. (2019), "Quantitative regulatory impact analysis: Experience of regulatory agencies", *Utilities Policy*, Vol. 59, *https://doi.org/10.1016/j.jup.2019.100931*.

CGI.br (2019), *ICT Households 2018: Survey on the Use of Information and Communication Technologies in Brazilian Households*, Comitê Gestor da Internet no Brasil, São Paulo, *https://cetic.br/pt/tics/domicilios/2018/domicilios/* (accessed on 11 September 2019).

CGI.br (2018), *ICT Enterprises 2017: Survey on the use of Information and Communication Technologies in Brazilian Enterprises*, Comitê Gestor da Internet no Brasil, São Paulo, *https://www.cetic.br/media/docs/publicacoes/2/TIC_Empresas_2017_livro_eletronico.pdf*.

Cloudscene (2019), *Markets: Brazil* (database), *https://cloudscene.com/market/data-centers-in-brazil/all* (accessed on 5 October 2019).

Convergência Digital (2019), *.br Completa 30 Anos com 4 Milhões de Domínios Registrados* [.br Celebrates 30 Years with 4 Million Registered Domains], Convergência Digital, *https://www.convergenciadigital.com.br/cgi/cgilua.exe/sys/7}start.htm?UserActiveTemplate=site&infoid=50498&sid=4* (accessed on 20 February 2020).

Google (2020), "Per-country IPv6 adoption", *https://www.google.com/intl/en/ipv6* (accessed in February 2020).

IEA (2019), *Energy Prices and Taxes for OECD Countries 2019*, OECD Publishing, Paris, *https://dx.doi.org/10.1787/71612f7e-en* (accessed on 18 February 2020).

Katz, R. (2019), *Alterações nos Mercados de Audiovisual Global e Brasileiro: Dinâmica Competitiva, Impacto no Bem Estar do Consumidor e Implicações em Políticas Públicas e no Modelo de Concorrência* [Changes in the Global and Brazilian Audiovisual Market: Competitive Dynamics, Impact on Consumer Welfare, and Implications for Public Policy and Competition Model], Telecom Advisory Services, *www.teleadvs.com/wp-content/uploads/PTBR-Changes-in-the-Global-and-Brazilian-Audiovisual-Market-Raul-Katz.pdf* (accessed on 14 February 2020).

Maigron, P. (2020), *Regional Internet Registries Statistics* (database), *https://www-public.imtbs-tsp.eu/~maigron/RIR_Stats/* (accessed on 19 February 2020).

Mendel, T. and E. Salomon (2011), *The Regulatory Environment for Broadcasting: An International Best Practice Survey for Brazilian Stakeholders*, United Nations Educational, Scientific and Cultural Organization, Brasilia, *www.unesco.org/new/fr/communication-and-information/resources/publications-and-communication-materials/publications/full-list/the-regulatory-environment-for-broadcasting-an-international-best-practice-survey-for-brazilian-stakeholders*.

M-Lab (2019), "Worldwide broadband speed league", *https://www.cable.co.uk/broadband/speed/worldwide-speed-league/* (accessed on 9 May 2019).

Moreira, V. (2004), *Estudos de Regulação Pública* [Public Regulation Studies - I. Centre for Public Law and Regulation Studies], Centro de Estudos de Direito Público e Regulação, Universidade de Coimbra Faculdade de Direito, Coimbra Editora.

NIC.br (2018), *Banda Larga no Brasil: Um Estudo Sobre a Evolução do Acesso e da Qualidade das Conexões à Internet* [Broadband in Brazil: A Study on the Evolution and Access], Comitê Gestor da Internet no Brasil, São Paulo, *https://cetic.br/media/docs/publicacoes/1/Estudo%20Banda%20Larga%20no%20Brasil.pdf* (accessed on 20 February 2020).

OECD (2020a), *OECD Telecommunication and Broadcasting Review of Brazil*, OECD Publishing, Paris.

OECD (2020b), *Broadband Portal* (database), OECD, Paris, *www.oecd.org/sti/broadband/broadband-statistics* (accessed on 20 May 2020).

OECD (2019a), *Economic Policy Reforms 2019: Going for Growth*, OECD Publishing, Paris, *https://dx.doi.org/10.1787/aec5b059-en*.

OECD (2019b), *OECD Peer Reviews of Competition Law and Policy: Brazil 2019*, OECD, Paris, *www.oecd.org/daf/competition/oecd-peer-reviews-of-competition-law-and-policy-brazil-2019.htm*.

OECD (2019c), *OECD Reviews of Digital Transformation: Going Digital in Colombia*, OECD Publishing, Paris, *https://dx.doi.org/10.1787/781185b1-en*.

OECD (2019d), *OECD Telecommunication and Internet Statistics* (database), OECD, Paris, *http://dx.doi.org/10.1787/tel_int-data-en* (accessed in May 2019).

OECD (2019e), "The road to 5G networks: Experience to date and future developments", *OECD Digital Economy Papers*, No. 284, OECD Publishing, Paris, *https://dx.doi.org/10.1787/2f880843-en*.

OECD (2018a), "IoT measurement and applications", *OECD Digital Economy Papers*, No. 271, OECD Publishing, Paris, *https://dx.doi.org/10.1787/35209dbf-en*.

OECD (2018b), *OECD Economic Surveys: Brazil 2018*, OECD Publishing, Paris, *https://dx.doi.org/10.1787/eco_surveys-bra-2018-en*.

OECD (2018c), *OECD Reviews of Digital Transformation: Going Digital in Sweden*, OECD Publishing, Paris, *https://dx.doi.org/10.1787/9789264302259-en*.

OECD (2017a), *OECD Digital Economy Outlook 2017*, OECD Publishing, Paris, *https://dx.doi.org/10.1787/9789264276284-en*.

OECD (2017b), "Revised OECD telecommunication price baskets", OECD, Paris, *http://www.oecd.org/sti/broadband/DSTI-CDEP-CISP(2017)4FINAL.pdf*.

OECD (2016), *Indicators of Regulatory Policy and Governance Latin America 2016: Brazil*, OECD, Paris, *www.oecd.org/gov/regulatory-policy/Brazil-regulatory-policy-ireg-2016.pdf*.

OECD (2014a), "International cables, gateways, backhaul and international exchange points", *OECD Digital Economy Papers*, No. 232, OECD Publishing, Paris, *https://dx.doi.org/10.1787/5jz8m9jf3wkl-en*.

OECD (2014b), *The Governance of Regulators*, OECD Best Practice Principles for Regulatory Policy, OECD Publishing, Paris, *https://doi.org/10.1787/9789264209015-en*.

OECD (2014c), "The Internet in transition: The state of the transition to IPv6 in today's Internet and measures to support the continued use of IPv4", *OECD Digital Economy Papers*, No. 234, OECD Publishing, Paris, *https://dx.doi.org/10.1787/5jz5sq5d7cq2-en*.

OECD (2008), *OECD Reviews of Regulatory Reform: Brazil 2008: Strengthening Governance for Growth*, OECD Reviews of Regulatory Reform, OECD Publishing, Paris, *https://doi.org/10.1787/9789264042940-en*.

Ookla (2019), "Speedtest", *https://www.speedtest.net/* (accessed on 10 July 2019).

Opensignal (2019), *The State of Mobile Experience, May 2019*, Opensignal, London, *http://dx.doi.org/www.opensignal.com/sites/opensignal-com/files/data/reports/global/data-2019-05/the_state_of_mobile_experience_may_2019_0.pdf*.

Packet Clearing House (2020), *Internet Exchange Directory* (database), *https://www.pch.net/ixp/dir* (accessed on 18 February 2020).

Steam (2019), "Steam Download Stats", *https://store.steampowered.com/stats/content* (accessed on 10 July 2019).

Strategy Analytics (2019), "Teligen tariff & benchmarking market data using the OECD methodology", *https://www.strategyanalytics.com/access-services/networks/tariffs---mobile-and-fixed*.

Tele.síntese (2019), *Morais: Roaming em Cidades Pequenas, uma Realidade em Transformação* [Morais: Roaming in Small Cities, an Ever-changing Reality], Tele.Síntese, *www.telesintese.com.br/morais-roaming-em-cidades-pequenas-uma-realidade-em-transformacao* (accessed on 30 October 2019).

Teleco (2019), *Market Share das Operadoras de Celular no Brasil* [Market Share of Cellular Operators in Brazil], webpage, *https://www.teleco.com.br/mshare_3g.asp* (accessed on 30 October 2019).

TeleGeography (2020), *Submarine Cable Map*, TeleGeography, *https://www.submarinecablemap.com* (accessed on 20 February 2020).

The World Bank (2020), *World Bank National Accounts Data, and OECD National Accounts Data Files: GDP Constant LCU Brazil*, The World Bank, Washington, DC, *https://data.worldbank.org/indicator/NY.GDP.MKTP.KN?end=2018&locations=BR&start=2006*.

Weller, D. and B. Woodcock (2013), "Internet traffic exchange: Market developments and policy challenges", *OECD Digital Economy Papers*, No. 207, OECD Publishing, Paris, *http://dx.doi.org/10.1787/5k918gpt130q-en*.

Notes

Israel

The statistical data for Israel are supplied by and under the responsibility of the relevant Israeli authorities. The use of such data by the OECD is without prejudice to the status of the Golan Heights, East Jerusalem and Israeli settlements in the West Bank under the terms of international law.

1. Using an exchange rate of 3.8742 BRL/USD for the year 2018 from *https://stats.oecd.org*.
2. Total communication access paths = Total access telephone lines + total fixed broadband subscriptions + cellular mobile subscriptions.
3. It is worth noting some of the features of the different measuring tools for download speeds when drawing conclusions from these data. M-Lab and Ookla compile results from speed tests conducted by users who actively measure their actual speed to access the Internet. Steam data are a further way to consider download speeds across countries, which reflects the speeds of users using one of the most Internet Protocol (IP)-intensive applications: online games.
4. To calculate the number of M2M embedded mobile cellular subscriptions, the OECD defines M2M on mobile networks as "the number of SIM cards that are assigned for use in machines and devices (cars, smart meters and consumer electronics) and are not part of a consumer subscription".

Chapter 3

FOSTERING DIGITAL UPTAKE AND USE AMONG PEOPLE, FIRMS AND IN GOVERNMENT

The Brazilian Digital Transformation Strategy recognises that "digital transformation is an opportunity for the entire nation to take a leap forward. Digital technologies provide the tools for a profound transformation in government actions, in competitiveness and productivity in the private sector, and in empowerment and inclusion in society, so that everyone can develop economically and socially, and thrive in quality of life" (MCTIC, 2018). The Brazilian Civil Rights Framework for the Internet (Marco Civil da Internet) recognises that "access to the Internet is essential to the exercise of citizenship". For Brazil to realise these premises, policies have to ensure inclusion, so that digital divides do not reproduce the "analogue" divides of the Brazilian society.

This chapter examines access to and use of digital technologies in Brazil. It first looks at how Internet use by individuals and households hinges on socio-economic and geographic conditions, and examines the government programmes that aim to overcome these barriers. It then explores the use of digital technology by firms and at the government policies devised to foster greater adoption. The third section looks at how government uses digital technologies to increase efficiency, provide services and increase transparency.

Internet use by individuals and households

More people are connected, but important gaps remain

Brazil has made progress in recent years in improving the population's access to the Internet, with 67% of households and 72% of the population (16-74 years old) being connected in 2018, compared to 40% and 50% in 2013. However, while Brazil compares well with Latin American, Caribbean and upper middle-income countries, it lags behind OECD countries (Figure 3.1). Despite progress in Internet penetration, there is ample room to enhance digital inclusion, as 42 million people, or 23% of the population, have never used the Internet (CGI.br, 2019a).

Figure 3.1. Internet users in Brazil and the OECD, by education level, 2019 or latest available year

As a percentage of individuals using the Internet in the last three months

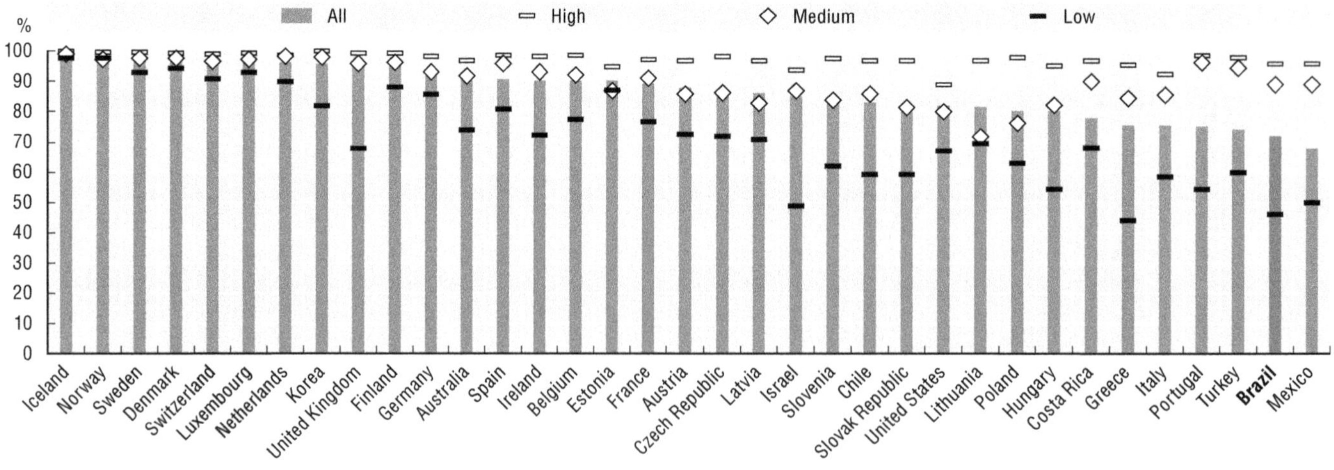

Note: Data for 2016 for Australia; for 2017 for Chile, Israel and the United States; for 2018 for Brazil, Costa Rica, Korea and Mexico.

Source: OECD (2020a), *ICT Access and Usage by Households and Individuals* (database), *http://oe.cd/hhind* (accessed in February 2020).

The digital divide tends to reflect the "analogue" divides of the Brazilian society, with education being the most important factor affecting Internet use. The highly educated use the Internet at rates comparable to most OECD countries, whereas usage by people with lower educational levels is considerably below the OECD average (73%) (Figure 3.1). Age is another key determinant for Internet use, as the gap between the younger and the older cohorts of individuals has been widening over time. Income also plays a very important role, as there is a particularly wide gap between high- and low-income individuals (Figure 3.2). The rural-urban divide is also considerable, with 75% of the urban population (aged 16-74) using the Internet, compared to 49% in rural areas (CGI.br, 2019a). People living in the Northeast region, in particular, are at risk of digital exclusion. While the digital transformation provides opportunities to foster inclusive growth, the current patterns of digital uptake point to a risk that the digital divide may aggravate the existing social divide, thus deepening social exclusion.

Figure 3.2. Internet users in Brazil, by region and socio-demographic group

As a percentage of individuals, aged 16-74, having used the Internet in the last three months

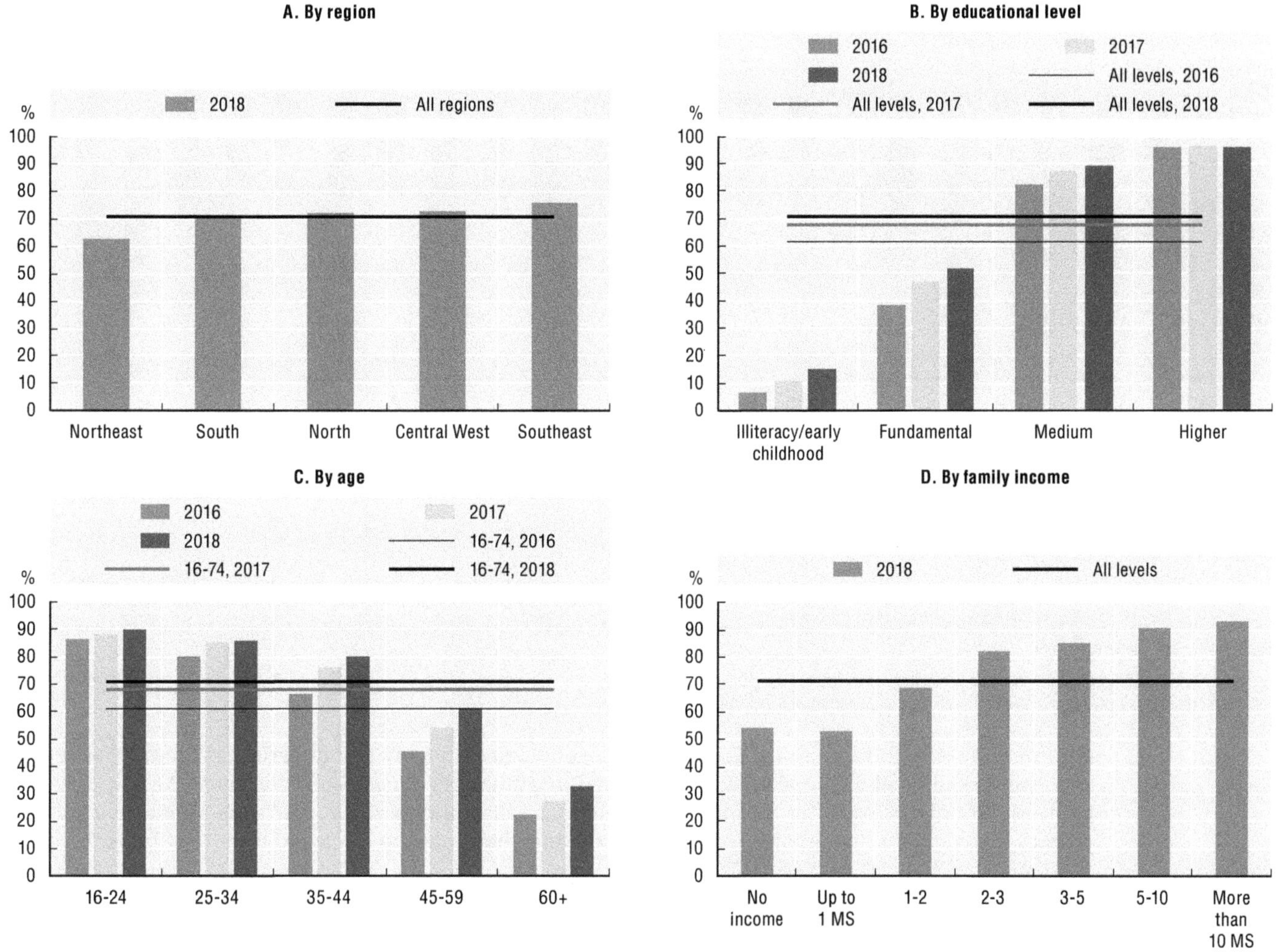

Note: MS = minimum salary.

Source: CGI.br (2019a), *ICT Households 2018: Survey on the Use of Information and Communication Technologies in Brazilian Households* (database), *https://cetic.br/en/pesquisa/domicilios/indicadores/* (accessed in February 2020).

Rapid diffusion of mobile technology is one of the key factors explaining the increase of Internet access among the Brazilian population. Mobile broadband subscriptions more than tripled in the 2012-18 period (see Chapter 2) and mobile phones are nowadays the primary device to connect to the Internet. In 2018, 122.5 million Brazilians accessed the Internet through a mobile phone, representing 97% of Internet users, up from 76% in 2014 (CGI.br, 2019a). Furthermore, the mobile phone is increasingly the only device used to access the Internet, especially among the most vulnerable groups (low income and low skills), in rural areas and in the North (Figure 3.3). This may have led these segments of the population to consider mobile phone applications and the Internet as different platforms, thus not recognising they are using the Internet when they use mobile phone applications (based on differences between indicator "Internet users" and "Internet users – expanded indicators"; CGI.br, 2019a). On the other hand, fixed broadband subscriptions, although increasing, have been growing at a slower pace. Currently 40% of households have access to fixed broadband (MCTIC, 2018). Computer access is also limited, with only 42% of households declaring having a computer, notebook or tablet. Thirty per cent of households have neither a computer nor access to the Internet (CGI.br, 2019a). The exclusive use of a mobile phone to access the Internet has implications on the activities individuals can carry out on line, preventing them from performing more sophisticated activities. This is leading to the emergence of different classes of users, with a small share of the population having more access at a higher speed, using the Internet on different devices and performing a range of activities on line, with a second, wider group with reduced and slower access, limited to one device, mostly performing communication activities on line (CGI.br, 2019b).

Figure 3.3. Internet users in Brazil, by type of device used to access the Internet, 2018

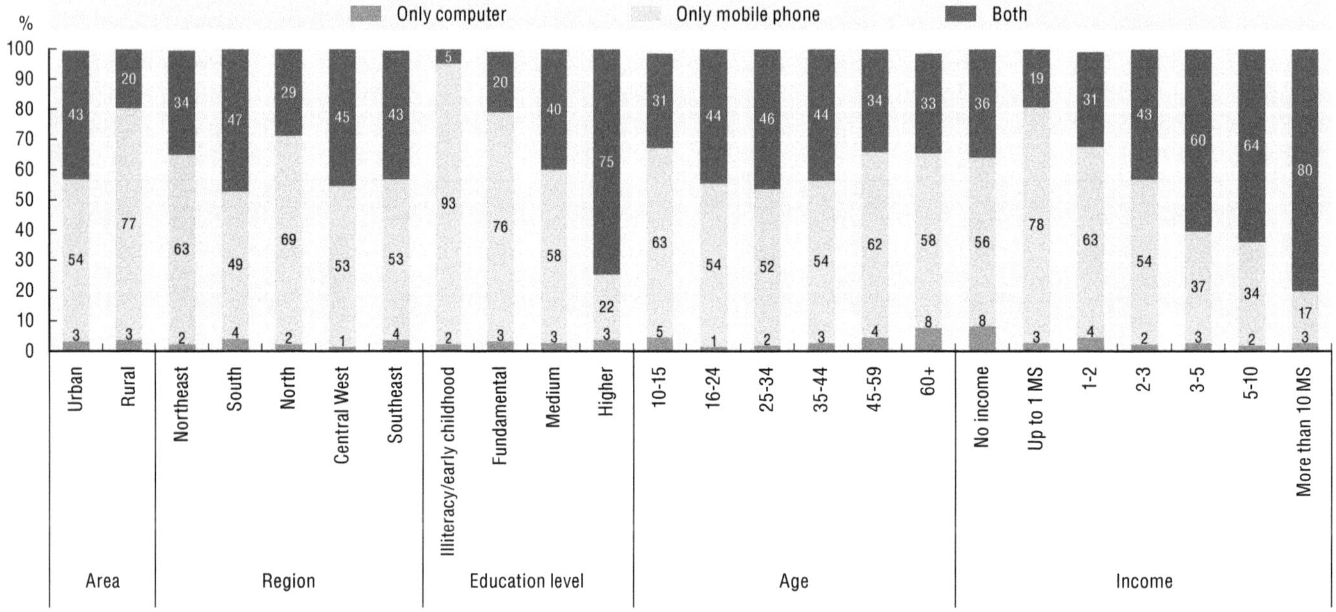

Note: MS = minimum salary.

Source: CGI.br (2019a), *ICT Households 2018: Survey on the Use of Information and Communication Technologies in Brazilian Households* (database), *https://cetic.br/en/pesquisa/domicilios/indicadores/* (accessed in February 2020).

Affordability is still the primary reason for households not having a connection at home (Figure 3.4), pointing to the need to increase Internet access at affordable prices (see Chapter 2). Lack of interest or need, lack of skills or of a computer are also important. Increasingly, concerns about security and privacy also prevent households from having the Internet at home (reported by 44% of households in 2018, up from only 5% in 2008).

Within its policies for digital inclusion, Brazil has programmes in place aimed at increasing access to the Internet in public places free of charge or at a lower price (Table 3.1). In addition, until 2016, the federal administration incentivised the purchase of digital routers, modems, tablets, PCs, laptops, chipsets, keyboards and mouse devices by establishing a federal tax exemption through the Good Law (Law 11.196/2005, known as Lei do Bem) for retail sales of these devices. Until 2018, the same law also incentivised mobile access to the Internet, through subsidised smartphone (and other devices) prices. Article 28 provided for a federal tax exemption for smartphones sold in retail for a price of up to USD 410 (BRL 1 500), manufactured according to a basic manufacturing process defined by the government, and meeting a minimum set of technical requirements developed in Brazil. A total of 17 companies participated in the programme, covering 425 different smartphone models and 429 applications.

When looking at Internet use by individuals, instead of households, affordability is no longer the main obstacle. Lack of computer skills was the most frequent reason (74%) reported by individuals for not using the Internet, followed by lack of interest (64%) and lack of need (48%) in the fourth position. High cost of the Internet services still matters when considering use (49%) but it is only the third most frequent reason (Figure 3.5). These findings point to the need for policies to increase digital literacy in the population and to raise awareness on the benefits of using the Internet, as well as for the development of specific content, services and applications that meet the needs of the groups of the population still off line. The government has a role to play here, by creating content and providing online services associated with education, health and other public services (UNESCO, 2017).

Figure 3.4. Barriers preventing Brazilian households from having Internet at home, 2018

As a percentage of households without an Internet connection, by reason declared for not having an Internet connection

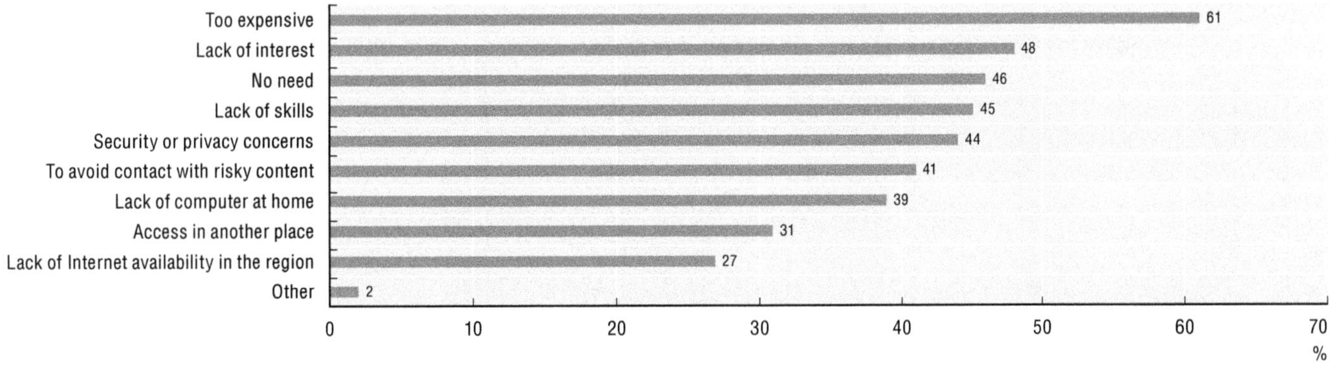

Source: CGI.br (2019a), *ICT Households 2018: Survey on the Use of Information and Communication Technologies in Brazilian Households* (database), *https://cetic.br/en/pesquisa/domicilios/indicadores/* (accessed in February 2020).

Figure 3.5. Barriers preventing individuals in Brazil from using the Internet, 2018

As a percentage of individuals aged 16-74 who never used the Internet, by main reason declared for not using the Internet

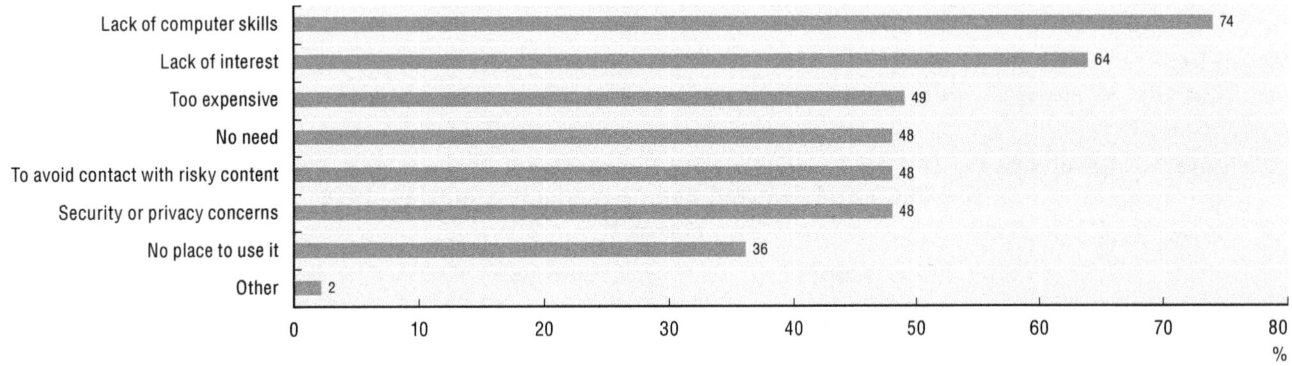

Source: CGI.br (2019a), *ICT Households 2018: Survey on the Use of Information and Communication Technologies in Brazilian Households* (database), *https://cetic.br/en/pesquisa/domicilios/indicadores/* (accessed in February 2020).

Improving digital skills among the population is necessary to avoid a second-level digital divide

Among the activities performed on line, those related to communication prevail, with connecting to social networks being the most frequent (58%), followed by calling/sending messages (55%), and looking for information about goods and services (46%). With the exception of following online courses and telephoning/making a video call, Brazil scores below the average of other OECD and Latin American countries in all activities performed on the Internet, in particular in e-banking, sending emails and online purchases (Figure 3.6).

Beyond the digital divide, between those that have access to digital technologies and those who do not, a second-level digital divide has been growing among Internet users in relation to their ability to use digital technologies effectively and benefit from them. Several factors may shape digital inequalities in use, such as age, gender, socio-economic background and geography. Skills appear to be one of the most important factors behind these differences (OECD, 2019a).

More than a half of all Brazilian adults have not reached secondary education levels; 17% have not even completed primary education, a figure well above the OECD average (2%). Despite the increase in education expenditures and the widespread access to free-of-charge primary and secondary education, educational attainments have remained low. The country's results in the OECD's Programme for International Student Assessment (PISA) suggest that challenges exist in achieving a quality education (Figure 3.7) and indicate vast disparities in outcomes depending on socio-economic background (OECD, 2019b).

Figure 3.6. Diffusion of selected online activities among Internet users in Brazil and the OECD, 2019 or latest available year

As a percentage of Internet users performing each activity

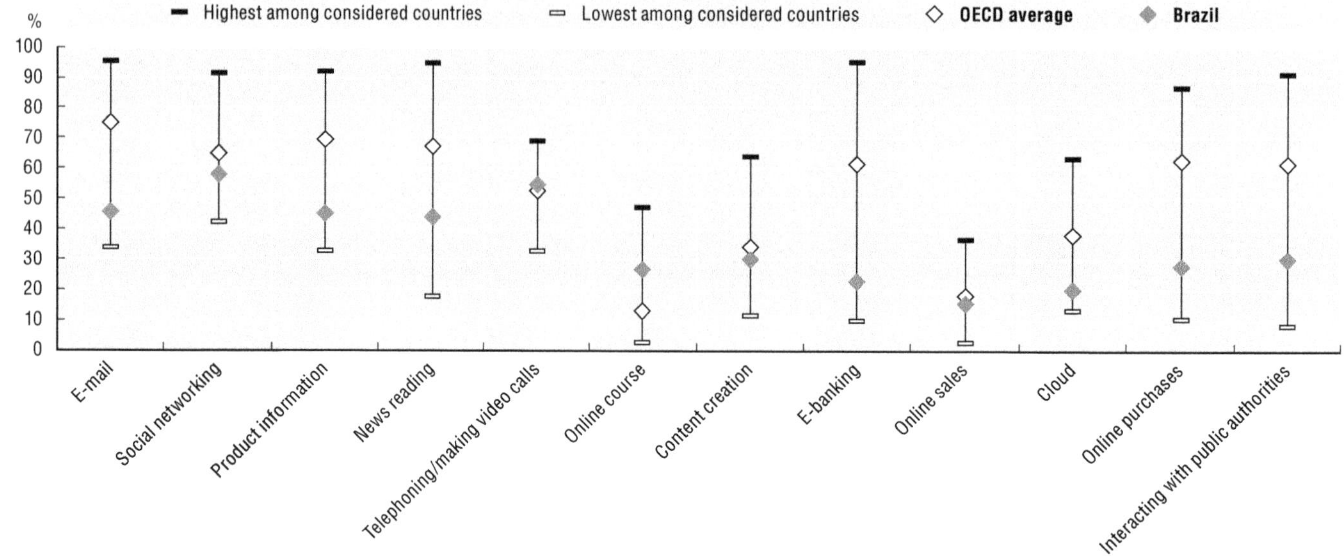

Notes: Data for 2018 for Brazil.

Source: OECD (2020a), *ICT Access and Usage by Households and Individuals* (database), *http://oe.cd/hhind* (accessed in March 2020).

Figure 3.7. Results in the OECD's Programme for International Student Assessment (PISA) in Brazil, the OECD and selected Latin American countries, 2018

Mean results

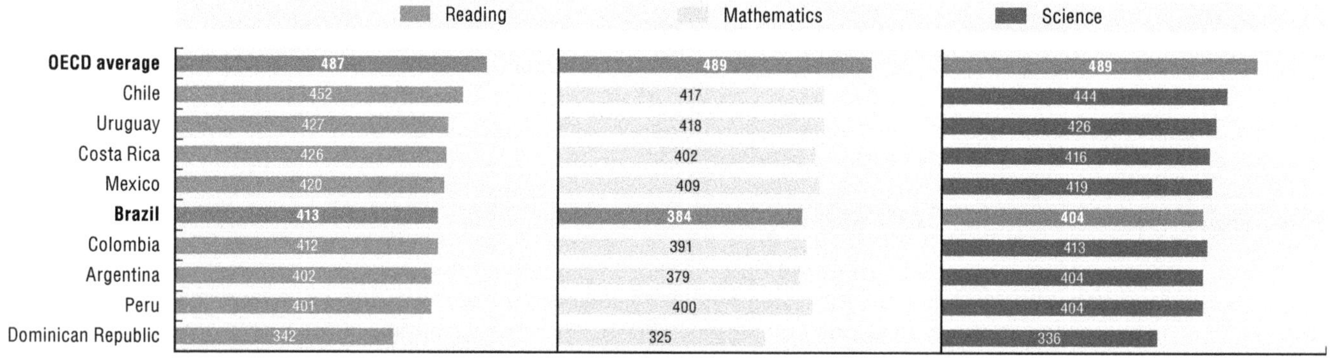

Source: OECD (2019b), *PISA 2018 Results (Volume I): What Students Know and Can Do, https://doi.org/10.1787/5f07c754-en.*

Based on the activities performed on line – i.e. communication, information searches, multimedia, education and work, content creation and sharing, and downloading – Brazilian Internet users can be grouped into four clusters: 1) instrumental; 2) interactive; 3) limited; 4) advanced (Araujo and Reinhard, 2018). Members of the instrumental group, which account for 17% of Internet users, are characterised by higher skill levels related to information searches and education and work-related activities. They tend to access the Internet through multiple devices (desktops, laptops and mobile phones), are mostly female, have higher educational levels and are 16-44 years old. The members of this group use the Internet as a tool for personal, professional and educational development. Users from the interactive cluster, accounting for 28% of total users, have higher skill levels in content creation and multimedia, belong to a younger age group (10-24 years old), prefer to access the Internet via mobile phones, are male and from the lowest socio-economic classes. Users from the advanced cluster, accounting for 20% of users, have higher skill levels in all six of the domains examined, whereas users with limited digital competencies, representing the majority of Brazilian users (35%), have the opposite profile, i.e. lower digital skill levels across all domains. In these two groups, social class appears to be the main discriminating factor and digital skills are correlated with the level of income and education.

Government policies for digital inclusion are mostly supply-side

Brazil has several initiatives in place to increase access to and use of ICTs and the Internet among its population. The Digital Inclusion Department in the Ministry of Science, Technology, Innovations and Communications (Ministério da Ciência, Tecnologia, Inovações e Comunicações, MCTIC) is responsible for executing and co-ordinating these initiatives, which may be grouped into four broad categories: 1) free public access to the Internet in public places and telecentres; 2) availability of digital services in public places; 3) support to telecentres; and 4) training and capacity building (Table 3.1). In the past, the government also provided incentives for the purchase of ICT devices (see above), which have, however, been discontinued. These policies are analysed in the following sections, except those related to access, which are discussed in Chapter 2.

One of the primary objectives of the Brazilian public policy for digital inclusion is to extend Internet access to remote areas and isolated communities of the country. Since 2002, Brazil has been running the Electronic Government Citizen Services programme (Governo Eletrônico – Serviço de Atendimento ao Cidadão, GESAC), established by the Ministry of Communications (2002) and lastly amended by the MCTIC (2017), with the objective of making Internet access universal throughout the country's vast territory, primarily targeting the most vulnerable groups. The programme is co-ordinated by the MCTIC, and is ran in partnership with the Ministry of Education (Ministério da Educação, MEC) and the Ministry of Health.

The GESAC programme aims to provide free-of-charge broadband Internet satellite and terrestrial connection to schools, public health clinics, indigenous villages, international border stations and "*quilombola*" communities (historical African-Brazilian communities), as well as telecentres (see below for a description) with difficult access. Participants in the GESAC programme are institutions earmarked by the public administration (either local or national) which have signed a co-operation agreement with the MCTIC. The telecommunication services are paid by the federal government and supplied by private companies, which benefit from an exemption of the tax on the movement of goods, transport services and telecommunication services (Imposto sobre Circulação de Mercadorias e Serviços, ICMS). To date, GESAC provides a connection to approximately 6 000 institutions and public places. The programme is implemented through a service provision contract, which is currently executed by Telebras (this is the fifth contract related to the programme). The current contract foresees the installation of 15 000 points. As of January 2020, 10 000 of them had already been installed. The largest majority of these points (80%) are schools, some of them with the connection paid for by the MEC's Connected Education (Educação Conectada) programme. Others are maintained with the MCTIC's own budget.

Smart Sustainable Cities and the National IoT Plan should be aligned

Providing high-speed networks in municipalities is the objective of the Digital Cities (Cidades Digitais) programme, established in 2011 (Ordinance 376/2011). It installed digital local networks in 160 municipalities, connected public offices and equipped them with digital tools for digital government services. Those networks are freely available to the population. Almost half of local governments with Internet access reported providing Wi-Fi connections in public spaces in the municipalities (45%), while the possibility was even more common among Brazilian state capitals (81%) and municipalities with more than 500 000 inhabitants (73%). It is, however, unclear whether the programme is also meant to include assistance and training in the use of the digital government services, and the degree to which it has contributed to the increase in the use of such services in these municipalities. Overall, the programme has been found to achieve modest results (CCT, 2017).

The Digital Cities programme is being replaced by the new Smart Sustainable Cities (Cidades Inteligentes Sustentáveis) programme. Based on the Smart Sustainable Cities Maturity Model and the Assessment Framework for Digital Transformation of Sectors in Smart Cities (ITU, 2016), Brazil is building a framework to evaluate the degree of maturity of cities. Further on, Brazil has created the Chamber of Cities 4.0, inside the structure of the IoT Chamber. When devising the policy and the implementation strategy, it will be important to align it to the National IoT Plan (Decree 9.854/2019; see Chapter 5), as Smart Cities is one of the four vertical sectors selected as priorities for the application of IoT in Brazil, so to not duplicate actions and exploit synergies among the two strategies. The programme should, for instance, foresee actions in support of the deployment of IoT solutions in municipalities, as a follow-up to the pilots funded by the Brazilian Development Bank (Banco Nacional de Desenvolvimento Econômico e Social, BNDES) (see Chapter 5), such as technical assistance or funding for those cities.

Table 3.1. Programmes for digital inclusion in Brazil

Year	Programme	Objective	Main activities/instruments	Budget
		Availability of free and public access to Internet in public spaces and telecentres		
2002	E-government Citizen Services programme (GESAC)	Ensure universal Internet access across the Brazilian territory.	Free-of-charge broadband Internet connection, terrestrial and via satellite, to public institutions and telecentres. Tax incentives for companies to provide Internet connections to these places.	About USD 6 million (BRL 24 million)/year.
2017	Internet for All (GESAC's extension)	Internet connections at reduced prices.	Tax incentives for companies to build broadband infrastructures and provide Internet connections.	USD 208 million (BRL 663 million) to connect 15 000 points.
		Deployment of high-speed municipal networks, digital government applications and Internet access points in public spaces		
2011	Digital Cities	Increase access to ICT and public services.	Install digital local networks connecting public offices and services with digital tools for digital government services and making them available for free use by the population.	USD 127 million (BRL 212 million) for 262 cities – it will not all be spent.
		Support to telecentres		
2009	Telecentros.BR	Develop joint actions (among federal government, states, municipalities and civil society) enabling the large-scale installation and maintenance of telecentres.	Installation and maintenance of public and community telecentres.	
2014	Community telecentres	Promote digital and social inclusion in the communities they are located in.	Training and financial support of monitors.	
		Training and capacity building		
2007	Computers for Inclusion	Training of low-income young people on reconditioning computer equipment.	Workshops, courses and training, focusing on reconditioning and maintenance of computer equipment, which is then provided to digital inclusion points.	
2017	National Digital Inclusion Agent Training Program	Provide training as digital inclusion agents for youth and adults who then will give support to users in telecentres.	Capacity building of young people and adults to act as knowledge multipliers in telecentres.	USD 246 000 (BRL 785 000).

Note: USD figures are based on the exchange rate for the year the programme was launched.

Source: OECD, based on responses from the MCTIC to the review questionnaire.

Telecentres are important for digital inclusion, but require more resources

The GESAC also provides connectivity to telecentres. These are public spaces with computers and other IT equipment, as well as broadband Internet connection, which offer ICT activities to promote digital and social inclusion among the communities they serve. The main objective of telecentres is to foster social and economic development in participating communities, with a view to reducing social exclusion and to creating opportunities for the population. Two programmes have supported the installation of telecentres throughout the country: Telecentros.BR, launched in 2009 (Decree 6.991, 27 October 2009) and the Community Telecentres programme, which started in 2014, and provided, in addition to the equipment, connection through GESAC and training of young people. Between 2006 and 2014, the federal government installed about 10 000 telecentres in 5 200 municipalities throughout the country: 6 400 through the Community Telecenters programme and 3 300 through Telecentro.BR. Once those were established, the municipalities were handed the responsibility to maintain them. Over the years, the responsibility of the Ministry of Communication, now merged into the MCTIC, has shifted from providing equipment and connection to providing training and refurbished computers.

The Integrated Monitoring System (Sistema Integrado de Monitoramento, SIMMC), developed by the MCTIC in partnership with the Federal University of Paraná (UFPR), is an embedded software that collects data on telecentres, including network availability, network use and application software installed on the computers. In a 2018 audit, the Brazilian Court of Auditors (Tribunal de Contas da União, TCU) pointed to the fact that several municipalities have had their telecentres established by the federal government, as well as by the municipality, while several others have not had any

(TCU, 2018). The ICT Public Access Centers 2019 survey (CGI.br, 2020a) reported 5 396 telecentres in the country, 55% of which were functioning (2 989). A higher proportion of telecentres is unused, compared to the last survey of this kind (CGI.br, 2014), which found 78% of active telecentres in the country. This might reflect the fact that many of these telecentres were decommissioned at some point. The original telecentre programme stipulated that after an initial five-year period of continued support by the federal government, the telecentre equipment would be donated to the municipalities. In terms of maintenance, CGI.br (2020a) reports that access to the Internet is limited in most cases by problems related to the equipment, such as not functioning or low-quality computers, and lack of technical assistance or financial resources to maintain computers. In order for these centres to foster digital inclusion, municipalities should be obliged to ensure that the equipment is maintained and replaced as required, with funding and technical assistance provided also from central sources. This last issue has been addressed, in part, by the MCTIC's Computers for Inclusion (Computadores para Inclusão, see below) programme, which provides refurbished computers to the telecentres.

The share of users accessing the Internet via telecentres grew between 2008 and 2018, reaching 21.8 million people (17% of the individuals 10 years old and above) in 2018 (CGI.br, 2019a). At the same time, there has been growth in access to the Internet from home (Figure 3.8). This may be linked to the low availability of computers and fixed Internet connections for several groups and areas across the country. Access to Internet in telecentres (or other public centres with free access) is concentrated among young (aged 16-34) individuals, and is less prevalent among older adults (aged 60 and above). People living in urban areas tend to access the Internet in telecentres or public centres more often than those in rural areas, and so do those with a higher education. In cities like São Paulo, where digital inequality is high (CGI.br, 2019b), telecentres are the only opportunity to have a better quality connection, allowing for more sophisticated activities than communicating (e.g. looking for a job or following an online course). Telecentres, however, fail to reach groups with a lower Internet usage (i.e. the elderly, the rural population, as well as low-income and/or low-skilled individuals). Measures specifically targeted at these groups should be put in place in order to reduce digital exclusion.

Figure 3.8. Internet users in Brazil, by place of access, 2008 and 2018

As a percentage of Internet users

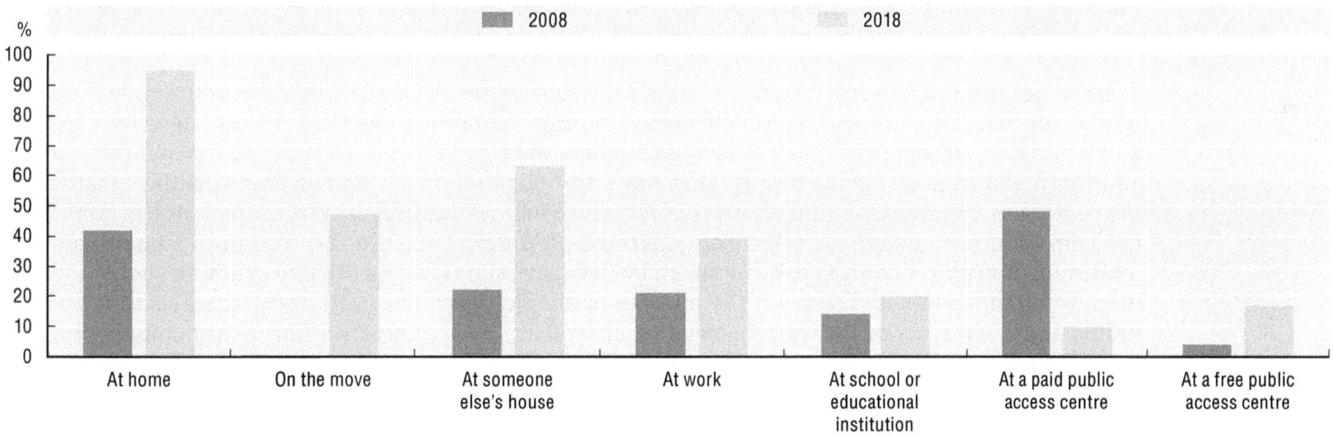

Source: CGI.br (2019a), *ICT Households 2018: Survey on the Use of Information and Communication Technologies in Brazilian Households* (database), *https://cetic.br/en/pesquisa/domicilios/indicadores/* (accessed in February 2020).

As accessing the Internet at home or from a mobile phone becomes more common, telecentres should become places where people can access computers to perform more sophisticated activities. They should therefore be equipped with better quality computers, and ensure Internet connections are functioning and their role in providing training should be strengthened. These centres are, in fact, important spaces for digital inclusion, where users receive support in accessing online public services and learning how to use digital tools (CGI.br, 2014). Training and assistance are key functions telecentres offer, although with great variations across the country and in terms of scope. In 2019, eight in ten telecentres had a monitor, guide or digital inclusion agents to assist its users (CGI.br, 2020a). Telecentres also offered courses on using a computer (55%), using the Internet (50%) and professional training (39%). The telecentres of the Northeast and Central West regions, in general, were the ones that most offered those types of service. Half of the telecentres from those two regions offered professional training, compared to 30% in the South region. Courses on the use of Internet were also more common among the telecentres of the Northeast (62%) and Central West (56%) regions, whereas this figure was 38% in the North (CGI.br, 2020a).

Federal programmes supporting training should be scaled up

The Computers for Inclusion programme offers training to socially vulnerable young students and professionals in dismantling or reconditioning IT equipment used by federal institutions, which is then provided to the digital inclusion points (DIP) and public spaces with free Internet access, including telecentres. Currently there are centres for computer reconditioning in 11 Brazilian states, which offered training to about 5 200 young people during the period 2014-18; 10 000 computers were provided to DIPs. Although, in principle, the refurbished material can be provided to DIPs across the country, the programme seems to have a limited geographic outreach (Figure 3.9).

This programme allows recovering and giving new life to used material, thus reducing electronic waste, while training young people and providing new equipment to public access centres. Partners of the Computers for Inclusion programme also provide training courses for women and older people. The initiative should therefore be stepped up, by increasing the number of centres for computer reconditioning in the country, also in co-operation with the private sector. The training dimension could also be strengthened, for instance by standardising training material and providing certification of the training undertaken. Centres for computer reconditioning could also collaborate with firms with a view of increasing youth employment opportunities, for instance by establishing programmes for traineeships. The "Computers for Schools" in Canada, which has inspired the Brazilian programme and Colombia's "Computadores para educar", relies on partnerships with the private sector, including with retired volunteers from the telecommunications sector who provide training courses to the participants.

The 2017 National Digital Inclusion Training Programme (Programa Nacional de Formação de Agentes de Inclusão Digital, PNAID) (Ordinance 2801/2017) aims at increasing monitoring and training services in telecentres. It trains young people to become digital agents and to act as "multipliers" of knowledge. The Federal Institute of Education, Science and Technology of Rio Grande do Norte has designed the programme's training curriculum and provided the technological platform for the online training activities.

To be part of this programme, the MCTIC selects telecentres, which, in turn, indicate which agents should receive training. The National Digital Inclusion Training Programme has selected 792 telecentres to date, and will train 1 200 agents in 2020. Selected beneficiaries receive a USD 100 (BRL 400) scholarship, and a 10-month, 480-hour distance training. They have the obligation to attend two hours per day and to train telecentre users for the duration of their course. The beneficiaries must also present a project benefiting the community in which the telecentre operates. In order to ensure the training's sustainability, a minimum duration of courses to be provided by the agent should be set. The programme should include monitoring indicators and tools on the number of people trained by each agent, their socio-economic profile and the impact of the training activity, as well as specific targets. Prior to launching a new call for selecting the agents, the MCTIC should evaluate the programme, with a view to improving it as required, and scale it up to increase its outreach, which is limited to date (Figure 3.9). Furthermore, as the training material is already developed, the MCTIC may consider distributing it to a wider number of people as educational material.

Digital literacy programmes should be accessible to all

To date, there have not been any programmes for improving digital skills among adults (beyond those offered in telecentres; see above). Programmes for digital skills could be run on line, with the objective of training large portions of the population. They could cover topics such as Internet safety and security, online banking, access to digital government services, e-commerce, and content creation. Given the digital divide affecting specific population groups, specific tools could also be developed for reaching the most vulnerable groups, such as older people or low-income, low-educated groups. Considering the widespread use of smartphones, trainings should also be considered for people using smart devices, such as tablets or smartphones. Several countries have adopted initiatives to train citizens for digital skills development, targeting citizens at large or specific segments of the population. Some national programmes are presented in Box 3.1. The MCTIC is considering launching a programme for improving the digital skills of the population along these lines. The programme will also count on co-operation with the private sector.

Figure 3.9. Percentage of telecentres participating in federal programmes in Brazil, 2018

As a percentage of functioning telecentres

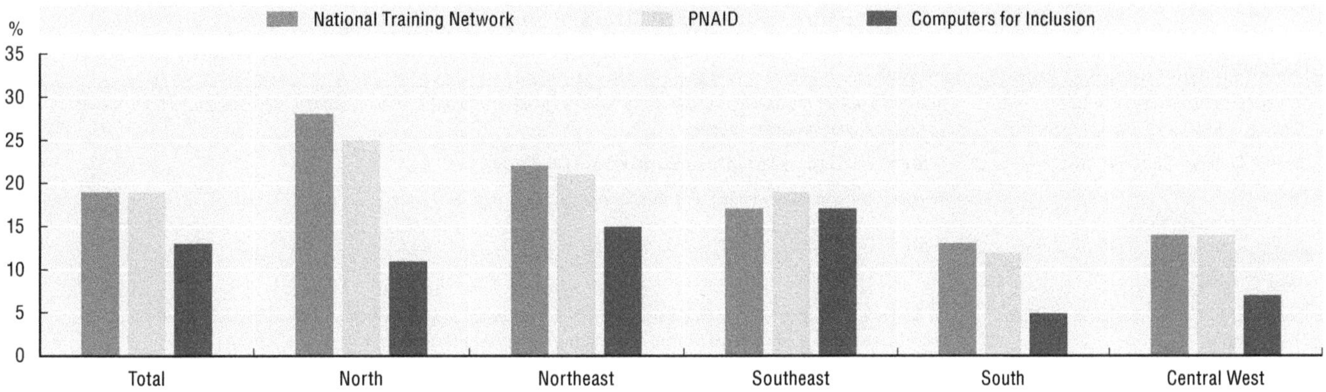

Note: PNAID = National Digital Inclusion Training Programme.

Source: CGI.br (2020a), *ICT Public Access Centers 2019: Survey on Public Internet Access Centers in Brazil* (database), *https://cetic.br/en/pesquisa/centros-publicos/indicadores/* (accessed in July 2020).

Box 3.1. Digital Skills for All: Programmes to bridge the skills gap

The **Australian** Be Connected programme aims to raise the digital literacy of older Australians. It takes a family and community centred approach to teach basic skills such as online shopping, sending email and using social media. It aims to reduce feelings of loneliness and increase community connection. The Department of Social Services is the lead agency, but provides grants to local partners and training for digital mentors. The programme received the support of 2 500 community organisations.

Israel has a National Programme for Digital Literacy, aimed at reducing the digital gap among citizens, with a special focus on disadvantaged populations, including senior citizens, the Arab population and the ultra-orthodox population. The programme focuses on finance, education, civil participation and use of rights, employment, health, transportation, and social life/communication.

Digidel 2017 was a national programme in **Norway** to strengthen co-operation and increase the efforts made by the public sector and information and communication technology sector as well as voluntary enterprises in the areas of digital competence and inclusion in Norway. Special focus groups included elderly people, women and immigrants that did not use ICT as part of their everyday life. The programme involved co-operation with a non-governmental organisation. A lot of training activities took place around the country, facilitated by local libraries, non-governmental organisations and industry.

Singapore has collaborated with non-profit organisations to set up senior-friendly infocomm learning hubs (Silver Infocomm Connections) island-wide, so that elderly people have access to affordable subsidised digital skills training. Digital clinics are also organised regularly in public libraries. Participants receive one-on-one assistance from corporate volunteers who help them with basic queries on phone usage, such as connecting to Wi-Fi hotspots, personalising accessibility tools on their devices and adjusting their phone settings to best suit their needs.

The **UK** Department for Education funds the Future Digital Inclusion programme, which supports adult learners to engage with digital technology and develop their digital skills in community settings through the 5 000 strong Online Centres Network.

Source: OECD (forthcoming a), *OECD Digital Economy Outlook 2020*.

Steps are being taken to prepare new generations for the digital world

Policies to increase digital skills in school fall under the responsibility of the Secretariat for Basic Education within the Ministry of Education. Brazil has programmes in place to increase the use of ICTs and Internet in schools, focusing on integration of digital literacy and skills in school curricula, the provision of infrastructures, training of teachers, and use of digital technologies (Table 3.2).

Table 3.2. Programmes for digital literacy and ICT use at school

Programme	Objective
National Education Plan 2014-2024	Includes goals for the development of digital skills, to make broadband access in schools universal and to triple the rate of computer/student in public schools.
National Common Curricular Base	Sets the general competences to be developed in basic education.
ProInfo (1997, changes in 2007)	To equip public schools with ICT and Internet access.
Broadband in Schools (2008-present)	
Connected Education Innovation Program (2017-present)	To structure a vision in schools on the use of digital technologies, develop pedagogical practices directed at innovation in classrooms, provide educational content and improve the infrastructure of technologies in schools.

Source: OECD, based on information provided by MCTIC.

The National Education Plan 2014-2024 (Plano Nacional de Educação, PNE), which states the 20 goals of the national education system, includes several objectives in relation to the development of digital skills and the use of ICTs, and considers innovation and technology as strategies to achieve the desired educational objectives:

- 5.3: Select, certify and promote educational technology for child literacy.
- 5.4: Encourage the development of educational technologies and innovative pedagogical practices that ensure literacy.
- 5.6: Promote and stimulate the initial and continued training of teachers for child literacy, building capacities related to new educational technologies and innovative pedagogical practices.
- 7.12: Encourage the development; select, certify and promote educational technologies for early childhood, elementary and high school education; and encourage innovative pedagogical practices.
- 7.15: Make high-speed broadband access universal, by the fifth year of the duration of the National Education Plan 2014-2024, and, by the end of the decade, triple the computer/student ratio in basic education public schools.

The National Institute for Research in Education (Instituto Nacional de Estudos e Pesquisas Educacionais Anísio Teixeira, INEP) is responsible for evaluating progress towards achieving these goals and targets. This is also done through an observatory showing the outcomes of the different actions (*www.observatoriodopne.org.br*). However, the observatory only has results for the objective related to the last goal listed above (Goal 7.15). The results show that the objectives of making access to broadband universal and the one related to the availability of computers are far from being achieved, with only 62.2% of schools of the basic education[1] having access to the Internet (INEP, 2017).

The National Common Curricular Base for Basic Education (Base Nacional Comum Curricular, BNCC) on the essential skills, attitude and values for the 21st century was approved in 2017 by the MEC after a long and comprehensive consultation process. All schools in Brazil had to implement the BNCC by the end of 2019. The BNCC defines a set of ten general competences to be developed throughout basic education. These competencies are cognitive and social-emotional, and include the exercise of intellectual curiosity, the use of digital communication technologies and the appreciation of individuals' diversity. Furthermore, in December 2018, the National Education Council – a government advisory body with representatives from schools, academia, local governments and civil society in the educational field – approved a resolution to include the theme "computational thinking" in elementary, secondary and high school curricula. Computational thinking, or the ability to frame problems in ways that computers can help to solve them, is increasingly put forward as an important skill for a growing number of jobs and a way to develop wider skills, such as creativity or critical thinking (OECD, 2019a).

The adoption of the BNCC is an important step in the attempt to improve education in the country and reduce the great variations in performance observed across regions. By providing uniform standards, it sets a clear framework for schools and teachers on what students should know and be able to do at different grade levels. Improving equity in education is the first and the most important step to reduce inequalities in the ability to benefit from digital tools (OECD, 2015). However, guidelines set by the federal government are not sufficient to promote convergence in educational outcomes, as primary and secondary education are the responsibility of states and municipalities. In order for the national guidelines to be effective in improving the performance of Brazilian schools and students, schools should align their performance assessments to such standards. Furthermore, instruction materials, such as textbooks, should be redesigned in line with the BNCC, and teachers should be given adequate training to acquire the content knowledge and pedagogical skills to bring the new standards into practice (Lemann Centre, 2016). A strict monitoring and evaluation system should be put in place to ensure that it is implemented equally across the country.

The main policy to improve the use of digital technology and the availability of ICT infrastructure and equipment in schools is the ProInfo programme, a government programme set up in 1997 and updated in 2007. Its main objective is to promote the use of digital technology as a pedagogical tool in public elementary and high schools (primary and secondary education levels). It focuses on enhancing students' digital literacy and includes trainings for teachers. In 2007, the programme was reformed ("ProInfo integrado") and basic education schools (including kindergarten for children up to five years old) were included among the programme's targets. ProInfo finances the purchase of computers, digital resources and education contents for public schools across the country, in co-operation with state and municipal administrations. The programme is jointly run by the MEC and the National Fund for Education Development (Fundo Nacional de Desenvolvimento da Educação, FNDE); the MEC is responsible for teacher training, curriculum design, teaching practices and evaluation, while the National Fund for Education Development is responsible for ICT infrastructure and resource development. There is no available evaluation on the results of the programme to date. One of the actions foreseen in the E-Digital Strategy (MCTIC, 2018) is a new national policy of educational technology to replace ProInfo, articulating the strategic dimensions of infrastructure, competencies, content and digital educational resources.

Several programmes support the provision of computers and Internet access in schools, particularly in rural areas (Figure 3.10). These include ProInfo, GESAC (see above), the Broadband in Schools Programme (Programa Banda Larga nas Escolas, PBLE), the recently launched Connected Education programme (see below) and the Direct Money in School programme (Dinheiro Direto na Escola, PDDE), providing financial assistance to schools to maintain or improve physical and pedagogical infrastructures. Furthermore, new draft legislation aims to approve the use of resources from the Universal Telecommunications Service Fund (Fundo de Universalização dos Serviços de Telecomunicações, FUST) – a fund financed through sector levies with a budget of USD 255 million (BRL 1 billion) per year – for broadband deployment in urban and rural schools. The bill (PL 172/2020) is currently scheduled for vote in the Senate. If approved, it would still have to be submitted to presidential approval.

Despite such programmes to finance the purchase of ICT equipment in schools, in 2015, the number of computers per 100 students in Brazil was much lower than the OECD average (20 vs. 77) (Figure 3.11). In addition, inequalities along regional, urban/rural and socio-economic lines persist. Internet usage, connection speeds and teacher training differ significantly depending on the type of school and geographic location (CGI.br, 2019c).

While nearly all schools in urban areas are equipped with computers and are connected to the Internet, on average only 34% of schools in rural areas are on line, with great differences across regions and according to the type of school (public or private). In the North, only 14% of rural schools are connected to the Internet. Overall, 94% of private institutions in rural areas have Internet access, compared with 34% of public institutions (Figure 3.12). In 45% of schools in urban areas, connection speed is 5 Mbps or more, compared to 11% of schools in rural areas. The difference is even larger for speeds greater than 11 Mbps, which are achieved by 21% of schools in urban areas and 1% in rural ones (CGI.br, 2019c).

Figure 3.10. Programmes financing technological infrastructures in Brazilian schools, 2018

As a percentage of schools, by programme of implementation of technological infrastructure

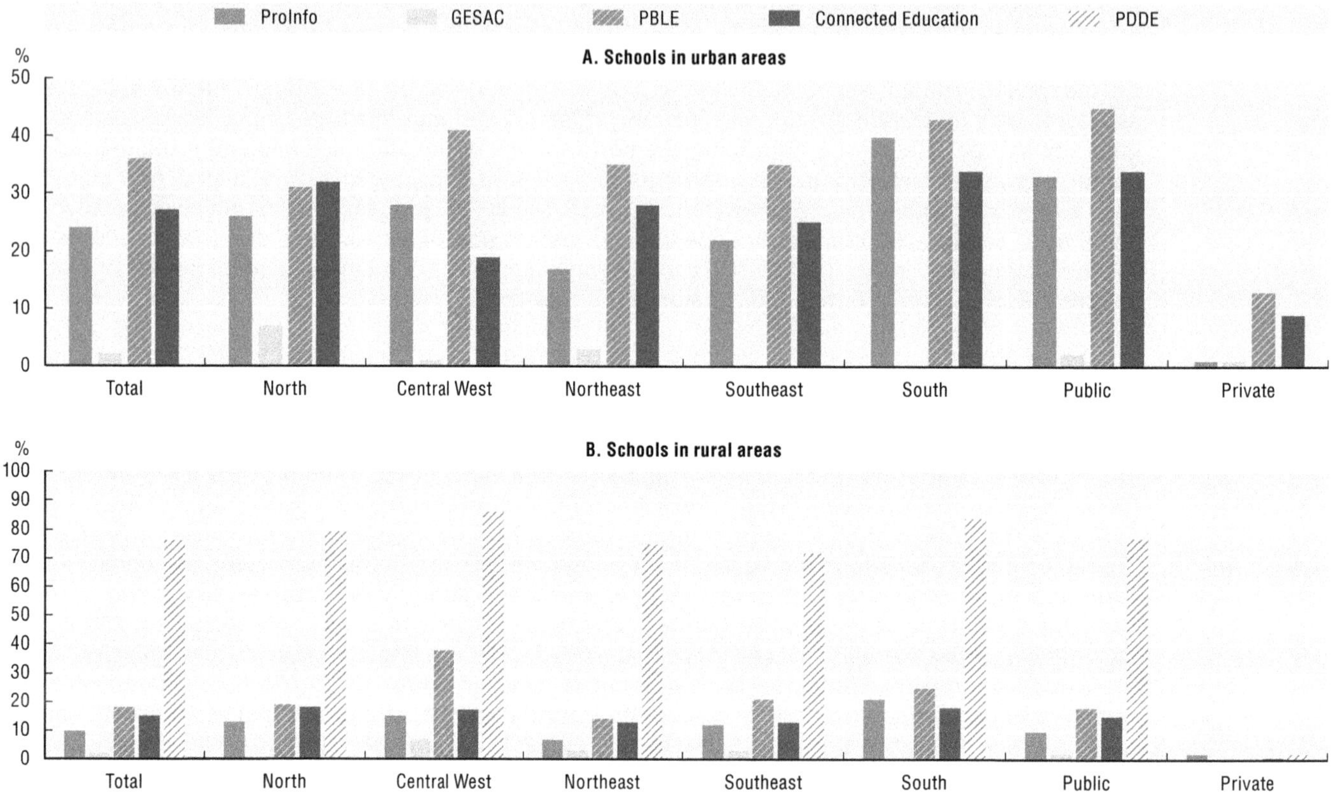

Note: ProInfo = National Educational Technology programme; GESAC = Electronic Government Citizen Services programme; PBLE = Broadband in Schools Programme; PDDE = Direct Money in Schools programme.

Source: CGI.br (2019c), *ICT Education 2018: Survey on the Use of Information and Communication Technologies in Brazilian Schools* (database), *https://cetic.br/en/pesquisa/educacao/indicadores/* (accessed in February 2020).

Figure 3.11. Number of computers per student in Brazil and the OECD, 2015

Results based on school principals' reports

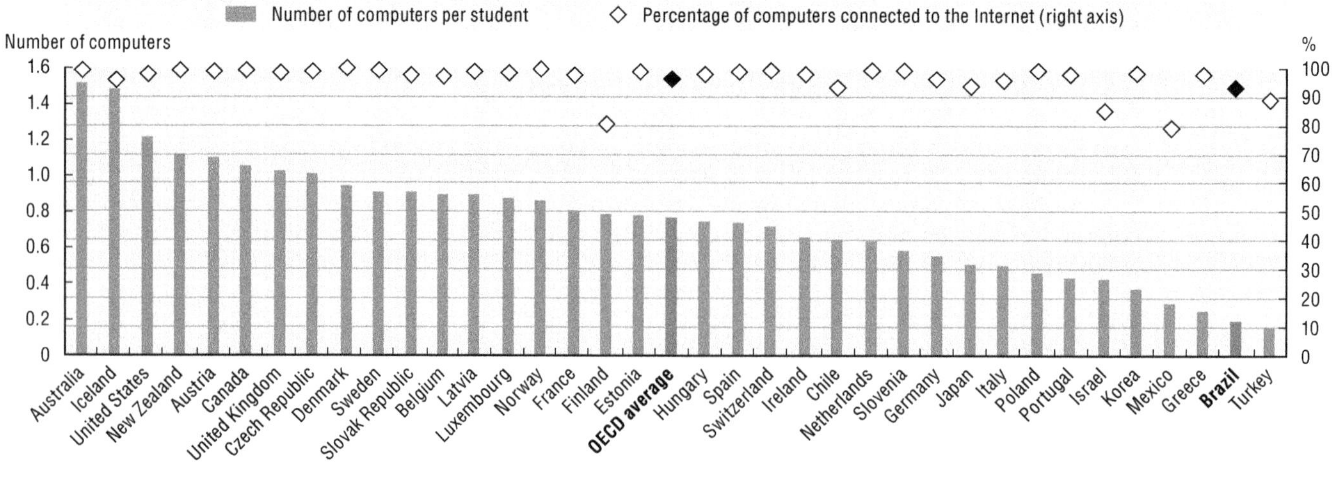

Source: OECD (2016), *PISA 2015 Results (Volume II): Policies and Practices for Successful Schools, http://dx.doi.org/10.1787/9789264267510-en.*

Figure 3.12. Connectivity in Brazilian schools, 2018

As a percentage of schools with Internet access in urban and rural areas

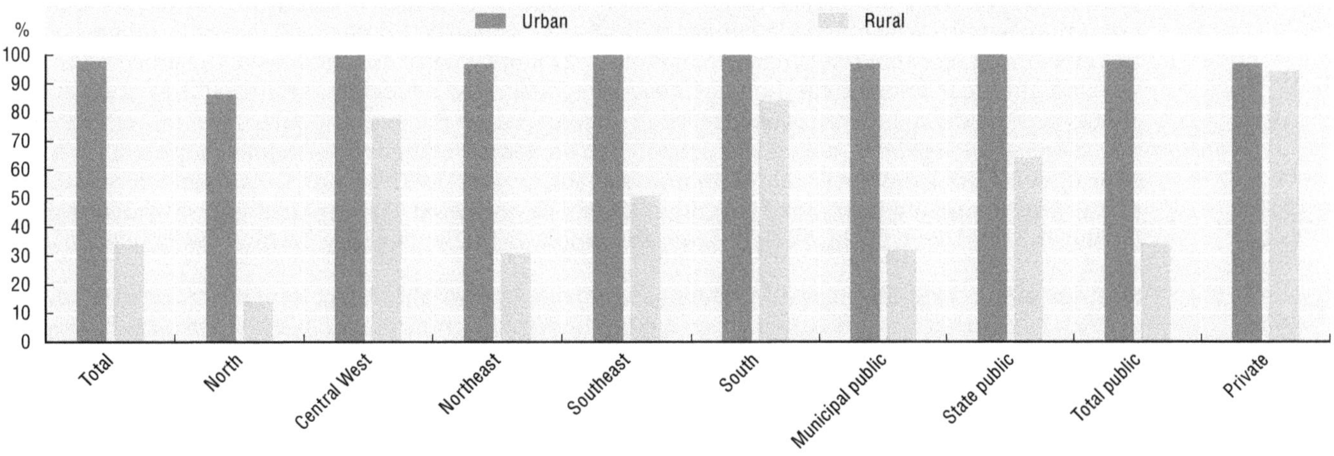

Source: CGI.br (2019c), *ICT Education 2018: Survey on the Use of Information and Communication Technologies in Brazilian Schools* (database), *https://cetic.br/en/pesquisa/educacao/indicadores/* (accessed in February 2020).

According to teachers in schools in urban areas, the low number of computers per student, the low number of computers connected to the Internet and the quality of connections are the main barriers to the effective use of technologies in education (CGI.br, 2019c). Only above one-third perceive there is a lack of pedagogical support for teachers for the use of computers and the Internet, but about 60% believe the absence of a specific course for the use of computer and the Internet in classrooms is a barrier. In rural schools, the development of training programmes for teachers and the development of new teaching practices, which include the use of computers and the Internet, are perceived as priority actions to improve and increase the use of Internet in schools (CGI.br, 2019c).

Overall, the pedagogical use of ICT in Brazilian classrooms remains below its potential. The programmes supporting diffusion of technology in education did not result in improvement in social inclusion in Brazilian public schools. This is due to physical and structural conditions, difficult access to equipment and, especially, insufficient or inadequate training of teachers on the use of digital technology resources. Technology will make a positive difference in education only if teachers are ready and able to use it effectively, and if schools and school systems sustain an atmosphere that promotes innovation. In addition to having access to the required hardware and software, teachers should be properly trained in the use of ICT – for instance, through communities of practice – and be encouraged to take risks (OECD, 2018a). It is also important for teachers to interact with peers, so as to spur real innovation in pedagogical practices (Brasilino et al., 2018). Improving initial and continuing training of primary, secondary and high school teachers is one of the strategic actions listed in the E-Digital Strategy concerning education, these insights should be taken into account while devising courses and guidance for teachers.

Connected Education is based on a holistic view of the use of ICTs in schools

The Connected Education programme, launched in 2017, complements the Proinfo and Broadband in Schools programmes. The programme, a joint venture between the MEC, the MCTIC, BNDES and the Internet Steering Committee (Comitê Gestor da Internet, CGI.br), is designed to combine efforts among public institutions at all levels of government, schools and civil society. The programme is built around four dimensions: 1) vision; 2) training; 3) digital educational resources; and 4) infrastructure. In order to benefit from federal funding, municipalities have to set their own vision on how digital technologies will be used in the school or network of schools. The programme makes use of local "articulators" (6 000 throughout the country), who assist municipalities in the implementation of the programme. In terms of teacher training, the programme foresees actions for initial and continuing education of teachers, including on the pedagogical use of technology. The federal government has set up an online platform, offering more than 20 000 educational multimedia resources for students and teachers of the basic education system. Through a contract with four universities, additional content is being developed in line with the BNCC and to include computational thinking. Looking forward, the MEC plans to also include courses on entrepreneurship, coding, robotics, cyberbullying and online behaviour. A second platform, AVAMEC, provides a virtual environment where teachers and students can follow online courses and interact with their peers. In terms of infrastructures, the programme provides the upgrade in speed, which is needed to use the interactive content, thus complementing other programmes which provide connectivity (Figure 3.10). The Connected Education programme is therefore much more comprehensive than ProInfo, as it has a more holistic view of the process through which digital technologies can be effectively integrated into education. Municipalities and schools should provide the right incentives to teachers to make use of the educational resources, both for their own learning and teaching, and to share them with students. Furthermore, despite online availability of education material and the virtual community enabled by AVAMEC, in-person courses where teachers can also exchange and learn from each other should be promoted. The Senate is currently discussing a bill which would formally make Connected Education the national policy for innovation in education.

Start-ups are also offering innovative solutions to provide schools with the tools for education in the digital age. There are presently 364 EdTech start-ups in Brazil (ABStartups and CIEB, 2019). Arco Educação, one of the Brazilian unicorns (see Chapter 5) focuses on educational solutions for basic education, providing technology, content and services from early childhood to high school. Mundo4D brings Education 4.0 to schools through experimentation of new technologies, whereas Faz Game provides teachers with a proactive and motivating way of teaching where students learn by creating educational games of diverse content, developing skills such as creativity, collaboration and resilience (BrazilLab, 2020). Other start-ups, such as QEDU, make use of publicly available data to provide in-depth analyses and present information in an innovative manner, so as to provide evidence for policy makers to improve schools.

Procuring services from start-ups is, however, not straightforward for the government. The general Procurement Law (Lei da Licitação, 8.666/93) does not formally exclude start-ups from public procurement. However, start-ups are often not capable of competing in public calls, as they lack experience or do not reach the turnover thresholds. The Innovation Law (Law 10.973/2004) and the Legal Framework for Innovation (Decree 9.283/2018) foresee the "technological order" of an innovative solution and the actual delivery of the innovative solution previously ordered. To contract such orders, however, civil servants need to have a deep understanding of industries, technologies and markets. High risk aversion among civil servants, who are personally liable for decisions taken as part of their duty, coupled with an increasing scrutiny from the Federal Court of Accounts, have limited the application of this law. The proposal for a legal framework for start-ups aims to make procurement from start-ups more agile, by introducing a trial period during which the public administration can test the solution offered by the company before proceeding to a full procurement. Such a provision, while safeguarding diligence in spending public resources, would allow young innovative enterprises to offer their solutions. Looking forward, it may also be necessary for Brazil to make its public procurement rules more suitable for start-ups to provide their services. Subsidies for schools to finance such solutions may also be envisaged.

Box 3.2. Policy recommendations to foster the use of digital technologies by individuals

Establish a wider set of demand-side policies to balance existing supply-side measures for digital inclusion, so as to foster digital skills and address the digital divide:

- Raise awareness on the benefits of Internet use among all people.
- Develop specific content, services and applications that meet the needs of those with low digital uptake, e.g. low-educated, low-income and elderly people.
- Offer large-scale online courses on Internet safety and security, online banking, access to digital government services, e-commerce, content creation.
- Increase the role of telecentres as training providers and ensure adequate funding and technical assistance from the federal government.
- Scale up the National Digital Inclusion Agent Training and the Computers for Inclusion programmes, in co-operation with the private sector.

Box 3.2. Policy recommendations to foster the use of digital technologies by individuals *(cont.)*

- Adapt textbooks, train teachers and align performance assessments in schools to the new National Common Curricular Base. Establish a sound monitoring and evaluation system to ensure equal implementation across the country.
- Develop a plan for regular monitoring and evaluation of the Connected Education programme.
- Foresee teachers' training courses for the use of ICTs in education that favour interaction and peer sharing of experiences.
- Reform regulation as to allow public procurement of innovative services and solutions from start-ups.

Uptake of digital technologies by firms

Digital technologies have the potential to increase productivity in firms and thus to boost economic activity across sectors. Online channels can increase exposure to a firm's products and services, therefore increasing their business potential. In embracing the digital transformation, different sectors may face challenges that are specific to their economic activity. Looking across sectors, however, there are also economy-wide factors at play. Brazilian enterprises operate within an economic environment that involves high costs, referred to as "Brazilian cost" (*custo Brasil*) (Dutz et al., 2018). This is the result of insufficient infrastructure, a complex taxation system with both high levels of taxation and compliance costs, high entry barriers and insolvency costs, and limited access to finance, especially for smaller enterprises. The lack of skills of the working population and the low quality of the education systems also hinder the development of more knowledge-intensive activities. Brazil's tariffs on imported goods, including for ICT goods, further increase the cost of inputs (OECD, 2019c). Finally, support of existing industry structures has been found to inhibit the reallocation of resources towards more productive uses and to reduce incentives for innovation (OECD, 2018b).

All of these factors tend to discourage competition, innovation and ultimately slow down the digital transformation of the country, as they favour incumbents and hinder experimentation with new ideas, technologies and business models, which are the drivers of productivity growth in the digital age (OECD, 2019d). For enterprises to invest in digital technologies, reforms are needed in the above-mentioned policy areas to strengthen incentives to innovate.

Brazil has recently approved new measures, such as the Declaration of Rights of Economic Freedom (Declaração de Direitos de Liberdade Econômica – Law 13.784 of 20 September 2019), the launch of the Growth Routes Plan (Rota da crescimento) in 2020, and Ordinance 2.023 of 12 September 2019 eliminating import tax on 34 IT and telecommunication goods. It is also discussing a comprehensive tax reform. These are crucial in fostering an environment conducive to innovation.

Brazilian firms are at an early stage of adoption of digital technologies

Internet connectivity and access to ICTs is quite widespread among Brazilian enterprises, as nearly all enterprises with ten or more employees had a computer (97%) and had accessed the Internet over the last 12 months (97%) in 2019, with no large differences across sizes, regions or sectors. However, among micro-enterprises, which account for the large majority of firms in Brazil, connections to the Internet (88%) and computer use (89%) were significantly lower (2017 data), pointing to a gap that needs to be closed. Micro-enterprises not using the Internet reported lack of skills as the main barrier to access, closely followed by lack of interest (CGI.br, 2018). These findings suggest a need for awareness-raising campaigns on the benefits of the Internet and digital technologies, as well as technical assistance and training for their uptake and use.

Enterprises tend to have quite slow connection speeds, with 52% (those with ten employees or more) reporting connection speeds between 1 Mbps and 30 Mbps and 42% above 30 Mbps. To ensure uninterrupted Internet connections, many enterprises contract more than one connection service. In 2017, this was the case of 76% of enterprises with 10 employees or more. This share increased to 91% in large enterprises and 82% in companies in the ICT service and telecommunication sector (CGI.br, 2018), which are also the enterprises with the greatest adoption of sophisticated digital technologies, e.g. Customer Relationship Management (CRM) and Enterprise Resource Planning (ERP). These patterns confirm that access to fast and reliable connections is an important factor for the uptake of more sophisticated digital technologies. Public policies to improve connectivity are, therefore, key to promote digital uptake by businesses.

Despite widespread access to the Internet, Brazilian enterprises lag behind those in OECD countries for the use of the Internet and digital technologies. In 2019, only 54% of Brazilian enterprises (10 employees or more) had their own website, against the OECD average of 78%. The use of CRM (22%) and ERP (29%) was also below the OECD average (31% and 36%, respectively). However, these average figures conceal a wide gap among large and small enterprises, as digital uptake among large enterprises is in line with OECD countries, in particular for websites and ERP (Figure 3.13). Brazilian enterprises are also catching up in the adoption of cloud computing services.

Small and micro-enterprises are much more prone to using social network accounts rather than websites. Brazilian Internet users are heavy users of social networks, which businesses are increasingly using as a communication channel with costumers. Overall, Brazilian enterprises stand out well above the OECD for the use of social networks (76% and 57%, respectively).

Figure 3.13. Diffusion of selected ICT tools and activities in enterprises in Brazil and the OECD, 2019 or latest available year

As a percentage of all firms with ten or more employees

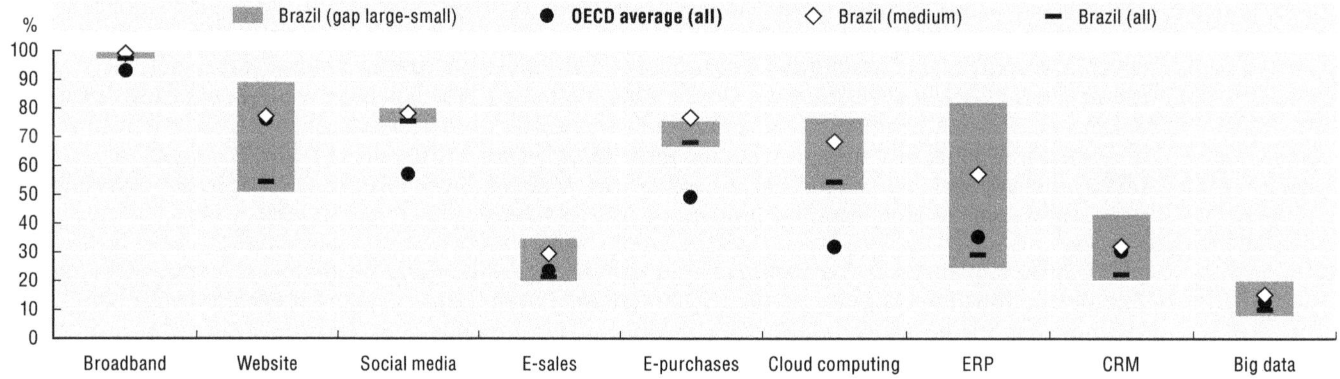

Notes: ERP = Enterprise Resource Planning; CRM = Customer Relationship Management. Average OECD is an unweighted average of available countries in each ICT tool and activity for all enterprises. Data for broadband for OECD countries refer to 2017. Data for e-purchases, cloud computing and big data for OECD countries refer to 2018. The indicator for cloud computing for Brazil is based on the use of four cloud services (e-mail, data storage, computing power and office software), instead of seven considered for the OECD countries.

Sources: OECD (2020b), *ICT Access and Usage by Businesses* (database), *http://oe.cd/bus* (accessed in March 2020); CGI.br (2020b), *ICT Enterprises 2019: Survey on the Use of Information and Communication Technologies in Brazilian Enterprises* (database), *https://cetic.br/en/pesquisa/empresas/indicadores/* (accessed in July 2020).

Based on the 2014 ICT Enterprises Survey microdata (Siqueira et al., 2017) calculated an ICT use index, showing that most small and medium-sized enterprises (SMEs) are still excluded from an effective use of digital technologies (Figure 3.15). Such a gap is likely to be even wider for the large number of informal enterprises, for which statistics are not available. Informality can inhibit digitalisation, as informal firms may wish to remain small to avoid detection. On the other hand, the government can use digital technologies to reduce informality, for instance by making electronic record keeping cash registers compulsory, as Latvia has done (OECD, forthcoming b). These findings point to the need for public policies to help smaller enterprises overcome barriers to the use of advanced digital tools, by providing technical extension services and targeted programmes to support skills development and investments.

The government can also provide incentives for the use of digital tools, for instance by offering a lower (or zero) fee for the completion of a compulsory service through online channels, as compared to the physical alternative (e.g. procurement of services). At present, for instance, paying taxes online is still used by only half of micro-enterprises and not by all bigger firms (Figure 3.16), and the proportion of firms using e-procurement services is even lower. Ninety-two per cent of firms (with more than ten employees) use the Internet to interact with public authorities or perform services on line, compared to 76% of micro-enterprises.

Figure 3.14. Adoption of digital technologies by Brazilian firms, by firm size, 2019 or latest available year

As a percentage of firms with an Internet connection,

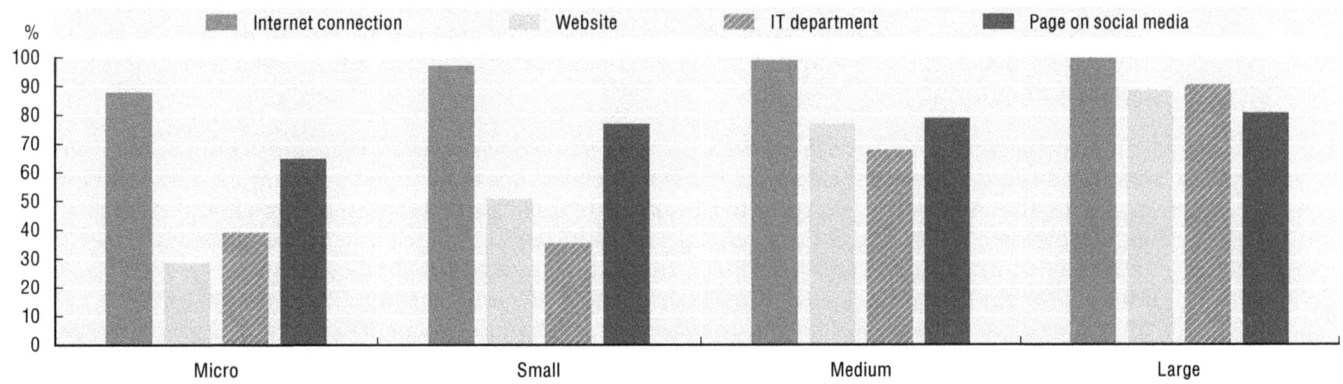

Notes: Data for micro-enterprises refer to 2017. IT department is one person for micro-enterprises.

Sources: CGI.br (2020b), *ICT Enterprises 2019: Survey on the Use of Information and Communication Technologies in Brazilian Enterprises* (database), *https://cetic.br/en/pesquisa/empresas/indicadores/* (accessed in July 2020); CGI.br (2018), *ICT Enterprises 2017: Survey on the Use of Information and Communication Technologies in Brazilian Enterprises* (database), *https://cetic.br/en/pesquisa/empresas/indicadores/* (accessed in February 2020).

Figure 3.15. ICT use index of Brazilian firms with ten or more employees, 2014

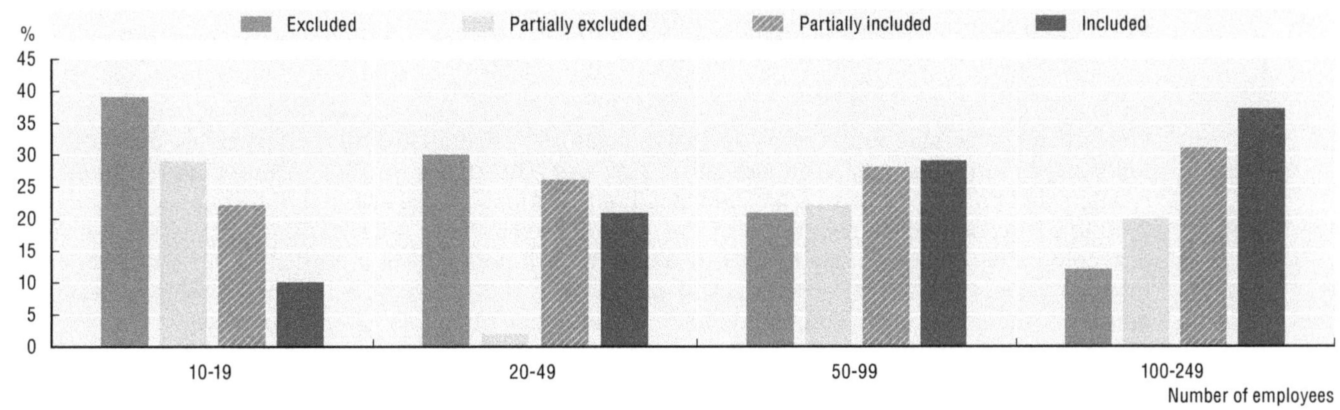

Source: Siqueira et al. (2017), "Using a Digital Divide Index among enterprises in the context of public policies in Brazil" *http://aisel.aisnet.org/confirm2017/41*.

Figure 3.16. Use of digital government services by Brazilian firms, 2019 or latest available year

Firms interacting with public authorities, by activity, as a percentage of firms using the Internet

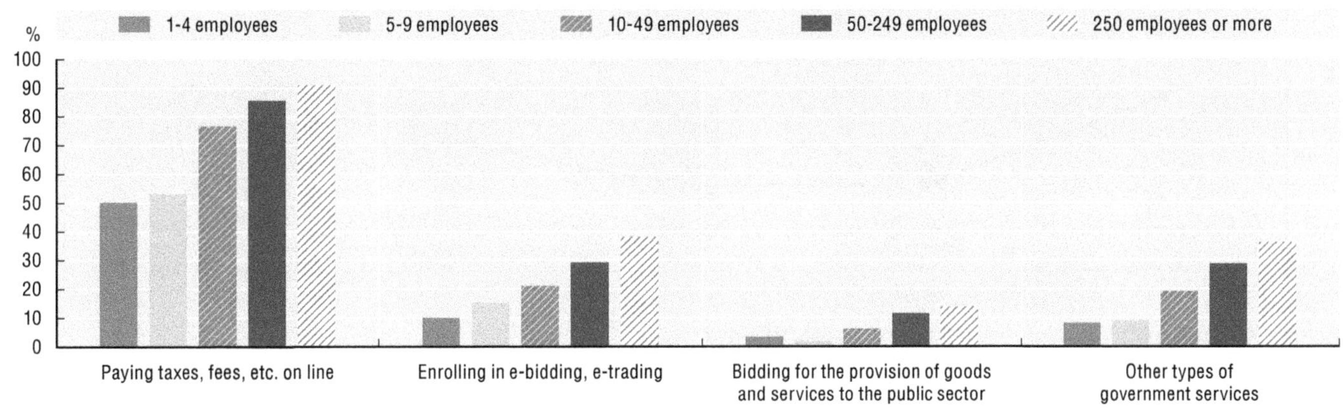

Note: Data for micro-enterprises refer to 2017.

Sources: CGI.br (2020b), *ICT Enterprises 2019: Survey on the Use of Information and Communication Technologies in Brazilian Enterprises* (database), *https://cetic.br/en/pesquisa/empresas/indicadores/* (accessed in July 2020); CGI.br (2018), *ICT Enterprises 2017: Survey on the Use of Information and Communication Technologies in Brazilian Enterprises* (database), *https://cetic.br/en/pesquisa/empresas/indicadores/* (accessed in February 2020).

Advanced manufacturing and the diffusion of the Internet of Things (IoT) are two key strategies adopted by the Brazilian government for digital transformation. Both require a set of technologies, such as sensors, software, data analytics and computing capacity, among others. Concerning IoT, in 2019, Brazil had a penetration of 10.6 machine-to-machine (M2M) SIM cards per 100 habitants, compared to the OECD average of 22. The number of M2M subscriptions was 22 million in 2019 (see Chapter 2).

For the manufacturing sector, the introduction of technologies related to the fourth industrial revolution is still at an early stage of development. Firms, especially large ones, report investing in these technologies or having the intention to do so in the near future (CNI, 2018). More than two-thirds of firms report high adoption costs as one of the main barriers. Other barriers, such as a lack of skilled workers (30%), inadequate infrastructure (26%), or difficulties to integrate new technologies and software (20%) were mentioned less frequently (CNI, 2016). The high cost of technology adoption is partly the result of high import tariffs on foreign ICT goods. Companies purchasing intermediate or capital goods are paying higher prices than in other countries (OECD, forthcoming c). Investments for Industry 4.0 need to be tailored to a firm's needs, while the technical solution has to be purchased by different suppliers. Integration companies play the role of intermediators between available technologies and enterprises. According to the National Confederation of Industry (Confederação Nacional da Indústria, CNI), only 50 such companies are currently operating in the country, mainly with a focus on large companies. A related issue is that, in most cases, SMEs lack a digitalisation plan. The recently launched Inovacred 4.0 programme by the Brazilian Agency for Innovation and Research (Financiadora de Estudos e Projetos, FINEP) aims to address these needs, by supporting investment in Industry 4.0 technologies, through the support of intermediary companies (see below).

E-commerce is growing, but structural problems hinder its development

E-commerce sales were valued at USD 14.6 billion (BRL 53.2 billion) in 2018, a 12% increase over 2017 and reflecting an estimated annual growth rate of 11% over 2015-19 (Figure 3.17). Several large multinational retailers and online platforms (e.g. MercadoLibre and Amazon) are active in the country. Although in 2015 Brazil accounted for about 40% of the e-commerce in Latin America (UNCTAD, 2015), the value of e-commerce in the country has not reached the full potential of a market of 107.5 million adult Internet users. Only 21% of enterprises sold on line in 2019. In 2017, e-commerce sales represented only 6% of total retail sales, compared to 20% in the People's Republic of China (hereafter "China"), 19% in Korea and 12% in the United States (McKinsey, 2019). Nonetheless, e-commerce sales in Brazil grew at an annual rate of 16% in 2019, far exceeding growth in the economy as a whole (Ebit Nielsen, 2020).

Figure 3.17. E-commerce turnover in Brazil, 2015-19

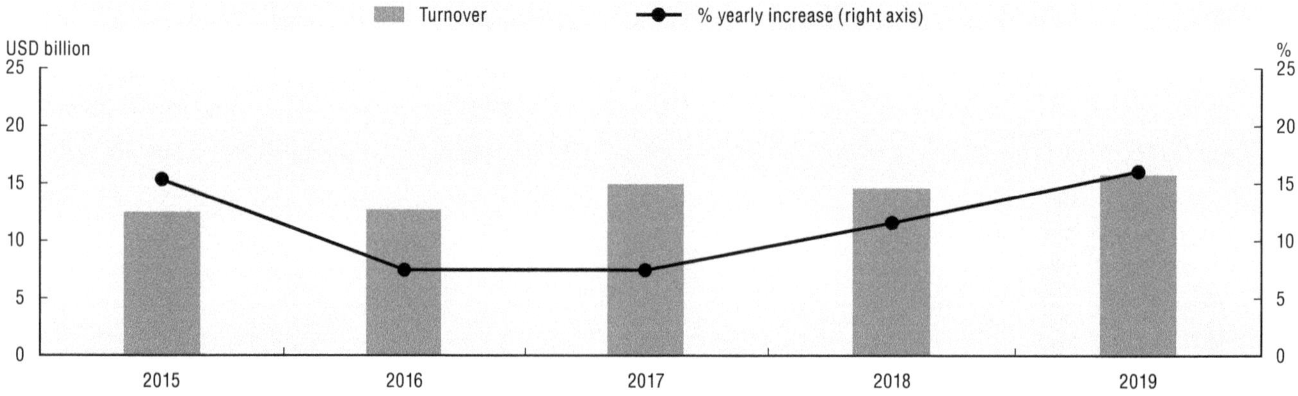

Source: Ebit Nielsen (2020), *Webshoppers 41ª Edição*, *www.ebit.com.br/webshoppers*.

Unlike most OECD countries, the gap between large and small enterprises in e-commerce engagement is not very wide (Figure 3.18). The gap with micro-enterprises is also small, with 19% reporting selling on line in 2017 (CGI.br, 2018). The rate of enterprises participating in e-commerce has grown for all sectors and regions. Some sectors, such as food and accommodation, stand out in terms of online sales (Figure 3.19).

Figure 3.18. Firm participation in e-commerce in Brazil and the OECD, by size, 2019

As a percentage of firms with ten or more employees

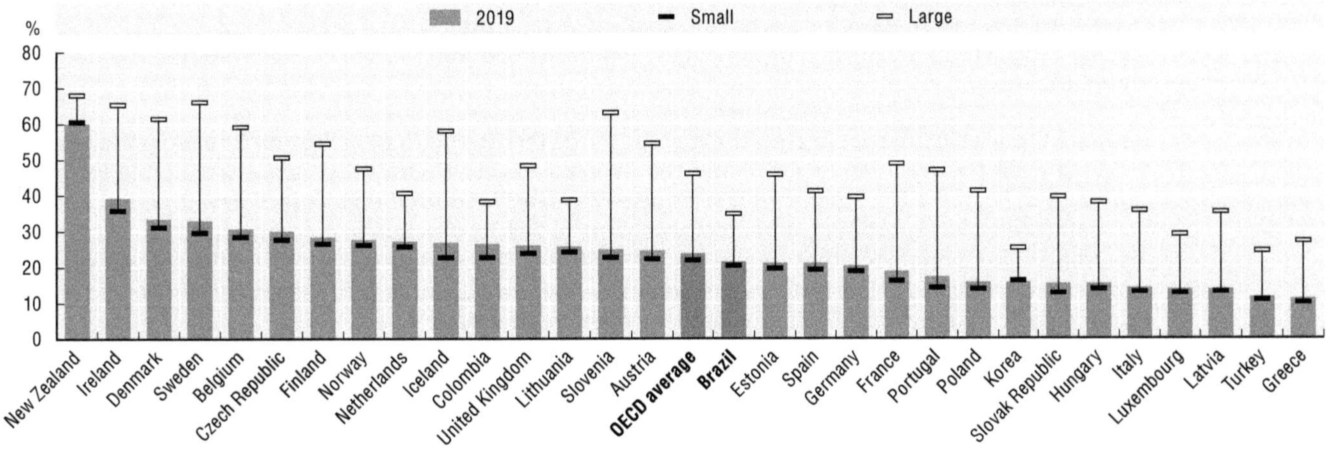

Notes: Firm participation is the percentage of all businesses employing more than ten employees receiving orders over computer networks. Small firms are defined as companies with 10 to 49 employees, and large firms as companies with 250 or more employees. Data for Colombia, Iceland, Korea and New Zealand refer to 2018.

Sources: Adapted from OECD (2019e), *Unpacking E-commerce: Business Models, Trends and Policies*, *https://doi.org/10.1787/23561431-en*. OECD calculations based on OECD (2020b), *ICT Access and Usage by Businesses* (database), *http://oe.cd/bus* (accessed in March 2020) and CGI.br (2020b), *ICT Enterprises 2019: Survey on the Use of Information and Communication Technologies in Brazilian Enterprises* (database), *https://cetic.br/en/pesquisa/empresas/indicadores/* (accessed in July 2020).

Figure 3.19. Evolution of e-commerce in Brazil, 2012 and 2019

As a percentage of firms with ten or more employees selling on line

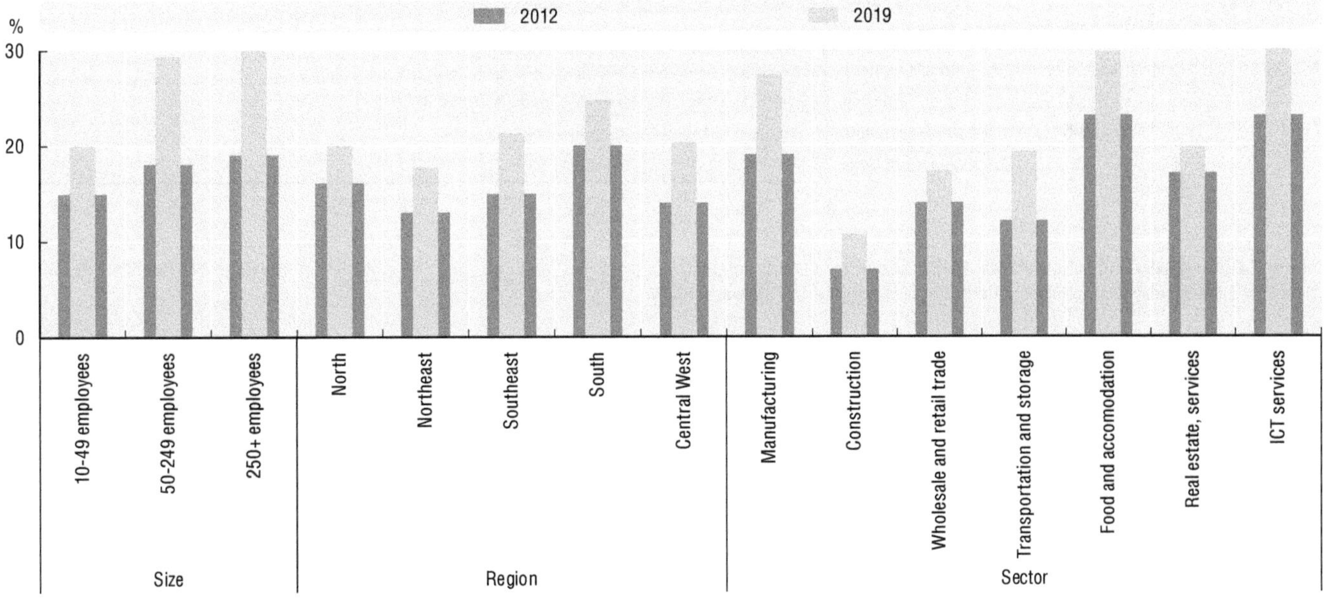

Note: ICT = information and communication technology.

Source: CGI.br (2020b), *ICT Enterprises 2019: Survey on the Use of Information and Communication Technologies in Brazilian Enterprises* (database), *https://cetic.br/en/pesquisa/empresas/indicadores/* (accessed in July 2020).

Enterprises in Brazil, and especially SMEs, still use emails as channels for concluding online transactions and increasingly use social media as marketplaces (CGI.br, 2020b). In a 2018 survey among SMEs engaged in e-commerce, email was the main service channel (90% of respondents), followed by WhatsApp (82%) and Facebook (64%) (SEBRAE and E-commerce Brasil, 2018). The share of enterprises engaged in e-commerce through Facebook was indeed found to be higher than the general population, as 67% of enterprises active on Facebook were selling on line (OECD, 2019e).

The market for e-commerce is concentrated, with the ten main marketplaces accounting for about 63% of total turnover (SBVC, 2018). Many SMEs use marketplace platforms to penetrate the market easily. By aligning themselves with a larger, known business, these stores can gain visibility and, in some cases, use the marketplace's options for payment. A majority (61%) of sellers on MercadoLibre (known as MercadoLivre in Brazil), one of the largest platforms operating in the country, are micro-enterprises or SMEs.

Among firms with Internet access, the main reasons reported for not selling on line are preference for their current business model (51%) and the perception that their products are unsuitable for online sales (49%) (Figure 3.22). Small enterprises also frequently reported high cost of development and lack of staff (CGI.br, 2018). Product suitability was reported as an obstacle to e-commerce in all sectors and is a challenge common to other countries (OECD, 2019e). This finding suggests that the perception about product suitability as an obstacle may be somewhat overrated among businesses and awareness-raising campaigns could increase their engagement with e-commerce.

On the consumer side, 38% of Internet users aged 16-74 had made purchases on line in the 12 months prior to the survey, with young (25-44 years old), wealthier and more educated consumers being more likely to shop on line. Brazil has the largest gap between the top and the bottom income quartiles (59 percentage points) among OECD countries and partner economies (OECD, 2019f). The main reasons among Internet users for not making purchases on line were the preference for seeing the physical product before buying it (86%) and trust-related issues (Figure 3.20).

Figure 3.20. Barriers preventing Brazilian Internet users from shopping on line, 2018

As a percentage of Internet users aged 16-74 who did not purchase goods or services on line in the last 12 months

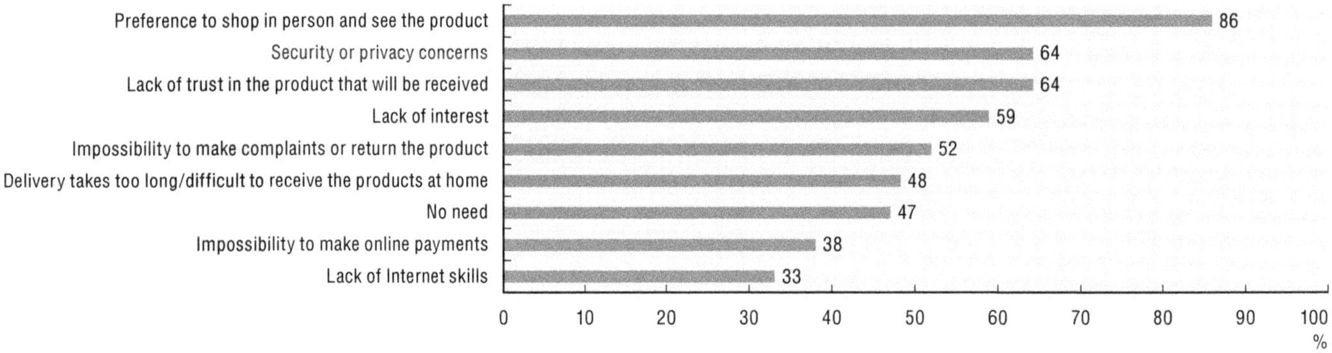

Source: CGI.br (2019a), *ICT Households 2018: Survey on the Use of Information and Communication Technologies in Brazilian Households* (database), *https://cetic.br/en/pesquisa/domicilios/indicadores/* (accessed in February 2020).

Financial inclusion is still low

Online financial services, including online bank accounts, credit, investments and insurance, are not widely diffused in Brazil (FEBRABAN/Deloitte, 2019). Financial inclusion is a challenge, as 30% of economically active people do not have a bank account and most payments are made in cash. Half of online shoppers in Brazil pay through a bank slip called *boleto bancário* and this is indeed one of the most diffused payment methods firms report on their online sales (Figure 3.21). Customers pay with cash banks, participating drugstores and ATMs and then send proof of payment to the company, with consequences on the business pace, as it takes a few days for these slips to be processed. The unbanked population, however, is driving the creation of new solutions, with many start-ups proposing financial services, thus breaking down barriers to financial inclusion (see Chapter 6). Platforms such as MercadoLibre have also introduced their own payment system, i.e. MercadoPago, which has developed from the platform-specific payment solution to a stand-alone online payment service available also for other online and off line stores.

Figure 3.21. Payment methods used for online shopping in Brazil, 2019

As a percentage of enterprises that sold on line in the past 12 months, 2019

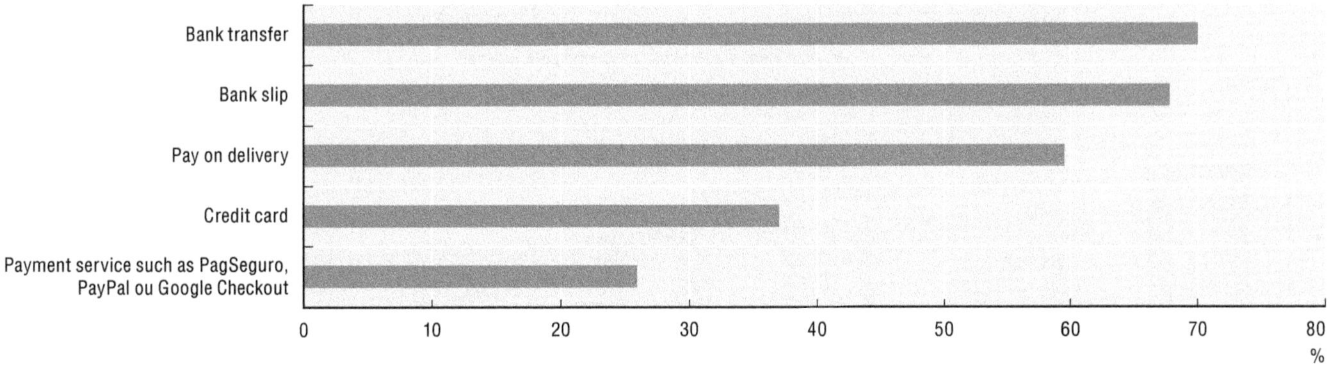

Source: CGI.br (2020b), *ICT Enterprises 2019: Survey on the Use of Information and Communication Technologies in Brazilian Enterprises* (database), *https://cetic.br/en/pesquisa/empresas/indicadores/* (accessed in July 2020).

The Central Bank of Brazil has also worked to implement an Instant Payment Ecosystem in Brazil (PIX), which will be implemented in November 2020. Work carried out in 2018 has resulted in a communication (Comunicado No. 32.927/2018, modified by 34.085/2019) on the fundamental requisites for the ecosystem. A permanent advisory committee, the Forum for Instant Payment (Ordinance 102.166/2019), has supported the Central Bank in defining rules for the instant payment ecosystem. In parallel, the Central Bank has developed the infrastructure and the centralised database. Importantly, Brazilians will be able to pay federal taxes through PIX, and all financial and payment institutions with more than 500 000 active customer accounts will be required to participate in PIX, offering their customers all their functionalities for initiating and receiving payments. The other financial and payment institutions, even those that have not yet reached the limits to request authorisation to operate as a payment institution, may, on an optional basis, participate in PIX since its launch. Instant payment will offer a quick and safe alternative for payments and is therefore expected to support e-commerce growth.

Logistics need to be improved

The other main factors hindering the development of e-commerce are logistics, particularly the high costs and long delays for last-mile delivery, and taxation, as consumption tax rates vary across states. Data from the Brazilian Micro and Small Business Support Service (Serviço Brasileiro de Apoio às Micro e Pequenas Empresas, SEBRAE) (SEBRAE and E-commerce Brasil, 2018) show that the main barriers for small businesses are the tax burden (43%), followed by logistics (42%), as well as marketing and competition/showrooming (30%). Interviews with large market players also confirmed that logistics and taxation are the main challenges faced by companies engaged in e-commerce.

Long distances, high traffic congestion in big cities and poor road conditions outside add up to long delivery delays (Figure 3.23).

The market structure also affects the costs and delays for product deliveries. The government-owned national post, Empresa Brasileira de Correios e Telégrafos (ECT, hereafter "Correios") is the mostly used delivery system. Online retailers relied on Correios freight in 88.6% of cases in 2018, while only 9.8% had their own delivery system and 58.7% used other private carriers (ABComm and Comschool, 2019).

Correios has a monopoly on mail delivery (exclusive right to receive, transport and deliver in the national territory, and to expedite abroad, letters, postcards and group mail) as established by Article 21 of the Constitution and Article 9 of Law 6.538/1978 (the "Postal Law"). It does not have a monopoly on parcel delivery. The company benefits from reciprocal tax immunity (exemption from taxes on property, rent and income), is exempt of the interstate checks from the Department of Federal Revenue (Receita Federal), and is under the procedural regime of a public company. The above privileges are granted to Correios so to ensure universal service provision of mail across the country. However, these privileges should not act as a barrier for the development of a competitive parcel delivery market.

Figure 3.22. Barriers to e-commerce reported by firms in Brazil, 2019

As a percentage of firms with ten or more employees using the Internet

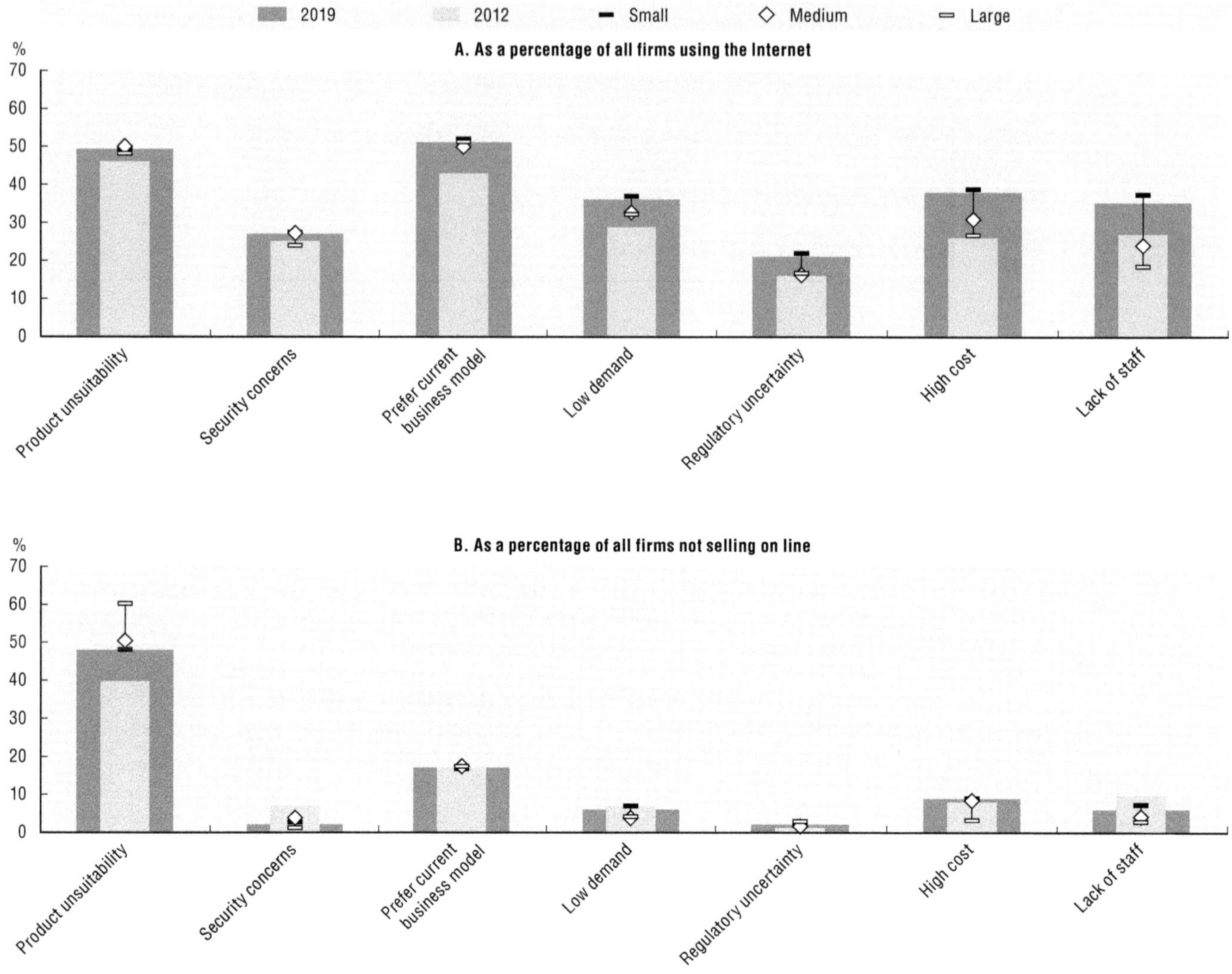

Source: CGI.br (2020b), *ICT Enterprises 2019: Survey on the Use of Information and Communication Technologies in Brazilian Enterprises* (database), *https://cetic.br/en/pesquisa/empresas/indicadores/* (accessed in July 2020).

Figure 3.23. Average time of delivery in Brazil, by region, 2013-19

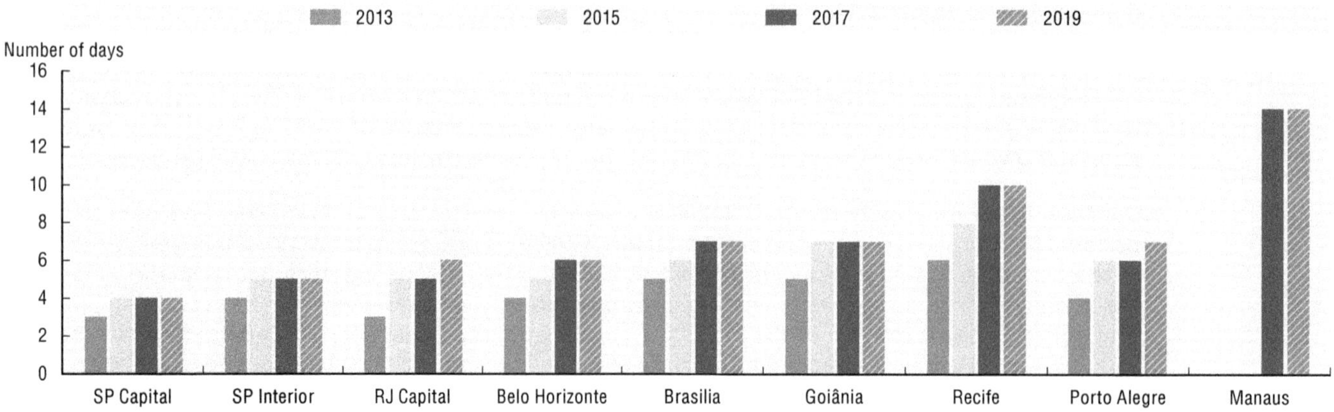

Note: SP = São Paolo; RJ = Rio de Janeiro.

Source: ABComm and Comschool (2019), *Pesquisa: Logística no E-commerce Brasileiro 2019 https://abcomm.org/noticias/pesquisa-logistica-no-e-commerce-2019/*.

Postal services across the globe are all experiencing similar challenges, due to the decreasing volume of postal mail, and an increasing volume of parcel deliveries, spurred by e-commerce. In this context, universal service providers are struggling to ensure universal service obligation requirements, while facing increased competition. Particularly in large countries, new entrants usually cherry-pick the most profitable consumers, leaving the incumbent with those consumers who provide insufficient revenue to cover their costs. The Brazilian postal market shows some similarities to the Canadian one, a country which also includes remote, sparsely populated areas. The postal service is not fully liberalised in either of these countries, i.e. the state-owned operator has a monopoly for the letter segment, while it has to compete with private operators in the parcel delivery market. Both countries also lack a national regulatory authority for postal services. This restricts transparency, as competitors cannot be confident that competition is fair, i.e. that there is no cross-subsidisation from monopolistic activities to the other market segments. Canada uses several measures to prevent such cross-subsidisation. A major tool is the Annual Cost Study Contribution Analysis. It is drafted by Canada Post and audited by an independent company (ERGP, 2019). Lacking an independent postal regulator, Brazil may wish to ensure greater transparency through regular reporting by Correios, audited by an independent body.

In the European Union, postal markets have been opened to competition in the past 20 years. This has been done through regulation aimed at liberalising the sector, while ensuring consumer protection through universal service obligation. Some countries, such as Germany, have established that if universal service cannot be fulfilled by the market, then all licensed operators must provide the service jointly. In Brazil, standing regulations require that private delivery companies pay a fee of 0.5% of their revenues to help support the universal service requirement. However, the fee is applied unevenly, and it is unclear which private companies are required to pay (Syndex/Uni Global, 2019).

For e-commerce to further develop, Brazil should ensure greater competition in the parcel delivery market. This may require that the government carry out an in-depth analysis of the postal service market. In the meantime, the country may apply some measures, such as those outlined above, i.e. transparent reporting and private sector contribution to universal service obligation.

The taxation system limits e-commerce potential

The taxation system affects the development of e-commerce in Brazil. Goods sold on line are subject to a state-level tax, which is applied to the movement of goods, transport services and telecommunication services (the ICMS). ICMS rates vary across states from 17% (standard rate) to 18% (e.g. São Paulo) and 20% in Rio de Janeiro. Interstate sales are subject to an interstate ICMS, at a rate of 4% (for interstate transactions with imported goods), 7% or 12% (depending on the region where the goods are sent to) (Figure 3.24), plus the difference between the ICMS rate of the destination state and the interstate rate (Diferencial de Aliquotas do ICMS, DIFAL) (Convênio ICMS 152/2015). A company based in one state and selling to another has to pay the ICMS at the interstate rate to the state of origin and the DIFAL to the state of destination.[2] The variation of ICMS rate across states and the compliance costs related to the payment of the interstate ICMS are clearly an obstacle to the development of e-commerce in Brazil. Establishing a harmonised value-added tax (VAT) system across states is among the most urgent reforms the country should undertake to foster e-commerce.

Figure 3.24. Interstate ICMS rates, 2019

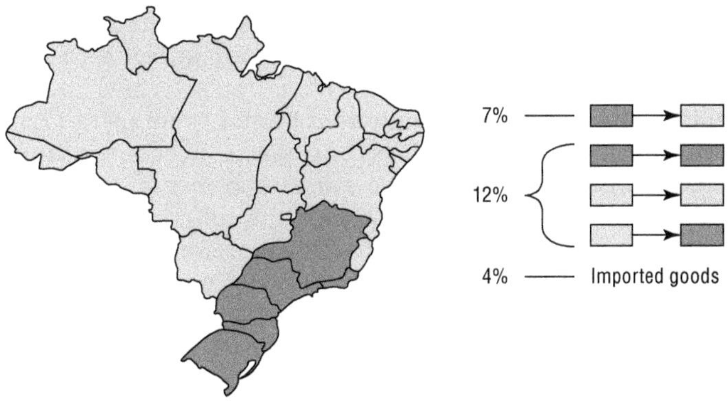

Note: ICMS = tax on movement of goods, transport and telecommunication services.

Source: MercadoLibre; original map by Koury Lopes Advogados.

Some of the ICMS rules may also be an obstacle to the development of multichannel e-commerce solutions, which combine buying on line with pick-up and return of goods in stores (multichannel e-commerce). The ICMS is applied to purchases and sales at the exit of merchandise from a company's establishment. Therefore, goods delivered to one's own or franchised stores for pick-up by the final consumer may be regarded by the fiscal authority as a resale and taxed again by the ICMS. Currently, there is a draft bill (PLP 148/2019) proposing an exception of the ICMS on the transfer of goods from the main seller to accredited product delivery stores. Additionally, the Secretary of Development of Industry, Trade, Services and Innovation of the Ministry of Economy (SCM/ME), which is part of the sub-committee on e-commerce and exports (see below), is interacting with the National Council on Tax Policy (Conselho Nacional de Política Fazendária, CONFAZ) – overseeing ICMS regulation implementation – to facilitate application of the current regulation. A resolution from this body would give legal certainty to operators, therefore providing a solution enabling omni-channel e-commerce.

The Digital Transformation Strategy has established a sub-committee on e-commerce and exports. Its main goal is to elaborate actions related to the promotion of domestic and international e-commerce activities, supporting the growth of Brazilian exports of goods and services, in co-ordination with different relevant Brazilian entities, including the Brazilian Trade and Investment Promotion Agency (Agência Brasileira de Promoção de Exportações e Investimentos, Apex), SEBRAE, the Brazilian Institute of Geography and Statistics, and CETIC.br. It is co-ordinated by the Secretary of Development of Industry, Trade, Services and Innovation of the Ministry of Economy and the Division for Technology Promotion of the Ministry of Foreign Affairs. The sub-committee is addressing some of the strategic actions, such as: data in e-commerce, the role of platforms, the measurement of e-commerce, taxation, logistics, international negotiations and digital payments. Up to September 2019, the sub-committee had supported the e-commerce negotiations at the World Trade Organization (Joint Statement on Electronic Commerce of 9 July 2019), and the negotiations of regional free-trade agreements with e-commerce chapters, such as Mercosul-Canada and Mercosul-Korea. In addition, it is working on developing statistics to understand how e-commerce takes place within and across states, based on invoices from the Receita Federal. It has also started a dialogue with the Central Bank of Brazil to support the organisation of a workshop on the Brazilian Instant Payments Ecosystem (see above). The sub-committee has also worked on policy actions for support to firms in domestic and cross-border e-commerce. In this context, the group could count on the participation of Apex and SEBRAE presenting their initiatives for e-commerce.

SEBRAE helps micro and small firms to build their online retail place

SEBRAE is an autonomous non-profit private entity, directly funded by a mandatory contribution from larger enterprises. It offers several services to micro and small enterprises across all sectors to promote their digital transformation, including business consulting, value chain support and export training. Through the programme SEBRAETEC, SEBRAE subsidises consulting services across four different areas: design, quality control, innovation and sustainability. SEBRAE manages a national web portal, as well as 13 portals at the state level, where enterprises and consulting companies can both register to ease the match between the demand for and supply of technology services.

As part of the work carried out within the E-digital sub-committee for e-commerce, SEBRAE has extended the information and practical guidance on e-commerce on its website. Based on the topics discussed by the sub-committee, SEBRAE has revisited its strategy regarding e-commerce. To further encourage micro and small enterprises to engage in e-commerce, SEBRAE offers financial support to companies for tailored business consulting activities on how to make their business more digital, through its newly launched initiative Digital Commerce (Varejo Digital). SEBRAE brought together five affordable solutions to help businesses accelerate their digital transformation, from social networks to e-commerce, online stores and virtual tours. Small firms can assess their degree of digitalisation, then proceed to purchase the solution offered, with SEBRAE financing up to 70% of the cost. Through this service, SEBRAE offers therefore a sort of "digitalisation voucher", i.e. a small grant to help companies digitalise. OECD countries such as Australia, Austria (KMG Digital) and Denmark (SMV:Digital) also offer similar support (OECD, forthcoming a) to foster digital transformation of SMEs. Such support could be extended to encompass more than just e-commerce, such as data protection, big data or online security.

Apex supports the internationalisation of Brazilian firms active in e-commerce

In 2017, Apex launched the e-Xport Programme to raise awareness about business opportunities in e-commerce among Brazilian firms. The initiative attracted interest from 700 Brazilian companies. The programme includes training and mentoring on how to develop an appropriate global marketplace strategy, market intelligence studies, promotion of strategic partnerships with main e-commerce players and customised consultancies. It was aimed at SMEs interested in operating via e-commerce in the international market.

Initially, Apex targeted Argentina, China, Mexico and the United States as key markets with the largest e-commerce opportunity for Brazil. However, in 2018, the e-Xport Programme was revised to focus only on China and the United States. Over the last two years, the following actions have been developed under the e-Xport Programme: 1) negotiation of strategic partnerships with more than ten marketplaces in the target countries, including Alibaba and Amazon; 2) hiring companies specialised in the Chinese and US e-commerce markets to mentor Brazilian companies interested in operating via e-commerce in these markets. The two hired companies mentored 60 companies throughout 2018 and 2019 and individually monitored Brazilian companies interested in operating through e-commerce in these markets. 3) A prospective mission to the United States e-commerce market for 24 Brazilian companies. During the mission, the companies had meetings with professionals from areas important to a US e-commerce operation (accounting, law, payment security) and with Brazilian businessmen who already operate successfully via e-commerce in the United States. In addition, Brazilian companies visited US e-commerce companies and e-commerce logistics companies. For 2020, the e-Xport Programme will be revised in order to carry out more e-commerce qualification actions for Brazilian companies and to increase the capillarity of the e-Xport Programme.

Brazil is stepping up support to the diffusion of digital technologies across the economy

Brazil currently does not have a unified programme supporting the digitalisation of firms. Under the momentum created by the adoption of the E-Digital Strategy, several programmes were launched in 2019 to increase ICT diffusion in the economy, and in particular IoT and technologies for Industry 4.0, and others are under preparation. Some initiatives in support of e-commerce have also been launched or strengthened, as part of the work of the E-digital sub-committee for e-commerce (see above). This is a positive sign, which shows the engagement of several stakeholders and institutions towards the achievement of the strategy's objectives. Furthermore, since adoption of digital technologies spans from investment in ICT capital to software acquisition, website, e-commerce related activities, software development or IT maintenance (IT services), a number of general cross-sector support programmes in Brazil also include provisions, which are relevant for ICT adoption by firms.

Such support programmes are both of a financial and non-financial nature and take the form of credit at more favourable conditions, subsidised business consulting programmes and export training. They are presented in Table 3.3 and are discussed below. Only programmes aimed at increasing ICT use by enterprises are analysed in this chapter; others related to supporting the overall development of the ICT sector through R&D and support to start-ups are discussed in Chapter 5.

BNDES and FINEP are increasingly supporting investments in digital technologies

The two main providers of business support in the country are BNDES and FINEP. This section looks at the support these two institutions provide for ICT adoption by firms.

BNDES is a federal public company whose goal is to provide long-term financing for endeavours that contribute to the country's development. It has a range of financial products earmarked for investment projects, the acquisition of new machinery and equipment, exports of machinery, Brazilian equipment and services, and the acquisition of goods and production inputs (BNDES, 2019).

BNDES supports the ICT sector directly by providing credit at preferential conditions for innovation activities related to software, data centres and IT services, and support to broadband development. Over the past five years, the volume of credit disbursed for the ICT sector amounted to USD 4 billion (BRL 13 billion; figures provided by BNDES). This figure includes credit provided through Cartão (Card) BNDES (see below), and working capital (FINEM Giro), but also credit for innovation (BNDES MPME Inovadora and BNDES FINEM Inovação) and for broadband deployment (FINEM Telecom). These figures also include credit for the digitalisation of the public administration (FINEM BNDES PMAT e BNDES PMAT Automático). The largest part of this credit was in support of large enterprises (gross annual operational revenue above USD 76 million, or BRL 300 million): 70% of the volume of credit (excluding telecom), 90% including funding for telecom. This is at odds with difficult credit market conditions faced by SMEs in Brazil, with low access to credit and an average interest rate of 25% per year (OECD, 2020c). In the past years, BNDES has increasingly focused its action on SMEs. In the first semester of 2018, spending on SMEs, including micro-enterprises, reached 48.6% of BNDES overall direct lending activities, up from 30.6% in 2016 (BNDES, 2019). Going forward, BNDES should further strengthen its focus on SMEs, in view of supporting their digital uptake.

Table 3.3. Business support programmes for the diffusion of ICT technologies in Brazil

	Support	Size of firms supported	Sector	Instrument specifically designed to foster ICT adoption
	Credit at advantageous conditions			
BNDES				
FINAME	Purchase of machinery and equipment, including IT.	All	All	
FINAME Industry 4.0 (launched in 2019)	Purchase of machinery and equipment that contain the technologies associated with advanced manufacturing solutions and Internet of Things services (IoT) categories in the list of BNDES' accredited suppliers.	All	All	✓
Automático	Financing up to USD 38 million (BRL 150 million) for investment projects of companies from all sectors.	All	All	
Card	Pre-approved credit for the purchase of accredited goods and services (such as machinery and equipment, including IT, software, IoT solutions).	Micro, small, medium (turnover up to USD 76 million, or BRL 300 million) Individual entrepreneurs	All	
FINEP				
FINEP Inovação (technological diffusion for innovation)	Purchase of informatics and automation goods.	Medium and large	All	
FINEP Inovacred 4.0 (launched in 2019)	Development and implementation of strategic business digital plans.	Small, medium (turnover up to USD 76 million, BRL 300 million)	Manufacturing	✓
FINEP Software (launched in 2019)	Investments from USD 38 000 (BRL 150 000).	All	All	✓
	Subsidised business consulting			
Ministry of Economy Brasil Mais (launched in 2020)	Consultancy services for the optimisation of production processes.	Small and medium (11-200 employees)	Manufacturing, trade and services	✓
SEBRAE Varejo Digital (launched in 2019)	Solutions for digital transformation are offered on a dedicated website. Firms can apply for purchasing the solution, which is financed up to 70% by SEBRAE.	Small and medium	All	✓
SENAI SENAI 4.0 portal	Training courses and a free assessment tool for enterprises to evaluate their degree of maturity in Industry 4.0.	All	Manufacturing	✓
	E-commerce export support			
Apex e-Xport	Training and mentoring to develop global marketplace strategy.	All	All	✓

Notes: Apex = Brazilian Agency of Promotion of Exports and Investments; BNDES = Brazilian Development Bank; FINEP = Brazilian Agency for Innovation and Research; MCTIC = Ministry of Science, Technology, Innovations and Communications; SEBRAE = Brazilian Micro and Small Business Support Agency; SENAI = National Service for Industrial Training.

Source: OECD, based on BNDES, FINEP, MCTIC, Ministry of Economy and SEBRAE.

BNDES also provides indirect support to the ICT sector, by financing the acquisition of ICT capital goods and software through several of its products and financial lines. By limiting its credit to the acquisition of products made in Brazil, BNDES supports domestic production, as acquisition of imported goods is financed only if the beneficiary firms can justify that equivalent products are not available domestically. IT and automation equipment are eligible for financing under the Financing Fund for the Acquisition of Machinery and Equipment (Financiamento de Máquinas e Equipamentos, FINAME), if acquired from suppliers accredited by BNDES. To be accredited, the supplier must prove that at least 50% of the value added of its product is produced in Brazil. Imported equipment with no domestic equivalent are eligible under the fund, as long as the payment does not imply international transfers. Since July 2019, BNDES has broadened the list of eligible products within the "BK Aquisição e Comercialização" line to include equipment related to advanced manufacturing and IoT solutions. BNDES offers more advantageous financial conditions (lower BNDES remuneration) to firms of all size investing in these assets, thus signalling its engagement for digital technologies diffusion in the economy.

An instrument which can also be used for purchase of machinery, equipment, software or software development services is the BNDES Card. This instrument, launched in 2003, is a pre-approved line of credit of up to USD 510 000 (BRL 2 million) to finance the acquisition of capital goods and is specifically designed for SMEs. The BNDES Card has subsidised interest rates – 1.3% per month in early 2019 – and is subject to a much simpler application process than other credit programmes. Since its launch, a total of USD 27.2 billion (BRL 68 billion) of credit has been disbursed through the card. Up to 2019, more than 36 000 companies had acquired ready-made software or software development services using the card, for total USD 273 million (BRL 999 million). As for similar BNDES instruments, there is a requirement for firms to buy machinery and upgrades by local producers accredited by BNDES. There are currently 2 500 recognised software vendors on the dedicated portal. The BNDES Card can also be used by micro, small and medium-sized companies from the ICT sector to purchase ICT goods and equipment, such as computers, security systems, furniture and technological services (including software certification). About 25% of the enterprises in the ICT sector (4 000) have used the card to date, for a total financing of over USD 118 million (BRL 464 million). The BNDES Card has proven to be one of the most innovative instruments for small enterprises in the country, thanks to its scope and its operational characteristics. Being primarily targeted at upgrading production processes, it has helped to increase productivity in SMEs (Noguiera, 2016). However, the local content requirement for ICT goods restricts firms' access to foreign technologies and inputs at the technological frontier, and may limit innovation and productivity gains (Pires and Russell, 2017).

BNDES is currently developing a new financial tool for the acquisition of services (e.g. for an IoT solution). A company can come to BNDES to propose a service solution. If approved, BNDES can finance the user and the provider, e.g. the monthly subscription. This would be also available to small producers and through the BNDES Card, as is already the case for software licences.

FINEP is a federal government organisation under the MCTIC, which funds science and technology in Brazil. It supports innovation through several credit lines, designed for firms of different sizes and for projects at different levels of technological readiness. One of the credit lines, FINEP Inovação, supports technological diffusion for innovation by providing support to all stages of innovation (from "critical" to diffusion), with different conditions and interest rates according to the stage of technological development. The highest interest rate is for the acquisition of informatics and automation goods.

FINEP has also recently expanded its offer in support of firms investing in digital technologies. In September 2019, it launched Inovacred 4.0. The programme is the result of collaboration with the CNI, the Ministry of Economy and the MCTIC and is the first initiative of the Brazilian Chamber of Industry 4.0 (see Chapter 6). FINEP Inovacred 4.0 aims to enhance productivity in Brazilian industry by fostering business innovation in areas such as IoT, big data, cloud computing, digital security, advanced robotics, digital and additive manufacturing, artificial intelligence (AI), and digitalisation. The novelty of FINEP Inovacred 4.0 lies in the use of an "integrating company", i.e. an intermediary who conceives and implements digitalisation plans in firms, by customising solutions, for example in terms of equipment, sensors, and software to be used to develop and implement a plan for adoption of enabling technologies tailored to the specific firm ("Strategic Business Digitalisation Plan"). The necessity of involving such a professional entity has been advocated by the CNI in several documents concerning Industry 4.0. SMEs generally lack awareness to estimate the impact of introducing business solutions which encompass technologies from Industry 4.0 in their processes, and even more so the technical information to identify and implement them. They also have lower investment capacity to finance Industry 4.0 digitalisation plans, whose costs for a large company are estimated at USD 380 000 (BRL 1.5 million) on average (estimate by the CNI).

The pilot programme has a budget of USD 50.9 million (BRL 200 million) and is targeted at SMEs in manufacturing (and soon agriculture), with annual revenues of up to USD 7.6 million (BRL 30 million). Each beneficiary will be supported with USD 1.4 million (BRL 5 million) to finance the development and implementation of the "Strategic Business Digitalisation Plan". Firms can only submit credit requests for their digitalisation plans if they are elaborated by FINEP-accredited integrating companies. As of January 2020, 7 companies had been accredited by FINEP and 4 loans had already been contracted, with the objective of reaching 25 accreditations and loans to 80 firms by the end of the year. Although the initiative will only benefit a limited number of firms, given the budget and size of each intervention, this is a promising initiative born from the collaboration between the private and the public sectors and could be an example for further actions aimed at implementing the E-Digital Strategy.

In June 2019, the agency also launched FINEP Software, which aims to support the acquisition of software and implementation services. The programme, which has a budget of USD 127.3 million (BRL 500 million) over three years, is open to Brazilian companies of all sizes and finances expenses above USD 38 000 (BRL 150 000) related to the acquisition and implementation of software, including training.

Brasil Mais aims at fostering productivity in firms, including through digital technologies

Brazil has recently launched a large plan – Growth Route – aimed at increasing productivity and improving the business environment. The plan is organised around six pillars, one of which is dedicated to Industry 4.0. The main initiative under this pillar is "Brazil More" (Brasil Mais), adopted through Decree 10.246/2020. Brazil More is the continuation and scale-up of the successful pilot programme "More Productive Brazil" (Brasil Mais Produtivo), which in 2016-18 supported about 3 000 manufacturing SMEs (11-200 employees) with consultancy services to optimise their production processes. With only about USD 14 million (BRL 50 million), the programme was found to be effective in increasing beneficiaries' productivity by 52% on average (ECLAC and IPEA, 2018).

The scope of the programme, which only included manufacturing, has been extended to the service and retail sectors, with the objective of reaching 220 000 SMEs by 2022. Co-ordinated by the Ministry of Economy, the programme will be managed by the Brazilian Industrial Development Agency (Agência Brasileira de Desenvolvimento Industrial, ABDI) and executed by the National Service for Industrial Training (Serviço Nacional de Aprendizagem Industrial, SENAI) and SEBRAE. In order to reach a greater number of firms, the programme will make use of an online platform; face-to-face consultancies will be reduced to 60 hours (as opposed to 180 in the previous programme). The programme does not have a new budget from the government, but will be financed through SENAI funds. Beneficiary firms have to contribute USD 380-1 500 (BRL 1 500-6 000). The programme recognises the potential that digital technologies have in boosting productivity, and 50 000 of the beneficiary firms will be supported to undergo more advanced stages of digitalisation of their processes and programmes.

Although it is too early to judge the programme, as its specific features and implementation aspects are yet to be defined, it goes in the right direction in actively supporting firms in their modernisation efforts and in a greater use of digital technologies. SMEs in traditional sectors need support to invest in technologies that are not necessarily new to the country but are new to them and can enable process and organisational improvements. Technical assistance programmes can help SMEs determine how to incorporate ICTs into their business model, acquire those technologies through supportive financing and learn how to use them effectively. To further increase the effectiveness of this programme, the government could also increase co-ordination with other existing initiatives to offer a full package of solutions, while also devising further mechanisms to promote technology adoption (see below).

Singapore's SMEs Go Digital programme could offer good practices. It supports SMEs in their digitalisation journey through a comprehensive suite of measures: enterprises can assess which digital solutions are suitable for them through sector-specific industry digitalisation plans and take up pre-approved solutions with grant support. Those that need advice receive support from an SME Digital Tech Hub and a network of SME centres (Box 3.3).

SENAI provides training and consulting activities for Industry 4.0

SENAI plays an important role in developing education applied to industry, in training, in offering technical services and technological support, and in disseminating technologies. SENAI is, in particular, focused on preparing industries and developing skills for Industry 4.0. Through the "SENAI 4.0" portal (*senai40.com.br*), it offers consulting services, training courses and a free assessment tool for enterprises to evaluate their degree of maturity in Industry 4.0. Training courses offered to prepare for Industry 4.0 are available at four education levels: technical, professional initiation, professional extension and post-graduate. They cover subjects such as IoT, blockchain, augmented reality, cloud computing, AI, big data and cybersecurity, among others.

Box 3.3. Singapore's SMEs Go Digital programme: Make going digital simple for SMEs

Launched in April 2017, the SMEs Go Digital programme aims to make going digital simple for small and medium-sized enterprises (SMEs). It includes a comprehensive range of initiatives to guide and support SMEs in their digital journeys.

The sector-specific industry digital plans (IDPs) provide SMEs with a step-by-step guide on the digital solutions to adopt and relevant training for their employees at different stages of their growth. The IDPs serve as a common reference for SMEs and are aligned with Singapore's industry transformation maps for each sector. To date, the Infocomm Media Development Authority (IMDA), which is responsible for the programme, has rolled out IDPs for the following sectors: retail, logistics, environmental services, security, food services, wholesale trade, media, sea transport, accountancy and hotel. The IMDA is developing IDPs for more sectors To make it easy for SMEs to adopt the digital solutions recommended in the IDPs, the IMDA provides a list of pre-approved solutions assessed to be market-proven, cost-effective and supported by reliable vendors.

SMEs interested in adopting these solutions can apply for the Productivity Solutions Grant through the Business Grants Portal. The Productivity Solutions Grant can help to offset up to 70% the costs of adopting these solutions. Together with Enterprise Singapore (ESG), the IMDA launched the Start Digital initiative in January 2019. Start Digital helps newly incorporated SMEs, and those that have yet to go digital, get started with foundational digital solutions in accounting, human resource management systems and payroll, digital marketing, digital transactions, and cybersecurity. SMEs can select any two solutions to be included in their Start Digital Pack.

Start Digital Packs are offered by banks and telecom partners. SMEs that sign up for a minimum 18-month contract receive cost waivers for at least 6 months.

The SMEs Go Digital programme not only provides digitalisation guides and digital solutions, it has consultancy and project management services too. The SME Digital Tech Hub provides digital consultancy to SMEs that require expert advice in specialised areas such as data analytics, cybersecurity, artificial intelligence and the Internet of Things. It complements SME centres, which help SMEs identify the pre-approved solutions that meet their business needs.

SMEs can also engage services from a ready pool of skilled digital project managers, at subsidised fees, to help with implementing their digital solutions. This can include the review of business processes and job redesign so that they can realise the full benefits of going digital.

Source: Infocomm Media Development Authority (2020), *SMEs Go Digital*, *www.imda.gov.sg/programme-listing/smes-go-digital* (accessed in March 2020).

Brazil lacks tax incentives to promote digital uptake

Brazil largely employs tax expenditures to support businesses and ICT is one of the sectors the most supported through this instrument. Tax credits are available to companies investing in R&D through the Informatics Law (Lei da Informática), specifically directed at enterprises operating in the ICT sector (producers within the computing, automation, telecom or microelectronics industries) and through the Good Law (Lei do Bem), which is applied across sectors.

The merits of these two instruments in promoting a local ICT industry and in increasing investments in R&D are discussed in Chapter 5. Despite the wide use of tax credits in Brazil (in 2015, tax expenditures accounted for 61% of total spending on business support policies and 2.9% of GDP; Dutz et al., 2017), there is currently no fiscal incentive for enterprises for technological upgrading, such as the acquisition of ICT machinery and equipment, or in investment in intangible assets, such as software or training related to ICT use. The Good Law foresees accelerated depreciation of machinery, equipment and intangible assets, but under the condition they are used for R&D activities. This therefore restricts the potential beneficiaries to those who carry out R&D. In the same vein, Normative Instruction 986/09 foresees tax breaks for firms in the ICT sector for expenses related to training of personnel developing software. This is also very narrow, as it targets a specific sector and skills development of ICT professionals, rather than employees at large. Furthermore, both of these two tax breaks are based on real profit (*lucro real*), whereas most SMEs operate in the deemed profit (*lucro presumido*) or Simples Nacional regimes, and are therefore excluded from these schemes. Recent changes to the Simples Nacional regime (Resolução CGSN 150/2019) may also affect the investment in intangibles (software and skills development), as informatics instructors will not qualify for a simplified tax regime and may, as a result, increase their tariffs due to an increase in the taxes they will be subject to.

Italy, for instance, has a policy foreseeing the accelerated depreciation of ICT investments in the context of strategies promoting Industry 4.0. Japan also offers tax credit or special depreciation for advanced IT investment to spur growth as part of the Fourth Industrial Revolution. Brazil could rethink its current business support policies, and in particular those related to tax expenditures, towards less sector-specific support and policies to foster broad diffusion of digital technologies across sectors.

A lack of skills in the workforce hinders the digital transformation

In order to increase the adoption of ICTs, firms require workers with the skills needed to make effective use of digital technologies. They need both workers with basic computer skills and ICT specialists to operate new systems. In addition, firms require workers with advanced literacy and numeracy skills and workers with a tertiary education, to take advantage of the new methods of working brought about by digitalisation.

Policies aimed at improving the quality of general education prepare students for the skills needed in the future, as they set the basis to further learn in line with the continuous transformation of technologies. On the other hand, lifelong training opportunities should also be available for workers, for them to upskill and reskill over the course of their careers. As the country progresses in the digital transformation of the economy, not only technical skills, but also cognitive non-routine skills, communication and interpersonal skills, managerial and negotiation skills will increasingly be in demand.

According to the OECD's *Skills for Jobs* database, ICT professionals was the second occupational category the most in shortage in Brazil in 2018 (OECD, 2018c). This category includes software and applications developers and analysts, as well as database and network professionals. ICT technicians (ICT user support technicians, web technicians, broadcasting and audio-visual technicians, among others) also showed a moderate shortage (OECD, 2018c). Industry estimates also suggest shortages of skills, difficulty in retaining talent, as well as dissatisfaction with the skills of the workforce. However, the survey on the use of ICT in enterprises (CGI.br, 2020b) provides little evidence of skills shortages or difficulty in recruiting ICT specialists, as only 6% of enterprises that wanted to recruit IT specialists did not find an adequate supply, whereas the largest majority (68%) declared they did not need to hire IT specialists (CGI.br, 2020b). This finding may also indicate the limited readiness of enterprises to adopt ICT, explaining the low demand for ICT specialists, which can be confirmed by the low growth of ICT capabilities in sectors (other than the ICT sector) in the period 2003-17 (Maciente Nogueira, Rauen Vianna and Kubota, 2019).

The share of 25-34 year-olds with at least an upper secondary education in Brazil is less than the OECD average (67% vs. 85% respectively). The share of 25-34 year-olds with a tertiary education (21%) is about half of the OECD average (44%), although it increased by 10 percentage points in the period 2008-18. Graduates in sciences, engineering and ICTs also represent a lower share of graduates than in developed economies and other Latin American countries (see Chapter 5).

Participation in vocational education – at both upper secondary and post-secondary levels – is still also relatively low. In 2017, only about 8% of students graduating from upper secondary education for the first time obtained a vocational qualification. This is the second lowest share across OECD countries and partner economies and well below the OECD average of 40% (OECD, 2019g). However, a considerable share of students from these vocational courses graduate in ICT (15%), well above the OECD average of 4%. Vocational programmes are also a way for adults to reskill or upskill to meet new demands from the labour market generated by the digital transformation. Brazil offers vocational programmes specifically geared towards adult education at both upper secondary and post-secondary levels. Some 0.5% of the population aged 25 and over are participating in either upper secondary or post-secondary vocational programmes, below the OECD average of 0.8%.

Figure 3.25. Upper secondary and tertiary attainment for 25-34 year-olds in Brazil and the OECD, 2018

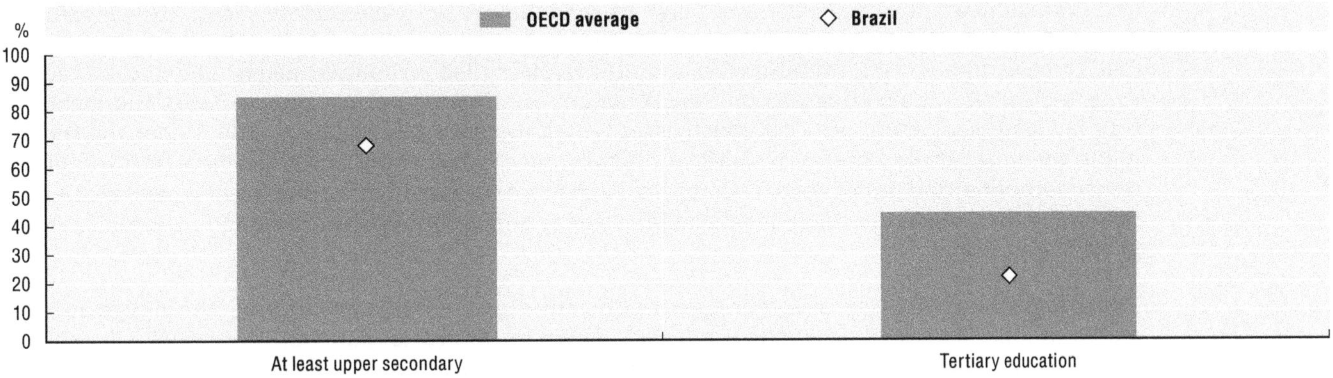

Source: OECD (2019g), *Education at a Glance 2019: OECD Indicators*, *https://doi.org/10.1787/f8d7880d-en*.

Steps are being taken to improve digital skills and reinforce training

Brazil is introducing reforms aimed at introducing digital skills both at the level of general education and of vocational and technical education. At the general education level, the NBCC has been approved since December 2018 also for upper secondary education (*ensino medio*, ISCED 3). The NBCC introduces digital competencies across study areas and computational thinking as part of maths and technology. The "New High School" (Novo Ensino Médio), which will be introduced in 2022, will include the national curriculum base and a "formative itinerary" of the student's choice, among five options. The formative itinerary will be the largest component of the overall training (1 800 hours out of a total of 3 000). These itineraries are: language and technologies, mathematics and technologies, life sciences and technologies, applied human and social sciences, and technical and professional training. The objective of this introduction is to provide more specialisation in general education, while exposing a higher proportion of students to technical and professional training. However, since general education does not provide a technical diploma to directly enter the labour market, and given the low share of students who enrol in tertiary education (15%, compared to 22% in OECD countries), more efforts are also being made to increase the number of students undertaking vocational training. The design of such itineraries is a state-level responsibility; therefore, there may be great variation across the country. Furthermore, the changes in curriculum, and in particular the introduction of the training itineraries, will require adequate training of teachers and additional hires to meet the new knowledge areas covered.

Professional and technological education is offered in upper secondary and in tertiary education. Upper secondary vocational training is of two types: one to three years of technical courses (*cursos técnicos profissionalizantes*) or short (three to six months) professional qualification courses meant to redirect workers to a new occupation or to deepen their occupation-specific expertise (*cursos de formação inicial e continuada*). While the former targets young individuals, potentially still in education, and leads to a qualification equivalent to a lower or upper secondary education, the latter is particularly aimed at individuals who have already left education and integrated the labour market or who are actively looking for a job. Tertiary vocational education and training requires completion of an upper secondary certificate and offers professional degrees (equivalent to university degree) in three years.

The Professional and Technological Education Secretariat (Secretaria de Educação Profissional e Tecnológica, SETEC) of the Ministry of Education is responsible for policies related to professional and technological education (*educação profissional e tecnológica*), implemented by public and private institutions. A key role among the private institutions is played by those of "Sistema S", a group of ten institutions partially financed by private sector companies, such as SENAI and SENAC, the two most important in terms of training provision. According to an agreement between these institutions and the federal government, SENAI and SENAC should allocate two-thirds of their annual revenues from compulsory taxation to the provision of free professional and technical education programmes.

The "New Paths" programme, launched in October 2019, aims to increase professional and technological training to 3.4 million by 2023 (from the current 1.9 million students). The programme is structured around three pillars: 1) management and results; 2) articulation and strengthening; and 3) innovation and entrepreneurship. Under the first pillar, in consultation with the private sector, the programme is updating the 2014 National Catalogue of Technical Courses (Catálogo Nacional de Cursos Técnicos, CNCT), so as to align the training offer with the evolving labour market needs. The new version is expected in 2020. It also foresees the regularisation of private providers of vocational and technical training, and recognition of 11 000 certificates issued by these schools since 2016. Under the second pillar, the programme foresees training and upskilling of more than 20 000 teachers in the subjects under vocational and professional training, through more courses in mathematics and natural sciences offered by the federal institutes of education, science and technology, whose role is to train teachers in basic education.

The programme also foresees changes in the funding model, establishing the obligation for states to link disbursement of training scholarships to the demands of the industrial, service and agricultural sectors, which have to be locally mapped following a methodology developed by the MEC (Ordinance 1.720/2019). Last, under the third pillar, the programme will encourage projects that stimulate applied research, innovation and technological activities, through competitive calls for groups of students, teachers and researchers, with an investment of USD 15.3 million (BRL 60 million) by 2022. A dedicated office at the MEC will promote private-public partnerships. This pillar also foresees the establishment of five innovation hubs in co-operation with the Brazilian Company of Research and Industrial Innovation (Empresa Brasileira de Pesquisa e Inovação Industrial, EMBRAPII), in addition to the nine currently existing, to disseminate the culture of entrepreneurship and leverage the development of applied research that meet the real demand of the private sector, bringing education closer to the labour market.

It is too early to judge the capacity of the "New Paths" programme to foster a higher level of digital skills among the workforce. Much will depend on the course catalogue, which will have to include both courses for specific ICT professions as well as digital literacy as a horizontal competence. The private sector's involvement in contributing to the catalogue's design, as well as the mapping undertaken to understand where needs lie, are certainly positive developments. Training scholarships should be directed as well to low-skilled, informal and unemployed workers, who do not seem to be the target of this policy, nor of the vouchers which will be distributed through SENAI (see below). Looking forward, Brazil should consider the use of digital technologies and big data to help increase the effectiveness of training programmes. The analysis of online vacancies provides more timely information on skills demand across small geographic areas. Big data allows tracking and evaluating the job placement of participants in vocational education and training, thus providing indications on how to improve them. The online collection and dissemination of timely information on the performance of higher education institutions, e.g. universities, helps prospective students' take informed decisions. In order to design skills policies and training programmes that effectively anticipate and tackle skills imbalances, as well as to respond to labour market needs, Brazil should establish rigorous and systematic initiatives to carry out skills assessment and anticipation exercises, which are currently missing (OECD, 2018c).

The recognition of acquired skills is also a positive feature of the programme, although it should be further extended, As put forward in the E-Digital Strategy (MCTIC, 2018), Brazil should facilitate the formal recognition of skills acquired in vocational training, through partnerships with vocational education institutions, companies or other entities. Brazil currently has a decentralised programme for the formal recognition of prior learning, "Rede CERTIFIC", which was never fully developed and implemented (OECD, 2018c). The creation of innovation hubs is also a very interesting component. Given the increasing specialisation of EMBRAPII's units in IoT and advanced manufacturing (see Chapter 5), these should certainly be among the fields for additional innovation hubs.

As part of the Growth Route Plan, the Ministry of the Economy has also recently announced the distribution of 1.3 million vouchers through 2022 for training workers at the S System. With the objective to tie training more to the actual market needs, professional training contracts will be based on performance, so that education institutes hired by the government are only paid if the beneficiary gets a job. This action will be realised without any additional budget, as SENAI will reallocate funding to finance a new National Qualification Strategy formulated by the government. SENAI will distribute the voucher, through an electronic platform, to companies in the sector and following guidelines from the Ministry of Economy. The companies will receive the vouchers, both for retraining their employees and for potential new employees who lack specific skills. The voucher quota will depend on the size of each establishment. All industries will receive at least one coupon upon registration on the platform. Micro and small companies (with up to 99 employees) will be entitled to vouchers corresponding to 20% of their workforce. Medium-sized companies (100-499 employees) may request a volume equivalent to 10% of the staff. In the case of large companies (over 500 people), it will be 5%.

To foster digital skills among young people aged 16-25, Brazil also has an online education programme, Brazil More Digital (Brasil Mais Digital). The programme is financed by the MCTIC and implemented by the industry association Softex. Several ICT companies are partners, contributing content and prospective opportunities for young professionals. It consists of a distance learning platform, which currently offers more than 35 courses (about 1 500 hours), from basic, intermediate and advanced IT courses to topics such as programming, software development and gamified content. By 2018, the platform had about 351 750 registered students, with a total investment of about USD 2.7 million (BRL 9.9 million). The figures suggest, however, that there is a high dropout rate, as only 41 811 courses have been completed. Also, there are no data on the effectiveness of the programme in terms of job placement. The ICT training provided should be equivalent to a technical high school/professional education, but the courses are not recognised by the MEC. The programme should be assessed and the evaluation outcomes taken into account to improve and extend the online programme to other age groups.

There are no policies to increase the number of STEM graduates

Presently, there are no comprehensive, national policies to increase the number of graduates in science, technology, engineering and mathematics (STEM), although a few initiatives have been carried out by a number of relevant players in these fields, particularly on vocational training in high school. Examples include the Brazilian Computer Society's Digital Girls Programme (Programa Meninas Digitais). The programme aims to discover and foster talents for STEM in undergraduate courses. With the same goal, academic entities organise several "Olympiads" in different STEM fields – maths, physics, robotics, astronomy, etc. – for high school students. Finally, the MCTIC is pledging to include incentives for STEM graduate courses in the National Innovation Plan. Nevertheless, Brazil may consider changes in the distribution of scholarships in relationship to the subject in favour of STEM degrees. Some countries, given the shortage of talent in these disciplines, particularly those related to digital technologies, are increasing funding for higher education in these fields (see Chapter 5).

Improving the links between firms and higher education institutions (HEIs) can also help HEIs provide students with the skills demanded in the labour market. In Latvia, for instance, some firms provide scholarships and offer traineeships to academic staff and students. Industry and academia also co-operate in the design and financing of university courses. The Riga Technical University, Riga Business School and the University of Latvia, in association with the Finance Latvia Association (an industry body) established a bachelor degree programme "Computer Science and Organisational Technologies" (OECD, forthcoming b).

Box 3.4. Policy recommendations to foster the use of digital technologies by firms

- Run awareness-raising campaigns on the benefits of the Internet and digital technologies, targeting in particular micro-enterprises.
- Introduce incentives for firms carrying out services on line, such as public procurement (e-procurement).
- Take measures to foster greater competition in the parcel delivery market.
- Remove regulatory barriers to the development of e-commerce business models, such as multi-channels models.
- Harmonise the rate of tax on goods and services (ICMS) across states, as a first step towards a federal VAT system.
- Improve co-ordination among programmes supporting digital uptake by firms; create a single portal where firms can access all information about these programmes.
- Introduce tax incentives for technological upgrade, training and ICT investments for all firms, irrespective of their sector and size.
- Integrate digital skills in professional and vocational courses and better align the training supply with labour market needs.
- Strengthen vocational training for low-skilled, informal and unemployed workers.
- Evaluate the effects of the online education programme "Brazil More Digital" on job placement; enrich the offer of online courses, with the co-operation of the private sector.
- Facilitate the formal recognition of skills acquired through online courses and vocational training, through partnerships with vocational education institutions, companies or other entities.
- Undertake sound skills assessment and anticipation exercises on a regular basis.
- Increase scholarships for STEM students as well as PhD candidates in engineering, natural sciences and ICTs. Increase the offer of Master and PhD courses in these disciplines, in co-operation with the private sector.

Digital government

Digital technologies are radically changing how citizens live, work, consume and interact. The capacity of governments to respond to the digital transformation and produce more inclusive, convenient and collaborative processes and services is crucial for securing citizens' trust.

The uptake of digital services is not improving

A key objective of the Brazilian government's and the public sector's use of digital technologies is to improve public service delivery to citizens and businesses. However, some basic indicators, such as the uptake of digital public services by individuals, show room for improvement. Brazilians still make limited use of the Internet to interact with public authorities and obtain information on line, compared to OECD countries (Figure 3.26).

In 2018, the percentage of Internet users who benefited from digital public services dropped to 55%, from 64% the previous year. The reasons behind this decrease need to be further investigated. Uptake of digital public services is also very unequal, with a 47 percentage point difference between individuals with a high versus those with a low education and a 44 percentage point difference between individuals with a high versus those with a low income. There is also a growing divide in the use of digital public services across urban and rural areas and across generations. These trends follow the general trends in use shown in Section 3.1, and they have been widening over the years (Figure 3.27).

Figure 3.26. Individuals using the Internet to interact and obtain information from public authorities, in Brazil and the OECD, 2018

As a percentage of all individuals

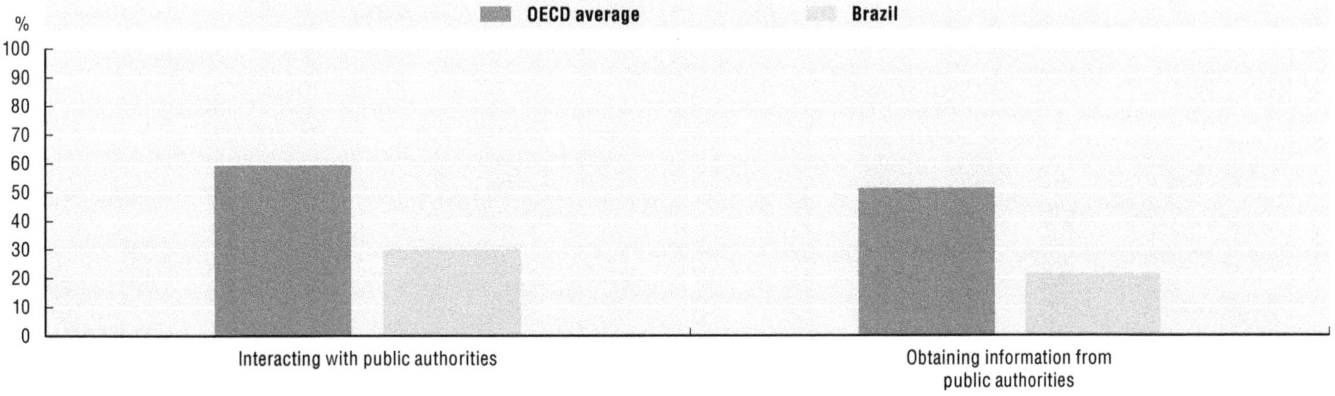

Note: OECD average is an unweighted average of available countries.

Source: OECD (2020a), *ICT Access and Usage by Households and Individuals* (database), *http://oe.cd/hhind* (accessed in February 2020).

Figure 3.27. Individuals using digital government services in Brazil, 2018

As a percentage of Internet users above 16 years old

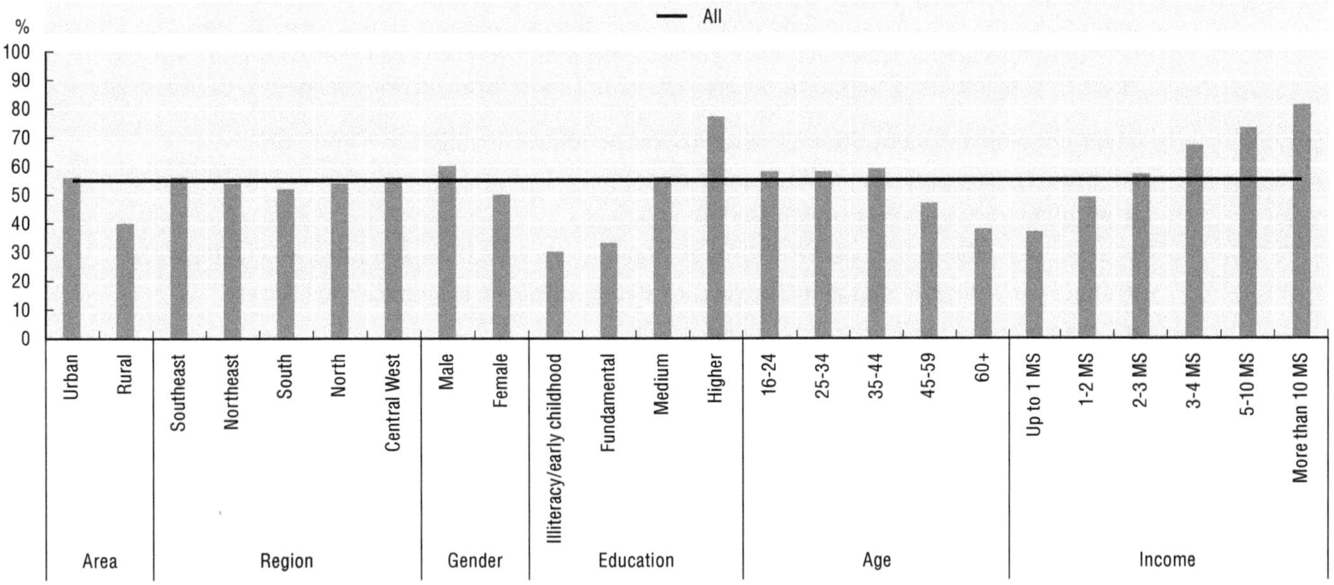

Note: MS = minimum salary.

Source: CGI.br (2019a), *ICT Households 2018: Survey on the Use of Information and Communication Technologies in Brazilian Households* (database), *https://cetic.br/en/pesquisa/domicilios/indicadores/* (accessed in February 2020).

Those using digital government mostly use services related to labour or social security rights, public education, personal documents, and taxes. However, only health and personal documents were used in 2018 at levels comparable to those in 2016, whereas the others had decreased (Figure 3.28).

Digital government is a priority for Brazil

The digital transformation of government is a priority for Brazil, whose ambition is to make the administration more efficient and citizen-friendly. The government expects annual efficiency gains in the range of USD 16.5-21.6 billion (BRL 65-85 billion), against annual inefficiency costs estimated at USD 333 billion (BRL 1.3 trillion). This priority also responds to the rapid changes foreseen in the public administration's workforce, which is expected to decrease by half in the next five years due to retirement and the government's efforts to rationalise and optimise the size of the public sector workforce.

Figure 3.28. Individuals looking for information or performing digital government services online in Brazil, by service, 2018

As a percentage of Internet users above 16 years old

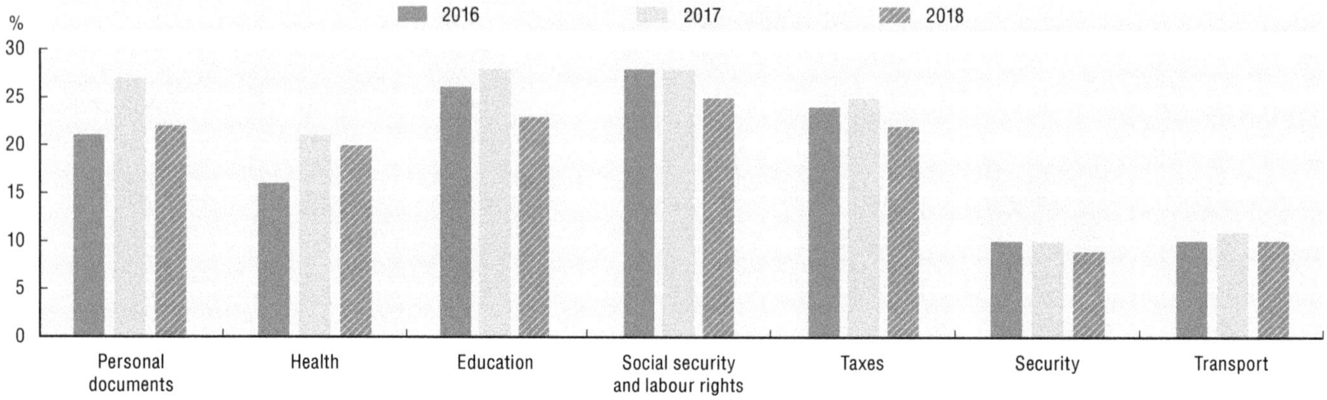

Source: CGI.br (2019a), *ICT Households 2018: Survey on the Use of Information and Communication Technologies in Brazilian Households* (database), *https://cetic.br/en/pesquisa/domicilios/indicadores/* (accessed in February 2020).

In 2016, the former Ministry of Planning (now the Ministry of Economy) drafted the Digital Government Strategy (Estratégia de Governança Digital), which defines the strategic objectives, goals, indicators and initiatives for the digital governance policy in the federal government. The Digital Government Strategy's main objective is to make public policy more efficient by using digital technologies. The Ministry of Economy, through its Secretariat of Digital Government (Secretaria de Governo Digital, SGD), is the main actor responsible for elaborating, co-ordinating and monitoring actions related to the strategy.

The Digital Government Strategy establishes the following objectives and initiatives:

- encourage the provision and use of open data
- promote transparency through the use of ICT
- increase public service delivery through digital transformation and improve its efficiency
- share and integrate digital infrastructure, data, processes, systems and services
- broaden social participation in public policy.

A new national Digital Government Strategy for 2020-22 was adopted in April 2020 (Decree 10.332/2020). The strategy has the vision of a government which will be:

- Citizen-centred: a government offering a more pleasant journey to citizens, responding to their expectations through high-quality services (simple, agile and personalised) and monitoring their experience.
- Integrated: a government that offers a consistent experience of citizen services and integrates data and services of all the levels of government.
- Smart: a government that implements effective policies based on data and evidence and proactively anticipates and addresses the needs of citizens and organisations.
- Trustworthy: a government that respects the freedom and privacy of citizens and ensures appropriate response to the risks, threats and challenges that arise from the use of digital technologies in the public sector.
- Transparent and open: a government that acts proactively in the provision of data and information and enables the monitoring and participation of society in the various stages of services and public policies.
- Efficient: a government that trains its professionals to adopt best practices and makes rational use of the workforce. In addition, it optimises the infrastructure and technology contracts, seeking to reduce the cost and expand the offer of services.

The E-Digital Strategy (MCTIC, 2018) also contains digital government priorities and establishes three guiding actions for public policies in the area of citizenship and digital government: 1) increased transparency and social control of government activities; 2) expanded social participation in the creation of public policies; and 3) higher quality digital public services.

Progress towards digital government

The Brazilian government has been iteratively moving towards digital government by prioritising policy issues such as connectivity, interoperability, open government data and citizen-driven service delivery (OECD, 2018d). The country's efforts to digitally transform its public sector have been thoroughly analysed in an *OECD Digital Government Review of Brazil* completed in 2018 (OECD, 2018d), which builds upon the analytic framework provided by the OECD *Recommendation of the Council on Digital Government Strategies* (OECD, 2014). It sets policy recommendations to help the Brazilian government capitalise on its digital government achievements, and to plan and implement a shift from e-government to digital government. This section updates and builds on the main findings and recommendations of the 2018 Review. The main policy recommendations are summarised in Table 3.4, which also indicates the key measures adopted to address them. Some of the key short-term recommendations and measures undertaken are discussed in the following sections.

Increased policy visibility and stronger high-level support for digital government

The *OECD Digital Government Review of Brazil* (OECD, 2018d) found that there is an opportunity to amplify the Brazilian commitment for a digital government through joint communication efforts with other strategic initiatives, such as the E-Digital Strategy and the Efficient Brazil Programme. The Review suggested the identification of a clear institutional function, e.g. a chief digital transformation officer, to lead and steer strategic co-ordination and help deliver on goals and priorities. It also suggested introducing a co-ordination process and mechanisms that allow public institutions to better communicate with each other, share resources and work together.

In terms of governance, since 2019, the Secretariat of Information and Communication Technologies has changed denomination – and enlarged its responsibilities – to become the Secretariat for Digital Government (SGD). This has also been accompanied by an increase in the number of staff: the SGD currently has 400 staff and co-ordinates 400 IT specialists that work in the agencies. The SGD is within the Special Secretariat of Red Tape Reduction (Secretaria Especial de Desburocratização) of the Ministry of the Economy.

The agenda for digital government is being implemented in partnership with the Special Secretariat of State Modernization of the General Secretariat of the Presidency of the Republic. The SGD has among its functions to define guidelines, standardise and co-ordinate projects to simplify services, governance and data sharing, and the use of digital channels. The SGD also has a reinforced role to optimise public IT expenditures. According to Decree 9.745/2019, which defines the structure of the Ministry of Economy, the SGD is responsible for

> *supporting the preparation and monitoring of the implementation of the information and communication technology budget within the scope of the Information Technology Resource Management System (Sistema de Administração dos Recursos de Tecnologia da Informação, SISP), in co-ordination with the Federal Budget Secretariat, and proposing actions to increase efficiency and public spending on ICT.*

All these elements point to an increased visibility of the digital government agenda and to a stronger governance framework for policy implementation, with high-level political support. Although Brazil has not institutionalised the role of a chief digital transformation officer, the SGD seems to have a comparable, clear and high-level mandate to lead and standardise the development of digital government. In 2019, the SGD also considerably stepped up communication efforts around the measures and the results in this field.

The government has also reduced the number of the public administration's committees (Decree 9.759/2019). In this context, the MCTIC and the Ministry of Economy mapped the committees related to the digital transformation of the state and the economy, and recreated those that are key to advance the digital transformation of the country. These are the CITDigital committee, responsible for the Brazilian Strategy for Digital Transformation (Decree 9.804/2019), the SISP and the Digital Governance and Information Security Committee (Ordinance 1.468/2019). However, despite the rationalisation of the number of committees and their respective roles brought about by the measure, further efforts may be needed in highlighting the relationship and synergies among the different policy instruments.

Table 3.4. Main policy recommendations for digital government in Brazil

Recommendation	Key measures adopted
Strengthening the governance framework for digital government	
Strengthen the communication efforts around the Digital Government Strategy and its relation to the Strategy for the Digital Transformation and Efficient Brazil.	No direct action, but the government has rationalised the number of policy committees through Decree 9.759/2019 and this is expected to increase clarity on respective roles and responsibilities.
Reinforce the role of the Secretariat of Information and Communication Technologies (SETIC), now the Secretariat of Digital Government (SGD) as the federal public sector organisation responsible for leading and standardising the development of digital government.	Increased responsibility, budget and staff. Close oversight and collaboration with the Special Secretariat of State Modernization of the General Secretariat of the Presidency of the Republic.
Consider the institutionalisation of the role of a chief digital transformation officer, supported by a clear and high-level political mandate and assigned clear responsibility to ensure cross-sectoral and cross-level co-ordination for digital government in Brazil.	No action, but the SGD seems to have a comparable, clear and high-level mandate to lead and standardise the development of digital government.
Consider adopting the pre-evaluation of ICT investments, business cases and project management standards, which can help SETIC (now the SGD) co-ordinate public ICT expenditures across the public sector to optimise investments and promote a coherent and sustainable implementation of digital government.	Normative Instruction No. 1 and No. 2 of 4 April 2019 promote transparency, guidelines, simplification in ICT procurement. Ordinance 103/2019 established the Internal Committee of Technical Reference evaluating major ICT expenditures.
Ensure coherency in digital government policies across the public sector by strengthening the communication in the Information Technology Resource Management System.	Normative Instruction No. 1 and No. 2 of 4 April 2019 promote transparency, guidelines, simplification in ICT procurement and mandatory evaluation of investments above USD 7.3 million (BRL 28.6 million)
Establish an inter-federative policy articulation to promote the expansion of a consistent digital offer to states and municipalities.	Five sectoral e-digital plans executed, ten under preparation.
Strengthening institutional capabilities for the sound implementation of digital government policies	
Include specific actions to develop digital skills within the new skills framework to promote the coherent development of user, professional, complementary and leadership digital capabilities among public servants.	Programme for Development of Digital Capabilities in the public sector (Capacita Gov.br) in collaboration with the National School of Public Administration (ENAP). Selection of digital transformation leaders. ICT work expansion strategy.
Consider strengthening the conditions for retaining and remunerating IT analysts.	Plan to elaborate a proposal for the adjustment of the position of ICT analyst within the public sector.
Update the Brazilian ICT procurement policy, promoting a shift towards a digital commissioning approach.	Normative Instruction No. 1 of 4 April 2019 establishes transparency in ICT procurement.
Strengthening the foundation for integrated, citizen-driven, digital service delivery	
Continue investing in the development of important digital enablers, such as digital identity and interoperability, and strengthening the foundations for coherent and integrated service delivery.	New Data Sharing Decree 10.064/2019. Digital Identity: Decree 9.723/2019, establishing the individual taxpayer registration number as sufficient for citizen's access to public services, is considered as a "preparatory act" for the implementation of the National Identity Document. Bill under discussion (PL 7316/2019) on digital certificates and signature. Planned for 2021.
Consider bringing in expertise from outside the public sector to update the existing open source software policy in line with digital government needs.	Work plan for restructuring the Brazilian Public Software Portal.
Continue updating the digital government legal and regulatory framework to incorporate emerging technologies, to ensure that it enables and drives the digital transformation of the public sector while protecting citizens' digital rights.	Bill under discussion (PL 3443/2019) to use technologies, such as blockchain and artificial intelligence, to improve service delivery.
Continue and strengthen an integrated digital service policy, linked to the Digital Government Strategy, to reinforce the coherence, effectiveness and commitment of the Brazilian public sector to delivering high-quality services to citizens.	Unique government portal (gov.br). Establishment of a user experience department within the SGD.
Take a multichannel approach to public services that includes mobile access to prevent the creation of new forms of digital divide to continue to promote the openness, auditability and accessibility of digital services, including transparency via the use, reuse and exchange of open government data.	Various actions.
Consider developing an action plan on the use of emerging technologies to promote inclusive and improved service design and delivery as a complement to the current Digital Government Strategy.	No action.
Consider leading and actively supporting other Latin America and Caribbean countries' efforts on cross-border service delivery, given the political and economic relevance of Brazil in the region as well as its experience in promoting interoperability across different federation levels.	Conference on digital signatures for cross-border services in 2019 in Chile.

Sources: OECD (2018d), *Digital Government Review of Brazil: Towards the Digital Transformation of the Public Sector*, *https://doi.org/10.1787/9789264307636-en* for the recommendations; OECD, based on information provided by the Ministry of Economy for the key measures adopted.

Decree 9.756/2019 established the unique portal "gov.br" and set the rules for the unification of the digital channels of the federal government. Gov.br is the single portal for several services. States and municipalities can also use the platform and some states have adopted the same platform for their state services. By April 2020, 18 portals had been migrated to the single portal "gov.br", including: Brasil.gov.br portal, Planalto, Civil House, General Secretariat, Government Secretariat, Comptroller General of the Union, the Access to Information Law website, the Ministry of Sport and the Ministry of Agriculture. The website offers a single sign-on platform, accessible through the individual taxpayer registration number (Cadastro de Pessoas Físicas, CPF), the unique identifier, which can be used for 400 services. According to the SGD, 45 million people are already using the platform, with the objective of reaching 70 million by the end of 2020. In terms of the digitalisation of federal government services, Brazil moved from 41% to 54%, with the objective to reach 100% by 2022.

The recently approved Digital Government Strategy 2020-22 includes a number of activities under the responsibility of the SDG aimed at increasing co-ordination. Among others, the SGD is responsible for approving the e-digital plans of entities of the public administration (see below), for offering shared technologies and services, as well as for defining technical norms and standards.

The "e-digital plan" was introduced in 2019 for designing digital transformation initiatives among entities in the Brazilian public administration. Responding also to the need to increase oversight of activities among sectors, the e-digital plan aims at matching the main needs and challenges of the sector/public entity with the various tools offered by the SGD. It comprises actions, goals and indicators for the sector in terms of digitalisation of public services for the upcoming one to two years. Fifteen plans are presently under implementation or in the process of being agreed (Table 3.5). In the first half of 2019, the National Institute of Social Security (Instituto Nacional do Seguro Social, INSS) completed the digitalisation of all its services, thus allowing those who want to apply for retirement to complete the procedure entirely on line.

Institutional capabilities are improving

Competencies and skills are fundamental pillars of a digitally enabled state. The 2018 Review found that Brazil faces challenges

> *not only related to attracting and retaining the best ICT professionals in the public sector, but also to developing digital skills and growing awareness among leaders, decision makers and policy implementers about the challenges and opportunities of digital transformation.*

It recommended that Brazil prioritise the development of digital skills in four key areas: user, professional, complementary (new skillsets necessary for public service professions that are profoundly transformed through digitalisation) and leadership. According to the recently adopted Digital Government Strategy, it is the SDG's responsibility to select and allocate the additional workforce required to execute the strategy and develop the digital talents and skills required for digital transformation teams, in conjunction with the National School of Public Administration (Escola Nacional de Administração Pública, ENAP).

In 2019, the Ministry of Economy, in co-operation with ENAP, launched the "Development of Capabilities for the Digital Transformation" Programme (Programa de Desenvolvimento de Capacidades para Transformação Digital). The courses are organised in seven knowledge areas: 1) leadership and innovation; 2) high technology; 3) data science; 4) agile transformation; 5) governance and management of ICT; 6) services for citizens; and 7) security and privacy. Training is provided in the form of short courses, seminars and other training events, in-person and on line, which consider the development of technical, communication and leadership skills. One of the innovations in the training concerns certification, with the aim to build talent banks for improving selection processes in the public administration. The SGD reported that in 2019, 18 000 people were trained through this programme.

Table 3.5. E-digital plans in Brazil

Digital government initiatives across sectors, 2019

Sector	Ministry	Plan status	Brief description	Public services to be transformed
Pension	Economy	Execution	Transformation of public services offered by the National Institute of Social Security in areas such as social benefits, retirement and fight against fraud. The objective is to achieve a 100% digitalisation rate in the sector (except for those services requiring in-person assistance) and consequently decreasing the counter assistance needed.	74
Economy and labour	Economy	Execution	The main objective of the initiative is to raise the level of digitalisation in the sector. Thus, actions relate to the provision of a digital channel for accessing public services mainly for companies that need to comply with labour legislation. The plan also seeks to implement the single sign-on (SSO) and evaluation solutions to existing systems. The SSO solution will enable citizens to access public services across agencies with the same username and password. In addition, the plan aims to simplify the process of starting a business through systems integration and process digitalisation.	58
Infrastructure	Infrastructure	Execution	The plan includes actions for transforming public services in the transport and traffic sector. Proposed actions aim at facilitating access, monitoring and assessment of public services, and reducing transaction costs. Further, the initiative fosters the promotion of competitiveness in the sector by removing barriers in the process of granting, authorisation, licensing and certification.	177
Industrial property	Economy	Execution	Transformation of public services in areas such as topographies of integrated circuits. The plan also includes actions which focus on revision, simplification, digitalisation and reduction of the timeframe for analysing brands and patents. Further, it aims to improve the experience citizens and enterprises have through the available service channels.	3
Energy	Mines and Energy	Execution	Transformation of public services offered by national regulatory agencies in areas such as energy, mining, oil and gas, with a focus on authorisations and inspection for exploitation, transmission and commercialisation activities.	182
Agriculture	Agriculture, Livestock and Supply	Preparation	To reduce fraud rates through digitalisation and data interoperability (pension, customs, Central Bank). Further, the plan aims at making processes such as registration and certification of agricultural and fishery products and facilities more agile. Ultimately, the planned actions will strengthen the transparency and competitiveness of the Brazilian agricultural industry in both domestic and foreign markets.	84
Public health	Health	Preparation	To increase the number of digital services provided by the Brazilian public health system to citizens. In addition, it seeks to reduce users' efforts in accessing the Ministry of Health's digital services and provide online access to healthcare data for citizens, health professionals and service providers.	27
Health regulation	Health	Preparation	To increase the number of digital services provided by the Brazilian Health Regulatory Agency with a focus on authorisations for the import and export of drugs, cosmetics and food. The plan also seeks to modernise the medicine traceability processes, which will improve authorities' capacity to co-ordinate public policies more effectively.	23
Citizenship	Citizenship	Preparation	The plan includes initiatives which focus on providing a digital channel to the public services offered by the sector. It also seeks to implement the SSO and evaluation solutions to existing systems. The main areas of the plan include culture, sport and social assistance.	70
Environment	Environment	Preparation	The plan aims at actions to help streamline the environmental licenses process, as well as to improve the monitoring and controlling processes of conservation areas and the execution of environmental conditionality.	68
Education	Education	Preparation	The proposed plan establishes guidelines and strategies for digital transformation and simplification of public services offered by the Ministry of Education and its related bodies. Initiatives relate to the adoption of the SSO and evaluation solutions to existing systems. The SSO will enable citizens to access public services across agencies with the same username and password.	115
Science and technology	Science, Technology, Innovations and Communication	Preparation	The Digital Science and Technology Plan is currently being developed and involves public institutions in the areas of scientific and technological development, telecommunications, nuclear energy, and space research.	80
Defence	Defence	Preparation	Transformation of public services offered by the Army, Navy and Air Force in areas such as sensitive material, aircraft and vessel registration.	30
Justice and security	Justice and Public Security	Preparation	The proposed e-digital plan focuses on providing a digital channel to the public services offered by the sector. In addition, it seeks the implementation of the SSO and evaluation solutions to existing systems. The mains areas of the plan include the prison system, trade unions, crime, refugees, consumers and human rights, among others.	35

Source: OECD, based on information provided by the Ministry of Economy.

Other actions undertaken or planned to strengthen capabilities are: selecting executives with a profile focused on digital transformation ("digital transformation leaders"); elaborating a strategy for expanding, strengthening and developing the ICT workforce; and preparing a proposal for adjusting the position of ICT analyst within the public sector (still at an early stage of development). Through the first, in 2019, ENAP and the SGD selected 17 professionals (out of about 290 applicants) through a transparent process to execute strategic functions in the area of ICT in public administration bodies. They will be responsible for enabling the digital transformation of their respective institutions; act strategically, by prospecting new solutions aligned to the needs of their respective bodies; manage ICT resources, in compliance with the provisions of the SISP's regulations; and mobilise teams that work with ICT. The second action foresees the mobility of public servants within the public administration, to take up roles related to the digital transformation. A call was published to this effect in February 2020, which defines the profiles sought and the application process, as well as the temporary additional remuneration the selected public servants will receive.

These actions are important steps in improving capabilities in the public sector. However, as challenges still persist, in particular in attracting and retaining a talented and competent workforce, the recruitment process in the public sector, as well as career paths, should be revised. Another action should be mapping the existing skills and a needs assessment across the public sector, so to measure the skills needs and the corresponding efforts in the short, medium and long terms.

In terms of institutional capabilities, a key element raised by the Review was the need for strategic planning and policy mechanisms to improve the coherence and sustainability of Brazil's public sector ICT investments, given the increasing share of ICT expenditures in the public sector budget. The Review recommended introducing mechanisms such as the pre-evaluation of ICT expenditures, business cases and project management standards.

The SGD has established an ICT Contracting Governance Model (Modelo de Governança das Contratações de TIC), which strengthens the governance of centralised or joint procurement of ICT solutions within the federal government. The model establishes the review of purchases by a committee and the definition of guidelines for action, of contracting amounts and of operational procedures. To formalise this model, in 2019 the Ministry of Economy published a new model for the purchase of ICT good and services by entities that are part of the SISP – Normative Instruction No. 1 and No. 2 of 4 April 2019.

Normative Instruction No. 1 extends the responsibility of public managers in the contracting process and prioritises the planning process, with an emphasis on comparative analysis of the solutions and justification of the choices made. Covering approximately 3 400 annual purchases, the new act makes mandatory the publication of preliminary technical studies on the Internet, even when dealing with public companies as suppliers. The new model also simplifies the process by eliminating documents (insertion plan, the inspection plan and the capacity plan) and incorporating them in the annual procurement plan. The ordinance also establishes that the government adopts cloud services to expand the capacity of its information systems.

The Review also recommended

> *institutionalising the pre-evaluation phase of digital technology investments through two distinct levels of budget thresholds: a first level directed at projects of medium ICT budget where the pre-evaluation would be considered best practice; a second level focused on strategic ICT projects with higher budgets where the pre-evaluation phase would be mandatory.*

Normative Instruction No. 2 establishes a threshold above which spending on ICT by the federal government agencies has to be submitted for approval to the Ministry of Economy. The threshold is USD 7.3 million (BRL 28.6 million). As this amount is rather high and would not be applicable to the majority of ICT spending in the public sector, the threshold corresponds to the "second level" suggested in the recommendation. For purchases below this threshold, there is no prior approval by the Ministry of Economy, but contracting agencies have to follow the procedure set by Normative Instruction No. 1.

The analysis and prior approval model involves the work of two boards, one advisory, the other deliberative, instituted by the Minister of Economy through Ordinance 103/2019. The Internal Board of Technical Reference (Colegiado Interno de Referencial Técnico, CIRT) analyses the planning of all major contracts submitted to the SGD for approval. Based on the opinion issued by the CIRT and depending on the size of the contract, the Internal Board of Procurement of Goods and Services of Information and Communication Technology (Colegiado Interno de Contratações de Bens e Serviços de TIC, CITIC) approves the spending. CITIC decides on the approval of large contracts up to USD 14.8 million (BRL 58 million); above that value, the expenditure has to be approved by the Centralized Procurement and Contracts Committee (Comitê de Compras e Contratos Centralizados, C4ME).

The SGD is also optimising the contracts the public administration has with big IT providers, negotiating 12-month framework agreements with them. Negotiating all the contracts at once allows obtaining lower prices, which are then made public and can also be used by states and municipalities. In terms of IT infrastructures, it is assessing the security of the 130 federal data centres, with the objective of reducing their number and increasing security levels.

Efforts are still needed for the development of important digital enablers

Brazil has made efforts in recent years to promote the development, use and reuse of digital key enablers across the public sector. However, the Review found several weaknesses in the current system, which results in inefficiencies and prevents the development of more integrated service delivery approaches. The review recommended that Brazil continue prioritising interoperability frameworks and digital identity systems, in order to build on existing efforts in integrated, multichannel and inclusive digital service delivery.

Brazil has interoperability frameworks for the public administration in place and recognises data as a strategic asset for the digitalisation of the public sector (Box 3.5). Nevertheless, the Review noted that due to the inexistence of the proper policy levers that can make data exchange among public sector entities mandatory, the connection and integration of central databases was still a problem in Brazil. It also noted that despite the development of legal instruments (such as Decree 8.789 of 26 June 2016), there was still room for improvement with regard to public sector data governance and a clearer link with several priorities, initiatives and projects listed in the Digital Government Strategy.

A new Data Sharing Decree (10.064/2019) adopted in October 2019 aims at clarifying issues related to the sharing of information between the bodies and entities of the federal public administration and the legislative and judiciary powers, at all level (states, municipalities and the Federal District). The decree establishes the creation of a Citizen Base Register, which will include in one platform all citizens' personal data, including biometric data. Data will be shared across government bodies with the objective of providing digital public services, according to criteria for interoperability defined by a Central Data Governance Committee. The decree also establishes the interoperability conditions. The SGD is also currently exploring the possibility to use blockchain for interoperability of public databases.

The Central Data Governance Committee will also oversee the sharing of public data with the private sector with a view to stimulating data-driven innovation. In continuity with the Open Data Policy, the Ministry of Economy is working on the "Government as a Platform" (GaaP) project, which will provide a legal mechanism for the private sector to use public data in a controlled environment. Through a consultative process, the SGD has been working with start-ups and companies to identify the data that will be most useful to share in this regard. GaaP refers to an entire ecosystem of application programming interfaces (APIs) and other shared components, open standards and established datasets, as well as the services built on these elements and the governance processes that can keep the system secure and ensure accountability. GaaP is based on the provision of new services from data sharing and on the promotion of civil society participation in co-creating services to meet public policy objectives and foster economic activity.

The Review also recommended considering reinvesting in open source software as a strategic key enabler. Despite Brazil's solid experience in the use of open source software, the topic's significance in the country's digital government policy has decreased in recent years. Brazil is currently developing a plan for restructuring the Brazilian Public Software Portal (PSPB); however, this seems to remain a lower priority for the government.

Diverse public identification documents have been digitalised in Brazil, including an electronic version of the driver's licence, the electronic payment card of the Bolsa Família programme, and several other labour and health documents. A decree adopted in March 2020 (Decree 10.278/2020) sets the technical conditions and "requirements for the digitalisation of public or private documents, so that the digitalised documents produce the same legal effects as the original documents". This is evidence of the federal government's efforts to increasingly use digital technologies to promote efficiency across the public sector and make citizens' interactions with government institutions more convenient. However, the development of a digital identification system, considered to be one of the central key enablers for digital government development, is delayed due to the complex digital and institutional environments and requirements to implement such a system, and the preponderance of other identity numbers used across the public sector to identify citizens.

Box 3.5. Interoperability and data-sharing architecture in Brazil

The ePing architecture, Standards of Interoperability of Electronic Government, reflects a Brazilian interoperability policy for the public sector. ePing defines a set of minimum requirements, policies and technical specifications governing the use of ICT in the public sector, establishing the basis for interoperability across public sector institutions.

In 2018, the Secretariat of Information and Communication Technologies also launched a new interoperability platform called Conecta GOV, which makes available a catalogue of application programming interfaces to be used by public sector organisations.

Brazil currently operates two open platforms that reflect the recognition of data as a strategic asset for the digitalisation of the public sector in Brazil:

- Portal brasileiro de dados abertos (*dados.gov.br*): A single national portal for open government data at the federal level.
- GovData (*govdata.gov.br*): A platform to cross-check information and produce strategic information, relaunched in 2018.

The mandate to develop a national digital identity framework has been given to the Supreme Electoral Court, which is also responsible for managing Brazil's electronic voting system. The National Identification Document (Documento Nacional de Identificação, DNI) is created from the national voter registration biometrics database, which currently only covers about 100 million Brazilians. The DNI will bring different registers together into one single document: the individual taxpayer registration number, the birth certificate and the voter's registration. In 2019, the individual taxpayer registration number replaced a number of other documents (Decree 9.723/2019) for citizens to access public services. This was considered to be a "preparatory act" for the implementation of the DNI.

The Brazilian Ministry of Economy is working with the Federal Electoral Court on a joint work plan for issuing the DNI to the population. USD 28 million (BRL 110 million) have been earmarked in the 2020 budget for the implementation of the voter identification automation system. The schedule is for the DNI to be made available to citizens at the end of 2021. However, the limited progress in the development of the digital identity system makes it unlikely that this objective will be met.

A related aspect for adoption of digital identity is the legal validity of electronic and digital signatures for proving authorship and confidentiality, as well as to regulate the provision of information services. Currently digital certificates are still the only technology to have the essential attribute of legal validity in the country. Digital certification was introduced in Brazil with the creation of the public keys infrastructure (Infraestrutura de Chaves Públicas, ICP-Brasil), through Provisional Measure 2.200-2/2001. The Digital Certificate is an electronic document that uses a cryptographic key and a specific standard containing the owners' data and guaranteeing their identity, thus ensuring confidentiality, authenticity and endorsement of any signed electronic transactions, as well as the exchange of information with integrity, confidentiality and security. Today, there are approximately 8.8 million active digital certificates in Brazil, corresponding to 3% of the total population.

New technologies such as blockchain, advanced biometric identification and quantum digital keys promise a large range of applications in this field, but they cannot be integrated, due to outdated laws, which has not kept up with the development of new technologies. A new bill (PL 7316/2019) aims to create the National Digital Signature and Identification System (Sistema Nacional de Assinatura e Identificação Digital, SINAID), which will amend the provisional measure, to take into account new digital identification technologies and the Civil Rights Framework for the Internet and the General Data Protection Law. The new regulation is a necessary step to include more secure technologies, such as cryptography, and to step up the use of digital certificates and signatures, both for the provision of public services and for use by the private sector.

The need to move to a data-driven public sector

In order to improve digital service delivery, the SGD established a user experience department, which is conducting research and evaluations with users of public services in various channels and agencies that offer public services. Although these efforts are very important, Brazil should move beyond simply digitalising what was previously analogue to open, user-driven service delivery, shifting from an e-government to a digital government approach (OECD, 2014). The government will also need to take a multichannel approach to service delivery in order to secure equitable and inclusive access to all segments of the population.

Efforts for the development of a data-driven public sector are already underway. These efforts should be continued so that data can become integral to policy making and service design and delivery. Achieving a true digitalisation of services implies better exploring integrated approaches such as life events, but also the application of the "once only principle". It also requires building a proactive service delivery capable of anticipating citizens' needs. Exploring the use of emerging technologies such as AI would be critical.

As part of the new strategy, the government foresees the use of blockchain to make the different base registers interoperable, to establish data analytics capability within the federal government and to use IoT to anticipate citizens' and services' needs. Brazil is currently in the discussion phase of a law (PL 3443/2019) which makes use of emerging technologies, such as blockchain and AI, for improving the efficiency and effectiveness and enhancing public sector intelligence. Brazil already has some advanced examples of the use of emerging technologies in the public sector (Box 3.6). It is also in the final phase of elaborating a national strategy for AI and is a signatory to the OECD AI principles (OECD, 2019h).

Box 3.6. Examples of the use of artificial intelligence in the Brazilian public sector

The Court of Accounts of the Union uses artificial intelligence (AI) to better analyse the procurement processes of the federal administration ("Alice" – Analysis of Bids and Tenders). Based on the information published on the public procurement portal, the system analyses the costs of tenders and compares the information with other databases. Based on this information, the system is able to identify risks and send alerts to auditors. AI also assists the auditor when writing a text ("Sofia" – System of Guidance on Facts and Evidence for the Auditor), pointing to possible errors and even suggesting information related to the parties involved or the topic addressed.

The Superior Labour Court (Tribunal Superior do Trabalho, TST) manages court cases with AI (Bem-Te-Vi). Since May 2019, the tool allows automatic analysis of compliance with the deadlines of the proceedings.

The Comptroller General of the Union (Controladoria-Geral da União, CGU) also uses an AI-based system for overseeing contracts and suppliers. The tool carries out a risk analysis, including not only that of corruption, but also of other problems, such as the possibility of a supplier not fulfilling the contract.

Source: MCTIC (2019), *Estratégia Brasileira de Inteligência Artificial, Consulta Pública*, *http://participa.br/profile/estrategia-brasileira-de-inteligencia-artificial.*

The Review also recommended that, given the political and economic relevance in the region, the government of Brazil consider leading and actively supporting efforts on cross-border service delivery in Latin America and the Caribbean. In this regard, a conference to discuss digital signatures in cross-border services took place in 2019 in Chile. The conference led to the signature of an agreement for mutual recognition of public key infrastructures within Mercosur, with a view of also reaching an agreement on the mutual recognition of signatures, on the basis of the European Union's (Electronic Identification, Authentication and Trust Services) eIdas (EU Regulation 910/2014).

Box 3.7. Policy recommendations for digital government

Brazil should push forward with those recommendations of the *OECD Digital Government Review of Brazil: Towards the Digital Transformation of the Public Sector* (OECD, 2018d) that are still valid. In particular:

- Continue reinforcing the responsibilities and resources of the Secretariat of Digital Government.
- Increase co-ordination and build synergies between the Digital Government Strategy and e-Digital.
- Continue prioritising digital skills development in any policy or framework for the public sector.
- Continue enhancing interoperability among the public administration's systems.
- Advance the new legislation on sharing of personal data among government bodies, initiated by the Data Sharing Decree (10.064/2019).
- Reinforce public efforts for the development of a digital identity framework.
- Speed up the establishment of the National Digital Signature and Identification System.
- Reinforce efforts to develop a data-driven digital government.
- Update the digital government legal and regulatory framework to seize the opportunities of emerging technologies.

References

ABComm and Comschool (2019), *Pesquisa: Logística no E-commerce Brasileiro 2019* [Research: Logistics in the Brazilian E-commerce 2019], Associação Brasileira de Comércio Eletrônico and ComSchool, *https://abcomm.org/noticias/pesquisa-logistica-no-e-commerce-2019/*.

ABStartups and CIEB (2019), *Mapeamento Edtech 2018: Investigacao Sobre as Tecnologias Educacionais no Brasil* [Edtech Mapping 2018: Survey on Education Technologies in Brazil], Associação Brasileira de Startups and Centro de Inovação para a Educação Brasileira, São Paulo, *www.cieb.net.br/wp-content/uploads/2018/08/Mapeamento-de-Edtechs-FINAL.pdf*.

Araujo, M. and N. Reinhard (2018), "Characterizing Brazilian Internet users: An analysis based on digital skills", in CGI.br, *ICT Households 2017: Survey on the Use of Information and Communication Technologies in Brazilian households*, Comitê Gestor da Internet no Brasil, São Paulo, *https://cetic.br/media/docs/publicacoes/2/tic_dom_2017_livro_eletronico.pdf*.

BNDES (2019), *BNDES* (website), *www.bndes.gov.br*, accessed in December 2019.

Brasilino, A. et al. (2018), "Teacher training and digital literacy: A correlation study on the ICT in education databases", in CGI.br, *ICT in Education, 2017: Survey on the Use of Information and Communication Technologies in Brazilian Schools*, Comitê Gestor da Internet no Brasil, São Paulo, *https://cetic.br/media/docs/publicacoes/2/tic_edu_2017_livro_eletronico.pdf*.

BrazilLab (2020), *BrazilLab* (website), *https://brazillab.org.br/*, accessed in February 2020.

CCT (2017), *Avaliação de Politícas Públicas, Ações e Execuções de Totos os Programas Relacionados à Banda Larga* [Evaluation of Public Policies, Actions and Executions of Programmes Related to Broadband], Comissão de Ciência, Tecnologia, Inovação, Comunicação e Informática do Senado Federal do Brasil, Brasilia.

CGI.br (2020a), *ICT Public Access Centers 2019: Survey on Public Internet Access Centers in Brazil* (database), Comitê Gestor da Internet no Brasil, São Paulo, *https://cetic.br/en/pesquisa/centros-publicos/indicadores/* (accessed in July 2020).

CGI.br (2020b), *ICT Enterprises 2019: Survey on the Use of Information and Communication Technologies in Brazilian Enterprises,* (database), Comitê Gestor da Internet no Brasil, São Paulo, *https://cetic.br/en/pesquisa/empresas/indicadores/* (accessed in July 2020).

CGI.br (2019a), *ICT Households 2018: Survey on the Use of Information and Communication Technologies in Brazilian Households* (database), Comitê Gestor da Internet no Brasil, São Paulo, *https://cetic.br/en/pesquisa/domicilios/indicadores/* (accessed in February 2020).

CGI.br (2019b), *Desigualdades Digitais no Espaço Urbano: Um Estudo Sobre o Acesso e o Uso da Internet na Cidade de São Paulo* [Digital Inequalities in the Urban Space: A Study on Internet Access and Use in the City of São Paulo], Comitê Gestor da Internet no Brasil, São Paulo,*https://cetic.br/media/docs/publicacoes/7/11454920191028-desigualdades_digitais_no_espaco_urbano.pdf*.

CGI.br (2019c), *ICT Education 2018: Survey on the Use of Information and Communication Technologies in Brazilian Schools* (database), Comitê Gestor da Internet no Brasil, São Paulo,*https://cetic.br/en/pesquisa/educacao/indicadores/* (accessed in February 2020).

CGI.br (2018), *ICT Enterprises 2017: Survey on the Use of Information and Communication Technologies in Brazilian Enterprises* (database), Comitê Gestor da Internet no Brasil, São Paulo, *https://cetic.br/en/pesquisa/empresas/indicadores/* (accessed in February 2020).

CGI.br (2014), *TIC Centros Públicos de Acesso 2013: Pesquisa Sobre o Uso das Tecnologias de Informação e Comunicação* [ICT Public Access 2013: Survey on the Use of Information and Communication Technologies], Comitê Gestor da Internet no Brasil, São Paulo, *https://cetic.br/media/docs/publicacoes/2/tic-centros-publicos-de-acesso-2013.pdf*.

CNI (2018), *Investments in Industry 4.0*, Confederação Nacional da Indústria, Brasilia, *https://bucket-gw-cni-static-cms-si.s3.amazonaws.com/media/filer_public/d4/c4/d4c48b24-0674-44a5-8799-b0fd5d0f8d11/investimentsinindustry40_2018.pdf*.

CNI (2016), "Industry 4.0: A new challenge for Brazilian industry", *Special Survey Industry 4.0*, Year 17, Number 2/April, Confederação Nacional da Indústria, Brasilia, *https://bucket-gw-cni-static-cms-si.s3.amazonaws.com/media/filer_public/13/e7/13e7e7bd-9b1d-4c16-8099-99b6d844d04e/special_survey_industry_40.pdf*.

Dutz, M. et al. (2018), *Jobs and Growth: Brazil's Productivity Agenda*, The World Bank, Washington, DC, *http://documents.worldbank.org/curated/en/226241530080563797/Jobs-and-growth-Brazil-s-productivity-agenda*.

Dutz, M. et al. (2017), *Business Support Policies in Brazil: Large Spending, Little Impact*, World Bank Group, Washington, DC, *http://documents.worldbank.org/curated/en/458011511799140856/pdf/121668-REVISED-Brazil-Public-Expenditure-Review-Business-Support-Policies.pdf*.

Ebit Nielsen (2020), *Webshoppers 41ª Edição* [Webshoppers 41st Edition], *www.ebit.com.br/webshoppers*.

ECLAC and IPEA (2018), *Avaliação de Desempenho do Brasil Mais Produtivo* [Performance Evaluation of Brazil More Productive], United Nations Economic Commission for Latin America and the Caribbean and Institute of Applied Economic Research, Brasilia, *https://www.ipea.gov.br/portal/images/stories/PDFs/livros/livros/181127_avaliacao_do_desempenho.pdf*.

ERGP (2019), *Report on Cross-Subsidization Practices*, European Regulator Group for Postal Services.

FEBRABAN/Deloitte (2019), *2019 FEBRABAN Banking Technology Survey*, Federação Brasileira de Bancos, São Paulo, *www2.deloitte.com/br/en/pages/financial-services/articles/pesquisa-deloitte-febraban-tecnologia-bancaria.html*.

Infocomm Media Development Authority (2020), *SMEs Go Digital*, *www.imda.gov.sg/programme-listing/smes-go-digital* (accessed in March 2020).

INEP (2017), *Censo Escolar*, Instituto Nacional de Estudos e Pesquisas Educacionais Anísio Teixeira, Brasilia, *http://portal.inep.gov.br/web/guest/censo-escolar*.

ITU (2016), *Overview of Key Performance Indicators in Smart Sustainable Cities*, ITU T Y.4900 Recommendation Series, International Telecommunication Union, Geneva, *https://www.itu.int/itu-t/recommendations/rec.aspx?rec=12627*.

Lemann Centre (2016), *Part I: Implementing the Base Nacional Comum Curricular: Lessons from "Common Core"*, Lemann Centre, Stanford, *https://lemanncenter.stanford.edu/sites/default/files/Implementing%20merged%20English%281%29_0.pdf*.

Maciente Nogueira, A., C. Rauen Vianna and L. Kubota (2019), "Tecnologias digitais, habilidades ocupacionais e emprego formal no Brasil entre 2003 e 2017" [Digital technologies, occupational abilities and formal work in Brazil, 2003-2017], in *Mercado de Trabalho, Conjuntura e Análise*, Year 25, Issue 66, April, Ministério da Economia and Institute for Applied Economic Research, Brasilia, pp. 115-129, *https://www.ipea.gov.br/portal/images/stories/PDFs/mercadodetrabalho/190520_bmt_66_dossie_tecnologias_digitais.pdf*.

McKinsey (2019), *Brazil Digital Report*, first edition, McKinsey & Company, *https://www.mckinsey.com/br/~/media/McKinsey/Locations/South%20America/Brazil/Our%20Insights/Brazil%20Digital%20Report/Brazil-Digital-Report-1st-Edition_Portuguese-vAjustado.ashx*.

MCTIC (2019), *Estratégia Brasileira de Inteligência Artificial, Consulta Pública* [National Strategy for Artificial Intelligence, Public Consultation], Ministério da Ciência, Tecnologia, Inovações e Comunicações, Brasilia, *http://participa.br/profile/estrategia-brasileira-de-inteligencia-artificial*.

MCTIC (2018), *Brazilian Digital Transformation Strategy: E-Digital*, Ministério da Ciência, Tecnologia, Inovações e Comunicações, Brasilia, *www.mctic.gov.br/mctic/export/sites/institucional/sessaoPublica/arquivos/digitalstrategy.pdf*.

MCTIC (2017), *Portaria n. 7.154, de 6.12.2017 - Aprova a Norma Geral do Programa Governo Eletrônico – Serviço de Atendimento ao Cidadão – GESAC* [Ordinance n. 7,154 of 6.12.2017 - Approves the Electronic Government Citizen Services Programme – GESAC], Ministério da Ciência, Tecnologia, Inovações e Comunicações, Brasilia, *https://www.mctic.gov.br/mctic/opencms/legislacao/portarias/Portaria_mctic_n_7154_de_06122017.html*.

Noguiera, M. (2016), "Cartão BNDES: Inovação no apoio às MPMEs" [BNDES Card: Innovation in Support of Micro and SMEs], *IPEA Radar* n° 48, December, Institute for Applied Economic Research, Brasilia, *www.ipea.gov.br/portal/images/stories/PDFs/radar/20170110_radar_48_art4.pdf*.

OECD (forthcoming a), *Digital Economy Outlook 2020*, OECD Publishing, Paris.

OECD (forthcoming b), *OECD Reviews of Digital Transformation: Going Digital in Latvia*, OECD Publishing, Paris.

OECD (forthcoming c), *OECD Economic Surveys: Brazil 2020*, OECD Publishing, Paris.

OECD (2020a), *ICT Access and Usage by Households and Individuals* (database), OECD, Paris, *http://oe.cd/hhind*.

OECD (2020b), *ICT Access and Usage by Businesses* (database), OECD, Paris, *http://oe.cd/bus* (accessed in March 2020).

OECD (2020c), *SME and Entrepreneurship Policy in Brazil 2020*, OECD Studies on SMEs and Entrepreneurship, OECD Publishing, Paris, *https://doi.org/10.1787/cc5feb81-en*.

OECD (2019a), *OECD Skills Outlook 2019: Thriving in a Digital World*, OECD Publishing, Paris, *https://doi.org/10.1787/df80bc12-en*.

OECD (2019b), *PISA 2018 Results (Volume I): What Students Know and Can Do*, PISA, OECD Publishing, Paris, *https://doi.org/10.1787/5f07c754-en*.

OECD (2019c), *Measuring the Digital Transformation: A Roadmap for the Future*, OECD Publishing, Paris, *https://doi.org/10.1787/9789264311992-en*.

OECD (2019d), "Productivity growth in the digital age", OECD Going Digital Policy Note, OECD, Paris, *https://www.oecd.org/going-digital/productivity-growth-in-the-digital-age.pdf*.

OECD (2019e), *Unpacking E-commerce: Business Models, Trends and Policies*, OECD Publishing, Paris, *https://doi.org/10.1787/23561431-en*.

OECD (2019f), *Going Digital: Shaping Policies, Improving Lives*, OECD Publishing, Paris, *https://doi.org/10.1787/9789264312012-en*.

OECD (2019g), *Education at a Glance 2019: OECD Indicators*, OECD Publishing, Paris, *https://doi.org/10.1787/f8d7880d-en*.

OECD (2019h), *Recommendation of the Council on Artificial Intelligence*, OECD, Paris, *https://legalinstruments.oecd.org/en/instruments/OECD-LEGAL-0449*.

OECD (2018a), "How can we effectively use technology in classrooms?", in *Teaching for the Future: Effective Classroom Practices to Transform Education*, OECD Publishing, Paris, pp. 75-95, *https://doi.org/10.1787/9789264293243-7-en*.

OECD (2018b), *OECD Economic Surveys: Brazil 2018*, OECD Publishing, Paris, *https://doi.org/10.1787/eco_surveys-bra-2018-en*.

OECD (2018c), *Getting Skills Right: Brazil*, Getting Skills Right, OECD Publishing, Paris, *https://doi.org/10.1787/9789264309838-en*.

OECD (2018d), *Digital Government Review of Brazil: Towards the Digital Transformation of the Public Sector*, OECD Digital Government Studies, OECD Publishing, Paris, *https://doi.org/10.1787/9789264307636-en.*

OECD (2016), *PISA 2015 Results (Volume II): Policies and Practices for Successful Schools*, PISA, OECD Publishing, Paris, *http://dx.doi.org/10.1787/9789264267510-en.*

OECD (2015), *Students, Computers and Learning: Making the Connection*, PISA, OECD Publishing, Paris, *https://doi.org/10.1787/9789264239555-en.*

OECD (2014), *Recommendation of the Council on Digital Government Strategies*, OECD, Paris, *https://legalinstruments.oecd.org/en/instruments/OECD-LEGAL-0406.*

Pires, J. and N. Russell (2017), *Assessing Firm-Support Programs in Brazil*, Inter-American Development Bank, Washington, DC, *https://publications.iadb.org/en/publication/17481/assessing-firm-support-programs-brazil.*

SBVC (2018), *Ranking das 50 Maiores Empresas do E-commerce Brasileiro 2018* [Ranking of the 50 Main Enterprises of Brazilian E-commerce 2018], Sociedade Brasileira de Varejo e Consumo, São Paulo.

SEBRAE and E-commerce Brasil (2018), "4ª edição da Pesquisa Nacional de Varejo Online" [E-Commerce National Survey, Fourth Edition], Serviço Brasileiro de Apoio às Micro e Pequenas Empresas, Brasilia.

Siqueira, E. et al. (2017), "Using a Digital Divide Index among enterprises in the context of public policies in Brazil", CONF-IRM 2017 Proceedings 41, *http://aisel.aisnet.org/confirm2017/41.*

Syndex/UNI Global (2019), *The Economic and Social Consequences of Postal Service Liberalisation*, UNI Global, *https://www.syndex.fr/sites/default/files/files/pdf/2019-07/The%20economic%20and%20social%20consequences%20of%20postal%20services%20liberalization.pdf.*

TCU (2018), *Acórdão 2.608/2018-TCU-Plenário* [Judgement 2.608/2018-TCU-Plenary], Tribunal de Contas da União, Brasilia.

UNCTAD (2015), *Information Economy Report 2015: Unlocking the Potential of E-commerce for Developing Countries*, United Nations Conference on Trade and Development, Geneva, *https://unctad.org/en/PublicationsLibrary/ier2015_en.pdf.*

UNESCO (2017), *Digital Society: Gaps and Challenges for Digital Inclusion in Latin America and the Caribbean*, United Nations Educational, Science and Cultural Organization, Montevideo, *https://unesdoc.unesco.org/ark:/48223/pf0000262860_eng.*

Notes

Israel

The statistical data for Israel are supplied by and under the responsibility of the relevant Israeli authorities. The use of such data by the OECD is without prejudice to the status of the Golan Heights, East Jerusalem and Israeli settlements in the West Bank under the terms of international law.

1. Basic education in Brazil includes kindergarten (*educação infantil*, 0-5 years), primary/secondary school (*ensino fundamental*, 6-14 years) and high school (*ensino médio*, 15-17 years).
2. CA 87/15 establishes that up to 2018, the DIFAL is divided between the states of origin and destination. From 2019 onwards, the DIFAL is due in full to the state of destination.

Chapter 4

ENHANCING TRUST IN THE DIGITAL ECONOMY

Digital security policy in Brazil

Brazil is increasingly being targeted by digital security attacks. CERT.br, the private sector Brazilian National Computer Emergency Response Team (Centro de Estudos, Resposta e Tratamento de Incidentes de Segurança no Brasil) maintained by the executive branch of the Brazilian Internet Steering Committee (Núcleo de Informação e Coordenação, NIC.br), received over 875 000 incident notifications in 2019, 78% of which originated from Brazil (Figures 4.1 and 4.2). The Brazilian Government Computer Security Incident Response Team (Centro de Tratamento e Resposta a Incidentes Cibernéticos de Governo, CTIR) also reports an increasing number of incidents (Figure 4.3). A brief analysis of data from other sources confirms this situation. In 2018, EUROPOL found that Brazil is both a leading target and source of attacks in Latin America, and further noted that 54% of digital security attacks reported in Brazil originate from within the country (EUROPOL, 2018) According to the LexisNexis Threatmetrix (2019), Brazil is the sixth country from which attacks originate globally (in volume).

The 2018 Norton Survey showed that 89 million Brazilians have been a victim of cybercrime, with 70.4 million in the last year alone (Norton, 2018). A Ponemon Institute's 2017 survey of 36 Brazilian companies in 12 sectors showed that they suffered an average of USD 1.1 million in losses for each digital security attack (Ponemon, 2017). The Marsh JLT13 Cyber Review 2019 survey, conducted with 200 medium and large Brazilian companies, found that 55% of these companies are totally dependent on the use of technology in their activities and that 35% may suffer severe downtime in the event of a technology-related problem (Insurancecorp, 2019).

Figure 4.1. Total number of incidents reported to CERT.br per year, 1999-2019

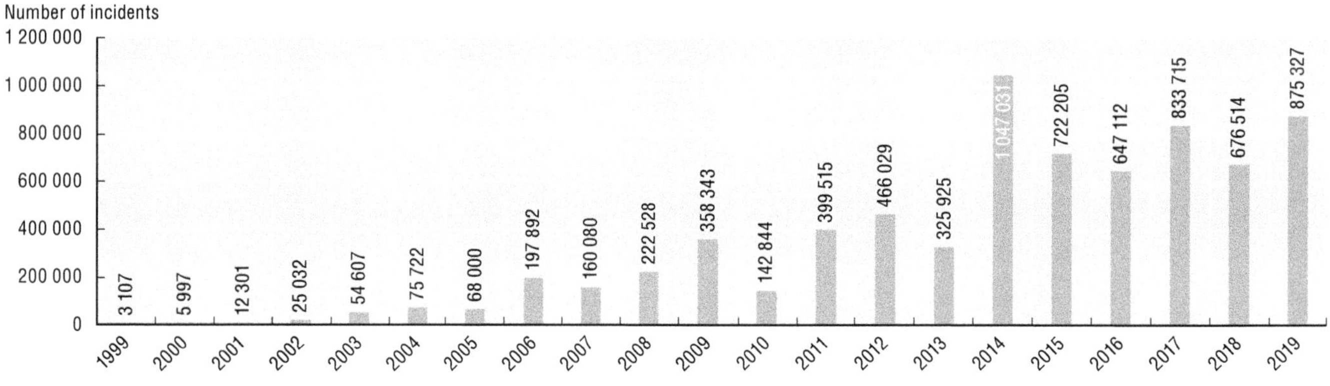

Source: Cert.br (2020), *Estatísticas dos Incidentes Reportados ao CERT.br*, *https://www.cert.br/stats/incidentes* (accessed on 8 March 2020).

Figure 4.2. Top 10 countries from which cyberattacks originate, 2019

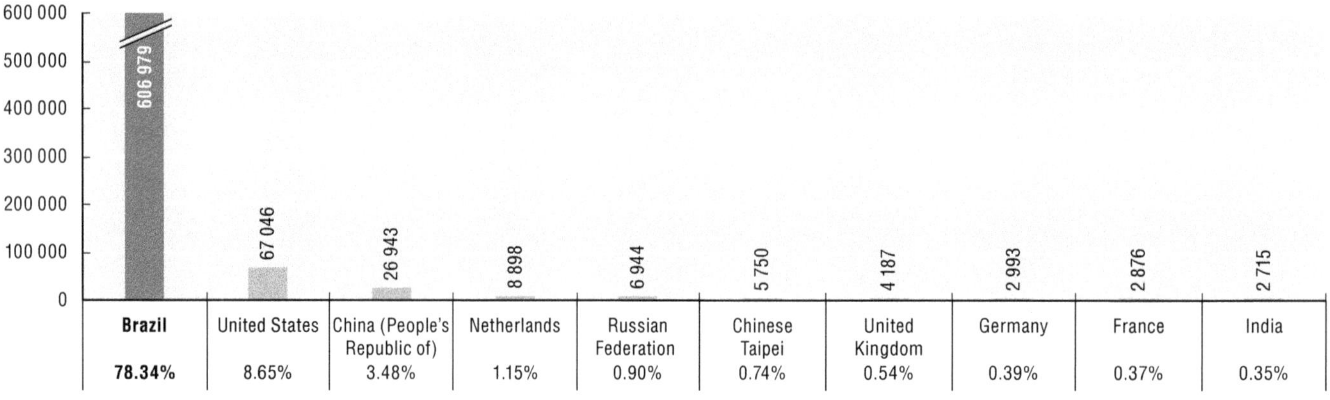

Source: Cert.br (2020), *Estatísticas dos Incidentes Reportados ao CERT.br*, *https://www.cert.br/stats/incidentes* (accessed on 9 March 2020).

Figure 4.3. Number of notifications and incidents registered by the CTIR, 2011-20

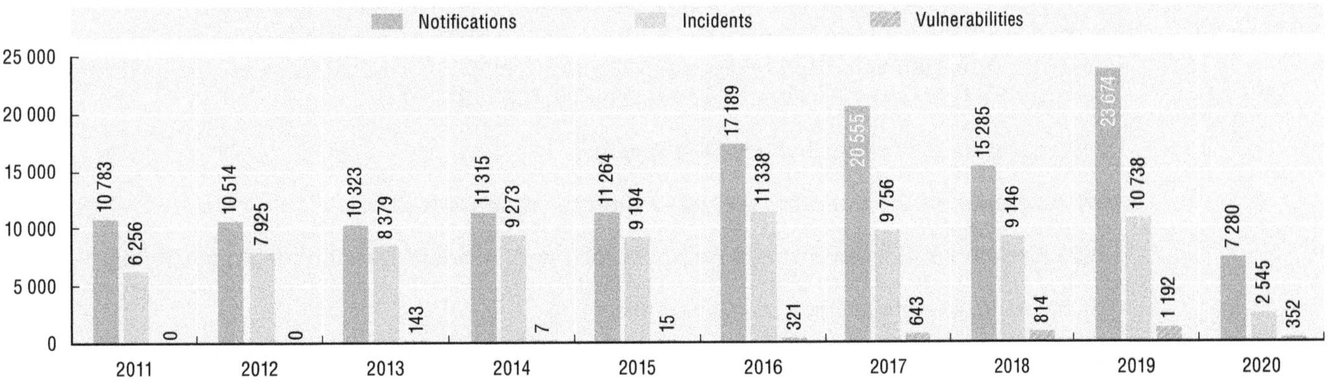

Source: CTIR.br (2020), *Estatísticas Resultantes do Trabalho de Detecção, Triagem, Análise e Resposta a Incidentes Cibernéticos, https://emnumeros.ctir.gov.br* (accessed on 9 March 2020).

However, 44% of companies surveyed did not have contingency plans or budgets to combat incidents and did not foresee, in their budgets, a response to a possible crisis.Eighty per cent of respondents estimated that a digital security incident would have significant operational impact across the enterprise (Insurancecorp, 2019). According to a survey of ICT practices in the health sector by Cetic. br (2018), only 23% of public and private health establishments had a document defining an information security policy in 2018.

To address this issue, Brazil is in the process of developing a broad digital security framework, starting with the adoption of its first National Cybersecurity Strategy.

This section provides an overarching description of digital security policies in Brazil and discusses their strengths and limitations from the perspective of the 2015 OECD *Recommendation of the Council on Digital Security Risk Management for Economic and Social Prosperity* (hereafter "Security Risk Recommendation") (OECD, 2015) and the 2019 *Recommendation of the Council on Digital Security of Critical Activities* (OECD, 2019b). Unless specified otherwise, "digital security" refers to the management of economic and social risks resulting from breaches of availability, integrity and confidentiality of hardware, software, networks and data. This chapter does not cover policies directly related to criminal law enforcement (i.e. cybercrime), national defence or national security.

The emergence of digital security policy in Brazil

Digital security is not a new policy area in Brazil. Since 2000, digital security policy has been evolving along three main phases.

2000-12: The first steps of digital security policy in Brazil

This period was characterised by the establishment of the fundamental building blocks focusing on digital security in the public administration (Box 4.1). In 2000, the government established an information security policy for the federal public administration and created and Information Security Management Committee (Comitê Gestor da Segurança da Informação, CGSI) tasked with advising the Executive Secretariat of the National Defence Council about its implementation.[1] The Brazilian Public Key Infrastructure (PKI) was created in 2001 (ICP-Brasil). The Government Computer Emergency Response Team (CITR Gov) was established in 2004. As of 2006, the Institutional Security Cabinet of the Presidency of the Republic (Gabinete de Segurança Institucional/Presidência da República, GSI/PR) was designated as the primary agency for digital security matters and, over the years, adopted 3 general instructions and 22 supplementary standards (as of 2019). The Federal Court of Accounts (Tribunal de Contas da União, TCU) monitored their implementation by the federal public administration through surveys followed by recommendations. The 2010 GSI/PR Green Paper on Cybersecurity in Brazil (GSI/PR, 2010), which included recommendations for the establishment of a national cybersecurity policy, can be viewed as the first attempt to approach digital security policy from a holistic and strategic perspective.

Box 4.1. The first steps of digital security policy in Brazil

2000: Establishment of an information security policy for the public administration and creation of the Information Security Management Committee (CGSI), co-ordinated by the Institutional Security Cabinet of the Presidency of the Republic (GSI/PR).

2001: Creation of the Brazilian PKI (ICP-Brasil).[1]

2003: Creation of the Internet Steering Committee in Brazil (CGI.br).

2004: Creation of the Government Computer Network Incident Handling Team (CTIR.Gov).

2005: First Government Security Conference.

2006: Creation of the Department of Information and Communications Security (DSIC) within the GSI/PR; creation of a partnership led by the GSI/PR to facilitate the co-ordination of various public sector bodies, including public companies (e.g. Petrobras, Bank of Brazil, etc.), and adoption of a budget to facilitate information security training in the public administration.

2008: First survey of digital security in the public administration and recommendations by the Federal Court of Accounts (TCU). Adoption of the National Defence Strategy, which establishes the "cybersector" as one of the three strategic sectors considered essential for national defence.

2008-18: Publication by the GSI of 3 general instructions and 22 supplementary standards for digital security in the public administration, covering various topics such as risk management methodology, business continuity management, use of cryptography, biometrics, cloud computing technologies and procurement of secure software.

2009: Establishment of a "Cyber Security Technical Group" to propose guidelines and strategies for cybersecurity.

2010: Second TCU survey. Publication of the GSI/PR Green Paper on Cybersecurity in Brazil.

2011: Law on Access to Information, which establishes a principle of transparency of information within the public administration (entering into force in 2012).

2012: TCU publishes recommendations.

1. *https://www.iti.gov.br/icp-brasil/icp-brasil-18-anos.*

Source: GSI (2015), *Estratégia de Segurança da Informação e Comunicações e de Segurança Cibernética da Administração Pública Federal 2015-2018, http://dsic.planalto.gov.br/legislacao/4_Estrategia_de_SIC.pdf/view.*

2012-17: Increased attention to and focus on national security aspects

As of 2012, key events created the conditions for increasing the country's operational digital security capacity while emphasising the national security dimension of digital security and raising awareness about privacy and civil liberties related to the Internet.

Between 2012 and 2016, the government significantly expanded its operational digital security capacity to protect several mega-events hosted in Brazil, such as the United Nations Conference on Sustainable Development (Rio+20 in 2012), World Youth Day (2013), the football Confederations Cup (2013) and the World Cup (2014), and the Olympics and Paralympics (2016). The Ministry of Defence played an important operational role, including by establishing a Cyber Monitoring Centre (Demetrio, 2012), and co-operating with several agencies as well as public and private incident response teams to successfully manage the situation (Hurel and Cruz Lobato, 2018).

In 2013, revelations of foreign espionage activities affecting Brazil led to the creation of a Parliamentary Committee of Inquiry on Espionage (CPI da Espionagem), which underlined weaknesses in the country's cybersecurity from a national security perspective. The committee's final report recommended the development of a National Cybersecurity Strategy, the adoption of measures to co-ordinate public and private actions in this area, and the creation of a cybersecurity agency within the federal public administration to address the issue in an overarching and more effective manner.

During the same period, a considerable amount of public attention was dedicated to privacy and civil liberties issues related to the Internet, in particular through the public consultations for and adoption of the Internet Civil Legal Framework (Marco Civil da Internet), establishing principles, guarantees, rights and duties for the use of the Internet in Brazil (April 2014).[2]

However, in 2014, the results of an audit carried out by the TCU emphasised a relatively low level of implementation of existing digital security requirements by the federal public administration. According to the TCU, most of the federal public administration was not aware of its exposure to IT risks, the likelihood of their occurrence or their possible impact on the achievement of their objectives, and many public organisations, despite being aware of IT risks, did not keep them at acceptable levels or costs by treating them appropriately. The TCU stressed the low level of maturity with respect to the risk management process in the public administration. The TCU underlined that this situation increased the likelihood of IT not delivering results to business in the agreed time, cost and level of quality, consequently affecting the achievement of the business objectives of the entities. For example, only 25% of audited organisations had established guidelines for the management of IT risks, and only 8% were fully aligned with existing requirements. Only 13 out of 355 audited organisations had formally defined their acceptable levels of IT security risk (i.e. risk appetite).[3]

In this context, the GSI/PR developed the Strategy for Information and Communications Security and Cybersecurity in the Federal Public Administration, 2015-2018. After describing the background and context, this document set the strategic mission and vision, defined 7 strategic values, 11 guiding principles, and 10 strategic objectives with targets to be reached by 2018.

2018 to present: Digital security in the context of the digital transformation of Brazil

A new phase started in March 2018 with the publication of the Brazilian Digital Transformation Strategy (see Chapter 1), which includes a thematic axis focusing on "building trust and confidence in the digital environment", with the objective of "making the Internet a safe and reliable environment that enables services and business transactions while respecting citizens' rights". This thematic axis addresses "defence and security in the digital environment" and the "protection of rights and privacy".

According to the Digital Transformation Strategy, important progress in the area of "cyber defence" has been accomplished over the years, but Brazil still needs to improve its regulatory and institutional framework to match the challenge of digitalisation of the society and economy. The strategy claims that digital security should be regarded as a national priority and that a comprehensive "strategy for cybersecurity and defence" should be developed. The Digital Transformation Strategy points out that co-operation between the public and the private sectors is a crucial factor for the effectiveness of the actions envisaged in the future strategy and plans. It identifies several strategic actions, including the need to enhance digital security in the public administration; protect national critical infrastructure; raise the awareness of the population; enhance digital security skills in the public and private sectors; invest in research and development; develop metrics and information sharing models; as well as increase international co-operation.

In December 2018, the government published a decree establishing the National Information Security Policy (Política de Segurança da Informação, PNSI).[4] Developed by the GSI/PR, this decree sets out 16 principles and 7 objectives. It establishes the legal basis for the development of a national information security strategy and of national plans detailing its implementation, such as planning, organisation, use of resources and attribution of responsibilities. The PNSI also includes measures related to roles and responsibilities with respect to information security within the public administration (see below).

In 2019, the GSI/PR started a process to draft the National Cybersecurity Strategy called for in the PNSI. To inform the development of the strategy, it organised a consultation process inspired by the one carried out for the digital strategy. The process included a 7-month, 31 meeting-long consultation of 40 experts from government agencies, businesses and academia gathered into 3 working groups. Based on this input, the GSI/PR developed a draft National Strategy for Cybernetic Security – E-Ciber, released in September 2019 for a 20-day public consultation through the participative government platform.[5]

Forty-one participants, including 31 individuals and 10 organisations, posted a total of 166 comments on the platform. The final strategy was adopted on 5 February 2020.[6]

The strategy's vision is for Brazil "to become a country of excellence in cybersecurity". The objectives of the strategy are to: make Brazil more prosperous and reliable in the digital environment; increase Brazilian resilience to digital security threats; and strengthen Brazil's performance in cybersecurity in the international scene.

The strategy focuses on the following ten actions:

1. **Strengthening digital security risk management governance in public and private sector organisations.** This action includes holding fora, establishing minimum requirements in contracts with the public sector, promoting GSI/PR standards and norms, promoting international standards for security by design and default, nominating a chief information security officer, recommending digital security certification in accordance with international standards, etc.
2. **Establishing a centralised governance model at the national level.** A national digital security system will be created to promote co-ordination of actors beyond the federal administration, promote the joint analysis of the challenges faced in combating cybercrime, assist in the formulation of public policies, create a national cybersecurity council, create discussion groups in different sectors, etc.
3. **Promoting a collaborative, participatory, reliable and secure environment involving the public sector, private sector and society.** This action aims to encourage information sharing about incidents and vulnerabilities, carry out exercises, strengthen the national CERT (CTIR Gov), issue alerts and recommendations, encourage the use of cryptography, etc.
4. **Raising the level of government protection,** including by encouraging the use of secure communication devices, keeping information systems' security up to date, recommending the use of backup mechanisms, including digital security requirements in privatisation processes, etc.
5. **Raising the level of protection of national critical infrastructures** by promoting interactions between sectoral regulatory agencies, encouraging the adoption of enhanced digital security policies by operators of critical infrastructures, encouraging their participation in exercises and the notification of incidents to CTIR Gov.
6. **Enhancing the legal framework on digital security**, including by reviewing the existing framework, modifying the penal code to include cybercrimes, creating incentives to reduce the cybersecurity skills shortage, preparing a draft law on cybersecurity.
7. **Encouraging the design of innovative digital security solutions** in order to align academic projects with the economic demand. For example, include digital security in research programmes, encourage the creation of research and development centres on digital security, stimulate the creation of digital security start-ups, encourage the adoption of global standards to facilitate international interoperability, establish minimum requirements for 5G technology.
8. **Expanding Brazil's international co-operation on digital security.** This includes promoting discussions in international groups of which Brazil is a member, expanding relations in Latin America, promoting international events and exercises, expanding co-operation agreements, etc.
9. **Expanding digital security partnerships between the public sector, the private sector, academia and society.** Possible actions include partnerships to encourage private investments in digital security, meetings with leading digital security actors, etc.
10. **Raising the level of digital security maturity in society.** For example, carrying out public awareness initiatives; encouraging public and private sector organisations to carry out internal awareness-raising campaigns; integrating digital security in basic education; encouraging the creation of higher education courses; creating professional training courses; improving mechanisms for integration, collaboration and incentives between universities, institutes, research centres and the private sector, etc.

The strategy includes a diagnostic distinguishing between thematic and transformative axes:

- Thematic axes: national cybersecurity governance, incident management and strategic protection, i.e. protection of the government and critical infrastructures identified in the National Policy for the Security of Critical Infrastructures (telecommunications, energy, transport, water, finance).
- Transformative axis: normative dimension, research, development and innovation, international dimension and strategic partnerships, and education.

In July 2019, the government expressed its intention to adhere to the Convention on Cybercrime (Budapest Convention). In December 2019, the Committee of Ministers of the Council of Europe invited Brazil to join the Convention (Ministry of Foreign Affairs, 2019).

Governance

According to the PNSI, the GSI/PR is the primary government body in charge of digital security in Brazil, a role it has been playing since 2000. According to the 2020 National Cybersecurity Strategy, the GSI/PR will continue to co-ordinate digital security at the national level.

The GSI/PR is at the centre of digital security governance

The GSI/PR's responsibility covers three areas:

- Information security standards and their implementation: establishing information security risk management standards for federal government agencies and entities; approving guidelines, strategies, norms and recommendations; and elaborating and implementing information security programmes aimed at raising awareness and training for the public administration and society.
- Public policy: following the doctrinal and technological evolution at national and international levels; elaborating and publishing the National Information Security Strategy, in collaboration with the Inter-ministerial Committee for Digital Transformation (see below); supporting the elaboration of national plans related to the National Information Security Strategy; establishing criteria for evaluating the execution of the PNSI; and proposing the publication of the normative acts necessary for its execution.
- Products: establishing minimum security requirements for the use of products incorporating information security features, which are binding for the federal administration; these requirements are not binding for the wider Brazilian market and only serve as a recommendation.

The GSI/PR is one of the organs of the Presidency of the Republic. It is led by a minister who reports directly to the President, as do all other Brazilian ministers. The Institutional Security Cabinet is responsible for analysing and monitoring issues related to potential risks of institutional stability; co-ordinating federal intelligence activities, and providing advice on military and security issues, in addition to other supporting functions for the President.[7] Until 2019, digital security matters were addressed by the GSI/PR's Department of Information and Communications Security (Departamento de Segurança da Informação e Comunicações, DSIC), within the Secretariat for Systems Coordination, which also addresses nuclear and space issues.

In 2019, the DSIC was elevated from a department to a secretariat. In contrast with a department, a secretariat reports directly to the minister, manages its own budget and has more resources. Figure 4.4 shows where the Secretariat for Information Security stands within the broader structure of the GSI/PR. This important evolution reflects the increased awareness of the importance of digital security in the government. With a budget of USD 433 000 (BRL 1.7 million), the secretariat comprised 30 staff in January 2020 (including 8 working for CTIR.gov, see below), which represents a 100% increase compared to the previous year.

Figure 4.4. Institutional governance for information security in Brazil

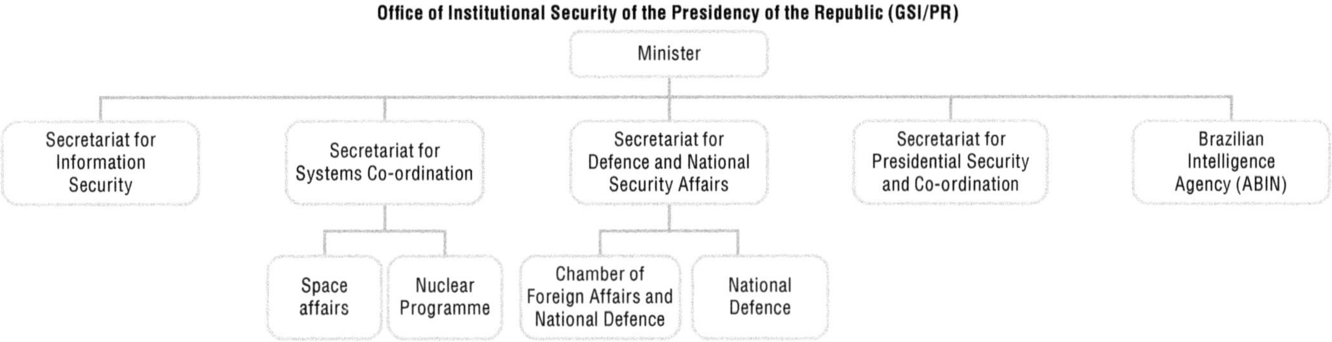

Note: This simplified overview of the Institutional Security Cabinet of the Presidency of the Republic structure does not include all of the entities of the office.

Source: OECD, based on *www.gsi.gov.br/sobre/estrutura*.

Most senior positions in the GSI/PR are held by high-ranking military officers.[8] The GSI/PR also hosts the Brazilian Intelligence Agency (Agência Brasileira de Inteligência, ABIN) and the Secretariat for Defence and National Security Affairs addresses issues related to the security of critical infrastructures, co-ordinates crisis management and carries out actions related to crisis prevention. However, many of the newly created positions created at the Secretariat for Information Security are filled by staff from other ministries, Anatel and public companies.

The Secretariat for Information Security is responsible for:[9]

- planning and supervising information security within the federal public administration, including incident management, data protection,[10] security accreditation and the handling of confidential information
- formulating and implementing the public administration's information security policies
- elaborating normative and methodological requirements related to information security in the federal public administration
- managing the government CSIRT (CTIR.Gov), co-ordinating and carrying out actions for the management of incidents, and co-ordinating the network of government agencies' and entities' CSIRTs
- proposing and participating in international treaties, agreements or acts related to information security
- acting as a central security accreditation body for the treatment of classified information
- supervising the security accreditation of individuals, companies, agencies and entities for the treatment of confidential information
- co-ordinating with the state, municipal and Federal District's governments; civil society; and organs and entities of the federal government, for the establishment of guidelines for information security policies for the public sector.

The secretariat includes three major branches:

1. The General Coordination of Security and Accreditation Centre (Coordenação-Geral do Núcleo de Segurança e Credenciamento, CGNSC),[11] which addresses issues related to information classification in the government.
2. The General Coordination of Information and Communications Security Management (Coordenação-Geral de Gestão da Segurança da Informação e Comunicações, CGSIC),[12] which elaborates proposals for information security guidelines, strategies, norms and recommendations; develops proposals for the National Information Security Plan; monitors its execution; plans and co-ordinates measures to guide information security implementation, such as for raising awareness and training; and monitors the doctrinal and technological evolution of activities related to information security at the national and international levels.
3. The General Coordination of Government Network Incident Handling Centre (CTIR.Gov), the government CSIRT[13] (described below).

The CGSI, gathering 21 ministries and government bodies covering a very large part of the federal public administration, provides advice to the GSI/PR. It meets at least twice a year and may establish up to four temporary sub-groups that cannot have more than seven members. The GSI/PR serves as the executive secretariat of the CGSI.[14] The further operationalisation of this committee and the creation of working groups is one of the secretariat's main objectives in 2020. For example, a working group within the Ministry of Economy is exploring the economic aspects of digital security in Brazil.

In November 2018, the Brazilian government published Decree 9.573 establishing the National Policy for the Security of National Critical Infrastructures. The policy aims to ensure the security and resilience of the country's critical infrastructure and the continuity of services. The policy's principles are: prevention and precaution; integration between government levels and branches, the private sector, and other segments of society; cost reductions benefiting the society resulting from investments in security; and safeguarding defence and national security. It also establishes the Integrated Critical Infrastructure Security Data System, the National Critical Infrastructure Security Strategy and the National Critical Infrastructure Security Plan. To address the complexity of digital security of critical infrastructures, a central organisation is expected to be established in order to co-ordinate all of the actors involved, public or private, as well as to call for accountability and action.

Each public sector entity is responsible for its digital security

The PNSI establishes a general principle whereby each organ and entity of the public administration is responsible for managing digital security in its own scope of action, including through the elaboration of its information security policy, designation of an internal information security manager, establishment of an information security committee, training, etc.[15]

The Ministry of Transparency and the Union Comptroller Office is tasked with auditing the implementation of the PNSI's activities under the responsibility of federal organisations and entities.

Central Bank of Brazil

In April 2018, the Central Bank of Brazil (BCB) published a resolution[16] to provide for the digital security policy and requirements on data processing and storage, including cloud computing. Such requirements shall be observed by financial institutions and other organisations authorised by BCB to operate in the financial market.

Financial institutions should implement and maintain a policy framework for digital security, respecting principles and guidelines for confidentiality, integrity, and availability of information systems and data.

The policy framework must include: the institution's digital security objectives; procedures and controls to reduce the institution's vulnerability; classification of data and information by relevance; definition of parameters to be used to assess incidents; mechanisms for dissemination of digital security culture in the institution; and information-sharing initiatives on relevant incidents.

BCB made other requirements, such as digital security policy disclosure to all employees; incident response and action plans; adoption of hard safety issues when contracting data-processing, storage and cloud-computing processes; and setting up monitoring and control mechanisms to ensure the implementation and effectiveness of the digital security policy.

BCB may rule out or restrict data-processing, storage and cloud-computing services contracts whenever it detects non-compliance with the provisions of the resolution or other BCB regulations. BCB may then establish a deadline for compliance.

BCB's technical digital security expertise relies in part on its CSIRT, which serves the financial sector and is in contact with large banks in the country.

ComDCiber (Ministry of Defence)

Issues related to national security and cyber defence, which are not in the scope of this section, are under the responsibility of the Cyber Defence Command (ComDCiber) and the Cyber Defence Centre (CDCIber), both specialised command bodies part of the Brazilian army. However, it is important to highlight the role played by ComDCiber, which has significantly more resources and staff than the GSI/PR, in particular at the technical level, and can take initiatives beyond the strict protection of the defence domain, such as the Cyber Guardian Exercise.

The second edition of the Cyber Guardian Exercise took place on 2-4 July 2019 at ComDCiber in Brasilia. About 200 members from 40 organisations participated in this simulated digital security exercise, including representatives from the financial, nuclear, electrical and telecommunications sectors. ComDCiber conducted the simulated training in a shared environment with other agencies. The initiative fostered collaborative action between government agencies, academia, private sector organisations, and the wider security and defence community.

The virtual simulation used the Cyber Operations Simulator (SIMOC) programme, which emulated computer systems used by participating agencies and companies. The constructive simulation used information technology, media, legal and senior management crisis offices, which provided solutions for security events which could impact those organisations. Discussions in crisis offices resulted in action at the decision-making and management level (crisis management) as well as at the technical level (incident response). Through SIMOC, attack situations against critical infrastructures were reproduced in electrical, telecommunications, financial and nuclear environments.

For example, the nuclear exercise comprised three groups working in co-operation: the crisis cabinet, the nuclear regulatory framework implementation team and digital systems test team. The digital systems test team used a simulator to test digital systems installed in nuclear plants, which serves as a cyber training tool. The simulator is part of a project by the National Atomic Energy Agency, developed by the Navy Technology Centre in São Paulo and the University of São Paulo. It is used by 17 institutions from 13 countries.

Participants acted collaboratively to prevent and resolve incidents involving information assets relevant to national defence. With this exercise, ComDCiber aims to integrate government, the private sector and academia in enhancing the protection of the national cyberspace.

Other actors of Brazil's digital security governance

The National Institute of Information Security

The National Institute of Information Security (Instituto Nacional de Tecnologia da Informação, ITI) maintains and implements the policies of the Brazilian public key infrastructure (ICP-Brasil), including the operation of Brazil's root Certification Authority. The ITI is also in charge of accrediting, discrediting, supervising and auditing the other participants in the trust chain.[17] The ITI is a federal agency linked to the Chief of Staff of the Presidency of the Republic (Casa Civil). It follows the operating rules established by the ICP-Brasil Steering Committee, whose members are nominated by the President of the Republic and include representatives of public authorities, civil society and academia.[18] The ICP-Brazil's Steering Committee, the ITI and accredited entities perform audits of the Brazilian PKI.[19] There are currently 17 first-level certification authorities in Brazil,[20] and 8 time-stamping service providers.[21]

Anatel, the telecommunications regulator

As Brazil's telecommunications regulator, Anatel also plays a role with respect to digital security in the country. Currently, there is limited co-operation and information sharing within the private sector on digital security, apart from trusted personal relationships between key individuals. Until now, security in the telecommunications sector is mainly self-regulated. Anatel started to focus on this issue through a public consultation launched at the end of 2018, which may result in the establishment of a committee of experts composed of all actors (e.g. operators, equipment providers, etc.) to share experiences, collectively discuss possible issues to be addressed, identify minimum requirements and best practices, etc. Anatel is responsible for certifying telecommunications equipment, including with respect to security requirements.

Anatel has adopted regulation with respect to protecting critical infrastructure and co-operates with the Ministry of Defence on exercises (cf. Cyber Guardian).

Computer emergency response teams and computer security incident response teams

There are over 40 computer emergency response teams (CERTs) and computer security incident response teams (CSIRTs) in Brazil, which can be grouped into 8 categories: 1) national responsibility; 2) international co-ordination; 3) critical infrastructures; 4) corporate; 5) providers; 6) academic; 7) government; 8) military. They co-operate in a broad ecosystem with a mix of institutional and personal trusted relationships. Two of them have a national responsibility and act as international contact points: CTIR.gov (mentioned above) for the federal government and CERT.br for the private sector.

CERT.br is maintained by NIC.br, the executive branch of the Brazilian Internet Steering Committee (CGI). It is responsible for:

- Handling voluntary computer security incident reports and activity related to Brazilian networks connected to the Internet. CERT.br collects incident reporting from any organisation and citizens. It provides a focal point for incident notification in the country, as well as co-ordination and support for organisations involved in incidents.
- Increasing security awareness. Together with NIC.br and CGI.br, CERT.br contributes to the portal internetsegura.br, which provides a wide array of educational material for various target audiences (children, teenagers, teachers, the elderly, etc.). The portal also provides links to many other awareness-raising and educational activities carried out by other entities in Brazil.[22]

- Carrying out network monitoring and trend analysis activities, including by maintaining an early warning project to identify new trends and correlating security events, as well as alerting Brazilian networks involved in malicious activities. CERT.br is an Anti-Phishing Working Group Research Partner, and a member of the Honeynet Project, with the HoneyTARG Chapter.
- Training and capacity building. CERT.br helps new CSIRTs to establish their activities in the country and delivers training for public and private sector information security professionals.[23]
- Participating in international CSIRTs fora. CERT.br leads LACNIC CSIRT initiatives that foster co-operation in the Latin American region. It also participates in the Forum of Incident Response and Security Teams (FIRST) as a member and through initiatives to improve global incident handling capabilities. CERT.br's general manager served as a member of the FIRST Board in 2012/13 and CERT.br staff currently take part in three FIRST working groups (CSIRT Services Framework, Membership Committee and Ethics SIG).

The Brazilian Government Response Team for Computer Security Incidents – CTIR.Gov, a division of the Institutional Security Cabinet of the Presidency of the Republic – addresses incidents on federal administration networks in Brazil. CTIR.Gov acts on the implementation of co-operation agreements with other federal incident handling teams, as well as with other national and international public and private CSIRTs, aiming at technical co-operation and mutual assistance on treating security incidents. CTIR.Gov provides:

- Reactive services initiated as soon as a notification arrives, followed by proper analysis of the incident and interactions with the originator. Patterns and tendencies revealed by continuous event observation serve as input to security recommendations issued to the concerned entities.
- Proactive services designed to prevent incidents or to reduce the impact of supervening events. These services are composed of information assets analysis and constitutive structures from different information technology environments in the federal administration, and provide a broad view of the available resources, their values, and associated risks.

CERT.br and CTIR have respectively a staff of ten and eight. CTIR doubled its staffing in 2019. Both CERTs work co-operatively with other trusted CERTs in Brazil and abroad. The National Education and Research Network has its own Security Incident Response Centre (CAIS).[24] With over 20 years of experience, CAIS was one of the first security incident response groups to operate nationally in the detection, resolution and prevention of incidents on the academic network.

Key findings and challenges

Brazil reached a turning point in 2018-19 with the adoption of its Digital Transformation Strategy and National Information Security Policy, as well as the preparation of its National Cybersecurity Strategy. A review of existing policy documents combined with elements collected during interviews reveal several key findings.

Brazil's primary digital security focus on national security is evolving to include economic and social aspects

The focus of digital security policies in Brazil has evolved from a technical dimension in 2000-11, to a national security dimension in 2012-18, driven in part by the organisation of mega-events and the revelations by Edward Snowden about cyberespionage by the United States. The overarching mission of the Strategy for Information and Communications Security and Cyber Security in the Federal Public Administration 2015-2018, which was to "ensure and defend the interests of the state and society for the preservation of national sovereignty", illustrates this evolution.

The 2018 Digital Transformation Strategy, which aims to "embrace digital transformation as an opportunity for the entire nation to take a leap forward", is the first Brazilian policy document to address digital security as part of a broad prosperity agenda and not solely from the national security perspective. Digital security is presented as part of an enabling thematic axis on "trust and confidence" and the recommended strategic actions primarily focus on measures that can support the digital transformation in Brazil from an economic and social perspective. The thematic axis also addresses the "protection of rights and privacy", echoing the trust policy dimension of the OECD Going Digital Integrated Policy Framework (OECD, 2019a). The Digital Transformation Strategy can therefore be viewed as a first step towards broadening the scope of Brazilian digital security policies to economic and social prosperity.

Nevertheless, the PNSI, published later in 2018, includes national sovereignty and human rights as the first and second principles, but does not consider economic and social prosperity as an objective of digital security.

A comparison of these two documents shows that this evolution is progressive. It is likely that each document reflects the perspective of the bodies that have developed it, namely the Ministry of Science, Technology, Innovations and Communications for the Digital Transformation Strategy, and the GSI/PR for the PNSI. The content of the National Cybersecurity Strategy and the consultation process carried out by the GSI/PR for its development demonstrate that Brazil is heading towards a more holistic approach to digital security, placing more emphasis on the economic and social dimension.

Brazil is at an early stage of promoting digital security across society

The general perception among experts in Brazil is that the government is starting to elevate digital security as a priority for the economy and society and that, apart from very large firms and some specific public sector bodies, most public and private stakeholders are not giving enough attention and resources to this issue.

In addition, over time, policy documents in Brazil have been using different concepts and terms to cover different aspects of digital security, including information security, cybersecurity, cyber defence, data protection, as well as related terms such as information assets, critical infrastructure, cyberspace, etc. Where available, definitions have not always been consistent over time, which can be explained by many factors, including that the approaches themselves have been evolving. However, definitions are sometimes confusing. For example, the PNSI defines information security as including cybersecurity, cyber defence, physical security and protection of organisational data; as well as actions to ensure the availability, integrity, confidentiality and authenticity of information (Article 2). This suggests that actions to ensure availability, integrity, confidentiality and authenticity are different from cybersecurity and cyber defence, which themselves are not defined.[25]

In addition, interviews carried out for this Review have shown that, beyond a circle of "information security" experts, there is widespread confusion between digital security and "data protection" (i.e. privacy protection). Many actors do not distinguish between the two areas and do not understand their relationship, including how they can strengthen or undermine each other. This situation is likely to evolve following the full implementation of the data protection law in Brazil.

This shows that the conceptual basis for approaching digital security policy in Brazil has considerably evolved over the last decade and is entering a new phase with the adoption of the National Cybersecurity Strategy.

At this juncture, a key challenge for Brazil is to recognise that, although in theory, "cybersecurity" (or "information security", depending on terminological preferences) can be viewed as a monolithic challenge, it is in reality a multidimensional policy area. In practice, it can cover at least four dimensions: 1) national security; 2) economic and social prosperity; 3) technology; and 4) law enforcement (Figure 4.5).

Actors and communities addressing each dimension have different cultures, backgrounds and objectives and can sometimes converge, overlap or compete, depending on the context and precise issue. Cryptography policy is a typical example of competing objectives, with businesses, organisations and consumers promoting the unregulated use of cryptography to support trust and facilitate e-commerce, digital governments and innovation on line, while law enforcement and intelligence call for more regulation to facilitate access to encrypted data in order to combat criminals and terrorists. Digital security of critical activities and infrastructure is another example where tensions can appear between economic and social prosperity and national security objectives, depending on the situation.

Ideally, terminology should reflect distinctions between the dimensions of digital security. For example, to reduce confusion and potential misunderstandings, the 2015 Security Risk Recommendation uses the term "digital" instead of the prefix "cyber". The term "digital" is consistent with expressions that characterise the economic and social perspective of ICT policy, as in "digital economy", "digital transformation", "digitalisation", etc. It is also common in business environments. In contrast, the prefix "cyber" is often used in relation to law enforcement (cybercrime) as well as national/international security (cyber warfare, cyber defence, cyber espionage, cyber command, etc.). The Security Risk Recommendation also uses the expression "digital environment" instead of "cyberspace", which is common in military doctrines as a domain of operations in addition to air, sea and land.

Figure 4.5. The four dimensions of "cybersecurity"

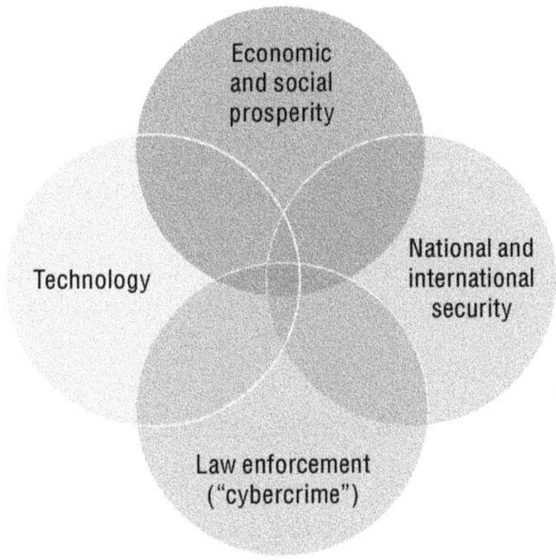

The main priority for Brazil is to raise awareness and promote the adoption of good digital security practices by all stakeholders

Brazil has made an important step forward with the acknowledgement of digital security as an enabler of economic prosperity in its Digital Transformation Strategy. In line with the first principle of the OECD Security Risk Recommendation (Box 4.2), the next step is to raise the awareness of businesses, public sector organisations and individuals about the importance of digital security to foster trust and support digital transformation; and to encourage them to adopt good digital security practices, enhance their digital security skills and empower them to manage digital security risk.

To do so, it is important to understand that, in organisations, digital security is primarily an economic and social challenge rather than only a technical issue and why digital security risk management should be a business, as opposed to a technical, process.

First, digital security incidents due to insufficient digital security risk management will potentially harm an organisation's economic and social objectives, operations, competitiveness, and reputation, as well as its customers' and users' trust and, potentially, privacy. Therefore, ensuring effective digital security risk management should be a business (as opposed to a technical) leadership's responsibility. To the extent that it can threaten the organisation as a whole, it should be owned by the highest level of leadership and followed at board level in an organisation-wide manner.

Second, although digital security measures aim to protect economic and social activities, they can also inhibit them by increasing costs, reducing performance and the openness and dynamic nature of the digital environment, which are essential to realising the full benefits of digital transformation. Business (as opposed to technical) decision makers should own digital security risk related to their business activities rather than delegate it to technical security experts. While technical security experts understand the technical aspects of digital security risk, they cannot assess the possible business impact of security measures on every line of their organisation's business and support activities. They should, however, support business decision makers as best they can to ensure their informed risk management decisions.

For example, one option to eliminate a virus from a system might be to shut down that system, clean it and turn it back on. While this may sound like a technical decision, it is in fact a business decision, because there might be negative business consequences in interrupting that system, such as stopping a production line or preventing customers from placing orders, etc. The decision maker owning the responsibility for shutting down the system should also own the responsibility for the possible negative consequences of doing it. S/he relies, however, on technical experts to most appropriately assess the technical risk and take the best-informed risk management decision.

Box 4.2. Principles of the OECD *Recommendation of the Council on Digital Security Risk Management for Economic and Social Prosperity*

The 2015 Security Risk Recommendation includes eight principles that describe how to approach digital security without inhibiting the economic and social benefits from digital technologies. It is based on the understanding that the overarching objective of digital security is to increase the likelihood of success of an economic and social activity rather than to create a state of security, i.e. entirely eliminating the risk. Security is an enabler for prosperity, not an end in itself, which is why it should be a business-driven rather than a technology-driven process. Decision makers in organisations should manage the economic opportunities and security risks from using digital technologies in tandem. To take the most appropriate risk management decisions from a business perspective, leaders and decision makers should own digital security risk management rather than delegating it to technical digital security experts. They should, however, work with them to understand the threats and vulnerabilities as well as the options to reduce the risk.

General principles

1. **Awareness, skills and empowerment**. All stakeholders should understand digital security risk and how to manage it.
2. **Responsibility**. All stakeholders should take responsibility for the management of digital security risk.
3. **Human rights and fundamental values**. All stakeholders should manage digital security risk in a transparent manner and consistently with human rights and fundamental values.
4. **Co-operation**. All stakeholders should co-operate, including across borders.

Operational principles

5. **Risk assessment and treatment cycle**. Leaders and decision makers should ensure that digital security risk is treated on the basis of continuous risk assessment.
6. **Security measures**. Leaders and decision makers should ensure that security measures are appropriate to and commensurate with the risk.
7. **Innovation**. Leaders and decision makers should ensure that innovation is considered.
8. **Preparedness and continuity**. Leaders and decision makers should ensure that a preparedness and continuity plan is adopted.

Source: OECD (2015), *Digital Security Risk Management for Economic and Social Prosperity: OECD Recommendation and Companion Document*, https://doi.org/10.1787/9789264245471-en.

Last, although they aim to create trust, digital security measures can also undermine confidence by raising suspicion related to human rights and fundamental values, in particular privacy. Digital security and privacy protection can reinforce or undermine each other depending on how they are managed. It is therefore essential that digital security and privacy protection be approached in a coherent manner, including from a legal and ethical perspective.

As a result, leaders and decision makers in organisations need to adopt a business-driven (as opposed to a technology-driven) approach that leads to the most appropriate selection and management of digital security measures, in light of the economic and social activities at stake as well as the need for trust and confidence. They should understand and be responsible for digital security risk and work in co-operation with technical security experts to take digital security decisions.

This means that public policies aiming at encouraging businesses and public sector organisations to step up their digital security should target leaders and decision makers as well as ICT professionals and experts, instead of only the latter.

Brazilian policies promote a risk management approach to digital security (e.g. the PNSI, Article 3-VIII) and encourage the implementation of information security risk management standards in the public administration. However, they primarily focus on the protection of information systems, networks and data rather than on the economic and social activities that rely on them. In other words, they approach digital security as a technical rather than as an economic and social matter. Most countries have followed the same steps, at different paces, and many are struggling to shift from a technical to an economic and social digital security approach. The development of the National Cybersecurity Strategy provides an opportunity for Brazil to make progress in this area.

Brazil should establish more robust and better resourced governance for digital security

The Digital Transformation Strategy, the PNSI and the National Cybersecurity Strategy cover many key aspects of an up-to-date digital security policy framework. These include standards and norms for digital security in the public administration, awareness raising, education and skills development, research and innovation, the protection of critical infrastructure, etc. However, most of them are addressed at a very high level, and implementation measures have not yet been defined. Implementation plans are expected to fill the gap. The definition and implementation of many of these implementation plans will require collaboration across several federal government agencies, regional and local bodies, as well as non-governmental stakeholders.

The Digital Transformation Strategy and the PNSI also mention human rights, fundamental values and privacy, as well as multi-stakeholder collaboration. These areas are particularly important, and can be challenging for Brazil.

Since 2006, digital security governance has been co-ordinated by the GSI/PR, an entity that has developed a certain degree of expertise in this area but which is characterised by its national security/military culture. During this period, some have criticised

> *the excessive securitisation and accentuated militarisation of cybersecurity; the exclusion of non-state actors from the definition of terms relevant to the political agenda; the increasing preference for solutions which seek to block applications and remove content; and the continuous difficulty of co-ordinating action at the level of the federal public administration (Hurel and Cruz Lobato, 2018).*

The GSI/PR's Secretariat for Information Security reports to the same minister as the Brazilian Intelligence Agency.

A key challenge for the GSI/PR will be to build trust with other government agencies at different levels (e.g. federal, regional, local, etc.), businesses (including foreign companies) and other non-governmental stakeholders in order to establish a long-standing partnership to promote digital security for prosperity in Brazil.

The Department for Information Security at the GSI/PR has significantly evolved over time. It has more and diversified staff, is better recognised at the political level, in particular following its elevation to a secretariat. It has also adopted a more open culture, illustrated by the working groups organised to develop the first draft of the National Cybersecurity Strategy through the public consultation held to gather input for the document. Many stakeholders have praised this evolution, noting, however, that the consultation process could have benefited from more publicity in order to involve more stakeholders. This is definitely a step in the right direction.

A key challenge is that the GSI/PR does not have competence to regulate the private sector. Instead of regulating, it publishes standards, makes their implementation mandatory by the federal administration, and encourages their voluntary adoption by other stakeholders. This includes various means, such as requiring compliance with these standards for public procurement. The general Brazilian governance approach with respect to digital security regulation is decentralised: as illustrated by the Central Bank example above, sectoral regulators are competent to regulate digital security in their area. As there is no centralised digital security agency in Brazil, sectoral regulators are invited to build upon the standards and good practices provided by the GSI/PR. This approach is closer to that of Sweden and the United Kingdom rather than France.

There is no universal model for digital security policy governance. Centralised and decentralised approaches have different pros and cons. For example, the decentralised approach enables sectoral regulation carried out by sectoral regulators to be better tailored to the sector's specificities. However, it raises the issue of each sectoral regulator aggregating a sufficient critical mass of expertise in order to be able to issue balanced and effective regulation, as well as to supervise its implementation. It also creates a situation where regulated entities may be reluctant to share digital security risk-related information with a government body tasked with regulating their activities more generally.

More generally, most governments have been struggling to set the most appropriate governance framework for cybersecurity, finding it difficult to strike the right balance between economic and social, national security, criminal law enforcement, and technical aspects. A good practice is to recognise the need for a whole-of-government approach co-ordinated at a high level of government with a view to balance the potentially competing objectives of each dimension. However, again, there is no one-size-fits-all model for how to implement this good practice. Governance frameworks and co-ordination mechanisms vary considerably, reflecting countries' history, style of government and maturity in this area.

For example, Australia, Japan and the United Kingdom have assigned policy co-ordination to the Prime Minister through the Cabinet Office. France established a national co-ordination agency within a pre-existing co-ordination body under the Prime Minister (ANSSI), and Israel created a national agency reporting directly to the Prime Minister (INCD); the United States established a Cybersecurity and Infrastructure Security Agency (CISA) in its Department of Homeland Security; Canada, Germany and the Netherlands have placed the main responsibility for digital security under an existing ministry (respectively Public Safety, Interior, and Security and Justice). In all of these cases, there are also different arrangements with respect to which agency or agencies) is/are responsible for policy and operational matters. For example, in the United Kingdom, the Department for Culture, Media and Sports is responsible for economic and social policy while the National Cyber Security Centre is responsible for operational aspects. In contrast, both aspects are addressed in a centralised agency in France. In Germany, the Ministry of Interior has the lead for public policy making but the Federal Office for Information Security has the technical competence and responsibility. Lastly, multi-stakeholder co-ordination is also concretely carried out differently across countries. In many countries, it took a couple of new versions of the initial cybersecurity strategy to set a relatively stable governance model.

Conclusions and recommendations

The new National Cybersecurity Strategy is clearly a step in the right direction. However, as the economic and social initiatives to promote digital security need to be scaled up to match the government's expectations reflected in the Digital Transformation Strategy, several issues arise.

Implementation of the strategy

The adoption of the strategy is an excellent first step, but it now needs to be translated into specific action items. In doing so, it is important to recognise that Brazil is at an early stage of development in this area and needs to take a step-by-step approach, distinguishing short-, medium- and long-term priorities.

Policy recommendations: To develop the agenda for the implementation of the National Cybersecurity Strategy, the government should build upon and expand the multi-stakeholder efforts undertaken to develop the strategy. For example, it could create a broad community of digital security leaders in the public and private sectors, academia, and civil society and hold annual meetings to develop the implementation plan and assess progress in its implementation over time. Such meetings would also provide an opportunity for the broader multi-stakeholder Brazilian digital security community to emerge, gather and dialogue, including through a national conference. It could aim at eventually becoming the main cybersecurity event in Brazil and Latin America, echoing, for example, the Israeli Cyber Week (Tel Aviv), the Dutch ONE Conference (The Hague), the French International Cybersecurity Forum (Lille) or the Singapore International Cyber Week.

Being at an early stage, awareness raising and education are particularly critical. In practice, Brazil should identify gaps in awareness and knowledge about digital security in society among businesses, governments and individuals. On this basis, it should develop an action plan to strengthen digital security training and education programmes at all levels (primary, secondary, higher education and vocational training), identify existing digital security experts who can teach and train the trainers, perhaps through a national register of digital security trainers; and encourage students to pursue carriers in digital security. The recently published National Cybersecurity Strategy points in this direction.

It will also be important for Brazil to periodically assess the effectiveness of its strategy, as experience from OECD countries demonstrate. Brazil would benefit from developing tools to evaluate the implementation of the strategy, assess progress and needs to revise the strategy.

Resources

To implement its National Cybersecurity Strategy and match the ambition of its Digital Transformation Strategy, Brazil will need to make a significant effort to allocate more resources to digital security. The government has doubled digital security resources at the GSI.PR in a single year. However, with only 30 staff addressing digital security, including 8 for incident response, more financial and human resources efforts will be needed over several years.

Policy recommendations: The government should consider allocating significantly more resources for digital security so as to ensure appropriate implementation of the National Cybersecurity Strategy. For example, each area covered by the implementation plan could be assigned a clear budget for a well-defined period in order to reach clear and measurable milestones. Resources should not be allocated only to technology, but also cover all other aspects. In addition, the government could work with the private sector and academia to better understand the cost of malicious digital security activities to the economy.

Co-ordination and decentralised responsibilities

According to the National Cybersecurity Strategy, the GSI/PR will continue to co-ordinate digital security at the national level. Is the GSI/PR the most appropriate institution to promote digital security risk management to the private sector, to encourage digital security innovation, to stimulate digital security education and training, etc.?

Policy recommendations: It seems that, to achieve the best results, Brazil should follow a co-ordinated decentralised approach, where different ministries and agencies would have the lead in their area of competence, leveraging their expertise and networks, with the GSI/PR having a co-ordination role. However, there is currently limited digital security expertise that can be leveraged outside of the GSI/PR to develop more tailored initiatives led by other ministries and agencies. One option would be for Brazil to train digital security policy experts to progressively enable each ministry and agency to start developing and implementing action plans in their respective areas.

Multi-stakeholder dialogue

Will the military and national security culture inherent to the GSI/PR be appropriate in the long run to promote digital security as an economic and social challenge and to facilitate trusted relationships with all economic and social actors? Digital security is an economic and social policy priority that requires the participation of all stakeholders. Sustainable trust between the co-ordinating government agency, other parts of the government and non-governmental stakeholders is essential. It aims to: establish a constructive public-public and public-private dialogue with a large number of stakeholders; ensure that policy measures are appropriately balanced and do not create unnecessary obstacles to the use of digital technologies for innovation and growth; create the conditions to share risk-related information with businesses; facilitate the promotion and dissemination of good practice throughout society by civil society; and ensure the protection of privacy and other human rights. The organisation and simplification of digital security governance in Brazil should aim at enabling digital security to grow while engaging all stakeholders in a sustainable manner.

Policy recommendations: One option might be to build on the lessons learnt from the Brazilian Internet governance model (CGI) to create a multi-stakeholder setting to facilitate debates and co-ordination. In addition, the government should encourage the establishment of a digital security governance structure for the private sector. It should also facilitate the creation of groups bringing together chief information security officers and other security professionals throughout Brazil, without necessarily taking part in their discussions. Such groups would then become discussion partners for the government, thereby facilitating the exchange of information on digital security threats, vulnerabilities, incidents, and risk management measures in both the public and private sectors.

Box 4.3. Policy recommendations for digital security policy in Brazil

In order to enhance digital security, Brazil should take action in the following areas:

- **Implementation of the National Cybersecurity Strategy**: Build upon and expand the multi-stakeholder efforts undertaken to develop the National Cybersecurity Strategy in order to build the agenda for its implementation.
- **Awareness raising and education**: Identify gaps in awareness, knowledge and digital security among businesses, governments and individuals, and develop an action plan to strengthen digital security training and education at all levels.
- **Resources**: Allocate significantly more resources for digital security in order to ensure appropriate implementation of the National Cybersecurity Strategy, covering all aspects rather than only technology.
- **Governance**: Follow a co-ordinated decentralised approach, where different ministries and agencies would have the lead in their area of competence, with the GSI/PR having a co-ordination role; and train digital security policy experts to overcome the current lack of experts in each ministry and agency.
- **Multi-stakeholder dialogue**: Build on the lessons learnt from the Brazilian Internet governance model to create a multi-stakeholder setting facilitating debates and co-ordination; encourage the establishment of a digital security governance structure for the private sector; facilitate the creation of groups bringing together chief information security officers and other security professionals.

Developing trust through greater privacy

Brazil passed the General Data Protection Law (Lei Geral de Proteção de Dados, LGPD) on 14 August 2018 (Law 13.709). It forms the main part of Brazil's legal framework for governing the collection, storage and use of personal data. Initially developed by the Ministry of Justice, the LGPD underwent extensive public consultation with a large number of stakeholders from civil society, academia and the business community over a seven-year period. Consultations were also held within government, involving different ministries and public organisations. Preliminary hearings and national consultations on the draft law were also subject to discussions in both the Senate and the Chamber of Deputies.

The LGPD was originally to become effective in February 2020. However, as a result of the enactment of the Executive Order MPV 869 of 27 December 2018, which was enacted into law as Law 18.583 of 8 July 2019, the term was extended to August 2020. On 3 April 2020, the Brazilian Senate approved a bill of law (PL 1179/2020) with several emergency measures to deal with the COVID-19 pandemic. The bill includes a specific rule that postpones the LGPD's entry into force until January 2021.

The next section examines in some detail the legal framework and how organisations (in both public and private sectors) are preparing for its implementation. In addition, it will review how the new law and existing data governance frameworks provide for the transfer of data to other countries.

Overview of Brazil's General Data Protection Law

Before the publication of the LGPD, Brazil's approach to privacy and data protection was either sector-specific or too broad. Privacy and data protection were regulated by different laws covering, for example, financial services, healthcare, telecommunications and consumer protection. At the same time, the Brazilian Constitution provides for a general level of protection. Enforcement was left to the discretionary powers of the national and local regulatory authorities and agencies.

The LGPD was drafted to create the conditions for greater consistency and uniformity in privacy and data protection legislation and the way individuals could exercise their privacy rights across the Brazilian territory. The law is largely based on the EU General Data Protection Regulation (GDPR) and the 1980 *OECD Recommendation of the Council concerning Guidelines Governing the Protection of Privacy and Transborder Flows of Personal Data* (hereafter "OECD Privacy Guidelines"; amended on 11 July 2013) (OECD, 2013), as well as in Convention 108 of the Council of Europe.

The LGPD takes a broad view of what data qualify as personal data, even more expansive than the GDPR and the OECD Privacy Guidelines. For example, the Brazilian law has a specific provision (Article 12, Paragraph 2) by which anonymous data may fall within the scope of the law if they are used to evaluate certain aspects of a natural person and create behavioural profiles (e.g. price discrimination methodologies).

Notably, the LGPD covers the collection and processing of personal data and information for both the public and private sectors. The processing of personal data has to be conducted in good faith and in accordance with the principles listed below, which are consistent with the principles of the OECD Privacy Guidelines:

- purpose specification
- suitability
- necessity
- free access
- data quality
- transparency
- secure safeguards
- prevention
- non-discrimination
- accountability.

Furthermore, the LGPD is concerned not only with an extensive qualification of consent, but also with empowering data subjects with meaningful control and choice regarding their personal information. The LGPD lists nine fundamental rights that data subjects have, which are essentially the same rights the GDPR mentions. Another similarity with the GDPR is that the LGPD applies to any business or organisation that processes the personal data of individuals in Brazil, regardless of where that business or organisation itself might be geographically located.

While the GDPR has six legal basis for processing personal data, Article 7 of the Brazilian LGPD lists ten (Box 4.4). There are, therefore, more legal authorisations for data processing, making it possible to interpret, at least theoretically, the LGPD as more flexible and less restrictive than the GDPR in relation to the processing of personal data.

Box 4.4. Legal basis of Brazil's General Data Protection Law

1. With the consent of the data subject.
2. To comply with a legal or regulatory obligation of the controller.
3. To implement public policies provided in laws or regulations or based on contracts or agreements.
4. To conduct studies by public research entities that ensure whenever possible the anonymisation of personal data.
5. To execute a contract or preliminary procedures related to a contract of which the data subject is a party, at the request of the data subject.
6. To exercise rights in legal, judicial, administrative or arbitration procedures.
7. To protect the life and physical safety of the data subject or a third party.
8. To protect health.
9. To fulfil the legitimate interest of the controller or a third party.
10. To protect credit (referring to a credit score).

Data portability

One of the new data subject rights in the GDPR is the right to portability, which has also been imported into the Brazilian law. Such a right mandates the controller to transfer, at the request of the data subject, their personal data to other controllers. In the Brazilian law, this right is not limited to data provided based on the data subject's consent, making it different from the GDPR.

The right to data portability is not a new right under the legal framework of Brazil. Portability is also present in other instances in Brazilian law. In the telecommunication services sector, for example, this right is currently regulated under Resolution 460/07,[26] better known as the General Portability Regulation of Anatel. Under this resolution, users of telecommunications services have the right to request the portability of their contracts (and, therefore, the related personal data) in relation to land and mobile telephone lines from telecommunication service providers of collective interest.

The LGPD imported the right to data portability from Article 20 of the GDPR, defining that the data subject may exercise this right through an express request to the provider of goods or services, according to further regulation to be provided by the ANPD. Nevertheless, there are major differences. One of them is that the GDPR establishes a major threshold that requires the specific consent of the data subject or that the request to data portability be based on an existing contractual relation in order to be able to request this right from a data controller, and as long as this is technically feasible. Further, the GDPR establishes an exemption to exercise this right when the processing of personal data is necessary for the performance of a task carried out in the public interest or in the exercise of an official authority vested in the controller.

National Data Protection Authority

Provisional Measure 869[27] of 27 December 2018 created rules for co-ordination within the government, mandating the creation of a permanent communication forum for technical co-operation between governmental bodies responsible for sectoral regulation. According to the provisional measure, the National Data Protection Authority (Autoridade Nacional de Proteção de Dados, ANPD) is considered the central governmental body of the public administration responsible for interpreting the LGPD and in enforcing the sanctions created by the law.

Provisional Measure 869 was voted into law by the Senate and by the House of Representatives and became Law 13.853 of 8 July 2019. It creates the ANPD in charge of the oversight of the LGPD. The ANPD is an entity of the federal public administration created as part of the Presidency of the Republic, with "technical and decision-making autonomy" guaranteed by the law (Article 55-B). It is composed of six main entities:

a) Board of Directors
b) National Council for the Protection of Personal Data and Privacy (Conselho Nacional de Proteção de Dados e Privacidade, CNPDP)
c) Internal Affairs
d) Ombudsman
e) legal advisory body
f) administrative specialised units.

The Board of Directors will be composed of five directors, which are appointed by the President after approval by the federal Senate. Until the LGPD's entry into force, technical and administrative support will be provided by the Executive Office of of the Presidency of the Republic (Casa Civil).

The CNPDP will be composed of the representatives of 23 organisations and bodies from the public, private and academic sectors. Its main activities will include proposing strategic guidelines and providing inputs for the preparation of the National Policy for the Protection of Personal Data and Privacy and for the activities of the ANPD, and preparing annual reports to assess the implementation of the actions of the national policies for the protection of privacy and personal data in Brazil.

Article 55-J grants the ANPD a wide range of responsibilities, from handling complaints, enforcing the law and applying sanctions to producing educational materials and guidance. The ANPD's main competencies and regulatory powers under the LGPD are listed in Box 4.5.

It is worth pointing out that the executive branch has vetoed certain sections of the LGPD. Specifically, Law 13.853 of 8 July 2019 that creates the ANPD contains a total of nine vetoes, most of them related to the administrative sanctions dealing with the processing of personal information to be imposed by the ANPD.

In addition to the above competencies, Articles 55-J, VI, and 58-B, V of the LGPD (as worded by Law 13.853, from 8 July 2019), attribute responsibility to the ANPD and its NDPPC for disseminating knowledge regarding policies and norms on personal data protection and privacy to society.

Other entities have traditionally contributed to education and awareness on privacy and data protection. Notably the National Consumer Defence System (Sistema Nacional de Defesa do Consumidor, SNDC), which congregates entities such as the consumer protection and defence programmes (Procons), the public prosecutor's offices, the public defenders' offices, specialised police offices (Decons) and civil organisations aimed at protecting consumer's rights, including the right to privacy and data protection.

Box 4.5. Competencies of Brazil's National Data Protection Authority

1. Ensure the protection of personal data, in accordance with the legislation.
2. Elaborate guidelines for the National Policy for the Protection of Personal Data and Privacy.
3. Supervise and apply sanctions for the processing of data in violation of the legislation.
4. Promote knowledge among the population of norms and public policies on the protection of personal data and of the security measures.
5. Stimulate the adoption of standards for services and products that facilitate the exercise of data subjects regarding their personal data.
6. Promote international co-operation with the data protection authorities of other countries.
7. Prepare annual activity reports.
8. Amend regulations and procedures on the protection of personal data and privacy, and conduct privacy impact assessments on the protection of personal data in cases where the processing represents a high risk to the guarantee of the general principles of personal data protection.
9. Conduct audits, or determine their performance, within the scope of the inspection activity.
10. Enact simplified and differentiated rules, guidelines and procedures, including deadlines, so that micro and small enterprises, as well as incremental or disruptive business initiatives that declare themselves to be start-ups or innovation companies, can adapt to this law.
11. Communicate any criminal offences they become aware of to the competent authorities.
12. Implement simplified mechanisms, including by electronic means, to register complaints on the processing of personal data in violation of the law.
13. Maintain a permanent forum for communication, including through technical co-operation, with entities of the public administration responsible for regulating specific sectors of economic and governmental activity, in order to facilitate the regulatory, oversight and punitive powers of the National Data Protection Authority.

Also, the Brazilian Institute for Consumer Protection (Instituto Brasileiro de Defensa do Consumidor, IDEC)[28] has conducted activities to educate consumers on privacy rights and the protection of their personal data. Idec's website contains a section with news concerning the scope of the LGPD to national consumers and has drafted an Anti-Privacy Map,[29] which seeks to help consumers protect their personal information and to not be tracked on the Internet based on the provisions of the LGPD.

Another relevant aspect of the ANPD that should be considered according to Article 55-B of Law 13.853, is "technical and decision-making autonomy" from other entities of the executive, in particular the Board of Directors, which will be composed of five commissioners including a chair (each with an initial four-year mandate), who will rotate on a staggered basis.

It should be noted that administrative and legal frameworks that leave open even a small possibility of a privacy enforcement authority being instructed by another administrative body on how to exercise its functions do not satisfy the independence criterion. Independence may not be fully achieved if, as per Article 55-A of Law 13.853, the ANPD: will be an organ of the federal public administration; will be a member of the Presidency of the Republic; will have a transitory legal nature; "may be transformed by the executive power into an entity of the indirect federal public administration, submitted to a special autarchic regime and linked to the Presidency of the Republic"; and will not be guaranteed funding in the annual budget law.

The OECD's 2019 questionnaire of privacy enforcement authorities (PEAs) collected information on the funding sources of the respondent authorities and their composition. Twenty of the 28 countries that responded (excluding the United States) were entirely funded by government grants. The remaining countries reporting mixed funding explained that other sources come from chargeable services, registration or licensing fees, fines and penalties. PEAs require considerable financial investment from governments. In 2019, for example, the Australian PEA was funded by AUD 15.85 million in government grants. The Canadian PEA was granted CAD 29.47 million and the Irish PEA received EUR 15.2 million. The United Kingdom's Information Commissioner's Office (ICO) is primarily funded by organisations paying the data protection fee, which accounts for 85-90% of the ICO's annual budget. From 1 April 2019 to 31 March 2020, the ICO projects that it will collect roughly GBP 46.6 billion through the data protection fee. In 2018/19, it collected GBP 39.3 billion in fee income (ICO, 2020).

The modifications to the LGPD creating the ANPD differ from the rest of the statute. They were legally enforceable since the enactment of the Law 13.853 on 8 July 2019, meaning that the LGPD is already valid in what relates to the constitution and functioning of the ANPD, regardless of the *vacatio legis* of its substantial parts.

However, for the ANPD to actually exist, the federal government must act to physically create it, by means of a decree and further regulation nominating its directors and establishing its composition and functioning. As of March 2020, this had not yet occurred. The emergency caused by COVID-19 adds to the uncertainty of the situation, as proposals to postpone the entry into force of the LGPD are currently being considered in Congress.

Technical measures for data protection

Article 46 of the LGPD establishes that processing agents shall adopt security, technical and administrative measures able to protect personal data from unauthorised access and accidental or unlawful situations of destruction, loss, alteration, communication or any type of improper or unlawful processing. The ANPD may provide minimum technical standards towards these measures, which shall be complied with from the conception phase of the product or service through to its execution.

Likewise, Article 13 of Decree 8.771[30] of 11 May 2016 that regulates Law 12.965 of 23 April 2014 (the Internet Civil Rights Framework, or Marco Civil da Internet) provides that connection and application service providers must observe guidelines on security standards in the custody, storage and processing of personal data and private communications. Among the obligations mandated by the guidelines are: the establishment of strict control over access to data, by defining responsibilities of persons who will have the possibility to access and exclusive access privileges for certain users; the provision of authentication mechanisms for access to records, by using, for example, dual authentication systems to ensure the individualisation of those responsible for data processing; the creation of detailed access logs to connection and applications records; and the use of records management solutions through techniques that guarantee the inviolability of data, such as encryption or equivalent protection measures.

Personal data breach notification

The notification of personal data breaches is a new right in Brazil, largely imported from Articles 33 and 34 of the GDPR, although with some major differences.

Article 48 of the LGPD establishes that the controller must communicate to the national authority and to the data subject the occurrence of a security incident that may create risk or relevant damage to the data subject. The communication must take place within a reasonable time period and in observance of the following requirements:

a) A description of the nature of the affected personal data.
b) Information on the data subjects involved.
c) An indication of the technical and security measures used to protect the data, subject to commercial and industrial secrecy.
d) The risks related to the incident.
e) The reasons for delay, in cases in which communication was not immediate.
f) The measures that were or will be adopted to reverse or mitigate the effects of the damage. After the communication, the national authority shall evaluate the severity of the incident and adopt any appropriate measures.

Where the GDPR establishes that the notification of security incidents shall be made to the supervisory authority as well as to the data subjects involved within undue delay and within 72 hours when the data breach represents a risk to the rights and freedoms of individuals, the LGPD establishes only that the communication must take place within "a reasonable time period"; a major difference that perhaps merits further clarification in the regulation of the law in the future.

Although the ANPD will officially start to function in August 2020, there is currently a Special Unit for Data Protection and Artificial Intelligence at the state level that is already monitoring the rights of data subjects, as well as conducting investigations for incidents involving breaches of personal data and information. The unit is part of the Public Prosecutor's Office of the Federal District and has handled several cases related to personal data protection, and created a mechanism for reporting data breaches and security incidents.

Likewise, Brazil also counts on CERT.br and CTIR.gov. for handling cybersecurity incidents. CERT.br is responsible for co-ordinating Brazilian entities in response to security incidents. CERT.br is part of NIC.br and acts on a multi-stakeholder basis (public/private co-operation). CTIR.br is a governmental body and is part of the GSI/PR. CERT.br compiles and has annual statistics on incident reporting.

Privacy management programmes

The accountability principle is one of the original eight basic principles of the 1980 OECD Privacy Guidelines. The 2013 revision of the Privacy Guidelines included a new part – "Implementing accountability" – which fleshes out the elements required of data controllers to implement the accountability principle, notably introducing the concept of "privacy management programmes" (PMPs). Under the revised guidelines, PMPs are the primary operational vehicle through which an organisation is expected to give practical effect to the basic principles contained in Part II of the guidelines. Specifically, the added section provides that a data controller should give effect to the guidelines for all personal data under its control by implementing a PMP that is tailored to the structure, scale, volume and sensitivity of its operations and that provides appropriate safeguards based on privacy risk assessment, including plans for responding to inquiries and incidents. In addition, the data controller should be prepared to demonstrate its PMP and provide notice, as appropriate, to authorities and data subjects where there has been a significant security breach affecting personal data.

The LGPD contains a specific section on responsibility that applies to infringements of the law as a result of the processing of personal data by public agencies and national authorities. Article 31 allows national authorities to send a report to public agencies with the applicable measures to stop the violation, while Article 32 grants the national authority the power to request agents of the public authorities to publish impact reports on the protection of personal data and suggest the adoption of standards and good practices for the processing of personal data.

Article 50 Section 2 (I) of the LGPD partially provides for the implementation of a governance programme for privacy and operation of procedures that may include complaints and petitions from data subjects, security norms, technical standards and other specific obligations for the various parties involved in the processing of personal information, educational activities, internal mechanisms of supervision and risk mitigation, and other aspects related to the processing of personal data.

Furthermore, under Article 50 Paragraph 2, Section I, data controllers are encouraged to implement governance programmes for privacy that at a minimum: demonstrate the controller's commitment to adopt internal process and policies that ensure broad compliance; are adapted to the structure, scale and volume of his operations, as well as to the sensitivity of the processed data; establish adequate policies and safeguards based on a process of systematic evaluation of the impacts on and risks to privacy; are integrated into its general governance structure and establish and apply internal and external mechanisms of supervision, among others.

International data flows

International transfers of data have increased and become very relevant for policy makers, especially with the deployment of cloud computing services and the expansion and growth of big data in recent years. The LGPD contains a full chapter on international data transfers (Articles 33-36), which largely reflects the language of the provisions of Chapter V on transfers of personal data to third countries or international organisations of the GDPR. International transfers of personal data in Brazil are only allowed under certain conditions described in nine sections of Article 33 and listed in Box 4.6.

Box 4.6. Conditions for international transfers of personal data under the General Data Protection Law

The international transfer of personal data is only permitted in the following cases:

1. Countries or international organisations that provide an adequate level of protection of personal data as provided for by the law.
2. When the controller offers and proves guarantees of compliance with the principles and the rights of the holder in the form of:
   a. specific contractual clauses
   b. standard contractual clauses
   c. global corporate rules
   d. issued stamps, certificates and codes of conduct.
3. When the transfer is necessary for international legal co-operation between public intelligence, investigative and prosecutorial authorities in accordance with international law.
4. When the transfer is necessary to protect the life or physical safety of the holder or third party.
5. When the national authority authorises the transfer.
6. When the transfer results in a commitment undertaken in an international co-operation agreement.
7. When the transfer is necessary for the execution of a public policy or legal attribution of the public service.
8. When the holder has given his specific consent, distinct from the transfer, with prior information about the international nature of the operation, clearly distinguishing it from other purposes.
9. When the transfer is necessary to fulfil the conditions of Article 7, II, V and VI, namely fulfilment of a legal or regulatory obligation; execution of a contract or preliminary procedures related to a contract to which the holder is a party; and to exercise rights in judicial, administrative or arbitral procedures.

Furthermore, Article 34 of the LGPD establishes that the level of data protection in a foreign country or international organisation shall be evaluated by the national authority taking into consideration six particular circumstances. Article 35 establishes that the verification of all of the legal instruments enlisted under Article 33 Section II will be carried out by the national authority and Article 36 mandates that changes to the guarantees presented for compliance with the general principles of protection of data subject's rights shall be communicated to the national authority.

The European Commission has not yet declared Brazil as a country that provides an adequate level of protection of personal data pursuant to the GDPR.

Likewise, Brazil, as an observer, has not yet signed and ratified the Council of Europe's Convention for the Protection of Individuals with regard to Automatic Processing of Personal Data (Convention 108) and its Additional Protocol regarding supervisory authorities and transborder data flows nor the modernised version of the Council of Europe's Convention 108+.

Cross-border enforcement co-operation

Due to the increasing demand for products and services available on the Internet and social media, co-operation in the enforcement of data protection laws is an important and decisive element to help strengthen consumer trust. The OECD *Recommendation of the Council on Cross-border Co-operation in the Enforcement of Laws Protecting Privacy* (OECD, 2007) represents a commitment of member countries to promote closer co-operation among privacy enforcement authorities to help them exchange information and conduct investigations with foreign counterparts. Section IV of the 2013 OECD Revised Privacy Guidelines highlights the importance of cross-border co-operation in the enforcement of privacy laws and facilitation of mutual assistance among privacy enforcement authorities.

Article 55-J, (IX) of the LGPD (as worded by Law 13.853 of 8 July 2019), attributes responsibility to the ANPD for promoting co-operation with international and transnational authorities on data protection. Since the ANPD has not formally been established, there are currently no bilateral or multilateral arrangements with other authorities or countries to co-operate in the enforcement of privacy laws.

Brazil is not yet part of the Global Privacy Enforcement Network[31] or similar international networks for the enforcement of privacy and data protection laws.

Data governance frameworks

Access to and sharing of data is crucial for innovation in the digital economy. For example, access to data can enhance public service delivery and facilitate the identification of emerging governmental and social challenges.

The legal frameworks and norms governing access to and sharing of personal data in Brazil presently consist of a complex regime of sector-specific laws and a patchwork of laws and regulations, including state and municipal laws that govern access to information and data protection in different sectors of the economy.[32] It should be clarified whether the aforementioned laws should coexist for some time or how they would be superseded once the LGPD fully comes into force, in order to avoid possible conflict of competencies across authorities and government agencies responsible for enforcing sectoral laws on data protection and the ANPD. For example, in Mexico, the Federal Law on the Protection of Personal Data Held by Private Parties contained a transitory article establishing that "state provisions on personal data protection are repealed, and other provisions opposing this law will be repealed" (Article 5). Although many of those provisions were not actually repealed, they are still written in law and in practice said laws should no longer be applicable.

Once the law enters into force, it will provide general rules that apply to all sectors of the economy as well as to federal, state and municipal governments. Thus, unless a provision expressly says that the LGPD is intended to pre-empt state and municipal laws that govern access to information and data protection in different sectors of the economy, one of the challenges of the ANPD would be to make sure that the old patchwork of federal laws governing the protection of information and personal data of citizens does not conflict with the LGPD. These efforts may consist of co-ordinating with the respective agencies and institutions responsible for the oversight and enforcement of the old legal framework, including the National Consumer Secretariat (Secretaria Nacional do Consumidor, Senacon) and the entities that are part of the National Consumer's Defence System (NCDS), among other law enforcement agencies at the state level.

The Ministry of Justice and Public Security through the Department of Protection and Defence of Consumers (Departamento de Proteção e Defesa do Consumidor, DPDC) of Senacon announced, on 30 December 2019, that it had fined Facebook Inc. and Facebook Serviços Online do Brasil Ltda. BRL 6.6 million (approximately USD 1.65 million). The fine is the result of an investigation after reports that Facebook users in Brazil may have suffered from misuse of data by the political marketing consultancy Cambridge Analytica. Further, the Ministry of Justice and Public Security outlined that Facebook is considered a supplier in accordance with Article 2 of the Consumer Protection Code and noted that Facebook had failed to provide appropriate information to its users regarding the consequences of their default privacy setting, especially regarding the data of users, their friends and those shared with application developers.[33]

The commercialisation of personal data of Brazilian citizens has been an ongoing national concern. The Public Ministry of Federal Districts and Territories (Ministério Público do Distrito Federal e Territórios, MPDFT) announced, on 16 January 2020, that it had launched a civil inquiry into BaseUp for the commercialisation of personal data of more than 10 million Brazilian citizens. The MPDFT highlighted that BaseUp operated a database which includes information such as names, addresses, zip codes, emails and taxpayer identification numbers which were then available for sale in different packages. The MPDFT requested the Brazilian Network Information Centre (NIC.br) to take down the website and domain name of BaseUp and to provide information on the person who registered the domain name in the Whois directory.[34] At the time of writing this report, the website (baseup.com.br) had been completely taken down and was no longer accessible.

Concerning policy initiatives for enhancing access to and sharing of data, Law 12.527 of 18 November 2011 (also known as the Transparency Law) governs access to information to public entities that are part of the direct administration of the executive; legislative, including the Courts of Accounts; the judiciary and the public prosecutor's office. This law establishes the rules and procedures for access to information requests to said entities.

Likewise, Decree 8.777 of 11 May 2016 establishes the Open Data Policy for the federal executive branch, which has nine fundamental objectives, as listed in Box 4.7.

Box 4.7. Main objectives of Brazil's Open Data Policy

1. Promote the publication of data contained in databases of direct, local and foundational federal public administration agencies and entities in the form of open data.
2. Improve the culture of public transparency.
3. Grant citizens access, openly, to data produced or accumulated by the federal executive.
4. Facilitate the exchange of data between entities of the federal public administration and the different spheres of the federation.
5. Foster social control and the development of new technologies for the construction of a participatory and democratic public management environment and better provision of public services for the citizen.
6. Foster empirically based scientific research on public management.
7. Promote technological development and innovation in the public and private sectors and promote new business.
8. Promote the sharing of information technology resources, in order to avoid duplication of actions and waste of resources in the dissemination of data and information.
9. Promote the provision of digital public services in an integrated manner.

The management of the federal executive branch's Open Data Policy is co-ordinated by the General Comptroller of the Union (Controladoria-Geral da União) through the National Open Data Infrastructure (Infraestrutura Nacional de Dados Abertos, INDA) as established in Decree 9.903 of 8 July 2019.

In addition, Brazil is part of the Open Government Partnership (OGP) and as mentioned on the OGP's website:

> *Brazil is currently implementing 11 commitments from their 2018-2020 action plan. This action plan features commitments related to local open government, open data, open science, climate change and water, legislative transparency and social control to nutritional policies.*

Recent developments

Two major public data-processing enterprises (Serpro and Dataprev), which are controlled and partially owned by the federal government, were included in a group of public companies to be privatised by the federal government. However, both companies process a substantial part of personal data in the interest of the federal government and other public bodies. There is currently a major debate on whether data subjects will lose control over their personal data as a result of the privatisation or to what extent these data could be accessed and used for other commercial purposes, as the companies will be given access to the information in the original contracts with the public entities, which include personal data. Calls for greater attention to and assessment of the data protection impacts of the privatisation should be heeded by the federal government.

Voter identification in every election in Brazil is almost entirely made by biometry (fingerprints). The electoral body, the Superior Electoral Court (Tribunal Superior Eleitoral, TSE), has collected enough fingerprints that in the 2018 elections, more than 87 million voters could be identified by biometric means. The TSE's biometric database is at the core of the National Civil Identity (Identidade Civil Nacional, ICN), a resource created by Decree 9.278 of 5 February 2019 in order to provide a backbone for the new National Identity Document (Documento de Identidade Nacional, DNI).

Brazil is currently in the final phases of preparing its National Artificial Intelligence Strategy, which has been elaborated through a multi-stakeholder process and has undergone public consultation (closed in February 2020).

There are currently three major draft bills aimed at regulating artificial intelligence (AI) in the Brazilian parliament. These three draft bills may likely be consolidated into two bills: the first is currently being discussed in the federal Senate, the other in the House of Representatives. Both propose principles to be observed in the implementation of AI, and specifically to preserve human agency and control. Both bills also go as far as to propose a national policy on AI, which, for some of the conditions and terms, is not completely aligned with the current draft National Artificial Intelligence Strategy currently being elaborated by the Ministry of Science, Technology, Innovations and Communications.

Conclusions and recommendations

Brazil passed the General Data Protection Law on 14 August 2018. The law creates a normative framework seeking to harmonise and expand the right to personal data protection. It is largely aligned with the OECD Privacy Guidelines and the GDPR, although some important differences remain, notably in relation to the governance and oversight structures.

In particular, it is noted that provisions of the 2013 OECD Privacy Guidelines in Part V ("National implementation") call on member countries to establish and maintain privacy enforcement authorities with the governance, resources and technical expertise necessary to exercise their powers effectively and to take decisions in an "objective, impartial and consistent basis" [Paragraph 19(c)]. This formulation, in the context of the guidelines, refers to the need for a privacy enforcement authority that is free from instructions, bias or conflicts of interest when enforcing laws protecting privacy.

The guarantee of the ANPD's independence is to ensure the effectiveness and reliability of the monitoring of compliance with the provisions of personal data protection and must be interpreted in light of that objective. It is established not to grant any special status to the authority or its agents, but in order to strengthen the protection of individuals and bodies affected by its decisions. It follows that, when carrying out its duties, the ANPD must act objectively and impartially. For that purpose, it must remain free from any internal and external influence.

However, the ANPD is currently strongly linked to the executive. According to the law and as specified in Article 58-A Paragraph 1 of Law 13.853, the members of the National Council for the Protection of Personal Data and Privacy will also be appointed by the President, not by the Board of Directors. Paragraph 2 of the same article mentions that each of the representatives of the CNPDP (executive, Senate, deputies, National Council of Justice, National Council of the Public Prosecutor, Internet Steering Committee) will be appointed by the respectively responsible entities of the public administration.

Besides overseeing compliance with the LGPD, the ANPD will have the main task of co-ordinating a range of different entities and engaging with the CNPDP and the Ombudsman, and other legal entities, which are likely to be distributed across the country. These various entities all play a relevant role in fostering and promoting policies on privacy and data protection. Although essentially an advisory body, the CNPDP's responsibilities and particular tasks do not seem, however, clearly or sufficiently defined under the law.

In addition, the LGPD does not specifically mention how the Board of Directors will implement the decisions and recommendations of said bodies or how said entities will address disagreement when it arises.

The development of a coherent and well co-ordinated national strategy on AI in Brazil may generate new and relevant public policies with a significant impact on the economy and social landscape of the country in the years to come. However, the strategy should be conceived and deployed with caution, taking into consideration existing policy frameworks and in co-operation with national stakeholders from different sectors. It should be well aligned with and complementary to the obligations and rights enshrined in the LGDP and other relevant national legal frameworks, and take account of ongoing international discourse in the field of privacy and data protection.

Box 4.8. Policy recommendations for enhancing privacy and data protection

In order to enhance privacy and data protection, Brazil should:

- Re-evaluate and amend the conditions establishing the National Data Protection Authority (ANPD) in Article 55-A of Law 13.709 to ensure that the Authority operates with full independence from the date of its establishment.
- Ensure that the rules for appointing the ANPD's Board of Directors and the National Council for the Protection of Personal Data (CNPDP) are transparent, fair and based on technical expertise.
- Clarify the responsibilities and tasks of the CNPDP.
- Set clear decision-making rules within the ANPD and for their implementation by the Board of Directors.
- Guarantee an adequate and predictable budget to the ANPD through a transparent process.
- Align the National Strategy on Artificial Intelligence to the General Data Protection Law and other relevant legal frameworks, in co-operation with all stakeholders.

Protecting digital consumers

Around the globe, consumers today are able to fulfil a significant proportion of their goods and service needs through e-commerce channels, in both developed and developing economies. They can do so at any time and from anywhere, and in particular across borders. Despite the many benefits that global e-commerce can bring to consumers, the complexity of the environment and the continued emergence of new business models and involvement of a myriad of economic operators may put their interests at risk. Consumers' understanding of their rights and obligations in the digital transformation are often challenged when they acquire digital content products, such as apps or games; when they purchase products through mobile devices; and when they transact with businesses located in foreign jurisdictions.

Protecting digital consumers is at the core of the OECD's *Recommendation of the Council on Consumer Protection in E-commerce* (hereafter "E-commerce Recommendation") (OECD, 2016), whose main high-level principles are listed in Box 4.9.

Box 4.9. The OECD *Recommendation of the Council on Consumer Protection in E-commerce*: Selected general principles for protecting digital consumers

1. Fair business and advertising practices.
2. Appropriate disclosures.
3. Effective processes for transaction confirmation and payment.
4. Product safety across e-commerce supply chains.
5. Meaningful access to effective mechanisms to resolve disputes.
6. Consumer education and awareness.
7. Authorities' powers to investigate and take action at domestic level.
8. Authorities' ability to engage in international policy and enforcement co-operation.

Source: OECD (2016), *Consumer Protection in E-commerce: OECD Recommendation*, https://doi.org/10.1787/9789264255258-en.

The E-commerce Recommendation was revised in 2016 to address a number of new and emerging e-commerce issues affecting consumers in the digital transformation. These include:

- growing consumer adoption and use of complex intangible digital content products and the related need for consumers to obtain clear, timely and conspicuous information about the limitations, functionality and interoperability of such products
- changing and more active consumer behaviour
- growing consumer use of mobile devices
- increasing risks associated with online and mobile payments and unsafe products.

The E-commerce Recommendation also highlights the need to provide redress to consumers involved in "free" transactions concluded in exchange for consumer data, and to address the privacy and security risks of e-commerce services, including payment methods.

E-commerce trends in Brazil

Growth of domestic and cross-border e-commerce

According to data from the Brazilian Consumer and Retail Association, B2C e-commerce sales are relatively small in Brazil, representing 3%[35] of all retail sales (export.gov, 2019; Administrative Council for Economic Defence of Brazil, 2018). Nonetheless, e-commerce sales in Brazil grew at an annual rate of 16% in 2019, far exceeding growth in the economy as a whole (Ebit Nielsen, 2020).

Brazil's e-commerce market, however, seems to offer outstanding opportunities for online retailers at local, regional and global levels. According to Euromonitor International, Brazil generates about 42% of all B2C e-commerce in Latin America. In 2017, an estimated 52.8 million people were shopping on line in the country, representing an increase of 11% compared to 2016 (Société Générale, 2019). A recent study conducted by PwC found that that 53% of Brazilians use their smartphones to research products, and 32% use online payments to purchase goods (export.gov, 2019). Increased consumer interest in, and adoption of, mobile devices to search and compare products on line, including on social media, is expected to further boost e-commerce transactions.

With respect to cross-border e-commerce, available data show that 23% of Brazilian consumers shop on US-based websites versus 9% of European consumers. Half of the Brazilian population (around 100 million people) has purchased through international websites, at least once. Chinese and other websites are also very popular, including AliExpress (45% of consumers), Amazon.com (40%), eBay (26%), DealExtreme (12%) and Apple Store (10%) (Société Générale, 2019).

Consumer complaints

Consumidor.gov.br[36] and the National Consumer Defence Information System (SINDEC)[37] are two main databases maintained by Senacon,[38] containing consumer complaint data about e-commerce transactions. As explained later in this report, while Consumidor.gov.br serves as an online dispute resolution system, SINDEC[39] provides all stakeholders with information concerning companies about which consumers have complained the most.

As shown in Figures 4.6 and 4.7, a growing number of e-commerce problems has been reported by consumers since 2017 on both platforms. The highest number of consumer complaints are related to non-delivery or late delivery of products. A number of consumers also experienced various problems throughout the transaction process, including payment confirmation and cancelling of transactions, and communicating with a business.

Figure 4.6. E-commerce complaints submitted to Consumidor.gov.br, 2017-19

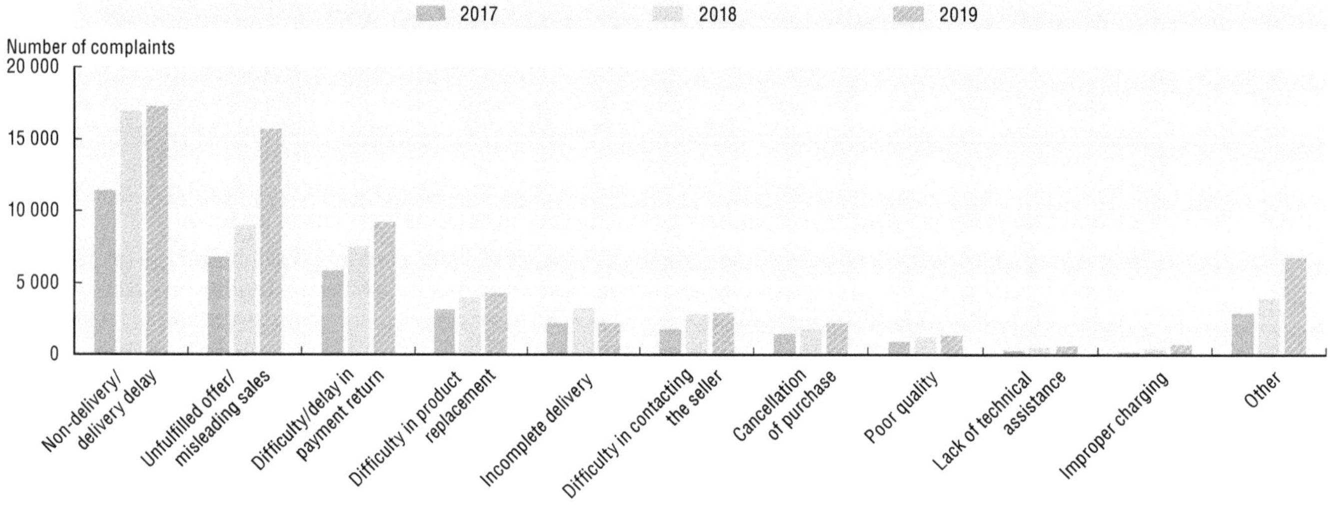

Source: Consumidor.gov.br (2020), *Indicatores* (database), *https://consumidor.gov.br/pages/dadosabertos/externo/* (accessed in March 2020).

Figure 4.7. Major e-commerce complaints reported on SINDEC, 2017-19

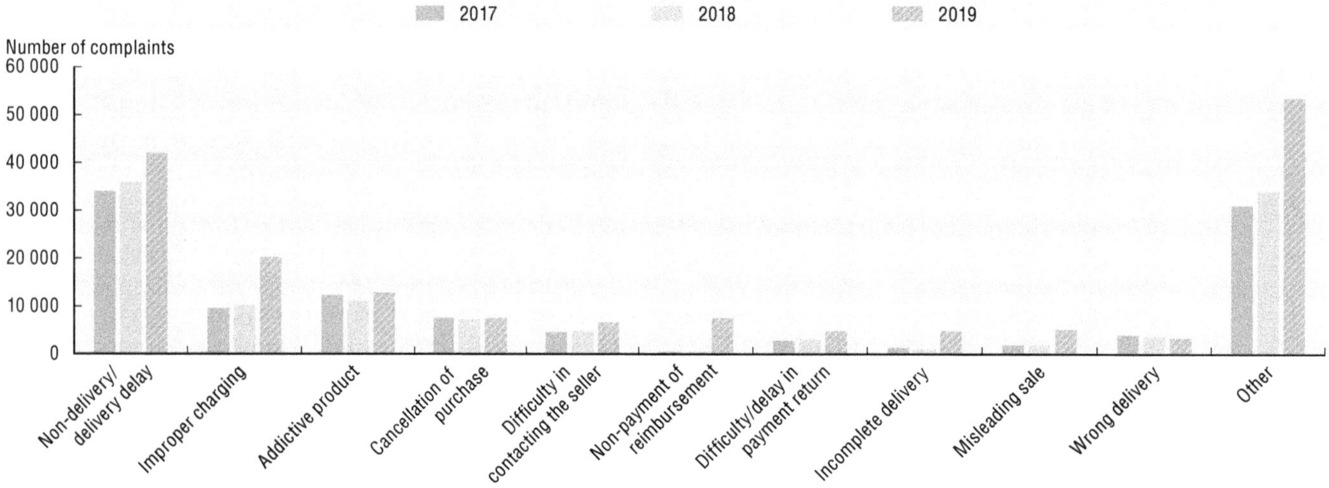

Source: OECD, based on information provided by the National Information System for Consumer Protection (Sistema Nacional de Informações de Defesa do Consumidor, SINDEC).

As shown in Figures 4.8 and 4.9, mobile phones attracted the highest number of consumer complaints on both platforms from 2017 to 2019. Consumers also encountered problems with a wide range of products, including furniture, electronic devices, clothing, and Internet and travel services. Figure 4.10 shows that a number of consumers faced problems with online retailers and marketplaces.

Figure 4.8. E-commerce complaints per product category submitted to Consumidor.gov.br, 2017-19

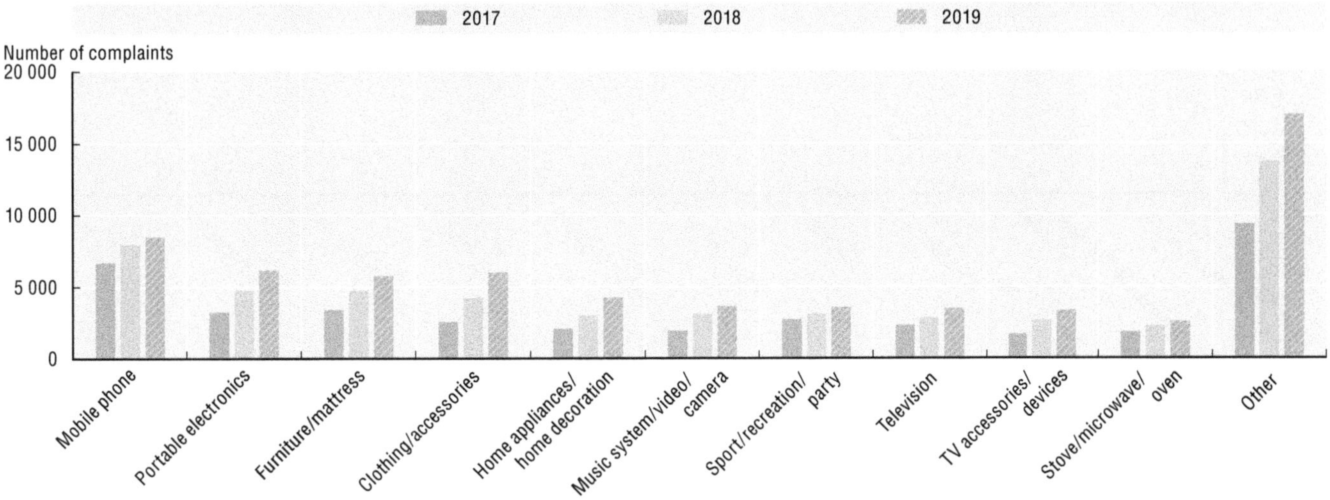

Source: Consumidor.gov.br (2020), *Indicatores* (database), *https://consumidor.gov.br/pages/dadosabertos/externo/* (accessed in March 2020).

Figure 4.9. E-commerce complaints per product category reported on SINDEC, 2017-19

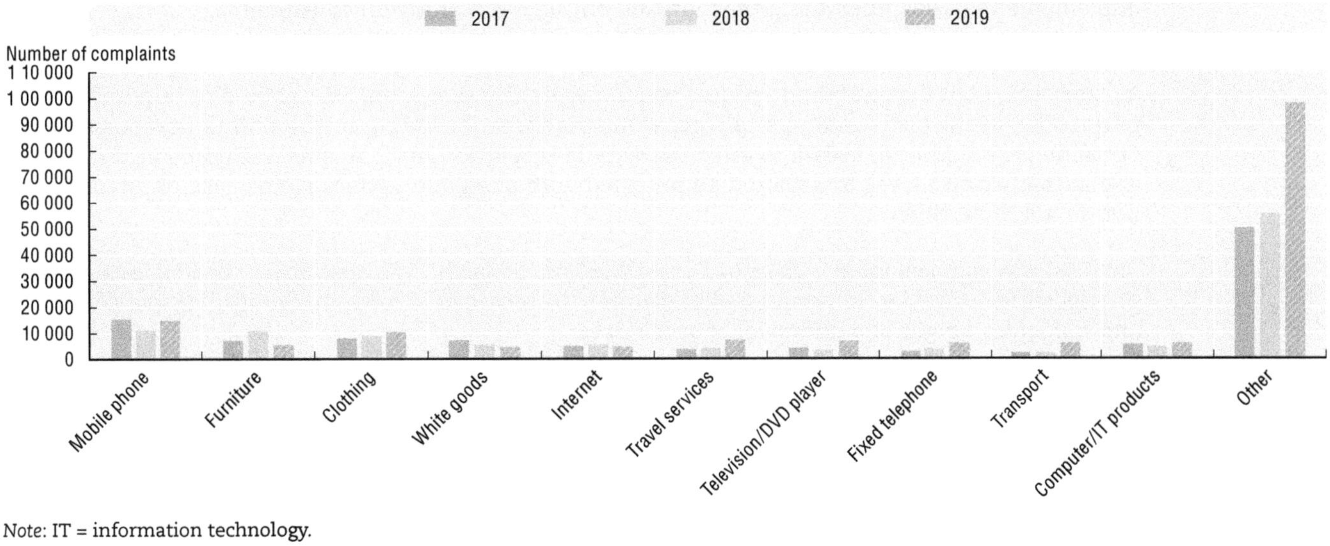

Note: IT = information technology.

Source: OECD, based on information provided by the National Information System for Consumer Protection (Sistema Nacional de Informações de Defesa do Consumidor, SINDEC).

With respect to cross-border transactions, issues associated with long delivery times (44% of consumers buying across borders) and a lack of security (31%) have also been reported by consumers (PagBrasil, 2018). However, it should be noted that neither Consumidor.gov.br nor SINDEC contains a specific issue category on cross-border transactions, thus information on available consumer complaint databases does not help to understand the degree to which Brazilian consumers experience problems with cross-border transactions.

Figure 4.10. Complaints by economic group reported on SINDEC, 2017-19

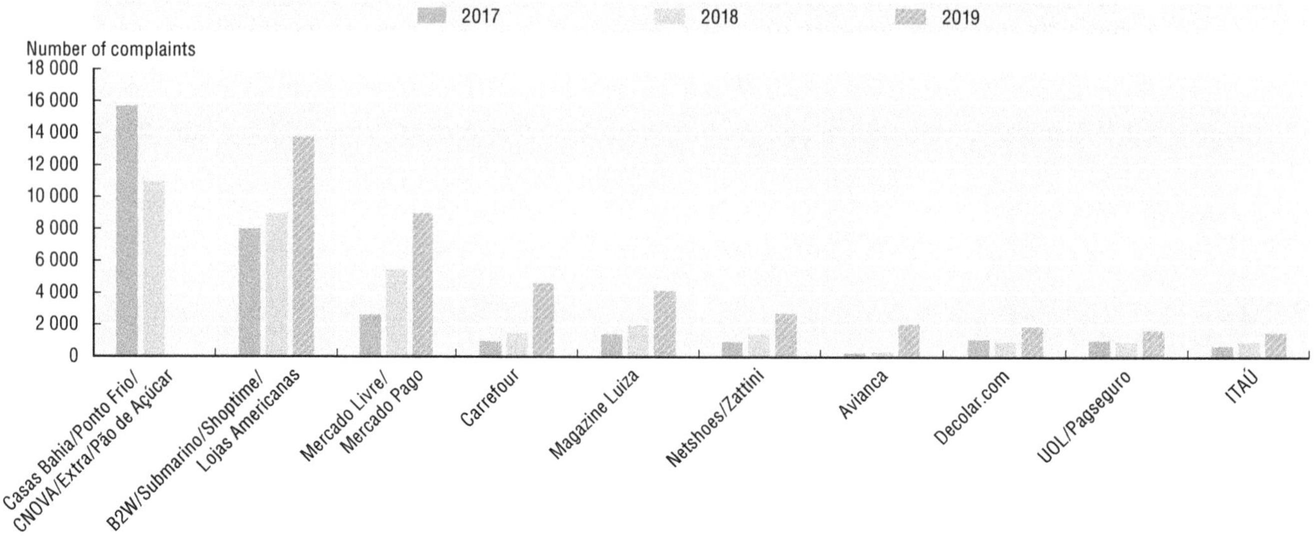

Source: OECD, based on information provided by the National Information System for Consumer Protection (Sistema Nacional de Informações de Defesa do Consumidor, SINDEC).

E-commerce policy framework

Over the past two decades, much has been done in Brazil to strengthen consumer trust in e-commerce. While most general consumer protection rights are enshrined in Brazil's Consumer Defence Code (CDC) adopted in September 1990, in recent years, a number of legislative developments have been implemented to strengthen the protection and engagement of digital consumers.

Under Article 6 of the CDC, consumers are to be provided by businesses with adequate and clear information about the goods and services on offer and the transaction. They should benefit from strong protections against misleading and fraudulent practices, including in the online advertising area. Consumers should have access to effective dispute resolution mechanisms, including at the judicial and administrative level, and should be provided with adequate redress in the case of financial and non-financial detriment.

The CDC was supplemented in 2013 by Decree 7.962 of 15 March 2013, specifically covering e-commerce. The decree identifies key information disclosures to be provided to consumers engaging in e-commerce and reinforces a right of withdrawal of seven days.

The protection of consumers on line has been further strengthened through the adoption in 2014 of the Internet Civil Rights Framework,[40] which provides the foundational principles, guarantees, rights and obligations for users of the Internet in Brazil, and lays out guidelines for action by the country's union, states, federal district and municipalities. More specifically, the law regulates the use of the Internet in the following areas: freedom of expression; privacy and data protection; net neutrality; preservation, stability, safety and functionality of the Internet; accountability of agents; preservation of the participatory nature of the Internet. Under Article 7, Internet access is essential to the exercise of citizenship and subsection XIII stipulates that citizens have the right to the correct application of norms for the protection and defence of the consumer in consumer transactions conducted through Internet.

With the entry into force on 20 December 2017 of Law 13.543/2017, rules on online advertising of goods and services sold through e-commerce have also been strengthened. The new law, which amends Law 10.962/2004 governing the establishment of prices for consumer goods and services, introduces new requirements for businesses to provide consumers with clear and conspicuous information about product prices, and with the image of the good or the description of the service.

In the area of consumer product safety, which is addressed under Chapter IV of the CDC, Brazil published two new ordinances in 2019 on product recalls (Ordinance 618/2019 on general rules, and Joint Ordinance 3/2019 on vehicle recalls). This updated recall legislation regulates the procedures for recalls of all products in Brazil, regardless of the medium or channel used by consumers to acquire the recalled product. Under the framework, a supplier who becomes aware of the unsafe nature of a good once placed on the market must immediately inform the authorities about it and alert consumers accordingly.

Institutional oversight

The E-commerce Recommendation highlights the need for authorities to have:

- the power to investigate and take action to protect consumers against fraudulent, misleading or unfair commercial practices and the resources and technical expertise to exercise their powers effectively
- the ability to co-operate and co-ordinate their investigations and enforcement activities with their counterparts in foreign jurisdictions.

Authorities with powers to act at the domestic level

The main Brazilian consumer protection authority is Senacon, which sits under the Ministry of Justice and Public Security. Created in 2012, Senacon succeeded to the DPDC, which was established in 1990 by the CDC.

Senacon's main powers and attributions are provided in Article 106 of the CDC and Article 3 of Decree 2.181 of 20 March 1997[41] that regulates the NCDS. Senacon oversees the development, implementation and enforcement of consumer protection laws, including through co-ordination with the NCDS. Senacon also maintains Consumidor.gov.br, which is a free public out-of-court service that can be used by consumers and companies to resolve their disputes arising from online transactions. In addition, Senacon has the power to engage in international co-operation with authorities in other countries. It does so mainly through the UN Conference on Trade and Development's (UNCTAD) Informal Group of Experts on Consumer Protection, the Southern Common Market (Mercosur), the Ibero-American Forum of Consumer Protection Agencies, and the Organization of American States.

The NCDS encompasses a number of public entities at the federal, state and local level, such as the Consumer`s Protection and Defence Authorities (Procons), the public prosecutor's offices, the public defenders offices, specialised police offices (Decons), as well as private entities and civil organisations promoting programmes and assistance in protecting consumers rights. Procons are responsible for co-ordinating their own local or state consumer policies. Moreover, Procons provide support for consumers and investigate consumer problems, while Senacon does not carry out these functions. Senacon's main objective is to co-ordinate the functioning of the NCDS in order to promote harmonised national policies for consumer relations.

The entities of the NCDS contribute to Senacon's general task to design and promote policies regarding consumer protection, including in an e-commerce context. Some of the programmes promoted by Senacon are: the National School of Consumer Protection, the National Consumer Policy programme, the National Information System for Consumer Protection (SINDEC), and the National Consumer and Citizenship Plan (Plandec).

In recent years, Senacon has explored ways to improve the effectiveness of Brazil's institutional framework. The agency has, in particular, signalled that it would need more resources and expert staff to engage in international co-operation.

Senacon currently has 90 staff, of which about 30 are technical experts. It has an annual direct budget of USD 950 000. According to a 2018 OECD study on cross-border enforcement co-operation across 31 countries, on average (despite great variations among countries), consumer agencies have 369 employees and a budget of USD 33 million (OECD, 2018).

The need for resources to assist in the implementation of Brazil's consumer protection framework may increase as the country introduces new measures for consumer data protection. On 14 August 2018, Brazil enacted a new General Data Protection Law (Law 13.709) and is working towards the establishment of a National Data Protection Authority (NDPA). Senacon is expected to co-operate with the NDPA to address consumer data-related issues. Moreover, following the adoption of Decree 10.197 in 2020, Consumidor.gov.br has become the official federal government platform for handling consumer dispute resolutions. As a result, issues associated with consumer data protection are within the scope of the platform, and consumer complaints regarding consumer data protection are filed at Consumidor.gov.br.

Cross-border co-operation

The E-commerce Recommendation puts a strong emphasis on enhancing and facilitating international co-operation in fights against fraudulent and misleading commercial practices across borders. The issue is becoming particularly important as global consumer complaint data show that the growing volume of cross-border transactions on line has been coupled with an increase in cross-border fraud, and a growing availability on line of unsafe products that have been banned or recalled from the offline marketplace.

In such a context, where new business models and technologies have made it easier to use virtual borders to evade regulations by setting up in one country and targeting consumers in another, deeper and more routine cross-border co-operation is needed. In 2018, more than 29 000 international complaints were reported to econsumer.gov,[42] a website dedicated to collecting cross-border complaints maintained by the International Consumer Protection Enforcement Network, which is an informal network comprised of consumer authorities from over 60 countries (including 14 G20 economies).

To date, there is no specific framework on cross-border co-operation in consumer protection in Brazil. Aside from the lack of resources to engage in cross-border co-operation, the lack of framework for cross-border co-operation has been identified as a barrier to international co-operation. Hence, Senacon should be equipped with the abilities and tools necessary to further enhance cross-border co-operation.

Senacon has signed a Memorandum of Understanding on consumer protection with seven countries, including Argentina, Germany, Korea, Paraguay, Peru, Portugal and Uruguay. Recently, it has also strengthened its engagement in cross-border co-operation within the framework of the OAS' Health and Safe Consumption Network, to address product recall issues. Senacon is one of the founders of the RCSS, which covers recalls of products, foods and medicines. Senacon has also co-operated with counterparts within the framework of the Mercosur in areas such as consumer complaints handling.

Until 2018, Senacon did not have the necessary resources to engage in cross-border co-operation with foreign consumer protection agencies nor to enhance its collaboration with the OECD and other fora, such as UNCTAD. Senacon is currently in the process of obtaining more resources (including budget and expert staff) to promote and engage in international co-operation, including to help enhance the capacity of the NCSD to collaborate with the international co-operation carried out by Senacon. Senacon has started a process for joining the International Consumer Protection and Enforcement Network, and intends to also participate in the econsumer.gov platform, once the Portuguese version of the platform is launched.

Role of industry associations

There is a large number of private associations and chambers involved in the development of guidance and policies related to information technology, including policies concerning digital issues and studies on e-commerce and Internet. These entities are not linked to the NCDS associations.

The most active private sector organisations focusing on e-commerce in Brazil are:

The Brazilian Chamber of Electronic Commerce (Camara e-net)[43] is the most representative Brazilian entity in the digital economy whose major role has been to promote security in electronic transactions, formulate public policies and improve sectoral regulatory frameworks that provide legal support to the incentive measures necessary for the development of the country. It also aims to encourage innovation, knowledge generation and the sustainable development of the digital economy. Camara e-net has eight special committees that companies may join and support their work: 1) Antifraud and Risk Management; 2) Trusted Digital Identities; 3) Insurtechs; 4) Legal; 5) Internet Payment Systems;

6) Micro, Small and Medium Enterprises; 7) Traveltech; and 8) Online Retail. Camara e-net also promotes consumer trustmarks like Clique e-Valide[44] and supports national campaigns to help consumers navigate and purchase safer on line, like Internet Segura[45] and DETONAWEB 2019.[46]

The Brazilian Electronic Commerce Association (ABComm)[47] is a non-profit organisation composed of a large number of national retail companies from the information technology sector. The association promotes the interests of technology companies with government institutions. ABComm's website contains useful information on e-commerce, including studies and surveys.

Senacon oversees the implementation of a number of co-regulation initiatives. For instance, in 2019, the telemarketing industry launched a "Do not call" initiative to ensure that businesses do not make unsolicited telemarketing calls to consumers. Similarly, in 2020, the Brazilian Federation of Banks will commence a "Do not call for credit offers" platform.

The role of consumer associations

Consumer associations play an important role in the development and implementation of Brazil's consumer policy framework. Some consumer associations, including Idec and Proteste, are members of the NCDS, and take part in the development and dissemination of consumer policy.

In addition, many consumer associations in Brazil help raise consumers' awareness through their website, publications and other promotional activities. For instance, a number of consumer associations have participated in annual consumer awareness campaigns in relation to Black Friday sales.

Dispute resolution mechanisms and redress for consumers

Dispute resolution schemes

Various private alternative dispute resolution schemes are available in Brazil to resolve disputes between consumers and businesses through the Internet. Among them is Reclame Aqui[48] ("Complain Here"), which has more than 15 million users and 120 000 companies registered.

In addition, in 2014, Senacon established Consumidor.gov.br, which is a free-of-charge public online dispute resolution scheme allowing consumers and businesses to resolve their disputes directly on line. The platform, which is monitored by Procons and the Ministry of Justice, contains a list of participating companies organised by area, including companies engaging in e-commerce. Consumers first need to register on the website or mobile app and file a complaint. Businesses have up to ten days to review it and provide a formal response to the consumer. Consumers have an additional 20 days to indicate whether they are satisfied with the feedback from the business.

It should be noted that if no settlement with a business has been reached through a private or public online dispute resolution, consumers retain the right to submit a complaint through the formal administrative procedures that are available via Brazil's government bodies in charge of consumer protection, such as the state and municipal Procons, public defenders, public ministries, and special civil courts.

According to a 2019 consumer survey conducted by Senacon, 97% of users of Consumidor.gov.br recommend the platform; and 80% of users reported that their problems were solved through the platform. However, there is a need for better communication to raise consumers' awareness of the platform. The same survey reveals that 59% of consumers did not know that the platform was also available as a mobile app; and only 25% considered the platform well publicised.

To address the issue and further promote and encourage the use of Consumidor.gov.br, Senacon has been co-operating with Brazil's national and state courts of justice. Such a strategic partnership between the judiciary and the executive has helped to reduce the volume of judicial disputes that included over 6 million consumer problems, even though the special civil courts were created to simplify legal processes. Senacon has already signed partnerships with 20 national courts of justice. In July 2019, it signed a technical co-operation agreement with the National Council of Justice to promote the integration between the Consumidor.gov.br and the PJe (electronic judicial process).

In addition, Senacon has engaged with businesses to expand the number of participating companies in Consumidor.gov.br. To broaden the membership, Senacon allows businesses to use a label "Participation Stamp" to indicate their participation in the platform.

Dispute resolution cases

In recent years, the DPDC of Senacon has opened the following administrative cases:

- Facebook Inc. and Facebook Serviços Online do Brasil Ltda (three *ex officio* cases opened discretionarily by the DPDC):
  - In one of the cases, the DPDC is in charge of verifying alleged illegal consumer data sharing by the above-mentioned Facebook companies. The case opened in 2018; the administrative process was launched in March 2019.
  - In another case, the DPDC found alleged illicit access of Facebook user accounts in Brazil through the Facebook platform collecting personal data, such as names, emails, phone numbers, visited places and Internet searches. The case was opened in 2018 and the administrative process launched in March 2019.
  - A third case concerns the verification of the use of sensitive personal data, including cardio-frequency and menstrual cycles, collected by associated apps, including from people that were not actual users of Facebook. The case started in February 2019 and is currently in a preliminary verification phase.
- Google Brasil Internet Ltda. The DPDC received a formal complaint by the Public Prosecutor's Office of the state of Piauí concerning access to personal emails sent via Gmail without the express consent of Gmail's users. An administrative procedure was launched in February 2019.[49]
- OI (TNL PCS S/A). The DPDC opened an investigation against the former Brazilian telecom company OI concerning alleged irregularities in the technology capable of mapping and tracking consumers' Internet browsing and purchasing history, for advertising purposes. The administrative process was launched in February 2019.

Education and awareness

One relevant instrument that Brazil developed in this area was the Foreign Consumer Guide[50] created by the Procon of the state of Parana under the supervision of the Brazilian Institute for Metrology, Standardisation and Industrial Quality (INMETRO).[51] The main purpose of the guide is to provide guidance to foreign consumers in Brazil on their rights and obligations in their relations with businesses and entities in different areas of the economy. The guide was drafted based on the rights and obligations of businesses and consumers in the CDC. It contained information such as where to file a complaint and how to obtain legal redress and provides a list of consumer and defence organisations and associations that may support consumers through their disputes. It has not, however, been updated.

The National School of Consumer Protection (NSCP)[52] was created on 13 August 2007, through Ministerial Ordinance 1.377. It is actively engaged in fostering knowledge and education on consumer protection by providing specially designed training to members of the NCDS across the country, as well as building specific knowledge on consumer relations, which are essential for the elaboration of public policies. The NSCP has a large number of digital manuals and guides to protect consumer rights. For example, it created a guide on data protection in consumer relations and credit information. The NSCP has a partnership with the University of Brasilia to implement an official certification system. It has expanded its public education programmes by engaging other national public agencies like the National Health Surveillance Agency; the National Civil Aviation Agency; the Central Bank of Brazil; the National Telecommunications Agency; the Ministry of Agriculture, Livestock and Supply; and the National Health Agency, among others.

New initiatives have been implemented in recent years to educate and raise consumer's awareness of their rights in e-commerce and to increase their digital competence. For instance, Senacon produced an educational video on consumer issues related to the digital economy.[53] In addition, educational programmes targeting vulnerable or disadvantaged consumers have been developed, which look at the impact of social media on the youths' consumption trends.[54]

Conclusion and policy recommendations

Box 4.10 contains proposed recommendations from the OECD for Brazil to enhance consumer protection and empowerment, and to improve its evidence base for consumer policy decision making.

Box 4.10. Policy recommendations for consumer protection and empowerment

In order to enhance consumer protection and empowerment, Brazil should:

- Establish a framework for analysing consumer complaints data and identify issues requiring policy and enforcement responses to protect digital consumers.
- Collect and analyse consumer complaints data that are specific to cross-border transactions to better understand the nature and scale of consumer issues associated with transactions across borders.
- Provide relevant domestic authorities, such as Senacon, with adequate powers, tools and resources to enhance their participation in cross-border co-operation for consumer protection. This could include participation in the activities of the International Consumer Protection and Enforcement Network.
- Improve the effectiveness of the government's dispute resolution and redress platform, Consumidor.gov.br, by evaluating consumer usage and satisfaction of the platform and further raising consumer awareness of the database, while looking into unresolved cases.

References

Administrative Council for Economic Defence of Brazil (2018), *Implications of E-commerce for Competition Policy: Note by Brazil*, *https://one.oecd.org/document/DAF/COMP/WD(2018)37/en/pdf*.

Baptista Luz (2017), *Current Legislation on Data Protection in Brazil*, white paper, Baptista Luz Advocados, *http://baptistaluz.com.br/wp-content/uploads/2017/11/Privacy-Hub-Leis-Setoriais.pdf*.

Cert.br (2020), *Estatísticas dos Incidentes Reportados ao CERT.br* [Statistics on the Incidents Reported to CERT.br], *https://www.cert.br/stats/incidentes* (accessed on 8 March 2020).

Cetic.br (2018), "A8. Estabelecimentos de saúde, por existência de documento que define uma política de segurança da informação" [Health establishments, due to the existence of a document that defines an information security policy], *TIC Saúde 2018*, Comitê Gestor da Internet no Brasil, São Paulo, *https://www.cetic.br/tics/saude/2018/estabelecimentos/A8*.

Consumidor.gov.br (2020), *Indicatores* [Indicators] (database), *https://consumidor.gov.br/pages/dadosabertos/externo/* (accessed in March 2020).

CTIR.br (2020), *Estatísticas Resultantes do Trabalho de Detecção, Triagem, Análise e Resposta a Incidentes Cibernéticos* [Statistics Based on the Work of Detection, Screening, Analysis and Response to Cyber Incidents], *https://emnumeros.ctir.gov.br* (accessed on 9 March 2020).

Demetrio, A. (2012), "Na Rio+20, Exército testa estratégias de defesa virtual em grandes eventos" [At Rio + 20, Army tests virtual defense strategies at major events], G1, *http://g1.globo.com/tecnologia/noticia/2012/05/na-rio20-exercito-testa-estrategias-de-defesa-virtual-em-grandes-eventos.html*.

Ebit Nielsen (2020), *Webshoppers 41ª* Edição [Webshoppers 41st Edition], *www.ebit.com.br/webshoppers*.

EUROPOL (2018), *Internet Organised Crime Threat Assessment (IOCTA) 2018*, European Agency for Law Enforcement Cooperation, *https://www.europol.europa.eu/sites/default/files/documents/iocta2018.pdf*.

export.gov (2019), *Brazil: eCommerce*, *https://legacy.export.gov/article?id=Brazil-e-Commerce* (accessed on 27 January 2020).

GSI (2015), *Estratégia de Segurança da Informação e Comunicações e de Segurança Cibernética da Administração Pública Federal 2015-2018* [Federal Public Administration Information and Communications Security and Cybersecurity Strategy 2015-2018], *http://dsic.planalto.gov.br/legislacao/4_Estrategia_de_SIC.pdf/view*.

GSI/PR (2010), *Livro Verde: Segurança Cibernética no Brasil* [Green Paper: Cybersecurity in Brazil], Presidência da República, Brasilia, *http://dsic.planalto.gov.br/legislacao/1_Livro_Verde_SEG_CIBER.pdf*.

Hurel, L.M. and L. Cruz Lobato (2018), *A Strategy for Cybersecurity Governance in Brazil*, Strategic Note 30, Instituto Igarapé, Rio de Janeiro, *https://igarape.org.br/wp-content/uploads/2019/01/A-Strategy-for-Cybersecurity-Governance-in-Brazil.pdf*.

ICO (2020), "How we are funded", Information Commissioner's Office, Wilmslow, United Kingdom, *https://ico.org.uk/about-the-ico/who-we-are/how-we-are-funded*.

Insurancecorp (2019), *MARSH/JLT Lança Estudo Sobre Segurança Cibernética* [MARSH/JLT Launches Cybersecurity Study], *http://insurancecorp.com.br/pt/2019/05/14/marsh-jlt-lanca-estudo-sobre-seguranca-cibernetica/*.

LexisNexis Threatmetrix (2019), *LexisNexis Risk Solutions Cybercrime Report: Global Insights from the LexisNexis Digital Identity Network January-June 2019*, LexisNexis Risk Solutions, *https://www.threatmetrix.com/wp-content/uploads/2019/09/lnrs-cybercrime-report-1568230431.pdf*.

Ministry of Foreign Affairs (2019), *Processo de adesão à Convenção de Budapeste – Nota Conjunta do Ministério das Relações Exteriores e do Ministério da Justiça e Segurança Pública* [Accession Process to the Budapest Convention – Joint Note from the Ministry of Foreign Affairs and the Ministry of Justice and Public Security], Note 309, *www.itamaraty.gov.br/pt-BR/notas-a-imprensa/21146-processo-de-adesao-a-convencao-de-budapeste-nota-conjunta-do-ministerio-das-relacoes-exteriores-e-do-ministerio-da-justica-e-seguranca-publica*.

Norton (2018), *Cyber Safety Insights Report Global Results*, *www.nortonlifelock.com/content/dam/nortonlifelock/pdfs/reports/2018-norton-lifelock-cyber-safety-insights-report-global-results-en.pdf*.

OECD (2019a), Going *Digital: Shaping Policies, Improving Lives*, OECD Publishing, Paris, *https://doi.org/10.1787/9789264312012-en*.

OECD (2019b), *Recommendation of the Council on Digital Security of Critical Activities*, OECD, Paris, *https://legalinstruments.oecd.org/en/instruments/OECD-LEGAL-0456*.

OECD (2019c), *Unpacking E-commerce: Business Models, Trends and Policies*, OECD Publishing, Paris, *https://dx.doi.org/10.1787/23561431-en*.

OECD (2018), "Consumer protection enforcement in a global digital marketplace", *OECD Digital Economy Papers*, No. 266, OECD Publishing, Paris, *https://doi.org/10.1787/f041eead-en*.

OECD (2016), *Consumer Protection in E-commerce: OECD Recommendation*, OECD Publishing, Paris, *https://doi.org/10.1787/9789264255258-en*.

OECD (2015), *Digital Security Risk Management for Economic and Social Prosperity: OECD Recommendation and Companion Document*, OECD Publishing, Paris, *https://doi.org/10.1787/9789264245471-en*.

OECD (2013), *Recommendation of the Council concerning Guidelines Governing the Protection of Privacy and Transborder Flows of Personal Data*, OECD, Paris, *https://legalinstruments.oecd.org/en/instruments/OECD-LEGAL-0188*.

OECD (2007), *Recommendation of the Council on Cross-border Co-operation in the Enforcement of Laws Protecting Privacy*, OECD, Paris, *https://legalinstruments.oecd.org/en/instruments/OECD-LEGAL-0352*.

PagBrasil (2018), *Brazil Ecommerce Report 2018*, PagBrazil, *https://www.pagbrasil.com/news/brazil-ecommerce-report-2018* (accessed on 27 January 2020).

Ponemon (2017), *2017 Cost of Data Breach Study: Brazil*, Ponemon Institute LLC, Traverse City, Michigan, *https://www.ibm.com/downloads/cas/EGGP7BBZ*.

Société Générale (2019), *Brazilian Market: E-commerce*, Société Générale, *https://import-export.societegenerale.fr/en/country/brazil/ecommerce?accepter_cookies=oui* (accessed on 27 January 2020).

Notes

Israel

The statistical data for Israel are supplied by and under the responsibility of the relevant Israeli authorities. The use of such data by the OECD is without prejudice to the status of the Golan Heights, East Jerusalem and Israeli settlements in the West Bank under the terms of international law.

1. Available at: *www.planalto.gov.br/ccivil_03/decreto/D3505.htm*.
2. Marco Civil da Internet, regulatory process of Law 12.965/2014, available at: *https://www.cgi.br/pagina/marco-civil-law-of-the-internet-in-brazil/180*.
3. Judgment 3117/2014-TCU-Plenary of 12 November 2014, referring to TCU Case No. 003,732/2014-2, available at: *https://portal.tcu.gov.br/lumis/portal/file/fileDownload.jsp?fileId=8A8182A14D78C1F1014D794C57073235*.
4. Decree 9.637 of 26 December 2018, available at: *www.planalto.gov.br/CCIVIL_03/_Ato2015-2018/2018/Decreto/D9637.htm*.
5. Available at: *http://participa.br/seguranca-cibernetica/estrategia-nacional-de-seguranca-cibernetica-e-ciber*.
6. Official Gazette, published on 6 February 2020, Vol. 26, Section 1, Page 6, Decree 10.222 of 5 February 2020.
7. Information available at: *www.brazil.gov.br/government/how-the-government-works/federal-executive-branch*.
8. Decree 9.668 of 2 January 2019, Article 26.
9. Decree 9.668 of 2 January 2019, available at: *www.gsi.gov.br/sobre/estrutura/secretaria-de-coordenacao-de-sistemas*.
10. Until the entry into force of the *General Data Protection Law*.
11. Information available at: *http://dsic.planalto.gov.br/coordenacoes-gerais/cgnsc*.
12. Information available at: *http://dsic.planalto.gov.br/coordenacoes-gerais/cggsic*.
13. Information available at: *www.ctir.gov.br*.
14. PNSI, Articles 9-11.
15. PNSI, Article 15.
16. Resolution No. 4.658 of 26 April 2018, available at: *www.bcb.gov.br/pre/normativos/busca/downloadNormativo.asp?arquivo=/Lists/Normativos/Attachments/50581/Res_4658_v1_O.pdf*.
17. Information available at: *https://www.iti.gov.br/icp-brasil*.
18. Information available at: *https://www.iti.gov.br/comite-gestor*.
19. Information available at: *https://www.iti.gov.br/auditoria*.

20. Available at: *https://estrutura.iti.gov.br*.
21. Available at: *https://www.iti.gov.br/icp-brasil/estrutura*.
22. Available at: *https://internetsegura.br/outras-iniciativas*.
23. Available at: *https://www.cert.br/cursos/index-en.html*.
24. Available at: *https://www.rnp.br/sistema-rnp/cais/tratamento-de-incidentes*.
25. Article 6 of the PNSI, which describes modules of the future National Cybersecurity Strategy, raises similar questions: cybersecurity; cyber defence; security of critical infrastructures; security of confidential information; and protection against data leakage.
26. Available at: *https://www.anatel.gov.br/legislacao/resolucoes/22-2007/8-resolucao-460*.
27. Available at: *www.planalto.gov.br/ccivil_03/_ato2015-2018/2018/Mpv/mpv869.htm*.
28. *https://idec.org.br*.
29. Available at: *https://idec.org.br/ferramenta/anti-mapa-de-privacidade*.
30. Available at: *www.planalto.gov.br/ccivil_03/_Ato2015-2018/2016/Decreto/D8771.htm*.
31. The Global Privacy Enforcement Network is an informal public network designed to promote cooperation on practical aspects of the enforcement of privacy and data protection laws. This network provides a list of official points of contact for participating authorities to facilitate investigations and enforcement co-operation on specific matters and to share experiences and best practices on enforcing issues and investigative techniques.
32. One study shows that Brazil currently has more than 40 sectoral laws and regulations that regulate data protection directly or indirectly (see Baptista Luz [2017]). For instance, the Civil Code sets forth the right to one's private life as a personal right that is neither assignable nor waivable by its subject in any circumstances. The Consumer Defence Code of 1990 establishes specific rules for the collection, processing, transfer, disclosure and storage of consumer data and the requirements for companies to obtain the unambiguous consent from consumers to conduct their activities, as well as specific data subject rights like access to information and the right to data rectification.

    The Internet Civil Legal Framework (Marco Civil da Internet) sets forth principles, rules, rights and obligations of Internet users in Brazil. The law contains specific rules on the collection, processing and storage of personal data and the transfer of data to third parties, as well as obligations on transparency, data minimisation and implementation of security measures by data controllers.
33. See the Ministry of Justice and Public Security's press release of 30 December 2019 at: *https://www.novo.justica.gov.br/news/mjsp-multa-facebook-em-r-6-6-milhoes*.
34. The MPDFT's Civil Inquiry No. 03/2020 of 16 January 2020 and its request to NIC.br for the takedown of the domain name is available at: *https://www.mpdft.mp.br/portal/index.php/comunicacao-menu/sala-de-imprensa/noticias/noticias-2020/11547-mpdft-investiga-empresa-que-vende-dados-de-cidadaos-na-internet*.
35. The OECD average in 2017 was around 9% (OECD, 2019c).
36. Available at: *https://www.consumidor.gov.br*.
37. Available at: *https://sindecnacional.mj.gov.br*.
38. Senacon is the National Consumer Secretariat of the Ministry of Justice and Public Security, and is in charge of developing, promoting, co-ordinating and implementing Brazil's consumer policy framework.
39. Senacon is introducing a new consumer complaint database "Pro Consumidor", which will gradually replace SINDEC from 2020.
40. Law 12.965 of 23 April 2014, available at: *www.planalto.gov.br/ccivil_03/_ato2011-2014/2014/lei/l12965.htm*.
41. Available at: *www.planalto.gov.br/ccivil_03/decreto/D2181.htm*.
42. Available at: *https://www.econsumer.gov/#crnt*.
43. Available at: *https://www.camara-e.net*.
44. Available at: *https://e-mpe.com*.
45. Available at: *www.internetsegura.org*.
46. Available at: *https://www.detonaweb.com.br/pme*.
47. Available at: *https://abcomm.org*.
48. Available at: *https://www.reclameaqui.com.br*.
49. A summary abstract of this case is available at: *https://globaldatareview.com/article/1180225/google-facing-proceedings-in-brazil-over-email-scanning*.

50. Available at: *https://www.justica.gov.br/seus-direitos/consumidor/educacao-para-o-consumo/guia-do-consumidor-estrangeiro/anexos-1/guia_eng.pdf*.
51. Available at: *www4.inmetro.gov.br*.
52. Available at: *https://defesadoconsumidor.gov.br/escolanacional*.
53. The video is available at: *https://www.defesadoconsumidor.gov.br/portal/ultimas-noticias/1165-mjsp-lanca-quarto-video-do-programa-se-liga-consumidor*.
54. More information is available at: *https://www.defesadoconsumidor.gov.br/escolanacional/cursos/lista-de-cursos-em-andamento*.

Chapter 5

UNLEASHING DIGITAL INNOVATION

After two years of recession in 2015 and 2016, the Brazilian economy was gradually recovering, when the coronavirus (Covid-19) outbreak hit. The economy is projected to contract by more than 9.1% during 2020 in the double-hit scenario, which assumes a second lockdown in Brazil at the end of the year. The recovery in 2021 would be moderate in this scenario, with projected growth of 2.4%. In the single-hit scenario, the economy is projected to contract by 7.4% during 2020, followed by an expansion of 4.2% in 2021. As lockdown measures are eased and activity resumes, the economy is projected to recover slowly and partially, but some jobs and firms will not be able to survive. Unemployment is predicted to reach historic highs before receding gradually (OECD, 2020a).

As productivity growth has remained stagnant and a declining working age population limits the prospects for further growth, Brazil may need to change its economic model. The digital transformation can offer new pathways for growth, through new and improved products and services, the improvement of traditional ones, and the creation of new business models. Digital innovation also has the potential to contribute to solving Brazil's most pressing social challenges, such as the efficiency of the health system, more sustainable agriculture, and urban mobility and security, to name a few.

This chapter examines the key features of the Brazilian system for science, technology and innovation. The first section provides an overview of its main strengths and weaknesses, and the policy responses adopted in recent years to overcome its main challenges. The second section looks at policies and instruments the country is devising to foster digital innovation.

Innovation in the Brazilian economy

Innovation is mostly state driven

Investment in knowledge is key to driving and adapting to the digital transformation. Brazil has made significant progress over the past two decades in modernising its policies and institutions to support R&D and innovation. It has succeeded in placing itself at the frontier of innovation in some "islands of productive excellence", such as oil and gas, aviation, agriculture, and the health sectors (Mazzucato and Penna, 2016). However, the overall innovation system continues to underperform and innovation activities have not resulted in productivity gains, competitiveness enhancement or a stronger presence in the global value chain (World Economic Forum, 2018).

In 2017 (latest available year), investment in R&D amounted to 1.26% of gross domestic product (GDP), higher than in other Latin American and Caribbean countries, but below most OECD countries (Figure 5.1A). The National Strategy for Science, Technology and Innovation (Estratégia Nacional de Ciência, Tecnologia e Inovação, ENCTI) 2016-2022 has set the ambitious target to increase R&D expenditure to 2% of GDP by 2022 (MCTIC, 2016). This target, however, may not be met, given the downward trajectory in spending in R&D since 2016. Economic recession and fiscal austerity have impacted the financing of R&D and innovation in the country. The adoption of a new fiscal rule in the federal Constitution in December 2016, which establishes a zero real growth for federal "discretionary expenses" for 20 years, maintains those expenditures at 2016 levels, with adjustments only allowed for inflation. This rule, therefore, limits public investment in R&D and innovation; the main agencies financing research in the country have all seen a decrease in their budget in recent years (Figure 5.7).

The gap with developed and emerging economies concerns in particular the source of funding for R&D (Figure 5.1B). Across OECD economies, businesses are the main source of R&D expenditure, with an average contribution of 62%. In Brazil, business expenditure represents only about half of total R&D. The contribution of the ICT sector, accounting for about 15% of the total R&D business expenditure in 2014 (the latest year for which data are available), is also much lower than the OECD average (35%) (Figure 5.2).

Data from the 2016 Brazilian Business R&D and Innovation Survey (Pesquisa de Inovação, PINTEC) show that only 36% of surveyed firms declared that they carried out innovations between 2012 and 2014. Firms in the ICT sector showed a higher propensity to innovate, particularly in products, whereas firms in the other sectors mostly report process-oriented innovations (Figure 5.3). Most of innovations, however, involve the adoption of existing technologies, as only a relatively small share of them are new to the Brazilian market. Firms in the ICT manufacturing and services sub-sectors have shown slight improvements over the years, compared to an overall deterioration in the innovative capacity of firms and of those in the telecommunications sub-sector (Figure 5.4).

Figure 5.1. R&D expenditure in Brazil, the OECD and selected countries

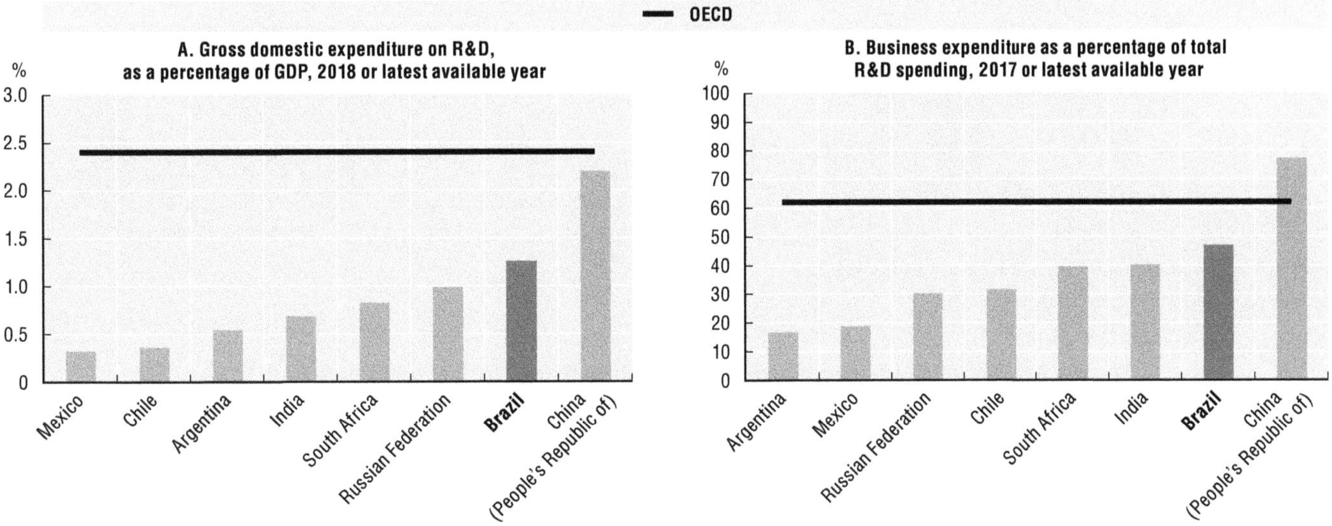

Notes: R&D = research and development; GDP = gross domestic product. Panel A: Data for India refer to 2015. Data for Argentina and South Africa refer to 2016. Data for Brazil and Chile refer to 2017. Panel B: Data for India and South Africa refer to 2016.

Sources: OECD (2020b), *Main Science and Technology Indicators* (database), *http://oe.cd/msti* (accessed in March 2020); data for Brazil are from MCTIC (2019a), *Indicadores Nacionais de Ciência, Tecnologia e Inovação 2018*, *https://www.mctic.gov.br/mctic/opencms/indicadores/indicadores_cti.html*; data for India are from Ministry of Science and Technology (2017), *Research and Development Statistics 2017-18.*

Figure 5.2. Business R&D of the ICT sector in Brazil and selected countries, 2016 or latest available year

As a share of total business R&D expenditure

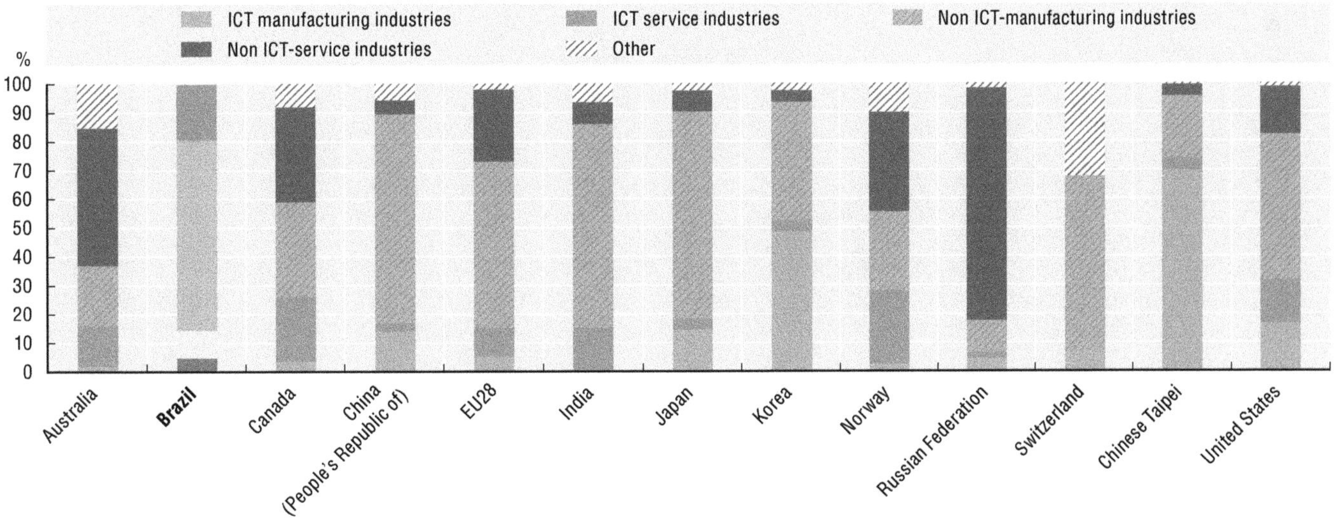

Notes: BERD = business expenditure on research and development; ICT = information and communication technology. "Other" includes: Agriculture, mining and quarrying, energy and construction. Data for India refer to 2013, for Brazil to 2014 and for Switzerland to 2015. "Other" includes non-ICT service industry for Brazil and service industries (ICT and non-ICT) for Switzerland.

Source: Mas et al. (2019), *2019 PREDICT Key Facts Report. An Analysis of ICT R&D in the EU and Beyond*, *https://doi.org/10.2760/06479*.

Figure 5.3. Innovative firms in Brazil, by sector, 2014

As a percentage of all firms

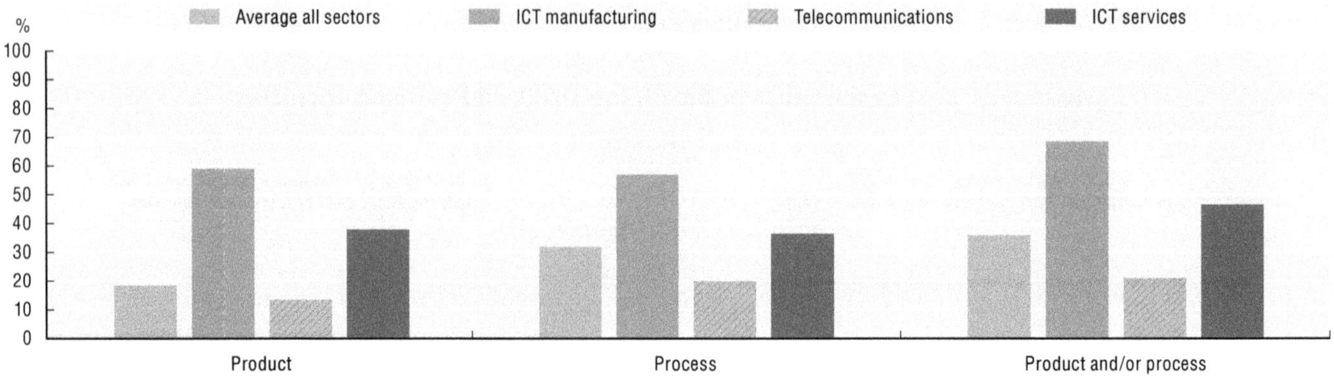

Note: ICT = information and communication technology.

Source: IBGE (2016), *Pesquisa de Inovação 2014*.

Figure 5.4. Novelty of innovation in Brazilian firms, by sector, 2008 and 2014

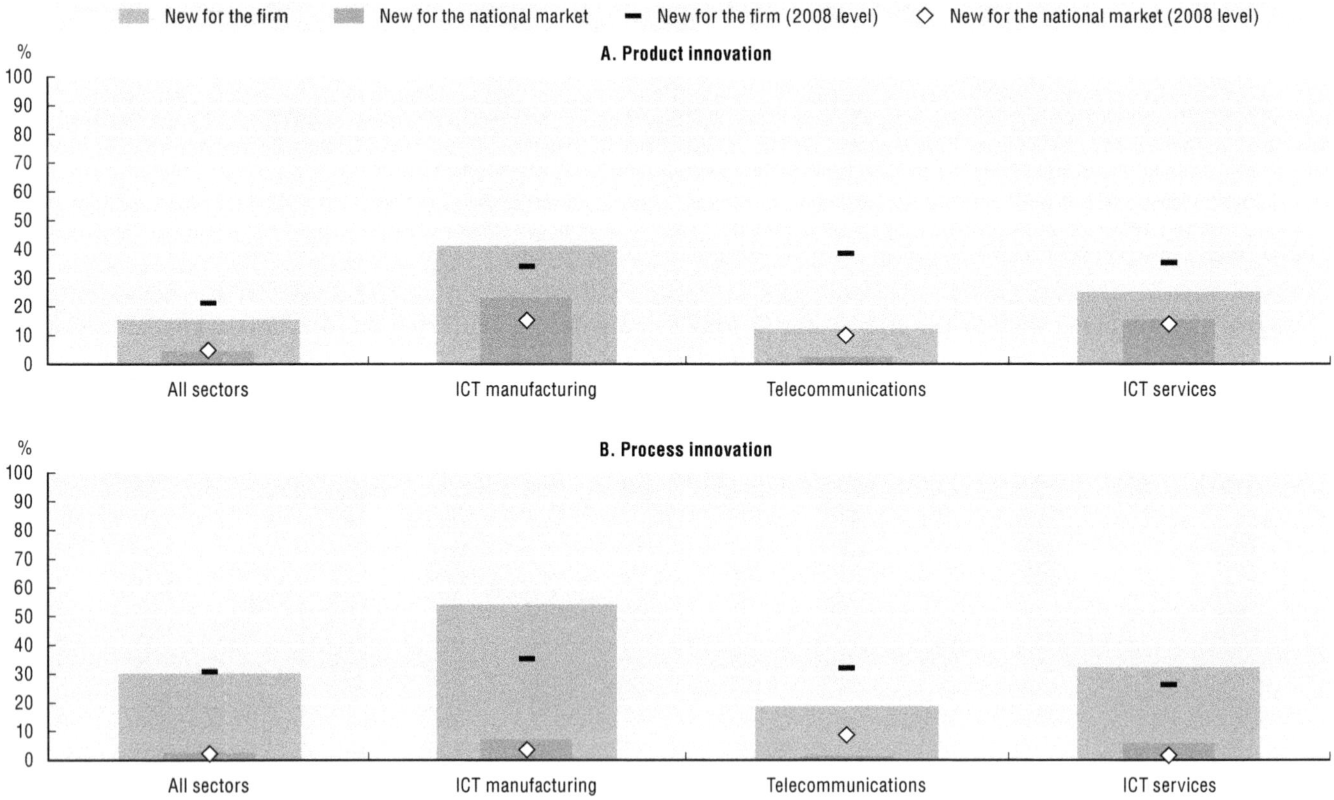

Note: ICT = information and communication technology.

Sources: IBGE (2016), *Pesquisa de Inovação 2014*; IBGE (2010), *Pesquisa de Inovação 2008*.

The business environment affects firms' investment decisions and innovative behaviour

Structural conditions in the overall economy affect firms' decisions to invest in innovation. Brazilian enterprises operate within an economic environment that incurs high costs, referred to as "Brazilian cost" (*custo Brasil*) (Dutz, 2018). This is the result of insufficient infrastructure, a complex taxation system with both high levels of taxation and compliance costs, high entry barriers and insolvency costs, and limited access to finance, especially for smaller enterprises. The lack of skills of the working population and the low quality of the education system also hinder the development of more knowledge-intensive activities. Brazil's tariffs on imported goods, including for ICT goods, further raise the cost of inputs (OECD, 2019a). Finally, support to existing industry structures has been found to inhibit the reallocation of resources towards more productive uses and to reduce incentives for innovation (OECD, 2018a).

All of the above factors tend to discourage competition, innovation and, ultimately, the digital transformation of the country, as they favour incumbents and hinder experimentation with new ideas, technologies and business models, which are the drivers of productivity growth in the digital age (OECD, 2019b). For enterprises to invest in digital technologies, reforms are needed in the above-mentioned policy areas to strengthen incentives to innovate.

Brazil has recently approved several new measures, such as the Declaration of Rights of Economic Freedom (Declaração de Direitos de Liberdade Econômica, Law 13.784 of 20 September 2019), the launch of the Growth Routes Plan (Rota da crescimento) in 2020, and Ordinance 2.023 of 12 September 2019, eliminating import tax on 34 IT and telecommunication goods. The country is also discussing a comprehensive tax reform. These are crucial in fostering an environment conducive to innovation.

Public funding of R&D is decreasing, thus calling for prioritisation

The federal government is the main contributor to the budget, although over the past decade, state research foundations (Fundações de Amparo à Pesquisa, FAPs), and in particular that of the State of São Paulo (FAPESP), have increased their funding of research. The majority of the federal budget for R&D is allocated to the Ministry of Education (MEC) to fund education and research in federal public universities. Most of the remaining budget finances "not-oriented" R&D (De Negri and Tortato Rauen, 2018), with the exception of agriculture and health, which receive a significant proportion of it (Figure 5.5).

The National Fund for Scientific and Technological Development (Fundo Nacional de Desenvolvimento Científico e Tecnológico, FNDCT), which is mainly financed by sectoral funds, including ICT, is the main source of funding for R&D, providing financing for public or non-profit research organisations and enterprises. The sectoral funds were established in the early 1990s with the objective to provide expanded and more stable financing to scientific and technological development. Since 2017, an increasing share of the FNDCT has been used as a contingency reserve for the federal budget, decreasing the amount of available resources for R&D (Figure 5.6).

Figure 5.5. Government expenditure in R&D, by ministry, Brazil, 2017

As a share of total federal expenditures in R&D

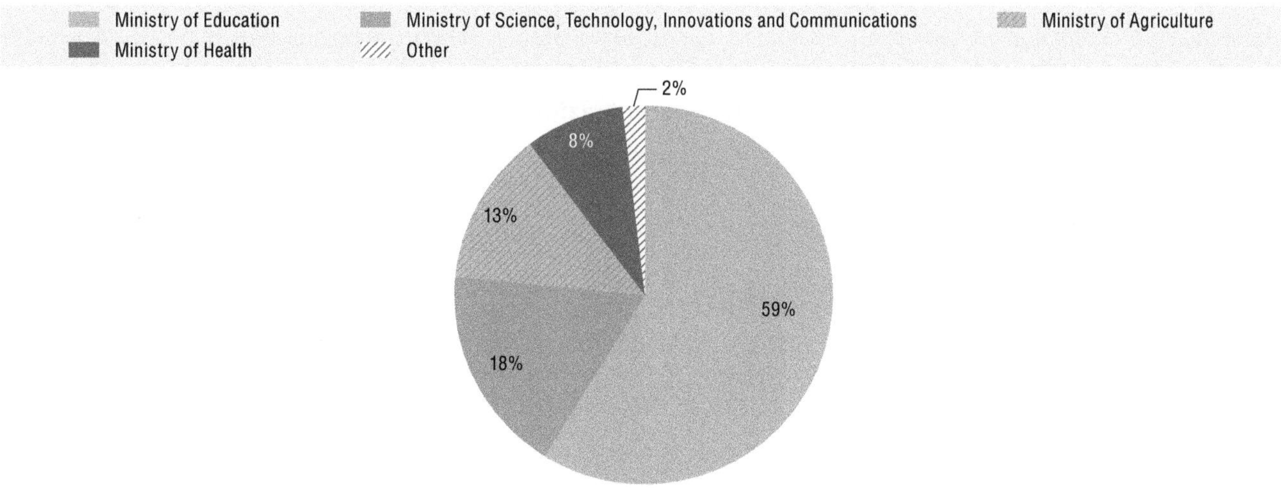

Source: MCTIC (2019a), *Indicadores Nacionais de Ciência, Tecnologia e Inovação 2018, https://www.mctic.gov.br/mctic/opencms/indicadores/indicadores_cti.html.*

The Ministry of Science, Technology, Innovations and Communications (Ministério de Ciência, Tecnologia, Innovaciones y Comunicaciones, MCTIC) is the main actor providing support to R&D and it leads two main funding agencies. The National Council for Scientific and Technological Development

(Conselho Nacional de Desenvolvimento Científico e Tecnológico, CNPq) finances research and training through scholarships for graduate students and through research funding programmes. The Brazilian Agency for Innovation and Research (Financiadora de Estudos e Projetos, FINEP) manages the FNDCT and finances R&D and innovation projects in the public and private sectors through grants and credit.

The MEC also provides support by leading the Foundation for the Coordination for the Improvement of Higher Education Personnel (Coordenação de Aperfeiçoamento de Pessoal de Nível Superior, CAPES), which awards a large number of scholarships and certifies higher education institutions (HEIs) and graduate programmes. The funding of the CNPq, FINEP and CAPES has decreased in recent years (Figure 5.7), impacting the Brazilian research base, which is mostly concentrated in public universities. The decrease in public resources will require co-ordination of actions and initiatives, prioritisation and stronger, more frequent public-private partnerships. However, the country should also secure funding for basic research, building human capital and investment in key technologies.

The MCTIC and MEC also finance, together with other sources, the Brazilian Company for Research and Industrial Innovation (Empresa Brasileira de Pesquisa e Inovação Industrial, EMBRAPII), which supports linkages between firms and research centres (Box 5.1). In addition, the Brazilian Development Bank (Banco Nacional de Desenvolvimento Econômico e Social, BNDES) is the main financing agent for development in the country, and provides credit and equity capital for innovation projects and technology acquisition.

Figure 5.6. Budget of the National Fund for Scientific and Technological Development, by destination, 2014-18

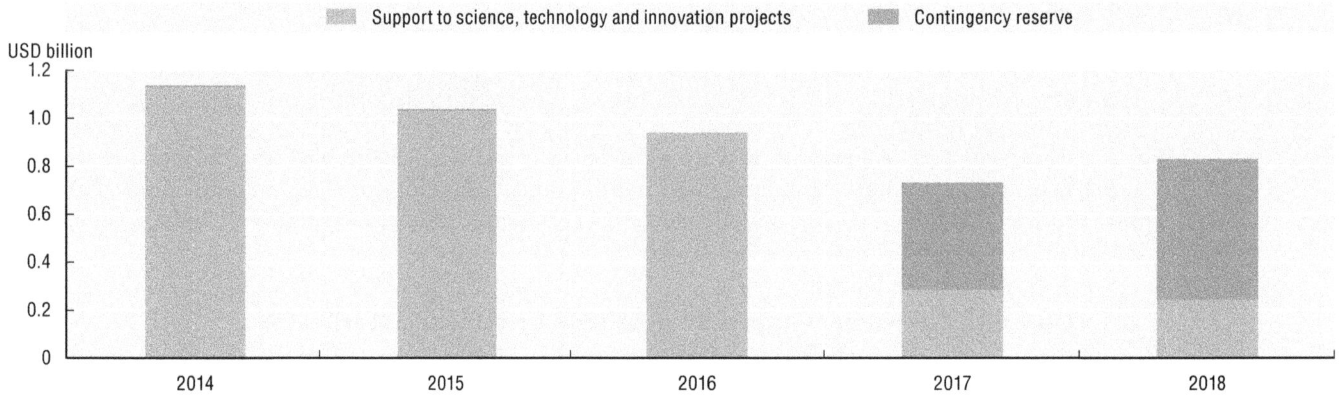

Source: MCTIC/FINEP (2019), *Relatório de Gestão do Exercício de 2018, www.finep.gov.br/images/a-finep/FNDCT/05_06_2019-Relatorio_de_Gestao_Finep_2018.pdf.*

Figure 5.7. Yearly expenditures of the federal Brazilian agencies fostering R&D, 2010-18

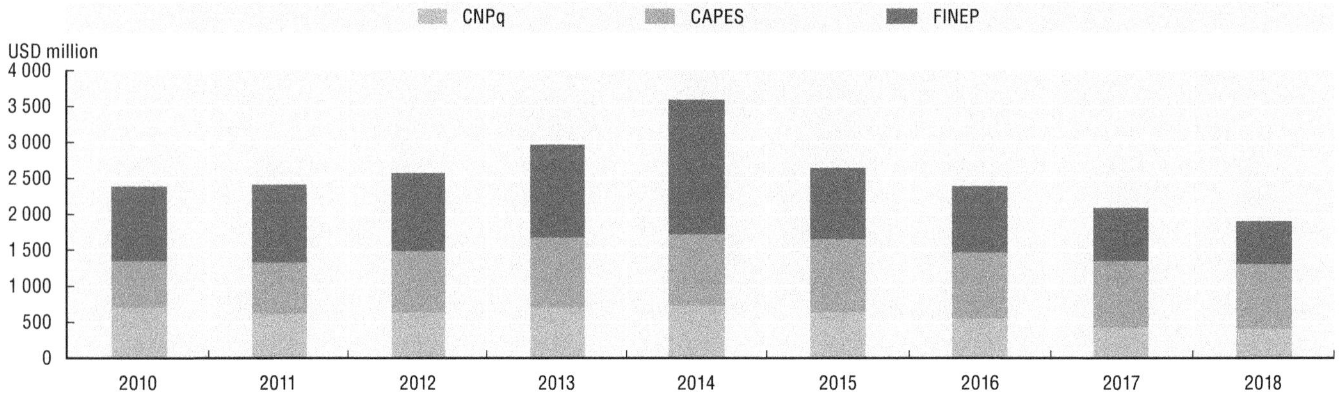

Note: CNPq = National Council for Scientific and Technological Development; CAPES = Foundation for the Coordination for the Improvement of Higher Education Personnel; FINEP = Brazilian Agency for Innovation and Research.

Source: SBPC (2019), *A Política Brasileira de CT&I e as Manifestações da Comunidade Científica, http://portal.sbpcnet.org.br/wp-content/uploads/2019/12/cartilha_manifestos_SBPC_online.pdf.*

Human capital is a bottleneck in the innovation system

The Brazilian higher education system includes both public and private universities, and different types of institutions, with the largest majority of them (*faculdades* and *centros universitários*) being education-oriented. Most of the research is carried out in public federal and state universities (*universidades*), together with research centres and non-profit organisations. Over the past decade, Brazil has seen rapid growth in participation in higher education, mostly as a result in expansion of private higher education establishments (OECD, 2018b), which currently represent 88% of the more than 2 530 HEIs (MEC, 2018). This marks a considerable increase in tertiary attainment among the younger generation (25-34 year-olds), from 11% in 2008 to 21% in 2018. Overall, however, the share of graduates among the adult population remains low, at 18%, compared to 39% in OECD countries, but also Latin American countries such as Argentina (36%), Chile (25%), Colombia and Costa Rica (23%) (OECD, 2019c).

Graduates in sciences, engineering and ICTs also represent a lower share of graduates than in developed economies and other Latin American countries (Figure 5.8). Among PhD graduates – whose absolute number has increased fourfold in the past two decades (MEC, 2018) – the preferred specialisations are health and human sciences, whereas engineering increased less than the average (CGEE, 2016). Increasing Masters' and PhD graduates is an objective of the National Education Plan (Plano Nacional de Educação, PNE). Whereas the goal of reaching 60 000 Masters graduates by 2024 was attained in 2018 (64 430 in 2018), the one of achieving 25 000 PhDs was still not realised (22 900).

Figure 5.8. Tertiary graduates in the natural sciences, engineering, ICTs, and creative and content fields of education in Brazil, the OECD and selected countries, 2016

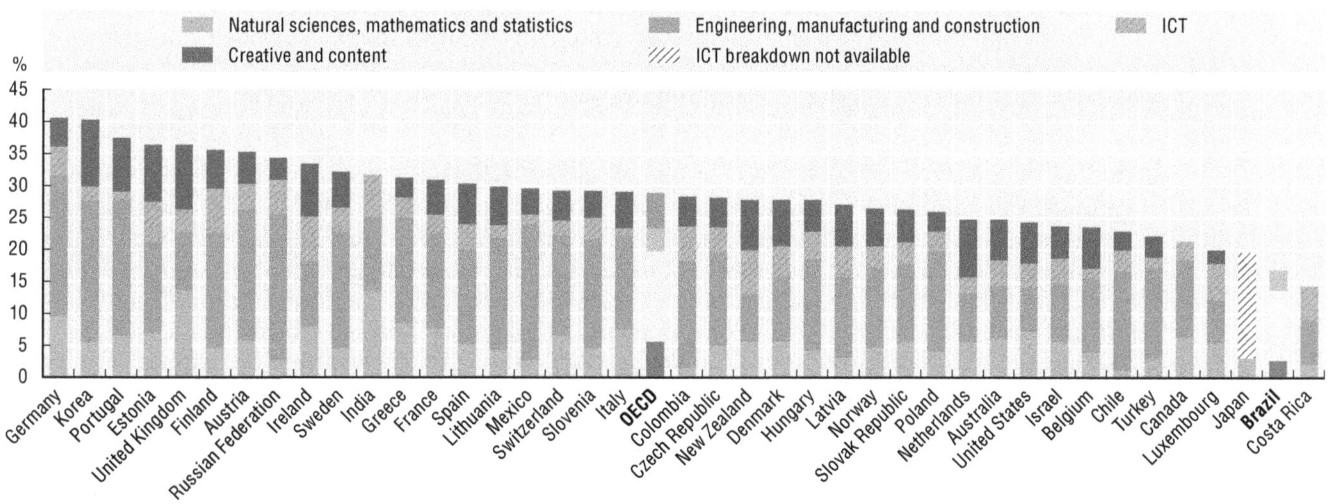

Notes: ICT = information and communication technology. The "Creative and content" field includes arts (including graphic design), journalism and information. For Japan, "Creative and content" fields of education are not presented due to data availability.

Source: OECD (2019a), *Measuring the Digital Transformation: A Roadmap for the Future*, *https://doi.org/10.1787/9789264311992-en*.

Human capital is the most important asset for establishing of a strong ICT sector, as shown by the "Start-up Nation" Israel, which has managed to attract R&D operations from leading ICT multinationals through the presence of highly skilled human capital and government policies. Strong investment in education, especially in maths, is also a core feature of Singapore's success in the digital economy (Getz and Goldberg, 2016). For the Brazilian economy to shift towards higher levels of knowledge intensity, Brazil needs to broaden and deepen its human resource base, by increasing the number of graduates in science, technology, engineering and mathematics (STEM). CAPES has recently announced a change in its funding mechanism, which, among others, will distribute an increased share of scholarships to PhD courses, as compared to Masters. The country may also consider making changes in the distribution of scholarships in relationship to the subject, in favour of STEM degrees. Some countries, given the shortage of talent in these disciplines, particularly those related to digital technologies, are increasing funding for higher education in these fields. Introducing interdisciplinary dual learning programmes may also be an option.

Several OECD countries have included in their national artificial intelligence (AI) strategies specific initiatives to develop AI talent, through the creation of AI Master or PhD programmes, and initiatives to attract, retain and train domestic and international AI talent. Brazil also needs to increase the attractiveness of its HEIs for foreign students, by encouraging the use of English in courses. Canada and France created AI Chairs Programmes to attract and retain top researchers and to train young researchers. The AI Sector Deal in the United Kingdom supports AI fellowship programmes, government-funded PhDs and industry-funded Masters. The AI Technology Strategy in Japan plans to tackle the shortage of AI talent by creating new programmes and providing higher salaries to researchers (Planes-Satorra and Paunov, 2019). Other emerging economies, such as Indonesia, have also increased their support to skills development in key digital technologies in recent years. In 2019, the Indonesian Ministry of Communication and Information funded 25 000 digital talent scholarships in areas such as AI, the Internet of Things (IoT) and cybersecurity, and it has recently announced it will double the number of supported students in 2020.

Brazil should also consider demand-side initiatives to actively orient more students towards STEM disciplines. A few initiatives of this type have been carried out in the country (see Chapter 3). Effective actions in this regard concern early exposure of students to STEM subjects at primary and secondary education levels, including through extra-curricular activities in the form of coding bootcamps, so as to boost their interest in science. Role models are also important, particularly for girls, who usually find it difficult to picture themselves in a STEM career. Girls have a higher fear of failure and less positive attitudes towards competition than boys, which also influences their career choices (Encinas-Martin, 9 March 2020). Exposure to real-world applications of STEM knowledge can change their attitude (Microsoft, 2018). Other actions include initiatives at the higher education level, such as increasing courses in particular subjects, offering scholarships to support students engaging in these disciplines or offering opportunities to a greater number of students to study them. In Sweden, students who did not follow STEM related-courses in secondary education can get a first year with basic knowledge in STEM so that they are eligible to study at university level.

High-quality research is concentrated in a few institutions and fields

Although the number of researchers has seen a threefold increase in the past two decades (MCTIC, 2019a), their proportion in the total employed population is very low compared to OECD countries (Figure 5.9). The increase in the number of researchers has resulted in growth of the country's scientific output, and Brazil currently ranks 11th worldwide in terms of total number of scientific publications. Publications in science and engineering increased at an annual average growth rate of 5.2% between 2000 and 2018 (US National Science Foundation, 2019), although at a lower pace than that of other major emerging economies, such as the People's Republic of China (hereafter "China") (7.8%) and India (10.7%).

There is high variation in the quality of research outputs, with excellence concentrated in a few public universities, mainly in the Southeast region, and in fields of research, which have benefited from targeted sector investment. Medicine and biochemistry are the most influential research areas of publication (Zuniga et al., 2016; Clarivate Analytics, 2018), whereas technological areas are less prominent internationally. Publications on computer science have a higher citation rate compared to the country's overall scientific production, but remain well below the average for OECD countries or other developed and emerging economies (Figure 5.10).

Out of the 197 universities in Brazil, 6 are ranked among the world's top 500, but only 3 in the computer science and engineering field (ShanghaiRanking Consultancy, 2020: the University of São Paulo, the University of Minas Gerais and the University of Campinas, all located in the Southeast region of the country. These are the digital economy poles in Brazil, which have also built large ecosystems of public-private co-operation, and where most of the research infrastructure in ICT is located (De Negri and de Holanda Schmidt Squeff, 2016).

There is a gap between basic and applied research

The increase in scientific publications has not been mirrored by an improvement in patenting activities, with the notable exceptions of the Brazilian high-performing industries, such as aerospace, oil and gas, and agroindustry. Research networks around Embraer (aircraft technologies), Petrobras (oil and gas) and

Embrapa (agriculture) have significant patenting outputs. These exceptional cases are characterised by a long-term involvement of both government and business, as well as specific features, which have been difficult to replicate in other industries (Zuniga et al., 2016).

Figure 5.9. Researchers in Brazil, the OECD and selected countries, 2017 or latest available year

Total researchers in full-time equivalent per 1 000 total employment

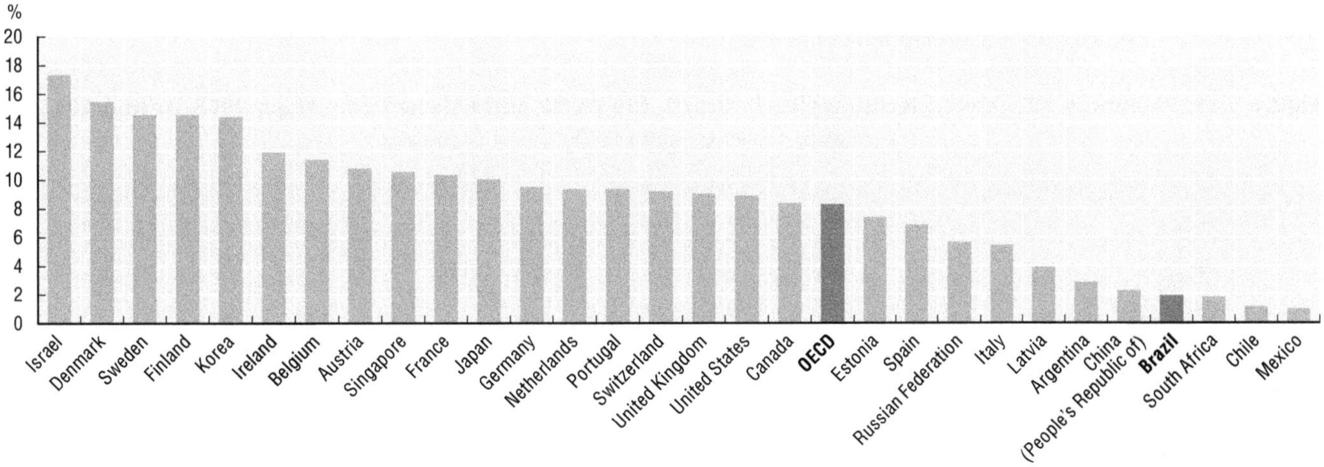

Note: Data for Israel refer to 2012 and for Brazil to 2014.

Sources: OECD (2020b), *Main Science and Technology Indicators* (database), *http://oe.cd/msti* (accessed in March 2020); data for Brazil are from MCTIC (2019a), *Indicadores Nacionais de Ciência, Tecnologia e Inovação 2018, https://www.mctic.gov.br/mctic/opencms/indicadores/indicadores_cti.html.*

Figure 5.10. Top 10% most-cited documents in computer science in Brazil, the OECD and selected countries, 2016

As a percentage of documents in the top 10% ranked documents, by field, fractional counts

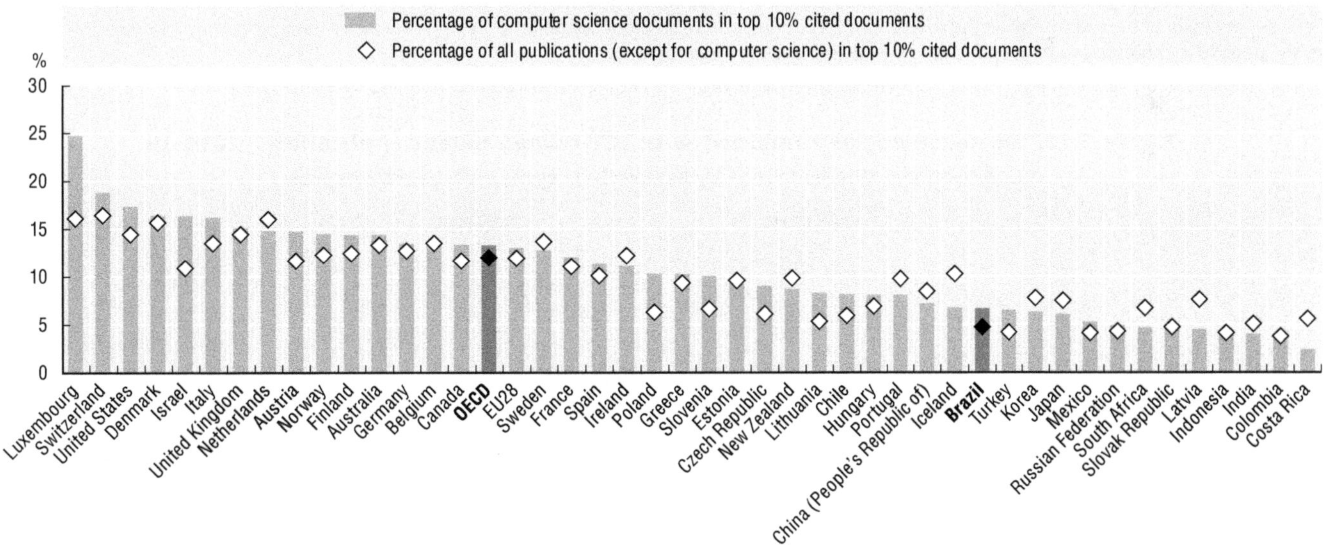

Notes: "Top-cited publications" are the 10% most-cited papers normalised by scientific field and type of document (articles, reviews and conference proceedings). The Scimago Journal Rank indicator is used to rank documents with identical numbers of citations within each class. This measure is a proxy indicator of research excellence. Estimates are based on fractional counts of documents by authors affiliated to institutions in each economy. Documents published in multidisciplinary/generic journals are allocated on a fractional basis to the ASJC codes of citing and cited papers. The field Computer Science comprises the following sub-fields: Artificial Intelligence, Computational Theory and Mathematics, Computer Graphics and Computer-Aided Design, Computer Networks and Communications, Computer Science Applications, Computer Vision and Pattern Recognition, Hardware and Architecture, Human-Computer Interaction, Information Systems, Signal Processing and Software.

Source: OECD (2019a), *Measuring the Digital Transformation: A Roadmap for the Future, https://doi.org/10.1787/9789264311992-en.*

The ICT sector does not show the same innovation outputs as the leading sectors. Only 10% of the country's patents were in ICT between 2013 and 2016, compared to about one-third in the OECD and 60% in China (Figure 5.11). Brazil has a revealed technology advantage in biotechnology, but lags behind OECD and BRIICS (Brazil, Russian Federation, India, Indonesia and South Africa) countries in ICTs (OECD, 2016). ICT-related innovations are diffused to other science and technology fields where they can play an important role in further innovation. Brazil has a share comparable to the world average of ICT-related patents in the area of measurement, but also a relative specialisation in control instruments and digital communications, probably in relation to the use of these technologies in sectors such as agriculture and aviation (Figure 5.12).

Figure 5.11. Patents in ICT-related technologies in Brazil, the OECD and selected countries, 2003-06 and 2013-16

As a percentage of total IP5 patent families, by country of ownership

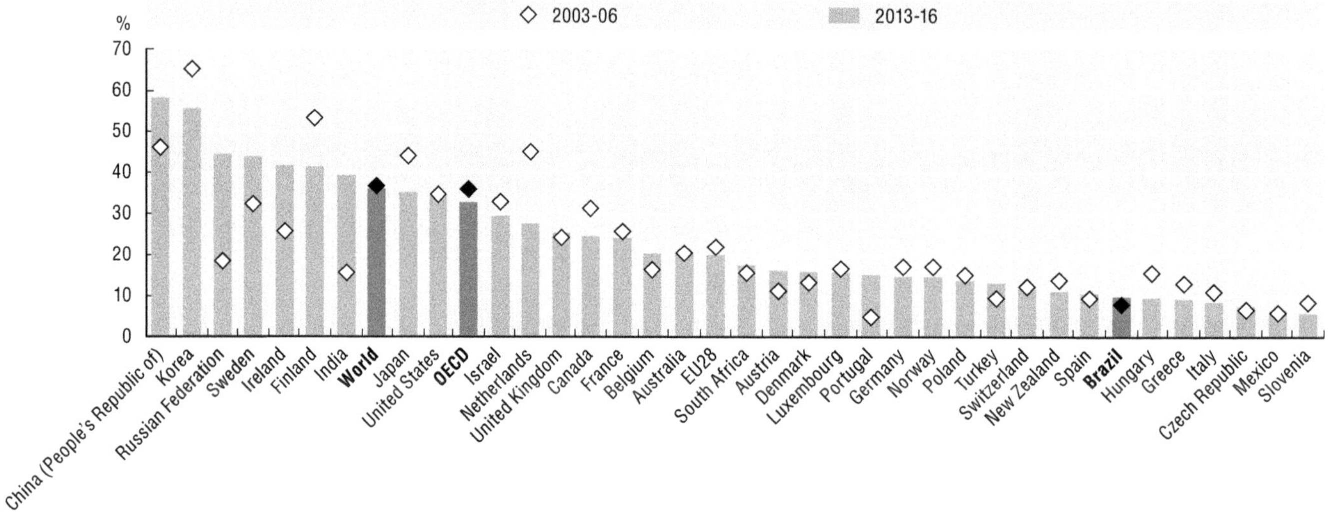

Notes: IP5 = five largest intellectual property offices. Data refer to IP5 families, by filing date, according to the applicants' residence using fractional counts. Patents in ICT are identified using the list of IPC codes in Inaba and Squicciarini (2017). Only economies with more than 250 patents families in the periods considered are included. Data for 2015 and 2016 are incomplete.

Source: OECD (2019a), *Measuring the Digital Transformation: A Roadmap for the Future*, *https://dx.doi.org/10.1787/9789264311992-en*.

Figure 5.12. Top technologies combined with ICT-related patent applications, 2014-16

As a percentage of ICT-related patent applications also belonging to other technology fields

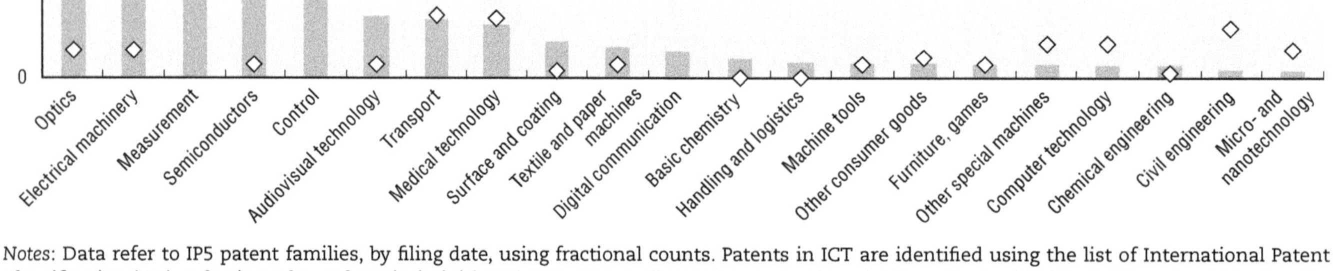

Notes: Data refer to IP5 patent families, by filing date, using fractional counts. Patents in ICT are identified using the list of International Patent Classification (IPC) codes in Inaba and Squicciarini (2017). Patents are allocated to technology fields on the basis of their IPC codes, following the concordance provided by WIPO (2013).

Source: OECD (2019d), *STI Micro-data Lab: Intellectual Property Database*, *http://oe.cd/ipstats* (accessed in September 2019).

The low patenting activity is affected by the backlog in the analysis of applications at the National Institute for Patents (Instituto Nacional da Propriedade Industrial, INPI), which results in an average 10-year delay for a patent application to be processed, with peaks of 13 years for pharmaceuticals and telecommunications patents. The INPI has started working on measures to address this problem, including a 25% increase in staff and restructuring of the internal processes. It also has a plan to digitalise its services and expand its IT infrastructure. Patent prosecution highways (PPH), i.e. examining patent applications based on the decisions already published by other jurisdictions programmes, are proving effective in accelerating patenting process, with an increase of 77.4% in the granting of patents in 2018 compared to the previous year. The INPI currently has six PPH programmes in force, for specific fields of technology. To further accelerate patenting processes, the INPI should work towards abolishing the restrictions on the technological fields included in the existing PPH pilot projects (information technology, for instance, is not included in the PPH with the European Patent Office).

Collaboration between enterprises and academia is still limited

Collaboration across sectors and disciplines, and technology transfer from academia to industry, are highly relevant for digital innovation. In Brazil, this relationship, although increasing, is still limited and is often given as another key explanation for the country's low innovation results. Heavy bureaucracy and low incentives in universities (Reynolds and De Negri, 2019), as well as a lack of qualified personnel in firms (Rapini, Chiarini and Bittencourt, 2016) hinder such collaborations.

Policies that foster university-industry collaborations have succeeded in stimulating growth in papers co-authored with researchers from industry (2.4% of all scientific publications), but to a level which is still low in international comparisons, e.g. 3.8-4.4% in France, Germany and Korea. Public universities are at the forefront of collaborations with industry, but with an uneven quality of universities and research centres across the country. For instance, São Paulo and Campinas universities have comparable and even higher rates of co-operation with industry than some of the leading universities in the United States (Cruz, 2019). The number of start-ups spun off from these universities is also high: the University of Campinas Unicamp generated over 100 start-ups between 2014 and 2016, most of them in the field of ICT (Cruz, 2019).

Researchers collaborate little with the private sector

A key feature in the Brazilian STI system is the high rate of researchers engaged in careers in academia and government, contrary to those in OECD countries and China, who mostly contribute to R&D innovation in the private sector (Figure 5.13). This seems to be driven by a lack of demand by enterprises, which do not compete with academia in terms of salary (Figure 5.14). Only some state-owned enterprises absorb researchers due to their big research centres, whereas the academic job market remains more attractive to PhD holders, who can benefit from a public servant status and guaranteed tenure after three years. Weak demand of high-skilled workers signals a lack of technology absorption capacity of firms. With regard to digital technologies, Brazilian firms are still at an early stage of adoption. To strengthen this, Brazil needs to reinforce policies for outreach, technology extension and skills for innovation, including managerial skills (see Chapter 3).

The CAPES system, through which post-graduate courses are evaluated, ascribes the greatest weight to scientific publications. Although patents and technical outputs are also considered in the assessment, there are no metrics on collaboration with industry, or the impact of scientific research on the marketplace, business strategies or public policy (Mazzucato and Penna, 2016). Introducing indicators on research's impact on the economy and society would help focus research towards areas that are better linked to economic, social and commercial applications, and would orient researchers towards perspective careers in the private sector. Higher exposure to the private sector during their studies, for instance allowing business experts to take up teaching assignments, may also increase openness to careers in the private sector, while bringing in knowledge about applications in economic sectors. Promoting an entrepreneurial culture throughout the education system will also be key in altering cultural factors, which influence preference for lifelong careers.

Figure 5.13. Researchers in Brazil and selected countries, by sector, 2017 or latest available year

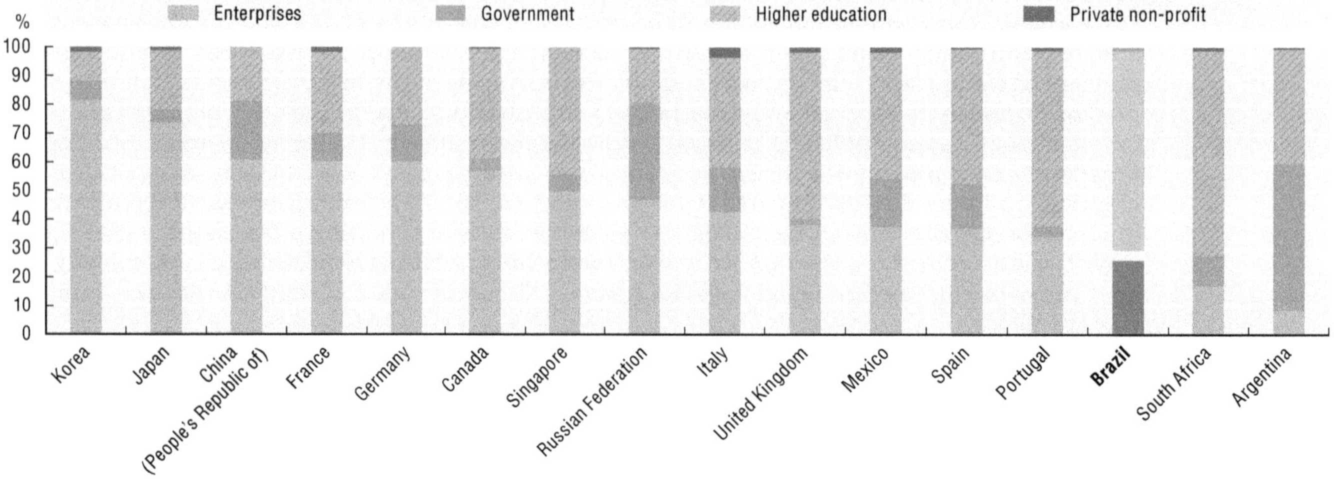

Sources: OECD (2020b), *Main Science and Technology Indicators* (database), *http://oe.cd/msti* (accessed in March 2020); data for Brazil are from MCTIC (2019a), *Indicadores Nacionais de Ciência, Tecnologia e Inovação 2018*, *https://www.mctic.gov.br/mctic/opencms/indicadores/indicadores_cti.html*.

Figure 5.14. Average monthly remuneration of PhD holders in Brazil, by sector, 2014

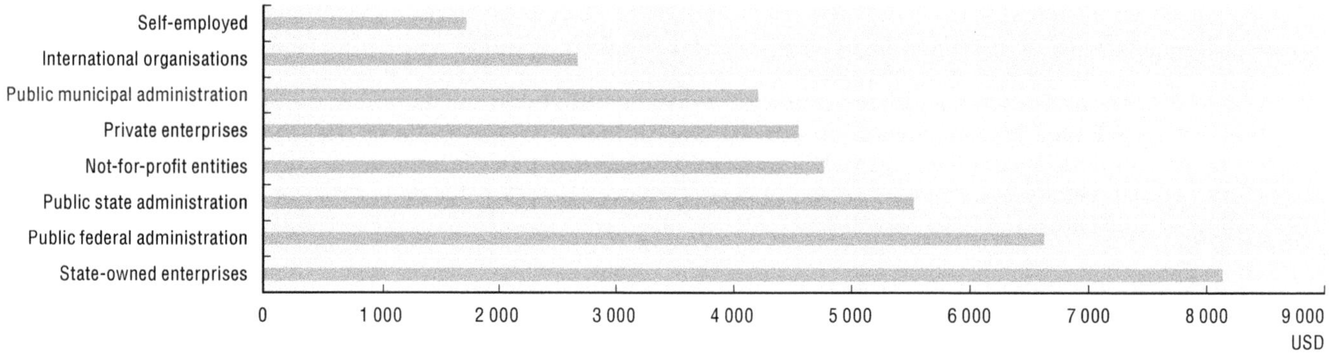

Source: CGEE (2016), *Mestres e doutores 2015: Estudos da Demografia da Base Técnico-científica Brasileira*, *https://www.cgee.org.br/documents/10182/734063/Mestres_Doutores_2015_Vs3.pdf*.

Efforts have been made to enhance public-private co-operation and businesses' investment in innovation

In the past 15 years, Brazil has introduced new regulatory measures to enhance firms' collaboration with universities and research centres. The Innovation Law (Lei Federal de Inovação, Law 10.937/04) aimed to facilitate collaboration between academia and industry by formalising the rules for interactions between researchers and firms. The law also created the possibility for the government to provide direct funding to businesses, which was not allowed until then. However, the law did not lead to a straightforward process of co-operation across sectors (Rauen, 2016). The law was profoundly revised in 2016 through the Legal Framework for Science, Technology and Innovation (Marco Legal de Ciência, Tecnologia e Inovação, Law 13.243/16), followed by a regulatory decree two years later (Decreto Federal de Inovação, Decree 9.283/18). The government also created EMBRAPII in 2013, a new "social organisation" – a private non-profit entity which manages public research facilities under contract to federal agencies. Through its agile, flexible and performance-based working model, it may be considered as one of the most effective novelties in the Brazilian innovation system for promoting industry-research collaboration (Box 5.1).

The overall objective of the Legal Framework for Science, Technology and Innovation is to bring more legal clarity to the interactions between the public and private sectors. To this end, a number of provisions specify, for instance, the number of hours that a university professor can spend on non-university activities, or the requirements firms must fulfil in order to rent laboratories in public research institutes. The framework clarifies the management of intellectual property rights generated by academia, by tasking the technological innovation hubs (*núcleos de inovação tecnológica*, NITs) with this role. NITs, however, are not new institutions to the country, as they were established by the Innovation Law.

One of the main novelties brought about by the new framework concerning NITs is the possibility for these entities to have their own legal personality, and thus more agility in operating than if they were subject to public sector regulations. This will be particularly important in relation to their hiring capacity, both in terms of the speed of recruiting and in the variety of profiles they will be able to attract. Both the size and composition of technology transfer offices' (TTOs) staff are crucial for them to play a central role in university productivity (Pojo et al., 2016). Staff need to be diversified in terms of background (science, economics, law, etc.), but also have a strong component from the business environment. The Israeli network of TTOs linked to research hubs, which is considered one of the key factors of the country's innovativeness, can be a model in this sense. Business leaders are on the TTOs' boards, so the market dimension is brought to the scientific ecosystem. They can act as intermediaries between researchers and business investors.

Box 5.1. Promoting industry-research collaboration: EMBRAPII, a new player in Brazil's innovation landscape

EMBRAPII is a governmental agency established in 2014. It is funded by the Ministry of Science, Technology, Innovations and Communications and the Ministry of Education, but decides the allocation of its resources independently. Its main objective is to stimulate private-public co-operation by linking research institutions and universities with the industrial sector. EMBRAPII selects private and public research institutions in specific areas of competence ("units"). The selection is based on previous co-operation with businesses, technical capacity and the quality of the research infrastructure. Selected institutions have a six-year agreement with EMBRAPII to undertake innovation projects in co-operation with firms, and are evaluated on a regular basis.

To date, EMBRAPII has 42 accredited units across 5 technological areas, 18 of which are in the Internet of Things and advanced manufacturing (Table 5.4). After accreditation, the institution receives funding from EMBRAPII to be spent exclusively on innovation projects with industry. Firms looking for innovative technological solutions can approach the accredited institutions of their choice and sign a contract with them. EMBRAPII does not interfere in the contract formulation, but supervises its execution. EMBRAPII therefore has a very agile way of working, with minimal bureaucracy. The project costs are shared by EMBRAPII (generally, one-third, through non-refundable grants), the enterprise (at least one-third) and the research institute (in-kind via its infrastructure and personnel).

Micro and small firms can also collaborate with EMBRAPII units and receive financial support for it. The Brazilian Micro and Small Business Support Agency (Serviço Brasileiro de Apoio às Micro e Pequenas Empresas, SEBRAE) can finance up to 70% of a firm's contribution to the project, and 80% for projects carried out in partnership with another firm (a start-up or a large firm).

Out of the 500 firms involved in EMBRAPII's projects since its creation, 42% were small (annual gross billing up to USD 1.2 million, or BRL 4.8 million), 17% medium (USD 1.2 million to USD 76 million, or BRL 4.8 million to BRL 300 million) and 41% large (annual gross billing over USD 76 million, or BRL 300 million). Small firms are increasingly requesting co-operation with EMBRAPII units, particularly for projects focusing on the Internet of Things, health and agriculture.

EMBRAPII appears to be an important institutional innovation in Brazil, both for firms' R&D and for industry-research co-operation. In its five years of existence, the organisation has developed a portfolio of 800 projects, involving 570 firms collaborating with 42 research institutes and universities. The research outputs are also promising, with more than 300 intellectual property applications, and the model is proving effective in bringing researchers closer to the business environment. The units are able to attract talents to work on projects and to retain researchers for further projects, thus also influencing career mindset and research orientations.

Source: OECD, based on information provided by EMBRAPII and on EMBRAPII (2020), *EMBRAPII*, *www.embrapii.org.br* (accessed in March 2020).

Public support to business R&D has increased, but young and small firms have limited access to it

Brazil has shifted in recent years towards a greater reliance on tax relief *vis-à-vis* direct support for R&D towards the business sector. The foregone revenue through tax incentives for R&D is estimated at about USD 2.4 billion (BRL 8.6 billion) in 2018 (Figure 5.15). Most of these incentives benefit the ICT manufacturing sector through the Informatics Law (see below), and the Good Law, which applies to all sectors. Tax breaks are also granted to universities and research institutions, exempting them from the payment of import duties on purchases of scientific equipment and materials. Another type of tax incentive benefits the ICT firms established in the Manaus Free Trade Zone, through the exemption of federal indirect taxes on sales and import tariffs on inputs.

Figure 5.15. Support to R&D through tax incentives in Brazil, 2000-18

Value of foregone revenues due to tax incentives

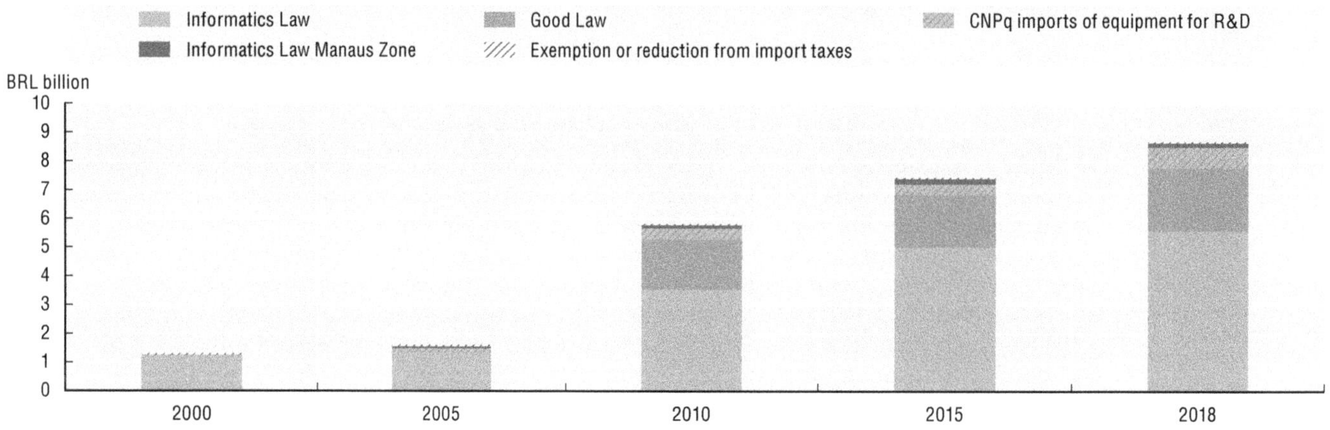

Note: Value for 2018 is an estimate.

Source: MCTIC (2019a), *Indicadores Nacionais de Ciência, Tecnologia e Inovação 2018, https://www.mctic.gov.br/mctic/opencms/indicadores/indicadores_cti.html.*

In 2005, the Good Law introduced a tax incentive for R&D investments available to firms in all sectors (Lei do Bem, Law 11.196/05). The law grants volume-based tax allowances on the corporate income tax for investments made in R&D. Firms can deduct up to 160% of their investment from the taxable base of corporate income, and this rate can increase up to 200% in case new researchers are hired and expenditures are related to patented products. Firms may also benefit from accelerated depreciation and amortisation for the purchase of new equipment and technology, along with a 50% reduction of the tax for industrialised products (Imposto sobre Produtos Industrializados, IPI) rate. Finally, they are also exempted from income tax on any international payments for the registration of intellectual property. Legislation also provides for a super deduction of up to 250% of eligible expenses made available for innovation projects executed by science, technology and innovation institutions (Instituições de Ciência, Tecnologia e Inovação, ICTs). Science, technology and innovation institutions are public or private non-profit legal entities, operating in basic, applied scientific or technological research for the development of new products, services and processes.

Deductible expenses are possible in a number of activities, namely: basic and applied research; experimental development; basic industrial technology; and technical support services. In order to benefit from the incentives, firms must: invest in RD&I activities; operate under the actual income (*lucro real*) tax regime; have earned a profit in the period referring to expenditures; and demonstrate fiscal regularity. The investments do not need prior approval, but activities and expenditures related to R&D and innovation are assessed *ex post* by the MCTIC, which can approve or reject the tax allowance. In 2014, 16% of the applications for the incentive were rejected (MCTIC, 2016).

Although the law has represented a turning point in support to firms through tax incentives compared to previous policies (Colombo, 2016), and despite a growing number of firms which have benefited from the incentive over the years (Figure 5.16), the number of applicants and beneficiaries is rather low. In 2017, only 1 476 firms applied for the incentive, or just over 2% of the potentially eligible firms (Figure 5.16).

Figure 5.16. The Good Law: number of applicant and beneficiary firms, 2006-17

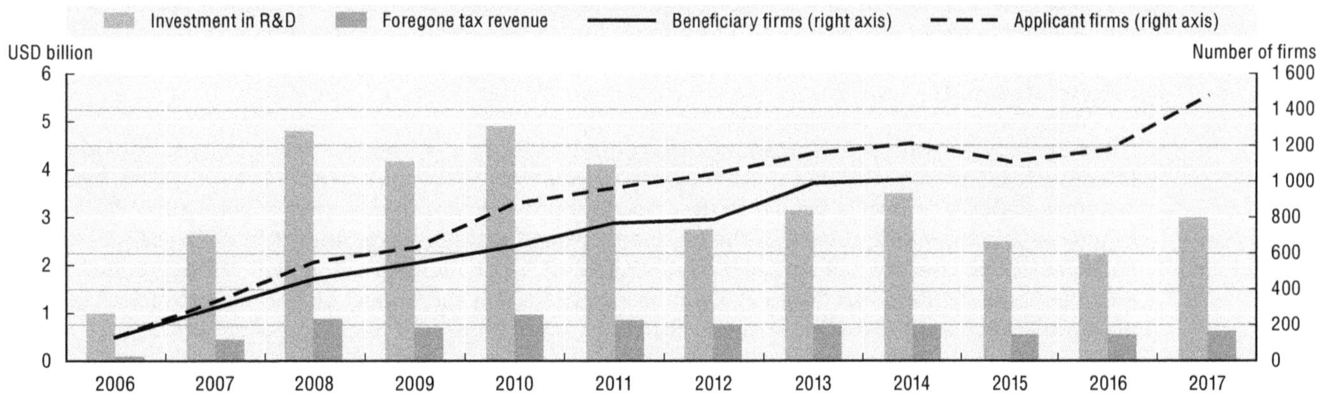

Notes: R&D = research and development. Yearly reports with data on beneficiary firms are only available up to 2014. Investments in R&D are those realised by beneficiary firms for the years up to 2014 and those realised by all applicants for the years 2015-17.

Sources: MCTIC/SETEC (2016), *Relatório Anual de Atividades de P&D (Retificado) 2014. Lei do Bem - Utilização dos Incentivos Fiscais à Inovação Tecnológica – Ano Base 2014: Capítulo III*; CGEE (2018), *Uma Análise dos Resultados da Lei do Bem: Com Base nos Dados do FormP&*, *https://www.cgee.org.br/documents/10182/734063/Mestres_Doutores_2015_Vs3.pdf;* MCTIC (2019a), *Indicadores Nacionais de Ciência, Tecnologia e Inovação 2018*, *https://www.mctic.gov.br/mctic/opencms/indicadores/indicadores_cti.html.*

The lengthy and burdensome application process, coupled with the uncertainty about the outcome may impact negatively on a firm's decision to apply. Kannebley and Porto (2012) pointed to the management and control processes as the main shortcomings of the law. Furthermore, two features of the policy design narrow its scope of application to a small minority of firms. First, as only businesses operating under the actual income tax regime are eligible, micro and small businesses – the majority of Brazilian firms – which typically operate under the deemed profit (*lucro presumido*) or the simplified (Simples Nacional) tax regime, are excluded. Second, the Good Law does not foresee provisions for refund of the tax allowance generated by the R&D expenditures, as it is the case, for instance, for the tax credits in the Informatics Law (see below). It also does not foresee the possibility to deduct the expenses in subsequent years when a profit is generated ("carry forward"). Young firms such as start-ups tend to fall outside the scope of the law, as they generally incur losses in their first years of activity when they perform R&D investments. Indeed, only 2% of the most innovative Brazilian Fintech start-ups used the incentive in 2018 (PwC and ABFintech, 2019). The law foresees an additional mechanism for start-ups to engage in activities. If they provide their services for R&D and innovation activities to a firm that fits the requirements of the Good Law, the revenues obtained from these services are not taxed. However, it is the partner company that benefits directly from the Good Law, as its expenditures are eligible for the tax allowance.

Evaluations of the law carried out to date point to additionality impact on research technical staff and on R&D spending (Kannebley and Porto, 2012; Kannebley, Shimada and De Negri, 2016; Colombo, 2016), and stimulus for firms to intensify their innovation strategies (Kannebley and Porto, 2012). Colombo (2016) also found that the policy has increased the base of firms investing in innovation and innovating, although there was no evidence of impact on firms' productivity or the sales and exports of new products.

Given the positive results of the Good Law, this tax incentive should be extended to a larger number of firms, first through advocacy actions to make the incentive known to a wider number of eligible firms operating in the actual income regime. Increasing clarity about what is included in the scope of the law would help firms to better assess their perspective projects and their potential to be granted the incentive, while making the application process less cumbersome would reduce costs. The MCTIC could also consider the possibility of using external audits from accredited firms to accompany the dossiers, to reduce the internal burden, while having an independent assessment (as is the case for the Informatics Law since 2018, see below). A measure undertaken by the MCTIC to address some of the above points has been the launch in 2019 of a "Guide to the Good Law" (MCTIC, 2019b), which explains the features of the law, including the main reasons which led in the past to rejections. Second, the incentive would benefit from some improvement in its design, such as allowing carry-forward or cash-refund provisions so that young companies can also become eligible. This would benefit smaller firms in general and would be particularly relevant for start-ups and software development firms. Although the software sector is among those with the most beneficiaries (15% of firms in 2018), they represent only about 5% of the 5 140 firms that are active in software development in Brazil. As 95.5% of them are micro and small enterprises (ABES, 2019), in most cases they likely do not meet the requirements of the law.

Offering carry-forward provisions and cash refunds if there is a negative tax liability is considered an effective measure for stimulating R&D in young innovative companies (Appelt et al., 2016). Tax credit schemes in OECD countries similar to the Good Law provide the opportunity for young innovative firms to receive an immediate refund of the tax credit gained through investments in R&D. France is one of such cases. The country has also recently introduced a new mechanism, which offers preferential tax arrangements for start-ups (Box 5.2). Evidence suggests that the impact of R&D tax incentives in terms of stimulating business R&D is stronger for young companies and SMEs (Ognyanova, 2017).

Box 5.2. Tax incentives supporting start-ups: The French Research Tax Credit and the Young Innovative Enterprise status

In France, the Research Tax Credit (crédit d'impôt recherche, CIR), grants businesses that invest in research a tax credit, which can be offset against the corporation tax they owe. All industrial, commercial or agricultural businesses taxed on the basis of their actual profits (under both the simplified and normal tax regimes) are eligible for the CIR. Scientific or technical research eligible for the scheme includes fundamental and applied research, as well as experimental development.

Since 2013, the Research Tax Credit has been extended to cover certain innovation investments by small and medium-sized enterprises (SMEs). These have to do with operations to design prototypes for new products not yet on the market, or which have superior features.

The CIR is deducted from taxes due by the business. Any remaining non-deducted CIR can be offset against taxes owed for the subsequent three years. The unused portion of the tax credit is refunded after this period. It is immediately refundable for SMEs and Young Innovative Enterprises.

The Young Innovative Enterprises/University status (Régime de la jeune entreprise innovante [JEI] or universitaire [JEU]) grants exemptions from taxes and social security contributions to new businesses (created before 31 December 2022) that invest in R&D.

To have JEI status, at each financial year-end, a business must: be an SME; have been set up for less than eight years; be independent (it must be a minimum 50% owned either by individuals or by certain firms in the venture capital sector, or by research and education institutions, or by non-profit organisations or scientific public interest foundations, etc.); not created out of a merger, restructuring, spin-off or takeover of pre-existing businesses; invest an amount for research representing at least 15% of tax-deductible expenses. To have JEU status, a business does not have to have to meet the criterion for research expenditure, but must fulfil a number of special conditions.

New businesses with JEI status are entitled to exemptions from:

- Personal income tax or corporate income tax: total exemption for the first financial year or the first period when they are taxed on profits (this may not be longer than 12 months), followed by a 50% exemption for the next year when they have a profit.
- The local economic contribution (CET) and property tax for seven years following a decision by the local government.

The exemption from tax on profits can be combined with the CIR and JEIs can also receive an immediate refund of their CIR credits.

Sources: OECD (2020c), *OECD Compendium of Information on R&D tax incentives, 2019, http://oe.cd/rdtax (accessed in March 2020)*; Ministère de l'Économie et des Finances (2020), *Innovation: Quels Sont les Aides et Crédits d'Impôt Existants?, www.economie.gouv.fr/entreprises/aides-financement-innovation.*

Digital innovation in Brazil

Digital innovation should be at the core of the economic and social agenda

At the federal government level, co-ordination of the research policy is under the responsibility of the MCTIC, the main body of the federal science, technology and innovation (STI) system. Other ministries are involved in the definition and execution of the research budget, including the Ministries of Education, Agriculture, Health, Energy, Economy and Foreign Trade.

The ENCTI 2016-2022 is the medium-term strategic document that sets out the main policy ambitions and provides guidance for the elaboration of STI initiatives. The strategy is based on a fundamental axis: the expansion, consolidation and integration of the National STI System. The strategy also identifies 12 key areas considered to be strategic for the development, autonomy and national sovereignty. Consolidating the digital economy is one of them. The strategy regards ICTs as a set of convergent and enabling technologies with the potential to bring innovation across several sectors. Despite the publication of an action plan in 2018, ENCTI remains an orientation document, lacking a roadmap for implementation. Furthermore, the innovation strategy does not seem to be connected to a broader economic, technological, industrial and social agenda, which would structure innovation efforts around Brazil's most pressing economic and social needs. Such an agenda would set key priorities and mobilise government, academia and the private sector around common goals.

R&D and innovation are "enablers" of the digital transformation in the Brazilian E-Digital Strategy (MCTIC, 2018), which calls for the development of an R&D and innovation policy for the 21st century. Both ENCTI and E-Digital stress the critical importance of R&D and innovation as well as the production of microelectronics, sensors, automation and robotics, supercomputers, artificial intelligence, big data and analytics, high-performance networks, cryptography, 5G networks, and cloud computing. The E-Digital Strategy also identifies priority areas for investment – i.e. security and defence, health, agribusiness and smart cities – along with a list of actions to increase productivity, competitiveness, integration in the global value chain, and thus income and employment. Compared to ENCTI, it nails down more concretely the areas in which digital could be most useful for the national challenges.

As part of the E-Digital Strategy, Brazil adopted (Decree 9.854/19) a National Internet of Things (IoT) Plan in June 2019. The plan's overall objective is to accelerate the uptake of IoT as a tool for the sustainable development of Brazil. The plan focuses on four key horizontal dimensions: 1) innovation and internationalisation; 2) human capital; 3) regulatory safety and privacy; and 4) infrastructure for connectivity and interoperability. It also identifies four key verticals (i.e. applications) regarded as having the largest growth potential in Brazil: agribusiness, smart cities, healthcare and manufacturing, in line with the E-Digital Strategy. The IoT Plan is a good example of a co-ordination effort at the national level, as it was promoted by the MCTIC, supported by BNDES and developed through several rounds of stakeholder interactions. BNDES and FINEP have opened lines of credit and provided grants to support business and academia to develop IoT networking technologies and applications in the priority areas. EMBRAPII is also supporting collaborative research in IoT (see below).

The National AI Strategy is set to promote high public-private co-operation around key national challenges

E-Digital also contains the mandate "to evaluate potential economic and social impact of AI and big data, and to propose policies that maximise effects and minimise negative results". Brazil is currently in the final phases of preparing its National AI Strategy, which has been elaborated through a multi-stakeholder process and has undergone a public consultation (closed in March 2020).

As part of the forthcoming national strategy for AI, the MCTIC and FAPESP, in co-operation with the Brazilian Internet Steering Committee (Comitê Gestor da Internet no Brasil, CGI.br), announced the creation of up to eight applied research centres (centros de pesquisa aplicada, CPA) in AI. These CPAs will be dedicated to applied scientific and technological research oriented to solving real challenges. The first four will focus on healthcare, agribusiness, manufacturing and smart cities, in alignment with the E-Digital Strategy and the IoT Plan. As they will be supported for a period of five years (possibly renewed for another five years, depending on the results achieved), the model ensures predictability of public funding, thus also stimulating the private sector's commitment. Each CPA may receive up to USD 255 000 (BRL 1 million) per year from FAPESP and an additional USD 255 000 from one or more partner companies. Multinational corporations also see Brazil as a potential AI innovation hub in the future. IBM has established a partnership with FAPESP to launch the first Latin American institution of IBM's AI Horizons Network, with USD 1.3 million (BRL 5 million) per year contributed by each of them.

Public-private partnerships are welcome, as innovation in key technologies such as data analytics and AI requires multidisciplinary and open research infrastructures where stakeholders can work together to advance AI responsibly. However, the rules regulating the CPAs' activities should be carefully designed. Private participation should not be limited to large companies, but needs to be extended to SMEs and start-ups. Setting high co-funding levels for the private sector may discourage the participation of small firms and start-ups; a more inclusive business model is therefore needed. These research centres should stimulate open innovation by establishing mechanisms for interaction of researchers with firms of all sizes and start-ups. The Alan Turing's Institute in the United Kingdom could provide a model for Brazil in this regard (Box 5.3).

Box 5.3. Digital technologies for the public good: The Alain Turing Institute in the United Kingdom

The Alan Turing Institute is the United Kingdom's national institute for data science and artificial intelligence (AI). Founded in 2015, it is an independent private sector legal entity formed as a joint venture between 13 universities. The institute undertakes basic research, and applies its cutting-edge science to real-world problems (revolutionising healthcare; delivering safer, smarter engineering; managing security in an insecure world; shining a light on the economy; making algorithmic systems fair, transparent and ethical; designing computers for the next generation of algorithms; supercharging research in science and humanities; fostering government innovation).

The national dimension of the centre allows delivering benefits that one single university could not deliver alone. The institute is a collaborative hub, with roots in universities and centres of research excellence across the country, counting on scientists from several disciplines and links to a network of industry, public sector and third sector partners. The Turing network encourages direct connections between universities, partners and other communities through a variety of models of engagement, ranging from one-week data study groups to multi-year research programmes, targeted projects and a membership programme for organisations and individuals in data science and AI.

One example of this way of working is the collaboration with the catapult centres, a network of ten physical centres that connect businesses with the country's research and academic communities. Each focuses on a strategic technology area and they offer a space with the facilities and expertise to enable businesses and researchers to collaboratively solve key problems and develop new products and services on a commercial scale. Digital Catapult runs a Machine Intelligence Garage programme to help AI and machine learning businesses gain access to technical expertise, computation power, knowledge and innovation.

Alan Turing and Digital Catapult provided support for nine start-up or scale-up companies to participate in "collaborative hackathons" with the aim to find data science solutions to real-world problems. These week-long events allow organisations to work with the institute, providing the start-ups access to a pool of researchers they may never otherwise have the opportunity to collaborate with.

Source: Alan Turing Institute (2020), *The Alan Touring Institute*, *www.turing.ac.uk*.

E-Digital, the national IoT Plan and the establishment of AI research centres around key areas are a step in the right direction for setting mission-oriented innovation. For the initiatives to deliver, Brazil should make such missions sufficiently granular, so that intermediate goals and deliverables can be set, and involve a wide array of stakeholders, enabling them to develop a shared sense of ownership (Mazzucato and Penna, 2016). The national IoT Plan was elaborated through a wide consultation and stakeholder involvement. The IoT Chamber is the advisory body accompanying its implementation, by monitoring the IoT Plan's initiatives and creating and encouraging partnerships between the public and private sectors. Although the chamber counts on the participation of various ministries (the MCTIC, the

Ministry of Economy, the Ministry of Agriculture, the Ministry of Health and the Ministry of Regional Development), it does not include the participation of stakeholders from businesses, academia or civil society. Involving a broader range of stakeholders is advisable for IoT deployment. Looking forward, a similar AI chamber should oversee and steer the implementation of the National AI Strategy, so that the government interacts with society at large for the advancement of this technology.

Missions are also an integral part of the 9th European Union framework programme for research and innovation, Horizon Europe, which will start in 2021. The programme has established five areas in which missions will be developed (cancer; adaptation to climate change including societal transformation; healthy oceans, seas, coastal and inland waters; climate-neutral and smart cities; soil health and food), with a mandate to solve a pressing challenge in society within a certain timeframe and budget. The European Commission will engage with citizens in a continuous process for the design, monitoring and assessment of the missions. Each of the areas has a mission board tasked with identifying one or more specific missions for implementation under Horizon Europe, i.e. to define specific challenges within the broad areas. The mission boards consist of 15 experts who have been selected through an open call for interest and come from innovation, research, policy making, civil society and relevant organisations. Each mission area also has an assembly that gathers a larger number of high-level experts. The assemblies provide an additional pool of ideas, knowledge and expertise that will be actively called upon to contribute to the success of the missions.

Mission-oriented innovation initiatives should rely on several instruments for their implementation, including demand-side initiatives such as public procurement. In Brazil, despite the conditions set by the new legal framework for innovation for the government to use instruments such as funding or placing direct orders and even minority equity in companies, to date their use has been limited (Tortato Rauen, 2019). High risk aversion among civil servants, who are personally liable for decisions taken as part of their duty, coupled with an increasing scrutiny from the Federal Court of Accounts (Tribunal de Contas da União, TCU), have limited the application of this law. Demand-driven innovation policies require civil servants to have a deep understanding of industries, technologies and markets. Appropriate actions should be taken to strengthen policy intelligence within procuring ministries. One way would be to engage with stakeholders to elaborate roadmaps for developing key technologies in strategic sectors, as suggested above, through formalised settings. BNDES may also provide expertise on the draft calls for tender or contracts. Brazil should also consider reviewing public procurement rules to contract solutions by innovative start-ups, for instance, those providing education services or using public sector data. Such start-ups are flourishing in Brazil and public demand would act as a stimulus for scaling them up.

Data governance frameworks must favour innovation, while respecting privacy

Data fuel innovation in the digital economy. To favour competition and innovation, data access policies should aim to ensure the broadest possible access to data and knowledge. At the same time, they must respect constraints regarding data privacy, ethics, intellectual property rights, and economic costs and benefits (OECD, 2020d). As businesses innovate with data, new policy issues are likely to arise, such as data portability or the treatment of non-personal sensor data, with different challenges at sectoral level (see Chapter 6). For instance, precision agriculture draws mainly on sensor and satellite data, and challenges often relate to data sharing and integration. The retail sector, on the other hand, exploits consumer purchasing and social media data to personalise services; therefore, the main concern is ensuring data privacy.

Brazil passed a General Data Protection Law in 2018. The law creates a normative framework seeking to harmonise and expand the right to personal data protection. However, the delay in establishing a data protection authority, as well as the features such an authority will have, may result in an ineffective application of the provisions (see Chapter 4).

Providing access to data generated by public services can foster data-driven innovation. Concerning policy initiatives for enhancing access to and sharing of data, the "Transparency Law" (Law 12.527/11) regulates access to information from public entities that are part of the direct administration of the executive, legislative, judiciary and public prosecution service. Decree 8.777/16 establishes the Open Data Policy for the Federal Executive Branch. The Ministry of Economy is also working on a "Government as a Platform" project (see Chapter 3), which will provide a legal mechanism by which the private sector will be able to use public data in a controlled environment. This is a positive initiative, as access to data can enhance public service delivery and facilitate the identification and resolution of emerging governmental and social challenges.

Brazil needs a balanced mix of policy instruments to spur digital innovation

Following the adoption of the E-Digital Strategy and the national IoT Plan, Brazil has been experimenting with new instruments for R&D and innovation in key digital technologies. These remain, however, relatively limited in number and volume of funding, whereas support to the ICT sector is mostly granted through tax incentives (Table 5.1).

Table 5.1. Main instruments supporting R&D and innovation in ICT in Brazil

Instrument	Type	Value (USD)	Type of beneficiary
Informatics Law	Tax credit	1.35 billion of tax credit resulting in 430 million/year in R&D investment (2016 values)	Firms in the ICT sector (manufacturing)
CNPq: Grants for research projects in computing sciences	Grants	3.8 million/year (average 2013-15)	Researchers
CNPq: Technology bonus and grants in advanced manufacturing	Grants (one-off)	547 000 in 2018	Small and medium-sized enterprises in partnership with large firms
BNDES IoT Pilot	Grants (one-off)	8.2 million in 2018	Consortia led by a public institution, with the participation of firms, municipalities and healthcare providers
FINEP IoT	Credit at preferential rate	410.5 million	Medium/large firms in the manufacturing sector
FINEP Inovacred 4.0 Pilot	Credit at preferential rate	50.9 million	Small and medium-sized enterprises in the manufacturing sector
EMBRAPII Programme of National Interest (PPI) in IoT, advanced manufacturing, robotics or mechatronics	Grants conditional to private-public collaboration	15.3 million/year	Firms in all sectors in co-operation with public universities or research centres

Notes: The purpose of the table is illustrative. It only shows programmes that are specifically designed for the ICT sector/digital technologies such as the Internet of Things (IoT) and advanced manufacturing. It does not include information about horizontal programmes, such as traditional credit lines, which may also support ICT innovation.

The Informatics Law needs to be revised

In Brazil, the Informatics Law (Lei de Informática, Law 8.248/91, last amended by Law 13.969/19) provides firms in the ICT manufacturing sector with tax credits for R&D expenditures. The law was issued in the early 1990s after two decades of highly protectionist policies, with the objective of increasing the national manufacturing capacity and generating jobs.

The law provides tax credits as a counterpart to investment in R&D and innovation, which firms can use to reduce the amount due on their corporate income taxes. They also benefit from an exemption on the IPI for intermediate goods used in the production of the incentivised goods.

In order to benefit from the tax credit, firms manufacturing ICT goods specified in the law (Article 16A of Law 8.258/91) must:

- produce according to the basic production process (*processo produtivo básico*, PPB), which is established by the Ministry of Economy and by the MCTIC and defined as "the minimum set of operations at the factory that characterizes the effective industrialization of a given product" [Law 8.387/1991])
- invest a minimum of 4% of their gross turnover from the sales of goods covered by the law and produced according to the relevant PPBs in R&D and innovation activities in the ICT sector
- be accredited by the MCTIC.

Firms have several options to invest in R&D and innovation. Part of the investment has to be directed to accredited STI or public research centres/HEIs, and to the FNDCT. Firms can also finance projects of national interest in the areas of ICT considered as government priorities (Programas e Projetos de

Interesse Nacional nas Áreas de Tecnologias da Informação e Comunicação, PPIs). Examples of such projects are those in IoT and advanced manufacturing under the management of EMBRAPII (see below). For the remaining amount, firms can invest in internal R&D, or, in funds supporting innovative start-ups, among others (Table 5.2).

The tax credit is a multiple of the amount invested, with multipliers varying depending on the firm's location and the object of the R&D and innovation. The credit, as calculated through the multiplier, cannot exceed a given ceiling, expressed as a percentage of the base of the R&D and innovation investment (the gross turnover from the sales of goods covered by the law and produced according to the PPB). Multipliers and related ceilings progressively decrease until 2029.

Multipliers and ceilings are established so that 4% is both the minimum and the maximum percentage of turnover firms would invest in R&D and innovation, as any additional expenditure would lead to a percentage above the ceiling, which will not generate any credit. The only incentive to spend higher percentages of gross turnover in R&D and innovation is for firms that do not fully reach the objectives set by the PPB (but still have to reach a minimum threshold), and can therefore compensate through higher expenditures. This seems to set less stringent local content rules, while strengthening the spending requirement. The Informatics Law has been reformed following a World Trade Organization (WTO) ruling that found it to cause taxation in excess and a less favourable treatment of imported goods (WTO panels WT-DS472 and WT-DS497). Under the previous rules, and until April 2020 (date of entry into force of the new ones), firms benefited from an 80% reduction of IPI on the incentivised products. The tax rate varies by product, and on average the rate applying to the incentivised products is 15%. This therefore made it possible for beneficiary firms to reduce the effective tax burden from 15% to 7%. In its new formulation, the law also maintains a similar or even higher level of reduction in the effective tax burden.

Table 5.2. Options for R&D and innovation spending set by the Informatics Law

% of resources		Modality of investment
4% of gross turnover from sales of ICT goods and services incentivised by the law	**Minimum 1.84%**	Co-operation with science, technology and innovation institutions, or public research centres/ higher education institutes - **Minimum 0.8%**
		Co-operation with science, technology and innovation institutions, or public research centres/ higher education institutes in the North (except Zona Franca de Manaus), Northeast and Central West - **Minimum 0.46%**
		National Fund for Scientific and Technological Development - **Minimum 0.4%**
		Application in Programmes and Projects of National Interest(PPIs) - **Minimum 1.84%**
	Remaining (maximum 2.16%)	Internal R&D and innovation, including outsourced to other firms, research centres or universities
		Support to development programmes for the ICT sector (up to two-thirds of resources)
		Investment funds or other instruments approved by the Securities and Exchange Commission directed at capitalisation of technological firms, or application in government programmes directed at supporting technological firms
		Application in priority programmes
		Application in social organisations that promote or realise projects R&D and innovation in ICT

Sources: Casa Civil (1991), *Lei n. 8.248, de 23 de Outubro de 1991 – Dispõe Sobre a Capacitação e Competitividade do Setor de Informática e Automação, e dá Outras Providências*, *www.planalto.gov.br/ccivil_03/leis/l8248.htm*; Casa Civil (2019), *Lei n. 13.969, de 26 de Dezembro de 2019 – Dispõe Sobre a Política Industrial Para o Setor de Tecnologias da Informação e Comunicação e Para o Setor de Semicondutores*, *www.planalto.gov.br/ccivil_03/_ato2019-2022/2019/lei/L13969.htm*.

The policy is therefore very generous, as it compensates firms with more than what they spent. Investments in R&D from this law are in fact only about one-third of its fiscal cost: in 2016, the lost revenues amounted to USD 1.35 billion (BRL 4.7 billion), while the investment in R&D was USD 430 million (BRL 1.5 billion) (Ministry of Economy, 2019). The law also has a low base of eligible firms, as under the old rules, software fell outside its scope (as it is not subject to the IPI). In this new formulation, while software is included, firms in IT services are still not eligible. As a result, the number of beneficiaries of the Informatics Law is small (673 in 2018) and mostly of medium/large size (54% in 2016), with less than 50 large firms accounting for most of the total volume of tax exemptions (Zuniga et al., 2016). The largest firms benefiting from the law are multinationals, such as Samsung, LG and Hewlett Packard, while Brazilian firms are more numerous, but smaller.

The policy also lacks transparency, as information about its implementation and results is not available in a timely manner. Firms have to submit their annual reports on the fulfilment of the R&D obligation to the MCTIC. Up to 2018, it was the MCTIC's responsibility to examine the annual reports, which resulted in a backlog of reports and approval of incentives. The new law seems to have a more agile application process, although the MCTIC only has 30 days to approve the credits. The MCTIC has introduced changes to improve efficiency, such as increasing electronic systems for the work processes and defining indicators to measure the results of the benefits granted. Establishing a monitoring framework and an evaluation plan is also needed. Using digital technologies can improve monitoring of the policies' outcomes (OECD, 2019e), for instance, by enabling the collection of increasingly granular datasets, which would allow text-mining project descriptions to analyse research subjects, discover patterns and get a more refined understanding of the R&D investments.

The government has not carried out a formal evaluation of the Informatics Law, as Brazil lacks a regulatory framework for a regular assessment of public policy. Several studies have analysed the effects of the law, sometimes with contrasting findings. Overall, the law has enabled Brazil to build a domestic manufacturing capacity, to generate employment, including of highly skilled workers (more than 7 000 working on R&D). By restricting the eligibility to the tax break to ICT goods produced domestically, the law has succeeded in attracting the world's leading ICT firms to Brazil, with results in employment and improving the sector's added value, which have remained stable over the past years (Figure 5.17). However, as PPBs concern mostly assembly, the productive capacity focuses on the low value-added production phases, and the sector remains dependent on the import of electronic parts and components, including for telecommunications devices. The law has also made it possible for firms outside the Manaus Tax-Free Zone to remain competitive (Prochnik et al., 2015). However, the law did not have an effect on exports, although this was not one of its stated objectives. Unlike Asian countries, where the ICT sector has strong international ties as part of a global value chains, in Brazil, firms usually sell consumer products domestically and are not export-oriented.

By design, the law does not stimulate additionality in R&D investment, as it is rather an instrument to attract foreign direct investment in the country, by offsetting the high taxation. Most of the activities carried out concern the development of existing solutions, such as adaptation to the local market, rather than innovation. Product innovation today in Brazil concerns a few niches, such as banking automation and telecommunications equipment (Barboza, Madeira and Lima, 2017). According to several evaluations, the law has not had any effect on additionality of R&D investments (Kannebley and Porto, 2012) or productivity, but rather hinders the reallocation of resources (Ribeiro, Prochnik and De Negri, 2011).

As the law mandates a minimum share of funding spent in collaborations with institutions accredited by the MCTIC, this spending is actually the main share of the overall investment (Figure 5.18). Over the years, a number of institutions, mainly private, have grown as a result of continuous co-operation with the investing firms. About USD 1.6 billion (BRL 6.2 billion) was spent by firms in collaborative research over the period 2006-17 (ABINEE, 2019). One such institution is CESAR, located in Recife, in the Northeast region of the country. Funding from the law has allowed consolidating the research centre through partnerships with the private sector and in 2000 led to the establishment of Porto Digital, a technological park affiliated with the Federal University of Pernambuco. The park is a cluster of over 300 firms, including multinationals, specialised in ICT and the creative economy (digital games, cine-video-animation, music, design and photography).

Among other institutions benefiting from the law are the CERTI foundation, Instituto Atlântico, and some public research or HEIs, although they are a minority. Several of them are also units selected by EMBRAPII for carrying out projects in IoT and advanced manufacturing (Table 5.4). Some of the main research centres engaging in collaborative research, however, although legally separated entities, are spinoffs of multinationals, such as the Samsung Institute for the Development of Informatics, Eldorado (Motorola), the Flextronics Institute for Technology and Venturus (Sony) (Zylberberg and Sturgeon, 2019). The linkages with the mother company, coupled with efforts to limit engineering mobility across research institutes has reduced the positive externalities of these R&D activities in Brazil (Zylberberg and Sturgeon, 2019). In terms of innovation outputs, collaborative research was less productive than internal one (Figure 5.19).

Figure 5.17. Value added and employment in the ICT sector in Brazil, the OECD and selected countries, 2006 and 2016

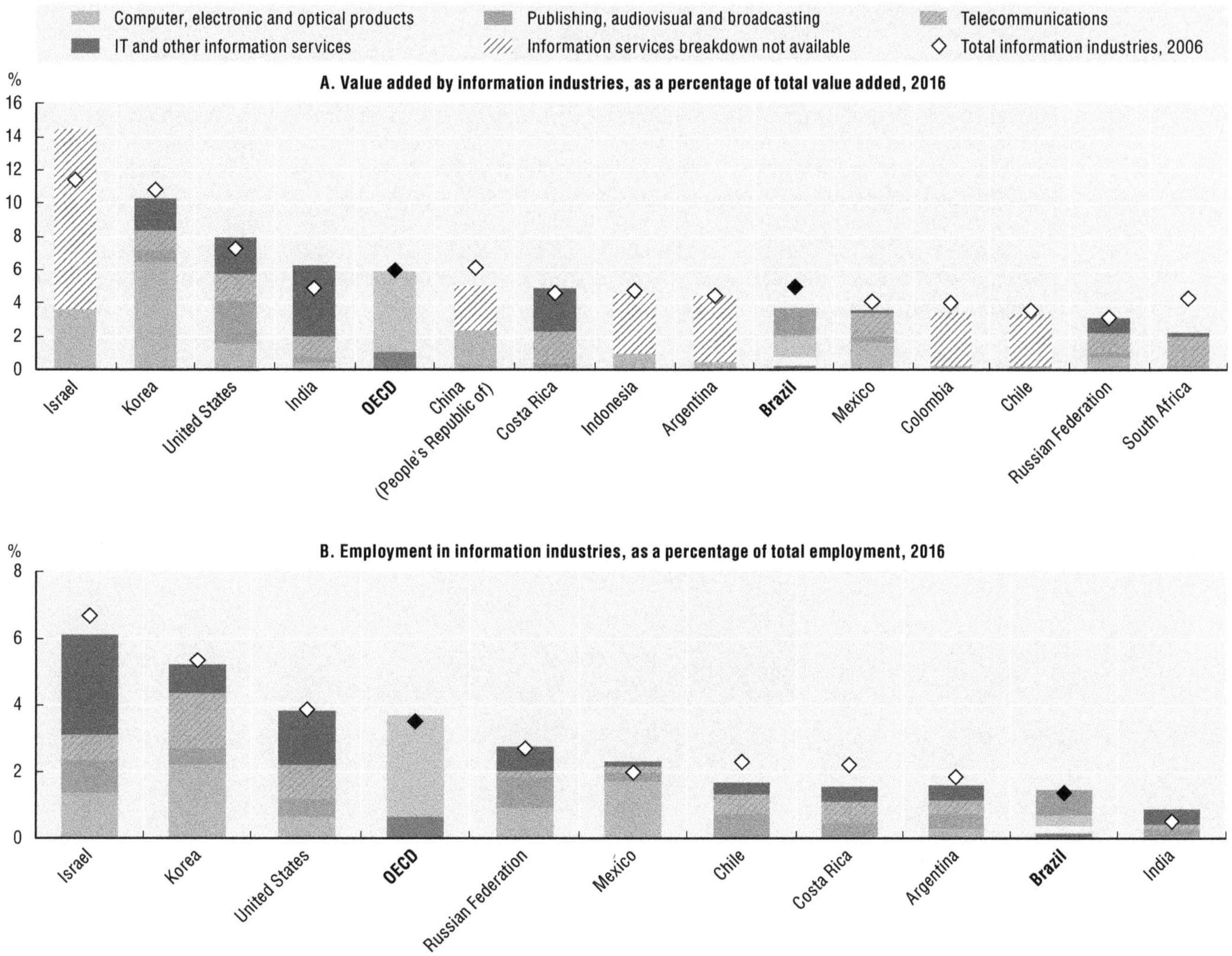

Notes: IT = information technology. Information industries cover the following ISIC Rev.4 divisions: Computer, electronic and optical products (26); Publishing, audiovisual and broadcasting (58-60); Telecommunications (61); and IT and other information services (62, 63). For Argentina, Brazil, the People's Republic of China, Colombia, Indonesia and South Africa, the value-added shares refer to 2015. For China and Indonesia, estimates are based on the OECD *Inter-Country Input-Output (ICIO) Database*. For Brazil and India, employment shares refer to 2015.

Sources: OECD (2019a), *Measuring the Digital Transformation: A Roadmap for the Future, https://dx.doi.org/10.1787/9789264311992-en.*

Summing up, the law has succeeded in its industrial objectives, and namely manufacturing capacity and employment, by subsiding firms through lower production costs. However, the policy does not seem to achieve its innovation objectives, which support productivity growth and competitiveness. Several aspects in the policy design should be improved.

First, the law currently favours large, established firms, and does not consider young, innovative companies, such as start-ups and spinoffs. For smaller firms to apply, the minimum threshold for investment may be lowered. Also, the cap on spending, which currently is equal to the minimum required, should be reviewed. Its scope, which has already positively been expanded to include software in the latest reform, should further include the ICT service sector, and also cover ICT-using sectors investing in digital solutions and services. As the next industrial revolution unfolds, manufacturing will be increasingly automated and make extensive use of digital technologies enabled through advanced services. Accordingly, the separation of manufacturing and services will increasingly be blurred and policies will need to be adapted (see Chapter 6).

Second, the definition of PPBs runs against quick developments in ICTs and the very nature of innovation (De Negri and Tortato Rauen, 2018). It does not include obligations for the most sophisticated stages of product manufacturing, thus reducing the high-value content of the domestically manufactured goods. For all of the above reasons, this requirement should therefore be removed. Instead, the law should revise the criteria for the tax incentive and limit it to firms with demonstrated innovation capacity. Favourable tax treatment may also be considered for investments in innovative start-ups. Furthermore, the policy could also pursue the objective of promoting linkages between domestic firms and subsidiaries of foreign multinational enterprises. This would enhance technology transfer, the capability of local firms and their integration in global value chains. Some South-East Asian countries provide good practice in this regard (Box 5.4).

Lastly, funds could be focused on the country's innovation priorities, for instance those set by the national IoT Plan and the National AI Strategy, instead of being dispersed around several, small-scale projects (about 3 000 carried out each year).

Figure 5.18. R&D expenditures from the Informatics Law, by destination, 2016

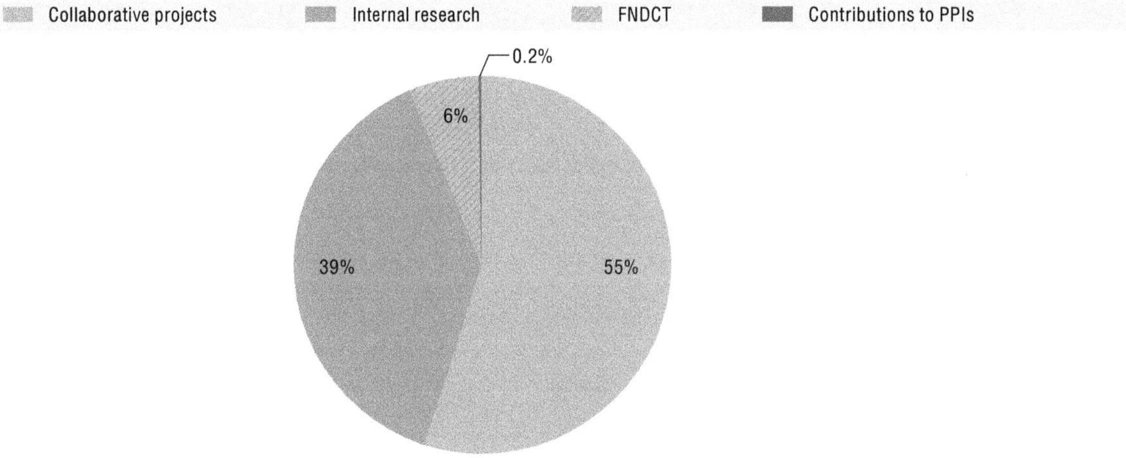

Notes: FNDCT = National Fund for Scientific and Technological Development; PPIs = Programmes and Projects of National Interest.

Source: MCTIC (2017), *Relatório de Resultados da Lei de Informática - Lei nº 8.248/91: Dados dos Relatórios Demonstrativos do Ano Base 2016 – Versão 1.*

Figure 5.19. Projects funded through the Informatics Law generating patents and publications, 2016

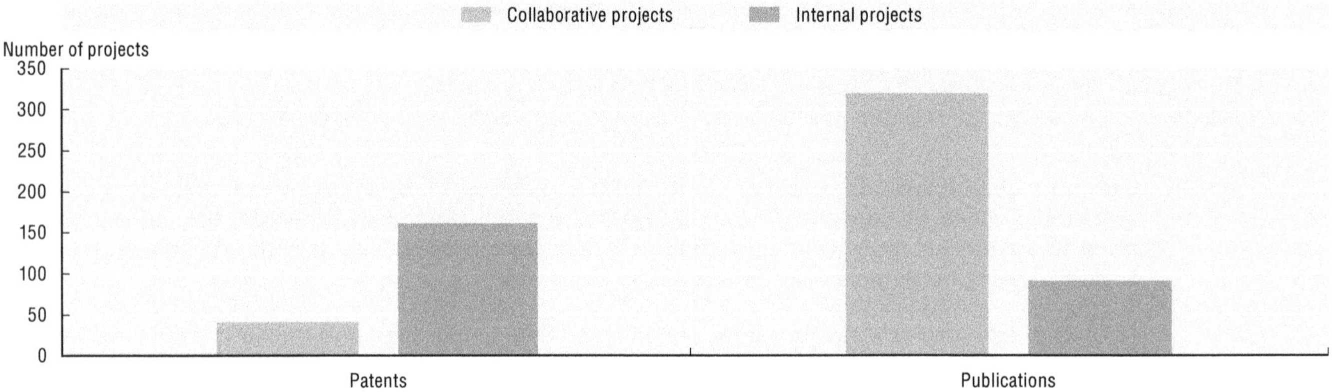

Source: MCTIC (2017), *Relatório de Resultados da Lei de Informática - Lei nº 8.248/91: Dados dos Relatórios Demonstrativos do Ano Base 2016 - Versão 1.*

The recent reform has responded to the need to ensure legal certainty for the sector, as the law stipulates that incentives will be maintained until 2029. Going forward, Brazil should perform a full-fledged evaluation of the effects of the law, with a focus on the type of innovation financed by the R&D tax credit, i.e. new-to-the-firm, new-to-the-market, etc. Such an evaluation would provide evidence for potential adjustments to the current formulation of the policy. It would also provide an objective and transparent justification for the policy continuation, as well as an opportunity to communicate broadly about its effects. In parallel, and well before the policy expires, the country should engage in a debate with all stakeholders on the perspective for the ICT sector. As it currently largely depends on public incentives and is one of the sectors with the highest protection from tariff and non-tariff barriers to trade (OECD, forthcoming), the objective should be to make it more competitive and better integrated into the global value chain.

Box 5.4. Tax incentives to foster linkages between subsidiaries of foreign multinational enterprises with domestic firms

Malaysia offers various incentives to encourage linkages between foreign investors and local small and medium-sized enterprises. Under the Industrial Linkage Program, investors can claim tax deductions for costs involved in providing support to local suppliers, including training, product development and testing, and factory auditing to ensure local supplier quality. A Global Supplier Program offers financial and organisational support to multinational enterprises (MNEs), if specialists from their foreign affiliates are seconded to local firms (for up to two years) for the purposes of local upgrading.

Singapore has the Pioneer Certificate Incentive and Development and Expansion Incentive, which encourages foreign MNEs to set up local upstream and downstream activities that are more typically conducted at companies' headquarters. The incentive provided is a corporate tax exemption or a reduced concessionary tax rate on eligible income. Companies that apply for this incentive must commit to upgrading their employment and business investments. The programme intends to foster technology transfers and the scale-up of the local economy.

Similarly, Thailand moved from a system of location-based incentives (economic zones) to an activity- and merit-based one. These new incentives also include the promotion of small and medium-sized enterprise linkages and skills.

Source: OECD (2019f), *OECD Investment Policy Reviews: Southeast Asia*, *www.oecd.org/investment/oecd-investment-policy-review-southeast-asia.htm*.

New approaches are being tested for digital innovation

The CNPq's technological bonuses for advanced manufacturing promote adoption by small and medium-sized enterprises

In 2018, the CNPq launched a call for a "Technology Bonus and Grants in Advanced Manufacture", making financial support available to R&D and innovation projects on solutions for advanced manufacturing projects, processes and services, performed by micro and small businesses in partnership with larger companies. The support includes a technological bonus to help finance the project, combined with grants for training and technology development. This is a new instrument introduced by the legal framework for innovation, intended to pay for sharing and using technological research and development infrastructure, hiring specialised technological services, or technology transfer (when it is merely complementary to those services).

The technology bonus is a valuable addition to the mix of instruments available to enterprises, as the development of solutions requiring digital technologies is often very costly for SMEs and requires training and adaptation of the solution to the specific SME's needs. The recent financial constraints of the CNPq may leave this as a one-off initiative, whereas to achieve sizeable effects, it should be continued on a larger scale in the forthcoming years.

BNDES Internet of Things pilots support real-time testing of solutions

BNDES is a federal public company whose goal is to provide long-term financing for endeavours that contribute to the country's development. It has a range of financial products earmarked for investment projects in areas of strategic priority.

In 2018, BNDES granted USD 8.2 million (BRL 30 million) to co-fund 14 pilots on IoT technology solutions in 3 priority areas: cities, health and agriculture (Table 5.3). Pilots in manufacturing will also be financed, in co-operation with the National Confederation of Industry (Confederação Nacional da Indústria, CNI). The pilots have been selected among over 50 proposals received to the call issued for this initiative, for a proposed investment 8 times higher than the budget initially available (USD 4.1 million, or BRL 15 million), which has since been doubled. The success of the call shows the high interest for IoT in the country, the readiness of the community, as well as the demand for grants to support development efforts. The leading institutions of the projects are public technology institutes, as BNDES can only provide non-reimbursable funding to public institutions, but all the consortia are made up of several private partners, with 11 technologies institutes, more than 70 companies and 6 hospitals overall. Over the two-year implementation period, the IoT pilots are aimed at testing the cost-effectiveness of these solutions in a real setting, with the objective of scaling them up across the country.

Experimentation is key to digital innovation, and in particular for IoT. Pilot tests in IoT are essential to check the seamless integration between the software and hardware components, the behaviour of the system in different connectivity conditions, and the potential security and privacy vulnerabilities. Pilot testing also checks the usability of devices, while gathering users' feedback to integrate them into further developments. Pilots also make it possible to assess performance when the number of users increases. Testing environments where new technology developments can be tested in controlled but near to real-world conditions are increasingly used across OECD countries (OECD, 2019g). The IoT pilots fall in this category and should be replicated. Also, there should be a plan for the follow-up phases of the pilots: government initiatives could provide technical support and funding to municipalities and hospitals to assist in the adoption of tested solutions, for instance as part of the Smart Cities strategy (see Chapter 3). In the United Kingdom, the National Health Service is running IoT pilots in healthcare, through a Test Beds Programme in partnership with industry. Successful innovations are then made available to the National Health Service and care organisations around the country (OECD, 2020d).

FINEP supports the development of IoT solutions and their uptake

FINEP funds several programmes supporting innovation in universities and firms, with funding conditions adjusted to the level of risk of the project, the innovation stage, as well as the profile of the beneficiary organisation. FINEP's support to IoT and Industry 4.0 has increased in recent years as a result of the government's efforts in this area. FINEP's support ranges from grants (Centelha), investments (FINEP Startup) and venture capital funds to support start-ups (Table 5.6), to credit for developing IoT and related technologies in the key four verticals.

As part of the national IoT Plan, FINEP launched the IoT programme in 2018, a new credit line with a budget of USD 410.5 million (BRL 1.5 billion). The action is directed at medium-sized and large firms (with minimum annual revenues of USD 4 million, or BRL 16 million) submitting an investment plan on IoT for at least USD 1.4 million (BRL 5 million). The programme offers preferential credit conditions (1% interest rate, instead of a market rate of 4-5%) to develop digital solutions with applications in industry, health, agriculture and cities based on IoT and other enabling technologies. The initiative supports the development of such solutions with applications in the above areas ("axis 1"); the formulation ("axis 2") and execution ("axis 3") of strategic business digitalisation plans in firms. These are business plans developed by a specialised company on how to integrate enabling technologies into the firm's production process and indicating the priorities for adoption.

Within the overall FINEP IoT programme, in September 2019 the agency also launched the USD 51 million (BRL 200 million) pilot Inovacred 4.0, specifically aimed at supporting the deployment and use in manufacturing and agriculture of advanced manufacturing solutions in SMEs. The initiative was prepared in partnership with the National Confederation of Industry, the Ministry of Economy and the MCTIC, and is the first of the Brazilian Chamber of Industry 4.0, formed by more than 30 entities representing the government, businesses and academia.

Overall, between 2018 and January 2020, FINEP contracted more than USD 356.5 million (BRL 1.4 billion) in projects supporting IoT and Industry 4.0. This offer of credit at a preferential rate plays a key role in the Brazilian system for innovation, given the absence of long-term credit markets. FINEP's portfolio of financed projects is a good indication of the use of ICT solutions across the economy, given that all the projects, except one, are in sectors other than ICT. Projects involving IoT solutions, for instance, are in the manufacturing of motor vehicles, machine manufacturing for agriculture and the plastic industry.

Table 5.3. BNDES Internet of Things pilot projects

Lead institution	Area/project	City or municipality/state
	Health	
Centre for Studies and Advanced Systems of Recife (CESAR)	Monitoring of inventory and automation of requests for replacement of oxygen cylinders, monitoring of consumption and registration of dosage.	Recife/Pernambuco
Hospital das Clínicas, USP Medical School (HCFMUSP)	1. Monitoring of hospital assets (infusion pumps, stretchers, wheelchairs and ambulances). 2. Screening for diabetic retinopathy by teleophthalmology.	São Paulo/São Paulo
Technological Integrated Systems Laboratory (LSI-TEC)	1. Remote monitoring for sepsis control in children with cancer. 2. Remote monitoring applied to sleep quality.	São Paulo/São Paulo
Pontifical Catholic University (PUC-Rio)	Development of solutions for a "Digital Hospital" involving automated and intelligent management of assets, patients, health agents, procedures and medical records.	Rio de Janeiro/Rio de Janeiro
National Research Network (RNP)	Remote monitoring of obese children and adolescents.	Fortaleza/Ceará
Federal University of Rio Grande do Sul	Remote monitoring of patients with hypertension.	Porto Alegre/Rio Grande do Sul
	Agriculture	
Telecommunications Research and Development Centre (CPqD)	Optimisation in the use of agricultural machinery, rainfall monitoring, pest management and precision livestock techniques for the welfare of cattle.	Diamantino/MatoGrosso, Correntina/Bahia, Pradópolis/São Paulo and Lucas do Rio Verde/MatoGrosso
Embrapa Informática	Pest and machinery management, animal welfare monitoring in dairy cattle farming and use of IoT systems for crop-livestock-forest integration.	Carazinho/Rio Grande do Sul, Santa Maria do Pará/Pará, Castanhal/Pará, Barbalha/Ceará, Valença/Rio de Janeiro, São Carlos/São Paulo, São João da Boa Vista/São Paulo, Itatinga/São Paulo, Sinop/MatoGrosso, Recanto das Emas/Distrito Federal, Parai/Rio Grande do Sul, Bom Despacho/Minas Gerais; Boa Esperança/Minas Gerais, Passos/Minas Gerais and Cel. Pacheco/Minas Gerais
Foundation for Technological Innovations (FITEC)	Integrated data platform (climate, soil, management, machinery, energy efficiency and water efficiency) for monitoring and recommendations on the use of natural resources, inputs and machinery.	Uberlandia/Minas Gerais
PUC-Rio	Optimisation of energy resources, natural resources, agricultural inputs, agricultural machinery, in addition to solutions aimed at small agricultural producers.	Holambra/São Paulo and Santiago do Norte/MatoGrosso
	Cities	
CPqD	1. Use of cameras and computer vision for public security. 2. Advanced climate prediction. 3. Provision of the shared electric vehicle service. 4. Complete remote management platform for public lighting.	Campinas/São Paulo
National Institute of Telecommunications Foundation (FINATEL)	Implementation of remote management in the intelligent lighting network and integration with video surveillance for public security.	Santa Rita do Sapucaí/Minas Gerais, Caxambu/Minas Gerais and Piraí/Rio de Janeiro
FITEC	Implementation of a public lighting network enabling IoT solutions, such as smart dumps, video surveillance for public security, civil defence and electronic parking meters.	Mar de Espanha/Minas Gerais
Instituto Atlântico	Implementation of public lighting networks that enable IoT solutions, aiming at reducing travel time, increasing the attractiveness of public transport and increasing the surveillance capacity for public security.	Fortaleza/Ceará, Juazeiro do Norte/Ceará and Petrópolis/Rio de Janeiro
Technological Integrated Systems Laboratory (LSI-TEC)	Use of Single Board Computer "Labrador" for: 1) intelligent control of the traffic light network in the city of São Paulo; and 2) monitoring of crime situations and threats to urban security.	São Paulo/São Paulo

Source: BNDES (2020), *BNDES*, *www.bndes.gov.br*.

EMBRAPII fosters collaborative research in the Internet of Things and advanced manufacturing

EMBRAPII is the co-ordinator of one of the Programmes and Projects of National Interest (PPIs) in IoT and Advanced Manufacturing. Since December 2018, firms financing PPIs have become eligible for the tax incentives under the Informatics Law; the 2019 reform of the law further expands the possibility to finance PPIs. Potentially all of a firm's R&D and innovation expenditure can contribute to PPIs (Table 5.2). The resources from the PPI are used as a financial counterpart for EMBRAPII according to its model (Box 5.1). By September 2019, over 520 projects in ICT (robotics, mechatronics, IoT and advanced manufacturing) had been launched through EMBRAPII, fostering collaboration among firms and the 18 research units (Table 5.4), for a total of USD 191.5 million (BRL 752 million). The projects have resulted in 128 intellectual property applications.

Some of the projects supported by EMBRAPII also involve more than one unit, or more than one firm, establishing partnerships to find solutions to more difficult challenges. Groups of units are therefore developing into innovation hubs, with their own specialisation, and spread across the country. This network of hubs should be strengthened and formalised, to become a reference for firms seeking support for their innovation efforts. In digital innovation, collaboration from different disciplines is often necessary, and having a network of excellence centres would ease the research for competences in a certain field.

These units also have infrastructures and demonstration facilities for them to evolve as testbeds for technologies, for firms, in particular SMEs, to pilot solutions before their adoption. Several countries are building such collaborative systems, to leverage existing knowledge and make it available to a large number of firms, and to link established companies with researchers or start-ups. The initiative "Testbeds for Industry 4.0", launched in May 2019 (see Chapter 6), which involves also EMBRAPII's units, goes in this direction.

Table 5.4. EMBRAPII's units for the Internet of Things and advanced manufacturing, 2019

Specialisation	Institution	City	State	Region
Optical communications	CPqD	Campinas	São Paulo	Southeast
Printed electronics	CSEM	Belo Horizonte	Minas Gerais	Southeast
Software for cyber-physical systems	DCC/UFMG	Belo Horizonte	Minas Gerais	Southeast
Internet and mobile computing equipment	Eldorado	Campinas	São Paulo	Southeast
Intelligent automotive systems	IFMG	Formiga	Minas Gerais	Southeast
Biophotonics and instruments	IFSC/USP	São Carlos	São Paulo	Southeast
Digital communications and radio frequency	INATEL	Santa Rita do Sapucaí	Minas Gerais	Southeast
Computational engineering solutions	TECGRAF/PUC RJ	Rio de Janeiro	Rio de Janeiro	Southeast
Software and automation	CEEI/UFCG	Campina Grande	Paraíba	Northeast
Embedded systems and digital mobility	IFCE	Fortaleza	Ceará	Northeast
Manufacturing systems	IFPB	João Pessoa	Paraíba	Northeast
Connected products	CESAR	Recife	Pernambuco	Northeast
Technology in health	IFBA	Salvador	Bahia	Northeast
Integrated manufacturing	SENAI/CIMATEC	Salvador	Bahia	Northeast
Intelligent systems	CERTI	Florianópolis	Santa Catarina	South
Embedded systems	ISI-SE	Florianópolis	Santa Catarina	South
Sensor systems	ISI METALMECÂNICA	São Leopoldo	Rio Grande do Sul	South
Embedded electronics	LACTEC	Curitiba	Paraná	South
Systems for manufacturing automation	INDT	Manaus	Amazonas	North

Notes: CPqD = Telecommunications Research and Development Centre; CEEI/UFCG = Electrical Engineering and Computing Centre/Federal University of Campina Grande; CERTI Foundation = Centres of Reference in Innovative Technologies; CESAR = Centre for Studies and Advanced Systems of Recife; CSEM = Swiss Centre for Electronics and Microtechnics; DCC/UFMG = Department of Computer Science/Federal University of Minas Gerais; IFBA = Federal Institute of Education, Science and Technology of Bahia; IFCE = Federal Institute of Education, Science and Technology of Ceará; IFMG = Federal Institute of Education, Science and Technology of Minas Gerais; IFPB = Federal Institute of Paraíba; IFSC/USP = Institute of Physics of São Carlos/University of São Paulo; INATEL = National Institute of Telecommunications; INDT = Institute of Technological Development; ISI METALMECÂNICA = SENAI Institute of Innovation in Metal-Mechanics Integrated Solutions; ISI-SE = SENAI Institute of Innovation in Embedded Systems; LACTEC = Institute of Technological Development; SENAI/CIMATEC = SENAI Integrated Campus of Manufacturing and Technologies; TECGRAF/PUC RJ = Institute of Technical-Scientific Software Development/Pontifical Catholic University of Rio de Janeiro.

Source: EMBRAPII (2020), *EMBRAPII*, *www.embrapii.org.br*.

If EMBRAPII's units scale up and network, the organisation will need to be able to ensure support to the current units, and possibly to increase their number to ensure greater thematic and geographic coverage. This will require additional resources, as, despite its success, funding remains limited, at USD 63.6 million per year (BRL 250 million). In this regard, the recent reform of the Informatics Law goes in the right direction, although the choice of funding destination is left to the firms, and therefore it is not foreseeable how this will impact PPIs' funding. As stressed above, in order to maximise the R&D and innovation investment from the Informatics Law, the MCTIC may become more stringent in terms of the funding destination, directing them to the innovation priorities set by the government.

Box 5.5. Linking competences in networks and diffusing them to firms: The role of digital innovation hubs

Digital innovation requires a high degree of co-operation across sectors and disciplines. In OECD countries, initiatives promoting this type of interaction are flourishing. Several instruments are used to this end, for instance clusters, grants conditional on collaboration, innovation hubs and innovation grants.

For example, since 2016, the European Commission has been promoting the establishment of digital innovation hubs across the European Union, in most cases with technical universities or research organisations at their core. Digital innovation hubs offer firms, especially small and medium-sized enterprises (SMEs), access to technology testing, financing advice, market intelligence and networking opportunities. These hubs also play a role in strengthening employees' preparedness to work with new technologies, by offering access to training and skills development. The European Commission also offers funding to SMEs to test and implement digital technologies. The "technological bonuses" available in Brazil could be used in this sense.

The Digital Hub Initiative in Germany supports the establishment of digital hubs across the country that connect medium-sized businesses and larger firms with new innovation partners from the scientific and start-up communities. Hubs aim to foster networking and co-operation within and between hubs, and are expected to serve as platforms for engaging in dialogue with global market leaders and foreign investors. There are currently hubs in 12 cities, each focusing on a particular industry (e.g. Internet of Things and Fintech hub in Berlin, artificial intelligence hub in Karlsruhe, digital chemistry and digital health hub in Ludwigshafen/Mannheim). The I 4.0-Testumgebung (I 4.0 Testbed) aims at improving the innovation potential of SMEs to test products, components and digital processes in real-life conditions. Aside from the infrastructure, the SMEs have access to expert knowledge that help them further develop their digital technologies with the right tools.

Sources: Planes-Satorra and Paunov (2019), "The digital innovation policy landscape in 2019", *https://doi.org/10.1787/6171f649-en*; European Commission (2020), *Digital Innovation Hubs (DIHs) in Europe*, *https://ec.europa.eu/digital-single-market/en/digital-innovation-hubs*; Digital Hub Initiative (2020), *The Digital Hub Initiative*, *www.de-hub.de*.

The policy mix in support of digital innovation is dominated by tax incentives, which currently mostly favour large incumbents and do not yet provide a suitable mechanism for smaller and younger firms. While seeking possibilities for making these mechanisms more effective in promoting innovation across firms of all sizes, Brazil should also rebalance the policy mix towards instruments supporting diffusion across firms, higher risk innovation, experimentation and collaboration across sectors.

The main research agencies in Brazil have shown dynamism in recent years in supporting new digital technologies, in particular advanced manufacturing and IoT solutions. Such co-ordination of efforts, which follows from the government's action in promoting the IoT Plan and advanced manufacturing as priorities, is a good example of aligning instruments to reach the set objectives. However, these initiatives remain dispersed and without predictability of funding. Co-ordination of the instruments and among institutions should be enhanced to articulate the innovation ecosystem and increase linkages among projects and teams.

Brazil should also take advantage of the existing innovation ecosystems, by establishing a network of competence centres, to avoid dispersing resources and make excellence spill-over to a broader community. In line with a definition of the key challenges and objectives to achieve, the available instruments should be clearly structured and the MCTIC should be the central entry point to innovators, with a centralised list of opportunities. Israel has recently restructured its offer of incentives and grants to fit the needs of the various target groups (Box 5.6).

Box 5.6. Making support instruments fit to their audience: Israel's innovation divisions

In 2016, a new authority was established in Israel, the Israel Innovation Authority (IIA). It replaced the Office of the Chief Scientist as the main Israeli government body that promotes and supports R&D, innovation and technology collaboration. The IIA provides a variety of practical tools and funding platforms aimed at addressing the dynamic and changing needs of the local and international innovation ecosystems. In 2017, the IIA formulated its strategy for 2018-23. This strategy formulates its vision to transform the Israeli innovation system from the start-up phase to the innovation-based growth phase, and increase the social and economic impact of the Israeli innovation system.

In order to meet the various needs of its wide range of clients, the IIA has developed a new internal structure focused on six primary innovation divisions. Each division offers a unique "toolbox" of customised and comprehensive incentive programmes. These divisions thus serve as a launch pad for successful innovative projects, providing entrepreneurs and companies with the most relevant plan for them to realise and implement their ideas, develop their products, and mobilise private investment. There are six innovation divisions: 1) Start-Up; 2) Growth; 3) Technological Infrastructure; 4) Advanced Manufacturing; 5) Societal Challenges; and 6) International Collaboration.

Source: OECD/EC (2020), *STIP Compass*, *https://stip.oecd.org/stip.html*.

Support to innovative entrepreneurship

A rising start-up scene

Brazil hosts one of the most active high-tech entrepreneurial communities in Latin America. An estimated 10 000 start-ups operate in the country (ABStartups and Accenture, 2018), mostly active in professional services, telecommunications, media and telecom, and finance. These start-ups flourish by developing new business models enabled by digital technologies, offering products and services based on data analytics (37% of all start-ups), the cloud (23%) and AI (14%) (ABStartups and Accenture, 2018). Brazilian start-ups are increasingly attracting investors: in 2018, eight of them became "unicorns", i.e. privately held start-up companies with a valuation of USD 1 billion or above (Table 5.5).

Brazilian start-ups are particularly successful in Fintech, edtech, health, agritech and mobility. In particular, Brazil has seen many new Fintech companies develop in recent years, with different target groups and business models. Both the high concentration and the high cost of services of Brazilian banks, which offered the opportunity to new entrants to provide new services, and regulatory changes encouraging competition have contributed to this success (see Chapter 6). Brazil has been highly responsive to innovative developments in this field. The Securities and Exchange Commission of Brazil (Comissão de Valores Mobiliários, CVM) has launched an experimental regulatory framework for the securities market, which encourages innovation in financial technology. The sandbox provides a controlled environment for businesses to test innovative products and services without incurring the regulatory consequences of pilot projects (see Chapter 6).

São Paulo is the biggest hub for start-ups in Brazil and the host city of most unicorns. The country, however, has several other hubs for start-ups, mostly concentrated in eight states and the Federal District. These hubs are becoming increasingly specialised, e.g. São Paulo on Fintech, Florianópolis on Industry 4.0 and automation, and Recife (CESAR, Porto Digital) on gaming. ANPROTEC, the Brazilian Association of Science Parks and Business Incubators, estimates that there are 369 incubators and 35 accelerators in Brazil. Public initiatives in support of technology parks date back to the 1980s, when researchers funded by the CNPq launched incubators attached to federal universities with a technological specialisation. In the 2000s, FINEP and the CNPq substantially increased their investments in technology parks. From 2006, as a result of the Good Law, the number of technological parks started to increase. In 2017, there were 43 technological parks in the country, up from 10 in 2000 (MCTIC, 2019c).

Table 5.5. Brazilian unicorns, 2019

Company (year of establishment)	Value (USD billion)	Headquarters	Sector	Description
Nubank (2013)	10	São Paulo	Fintech	Nubank is the largest Fintech in Latin America. It also has an engineering office in Berlin and an office in Mexico City. Among the company's products are NuConta (a digital account), an international credit card, both without fees, and personal loans. The company's distinguishing feature is that it offers a credit card entirely controlled via a mobile app.
iFood (2011)	1	Campinas	Food delivery	Food delivery platform.
Loggi (2013)	1	São Paulo	Logistics	This start-up is attempting to secure next-day delivery anywhere in Brazil. Businesses use Loggi's "logistics-as-a-service" platform to send out delivery requests, which automatically calculates the route and price.
QuintoAndar (2013)	1	São Paulo	House rental	QuintoAndar focuses on real estate rentals. It manages the rent payment to the landlord, exempting the tenant from presenting a guarantor, surety bond or deposit. The company eliminates the use of notary offices by using digital signatures, and claims that it can, due to the simplified process, rent real estate ten times faster than traditional real estate.
PagSeguro (2006)	14.5	São Paulo	Fintech	Online or mobile payment-based e-commerce service for commercial operations. It intermediates payment between sellers and buyers by offering a billing option via email for traders who do not have a site or a well-structured e-commerce. The company has agreements with several banking institutions so that sellers can offer buyers different payment methods. The service offers over 25 payment methods. PagSeguro also mediates disputes between sellers and buyers.
Ascenty (2010)	1.8	São Paulo	Data centre	The largest data centre in Latin America. It currently has 18 data centres around the world.
Arco (2006)	2.2	Fortaleza	Education	The platform offers basic education programmes for learning and development.
StoneCo (2012)	9.9	São Paulo	Fintech	Customer-oriented tailored payment solutions for businesses.
Gympass (2012)	1.1	New York (founder from Minas Gerais)	Health and fitness	Gympass allows users to access a global network of gyms and studios in 15 different countries. Companies pay a monthly fee for their employees to access the platform.
99 (2012)	1	São Paulo	Transport	Transportation network company acquired by DiDi.

Note: This table also includes public companies (Arco, PagSeguro and StoneCo).

The government has launched several initiatives to support start-ups in the past decade (Table 5.6). These initiatives are under the responsibility of different ministries (the MCTIC and Ministry of Economy) and depend on various agencies and private sector organisations for their implementation. They are designed to support start-ups at different phases of their development, and have different objectives and type of support. The Centelha programme assists entrepreneurs in turning their ideas into start-ups, through training, financial and technical support. Startup Brazil, BNDES Garagem and InovAtiva are all accelerator programmes. InovAtiva is an online programme and thus has the largest outreach. Interesting initiatives are those related to open innovation, i.e. calls with a technological challenge, which start-ups have to solve for medium/large companies. One of them, Programa Conexão Startup Indústria 4.0, focuses specifically on advanced manufacturing solutions.

All of these programmes show the interest in innovative entrepreneurship in Brazil. Some are very similar and run the risk of overlapping, yet a large supply is important to meet the growing demand. Given the variety of programmes in place, it would be useful to create a one-stop shop for start-ups. A review of the available programmes could also help streamline the offer and identify possible gaps.

Brazilian start-ups are mostly male businesses, as both the founders and the employees are mainly men. Until recently, the country lacked a programme for start-ups focused on strengthening innovative entrepreneurship among women. A pilot initiative jointly managed by the MCTIC, FINEP and the city of São Paulo has recently been launched. "Innovative Women" (Mulheres Inovadoras) will target 300 entrepreneurs and accelerate 20 start-ups. This initiative intervenes at the acceleration phase of an already existing company. While this may help start-ups founded or led by women entrepreneurs to grow, support may also be needed in stimulating entrepreneurial skills at earlier stages, or in securing funds in more mature phases.

Table 5.6. Programmes supporting start-ups in Brazil, 2019

Programme (year of launch)	Objectives	Supervising institution	Other implementing institutions	Cumulated funding to date	Start-ups supported to date
		Promotion of start-ups			
"Spark" Program – National Innovative Enterprise Support Programme (Programa Centelha) (2018)	Organised in three phases, the programme aims at transforming innovative ideas into projects by offering training, financial resources and technical support. It involves a network of local, mostly public, institutions active in innovation and technological research.	MCTIC	FINEP	USD 10.4 million (BRL 41 million)	31 contracted projects
		Acceleration			
Startup Brasil – National Start-up Acceleration Programme (2012)	Public-private partnership aiming to support newly founded Brazilian tech-based companies. Selected start-ups are awarded USD 50 000 (BRL 200 000) for R&D support and go through a one-year acceleration programme. The programme offers partnerships with accelerators; research, development and innovation scholarships; a 12-month visa for foreign entrepreneurs; international hubs; and access to investors and target markets.	MCTIC	Softex, CNPq, Ministry of Foreign Affairs and private accelerators	USD 89 million (BRL 350 million)	200
InovAtiva Brasil Acceleration Programme (Programa de Aceleração InovAtiva Brasil) (2013)	Large-scale online mentoring programme for innovative, Brazilian-based businesses in any productive sector.	Ministry of Economy	SEBRAE, CERTI, SENAI and a private mentoring network	USD 2.5 million (BRL 10 million)	2 000 have received training >800 have presented their solutions to investors and large companies
BNDES Garagem – Support to Start-up Development (2018)	Acceleration programme in co-operation with the private sector. It includes an incubation module ("Creation") that aims at creating start-ups and an "Acceleration" module focused on existing start-ups with revenues up to USD 4 million (BRL 16 million). The priority industries include health and well-being, social and environmental sustainability, the creative economy, safety, financial solutions, education, the Internet of Things and blockchain.	BNDES	Private firms	USD 2.5 million (BRL 10 million)	79 Given the high oversubscription of high-quality projects, it is foreseen to support through a platform about additional 300 applications
		Open innovation and linkages start-ups/larger firms			
Startup-Industry Connection Programme (Programa Conexão Startup Indústria 4.0) (2017)	It supports open innovation in the start-up ecosystem and connects start-ups with real demands from industry. It also promotes direct assistance by associating local innovative environments with international counterparts.	Ministry of Economy	ABDI		27
Startup Connection	It connects medium and large industrial companies, which define technological challenges, with start-ups, which apply to provide solutions. Start-ups receive USD 7 000 (BRL 30 000) in grants to finance their proof of concepts, but only after their idea is validated by the large company that has set the challenge. Additional grants of up to USD 15 000 (BRL 60 000) are awarded for product development after the validation of the proof of concept.	MCTIC	ABDI, Softex and the CNPq		
SEBRAE Nexos (2019)	It connects medium- and large-sized companies with technology-oriented start-ups through open calls for innovation. Medium- and large-sized companies define the technological domains of the calls, while start-ups are invited to develop products and services in the fields of the calls. Start-ups can use resources owned by large companies as well as those owned by incubators and accelerators involved in the programme. The government invests in the start-ups based on the achievement of development milestones, with investments of USD 25 500-64 000 (BRL 100 000-250 000). Large companies have to match government funding.	FINEP	ANPROTEC		

Table 5.6. Programmes supporting start-ups in Brazil, 2019 *(cont.)*

Programme (year of launch)	Objectives	Supervising institution	Other implementing institutions	Cumulated funding to date	Start-ups supported to date
		Support to internationalisation			
StartOut Brasil Programme (2017)	Insertion of Brazilian start-ups in international innovative environments.	Ministry of Economy	Apex, ANPROTEC, SEBRAE and the Ministry of Foreign Affairs	USD 610 000 (BRL 2.4 million)	110

Notes: ABDI = Brazilian Industrial Development Association; ANPROTEC = Brazilian Association of Science Parks and Business Incubators; Apex = Brazilian Agency of Promotion of Exports and Investments; BNDES = Brazilian Development Bank; CERTI = Centres of Reference in Innovative Technologies; CNPq = National Council for Scientific and Technological Development; FINEP = Brazilian Agency for Innovation and Research; MCTIC = Ministry of Science, Technology, Innovations and Communications; SEBRAE = Brazilian Micro and Small Business Support Agency; SENAI = National Service for Industrial Training. USD figures are based on the 2019 exchange rate.

Source: OECD, based on MCTIC, FINEP, BNDES, Ministry of Economy and OECD (2020f), *SME and Entrepreneurship Policy in Brazil 2020, https://doi.org/10.1787/cc5feb81-en.*

Venture capital and equity financing should be further developed

Venture capital (VC) is one of the main funding mechanisms for disruptive technologies. In 2016, new regulation was introduced which has improved the legal protection for angel investors with the market recording fast growth in the following two years. VC investments in Brazilian start-ups doubled in 2018, reaching USD 1.3 billion, i.e. about two-thirds of the VC raised in Latin America in the same year (Figure 5.20). Although it is growing fast, the VC market only represents 0.06% of GDP, compared to 0.55% in the United States or 0.18% in Canada (OECD, 2020e).

Figure 5.20. Venture capital investments in Brazilian and Latin American start-ups, 2011-18

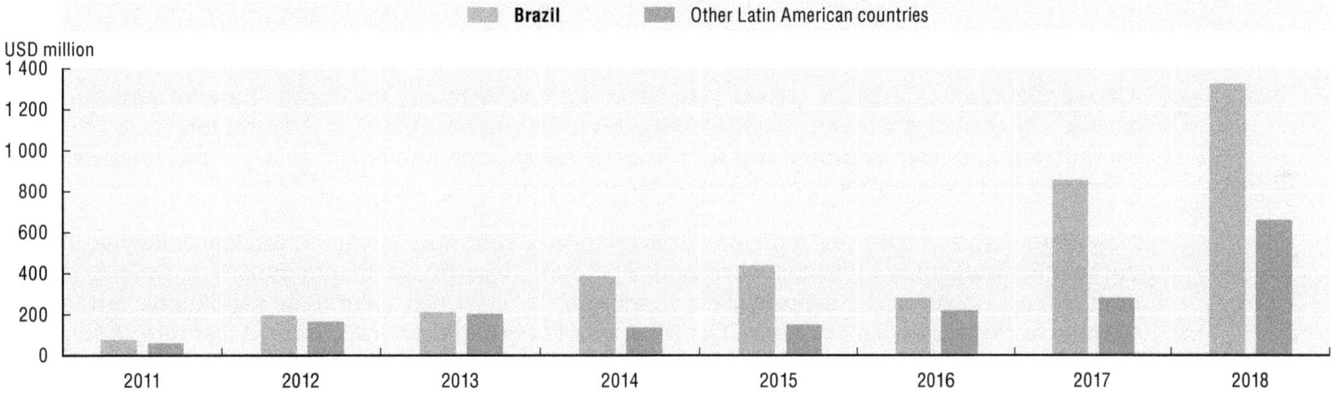

Source: OECD, based on LAVCA (2020), *LAVCA's Annual Review of Tech Investment in Latin America, www.lavca.org*, LAVCA (2019), *LAVCA's Annual Review of Tech Investment in Latin America, www.lavca.org* and LAVCA (2016), *Latin America Venture Capital: Five-Year Trends, www.lavca.org*.

Public funding institutions (namely, BNDES and FINEP) have also set up their own programmes to promote the development of the VC market in the country. BNDES is currently the main investor in seed capital and VC. The main seed capital funds are Criatec I, II and III and Primatec, all supporting small innovative companies with high growth potential with annual revenues up to USD 4 million (BRL 16 million). The three funding cycles together add up to USD 124.5 million (BRL 489 million), mostly in digital technologies, agro-businesses, nanotechnology, biotechnology and advanced materials (OECD, 2020f). The first two editions of Criatec invested in 72 companies, leading to 60 patents. The Primatec Fund is dedicated to seed VC investments in start-ups in a group of incubators and technology parks, known as Rede Primatec. It is funded by BNDES and FINEP, with a capital of USD 25.5 million (BRL 100 million). It focuses on investments in ICTs, the energy sector and creative industries, as well as socially responsible start-ups.

BNDES' Angel Co-investment Fund (Fundo de Coinvestimento Anjo) was introduced in 2018. In its first phase, its objective is to support about 100 start-ups with an annual income of up to USD 255 000 (BRL 1 million), with an investment ticket of USD 25 500-127 000 (BRL 100 000-500 000) per beneficiary, matched by VC funds for the same amount.

FINEP Startup was launched in 2017 with the objective to support small technology-based companies (annual revenues up to USD 1.2 million, or BRL 4.8 million) in the final stages of product development or that need to gain production scale. Calls are opened in specific sectors and technologies, including agritech, Fintech, healthtech, blockchain, AI, IoT, advanced manufacturing, and augmented and virtual reality technologies. The maximum investment for each start-up is USD 255 000 (BRL 1 million). FINEP Startup also encourages applicants to look for private investors, as those showing a letter of commitment from a business angel earn points in the selection, proportionate to the amount committed. After its first three calls, FINEP Startup has invested in or approved for investment 51 start-ups, for a total of USD 10 million (BRL 40 million). Out of these start-ups, 9 are active in IoT, 5 in AI, 2 in advanced manufacturing, 2 in virtual and augmented reality, and 1 in smart cities. Finally, since 2003, FINEP has supported 33 investment funds, in more than 220 companies and with USD 1.3 billion (BRL 5 billion) committed, resulting in an external funding of BRL 6.62, for each Brazilian real contributed by FINEP.

One of the obstacles to the VC and equity funding market in Brazil has been the lack of a legal provision for the "corporate veil", i.e. the assumption that the liability of the managers or shareholders of a company does not extend beyond the value of their shares. The absence of the "corporative veil" drastically increases the risk and uncertainty of VC investments.

Law 13.874/2019 of September 2019 establishes the Declaration of Economic Freedom Rights, marking progress in this direction. The law brings legal clarity on the applicable cases of disregard of legal entity (*desconsideração da personalidade jurídica*) and clarifies the nature of investment funds, allowing limited liability of their investors to the value of their shares. The Securities and Exchange Commission has to issue a regulation for this rule to also become operational for pre-existing contracts. However, this measure is a significant step towards enlarging the VC market in the country.

A legal framework for start-ups and innovative entrepreneurship is being developed

Among the main challenges for start-ups, the National Strategy for Digital Transformation points out the lack of skilled workers, notably computer programmers, the lack of entrepreneurial attitudes, bureaucratic and lengthy procedures for company registration and liquidation, a rigid labour law, and a complex and expensive web of state and federal taxes.

Interviews with some leading start-ups have confirmed that human capital is a key challenge, due to the limited availability of skilled workers at home and visa requirements making it difficult to hire from abroad. However, the main challenges reported by start-ups seem to be regulations, red tape in opening or closing a business, as well as the level of taxation (ABStartups and Accenture, 2018).

One of the first actions undertaken under the E-Digital Strategy has been elaborating a proposal for a legal framework for start-ups and innovative enterprises by the Sub-committee of the Inter-ministerial Committee for Digital Transformation (CITDigital). The proposal, which has been open to public consultation, focuses on four key areas for start-up development: 1) business environment; 2) work relations; 3) investment; and 4) public procurement. Brazil currently lacks a legal definition for start-ups and the consultation invites suggestions about the criteria defining a start-up, e.g. age, turnover, number of employees, R&D investment. The proposal also includes six "blocks" with concrete legislative proposals to amend existing legislation, with the following objectives:

- **Block A: Establish a new company model: the *sociedade anônima simplificada* (SAS).** The two types of company models in Brazil are limited liability companies (*empresa de responsabilidade limitada*) and corporations (*sociedad anônima*). This block proposes the introduction of a simplified corporation for companies with capital less than USD 4 million (BRL 16 million) that would allow start-ups to receive external funding, while having simpler reporting requirements.
- **Block B: Clarify joint liability.** Despite being companies with a high risk of failure, start-ups have several joint liabilities. This proposal aims at introducing legal certainty on the joint liabilities in case of business failure.

- **Block C: Extend the simplified tax regime (Simples Nacional).** This proposal aims at conciliating a company model able to issue stock options with the simplified fiscal regime.
- **Block D: Facilitate investment in R&D and innovation.** This proposal aims at expanding the sources of funding for start-ups. It introduces the possibility for sectors that have legal obligations to invest in R&D (oil and gas, electric sectors) to fulfil their duty by investing resources in equity funds or equity investment funds in categories associated with R&D and innovation.
- **Block E: Clarify the legal nature of stock options plans.** Stock options are an important talent retention mechanism, particularly for start-ups, which have fewer resources available for hiring employees. This proposal aims to give companies greater certainty on their legal nature.
- **Block F: Introduce a test for public procurement of innovative solutions.** Start-ups are seldom hired by the public administration, as they do not comply with legal requirements, such as previous experience to show their capabilities. This proposal introduces the Collaboration Term for Innovation Test (*Termo de Colaboração para Teste de Inovação*), the testing of innovative solution by start-ups prior to purchase by the public administration.

The legal framework for start-ups is a comprehensive proposal, built through consultation of interested parties. The MCTIC is analysing the inputs received during the consultation and will put forward a revised legislative text.

By creating a legal framework for start-ups, Brazil would follow in the footsteps of a number of countries that have already introduced specific legislation for start-ups or innovative entrepreneurship, such as Italy (Startup Act 172/2012) and Argentina (Entrepreneurs' Law of 2016). Some provisions improving the business environment have been introduced by recent legislation. For instance, Law 13.874/2019 has introduced the provision to constitute individual limited companies (*sociedade limitada unipessoal*). Although this does not fully reflect the proposal in "Block A", it introduces a new business typology, which addresses start-ups' needs. Other provisions, such as the legal clarity on the applicable cases of disregard of legal entity and the definition of the nature of investment funds mentioned above, are also positive elements to improve the legal environment and the investment options for start-ups. The Declaration of Economic Freedom Rights also reduces red tape for a number of operations, and therefore is likely to improve the business environment in Brazil.

Box 5.7. Policy recommendations to strengthen digital innovation in Brazil

Strengthen the role of innovation in the country's economic and social agenda

- Orient public support to digital innovation towards mission-oriented research, building on the model of the National IoT Plan.
- Ensure adequate, stable and predictable publicly funded resources for research in ICT.
- Develop clear roadmaps for advancement in key digital technologies, such as artificial intelligence and data analytics, in co-ordination with sectoral ministries and private stakeholders.
- Build capacity in the public sector to procure high-tech innovative solutions, borrowing expertise from businesses and institutions, e.g. BNDES.
- Increase legal guarantees for public servants contracting procurement for innovation.

Reinforce the human resource base for digital innovation

- Revise the current distribution of CAPES scholarships to increase the share of funding to support STEM graduates and PhDs in engineering, natural sciences and ICT. Increase the offer of Master and PhD programmes in these disciplines, in co-operation with the private sector.
- Increase the attractiveness of Brazil's higher education institutions for foreign students by encouraging the use of English in courses.
- Include indicators on the economic and social impact of research among the evaluation criteria of academic researchers.
- Increase knowledge and expertise transfer from business to academia, for instance by encouraging business experts to participate in technology transfer offices and in teaching.

Box 5.7. Policy recommendations to strengthen digital innovation in Brazil *(cont.)*

Reform the Informatics Law to strengthen its support to innovation

- Reform the Informatics Law so as to strengthen its support for innovation. In particular: remove the "basic production process" specifications; limit the eligibility for financial credit to firms with demonstrated innovation capacity or investing in innovative start-ups; extend the incentive to ICT services and to firms investing in R&D in digital technologies across all sectors; revise the calculation of the tax credit to incentivise R&D expenditures above the minimum threshold set by the law; better align the R&D investments in collaborative research to the innovation agenda.
- Carry out a full-fledged evaluation of the Informatics Law.
- Make an *ex ante* impact assessment of the phasing-out of the Informatics Law and engage stakeholders in discussions about future scenarios for the ICT sector in Brazil.
- Make more use of digital tools to monitor the Informatics Law, as well as for the implementation of other public policies.

Strengthen instruments for diffusion of digital innovation

- Increase co-ordination among FINEP and BNDES on the financing of innovation projects, and among these institutions and EMBRAPII, to strengthen the innovation ecosystem.
- Increase funding to EMBRAPII, including by increasing compulsory funding from the Informatics Law to programmes and projects of national interest.
- Identify and strengthen innovation hubs for experimentation and technological transfer to small and medium-sized enterprises, for instance by developing EMBRAPII units to be testbeds for digital technologies. Identify an appropriate co-financing model for the private sector.
- Establish and strengthen public-private partnerships for the advancement of artificial intelligence in a trustworthy way, ensuring participation by small and medium-sized enterprises and start-ups.

Adapt instruments and legal provisions to increase the participation of start-ups in innovative activities

- Consider introducing cash-refund or carry-forward provisions in the Good Law, to make it more suitable for young innovative firms.
- Introduce the possibility for the government to procure innovative solutions from start-ups.
- Establish a one-stop shop where start-ups can access information on existing support programmes. Evaluate the current programmes to streamline the offer and scale up the most successful initiatives.
- Strengthen programmes for start-ups targeting female entrepreneurship.

References

ABES (2019), *Mercado Brasileiro de Software: Panorama e Tendências, 2018* [Brazilian Software Market: Scenario and Trends, 2018], Associação Brasileira das Empresas de Software, São Paulo, *http://central.abessoftware.com.br/Content/UploadedFiles/Arquivos/Dados%202011/ABES-EstudoMercadoBrasileirodeSoftware2019.pdf*.

ABINEE (2019), Presentation at the seminary on "Resultados da PD&I no setor brasileiro de tecnologia da informação e comunicação" [Results of R&D&I in the Brazilian sector of ICT], Associação Brasileira da Indústria Elétrica e Eletrônica, São Paulo.

ABStartups and Accenture (2018), *Radiografia do Ecossistema Brasileiro de Startups 2017* [Radiography of the Brazilian Start-up Ecosystem 2017], ABStartups and Accenture, São Paulo.

Alan Turing Institute (2020), *The Alan Turing Institute* (website), *www.turing.ac.uk* (accessed in February 2020).

Appelt, S. et al. (2016), "R&D Tax Incentives: Evidence on design, incidence and impacts", *OECD Science, Technology and Industry Policy Papers*, No. 32, OECD Publishing, Paris, *https://doi.org/10.1787/5jlr8fldqk7j-en*.

Barboza, L., R. Madeira and R. Lima (2017), "Panoramas Setoriais 2030: Tecnologia da informação e comunicação", in *Panoramas Setoriais 2030: Desafios e Oportunidades Para o Brasil* [Sectoral Outlooks 2030: Information and communication technology, in Sectoral Outlooks 2030: Challenges and Opportunities for Brazil], Brazilian Development Bank, Rio de Janeiro, pp. 147-158, *https://web.bndes.gov.br/bib/jspui/handle/1408/14514*, *https://web.bndes.gov.br/bib/jspui/handle/1408/14514*.

BNDES (2020), *BNDES* (website), *www.bndes.gov.br* (accessed in March 2020).

Casa Civil (2019), *Lei n. 13.969, de 26 de Dezembro de 2019 – Dispõe Sobre a Política Industrial Para o Setor de Tecnologias da Informação e Comunicação e Para o Setor de Semicondutores* [Law n. 13.969, of December 26, 2019 - Provides for Industrial Policy for the Information and Communication Technologies Sector and for the Semiconductor Sector], Presidência da República, Brasilia, *www.planalto.gov.br/ccivil_03/_ato2019-2022/2019/lei/L13969.htm*.

Casa Civil (1991), *Lei n. 8.248, de 23 de Outubro de 1991 – Dispõe Sobre a Capacitação e Competitividade do Setor de Informática e Automação, e dá Outras Providências* [Law n. 8.248, of October 23, 1991 - Provides for Training and Competitiveness in the Computer and Automation Sector, and Provides Other Provisions] , Presidência da República, Brasilia, *www.planalto.gov.br/ccivil_03/leis/l8248.htm*.

CGEE (2018), *Uma Análise dos Resultados da Lei do Bem: Com Base nos Dados do FormP&D* [Analysis of results of the Good Law based on data from FormR&D], Centro de Gestão e Estudos Estratégicos, Brasilia.

CGEE (2016), *Mestres e Doutores 2015: Estudos da Demografia da Base Técnico-científica Brasileira* [Master's and Doctoral Graduates 2015: A Demographic Study of the Brasilian Technical and Science Base], Centro de Gestão e Estudos Estratégicos, Brasilia, *https://www.cgee.org.br/documents/10182/734063/Mestres_Doutores_2015_Vs3.pdf*.

Clarivate Analytics (2018), *Research in Brazil, A Report for CAPES by Clarivate Analytics*, *https://www.capes.gov.br/images/stories/download/diversos/17012018*.

Colombo, D. (2016), "Impact assessment of tax incentives to foster industrial innovation in Brazil: The case of Law 11,196/05", *Department of Economics Working Papers*, No 2016_30, University of São Paulo, *https://EconPapers.repec.org/RePEc:spa:wpaper:2016wpecon30*.

Cruz, B. (2019), "Benchmarking industry/university research collaboration in Brazil", in Reynolds, E.B., B.R. Schneider and E. Zylberberg (eds.), *Innovation in Brazil, Advancing Development in the 21st Century*, Routledge, London, pp. 206-227.

De Negri, F. and F. de Holanda Schmidt Squeff (eds.) (2016), *Sistemas Setoriais de Inovação e Infraestrutura de Pesquisa no Brasil* [Sectoral Systems of Innovation and Research Infrastructure in Brazil], Institute for Applied Economic Research, Brasilia, *https://www.ipea.gov.br/portal/images/stories/PDFs/livros/livros/livro_sistemas_setoriais.pdf*.

De Negri, F. and A. Tortato Rauen (2018), "Innovation policies in Brazil during the 2000s: The need for new paths", *IPEA Discussion Papers*, No. 235, Institute for Applied Economic Research, Brasilia, *https://www.ipea.gov.br/portal/images/stories/PDFs/TDs/ingles/dp_235.pdf*.

Digital Hub Initiative (2020), *The Digital Hub Initiative* (webpage), *www.de-hub.de* (accessed in March 2020).

Dutz, M.A. (2018), *Jobs and Growth: Brazil's Productivity Agenda*, The World Bank, Washington, DC, *https://doi.org/10.1596/978-1-4648-1320-7*.

EMBRAPII (2020), *EMBRAPII* (website), *www.embrapii.org.br* (accessed in March 2020).

Encinas-Martin, M. (9 March 2020), "Why do gender gaps in education and work persist?", OECD Education and Skills Today blog, *https://oecdedutoday.com/gender-gaps-education-work-persist*.

European Commission (2020), *Digital Innovation Hubs (DIHs) in Europe* (webpage), *https://ec.europa.eu/digital-single-market/en/digital-innovation-hubs* (accessed in March 2020).

Getz, D. and I. Goldberg (2016), *Best Practices and Lessons Learned in ICT Sector Innovation: A Case Study of Israel*, World Development Report background papers, The World Bank, Washington, DC, *http://documents.worldbank.org/curated/en/657111468185331183/Best-practices-and-lessons-learned-in-ICT-sector-innovation-a-case-study-of-Israel*.

IBGE (2016), *Pesquisa de Inovação 2014* [Survey on Innovation 2014], Brazilian Institute of Geography and Statistics, Rio de Janeiro.

IBGE (2010), *Pesquisa de Inovação 2008* [Survey on Innovation 2008], Brazilian Institute of Geography and Statistics, Rio de Janeiro.

Inaba, T. and M. Squicciarini (2017), "ICT: A new taxonomy based on the international patent classification", *OECD Science, Technology and Industry Working Papers*, No. 2017/01, OECD Publishing, Paris, *https://doi.org/10.1787/ab16c396-en*.

Kannebley, S. and G. Porto (2012), "Incentivos fiscais à pesquisa, desenvolvimento e inovação no Brasil: Uma avaliação das políticas recentes" [Tax incentives for research, development and innovation in Brazil: An assessment of recent policies], *IDB Discussion Papers*, No. 236, Inter-American Development Bank, *https://edisciplinas.usp.br/pluginfile.php/3512888/mod_resource/content/2/BID%20incentivos%20fiscais%20no%20Brasil.pdf*.

Kannebley, S., E. Shimada and F. De Negri (2016), "Efetividade da Lei do Bem no estímulo aos dispêndios em P&D: Uma análise com dados em painel" [Effectiveness of the Good Law in stimulating R&D expenditures: An analysis with panel data], *Pesquisa e Planejamento Econômico*, Vol. 46/3, pp. 111-145, Instituto de Pesquisa Economica Aplicada, Brasilia, *http://repositorio.ipea.gov.br/handle/11058/7504*.

LAVCA (2020), *LAVCA's Annual Review of Tech Investment in Latin America*, The Association for Private Capital Investment in Latin America, *www.lavca.org*.

LAVCA (2019), *LAVCA's Annual Review of Tech Investment in Latin America*, The Association for Private Capital Investment in Latin America, *www.lavca.org*.

LAVCA (2016), *Latin America Venture Capital: Five-Year Trends*, The Association for Private Capital Investment in Latin America, *www.lavca.org*.

Mas, M. et al. (2019), *2019 PREDICT Key Facts Report. An Analysis of ICT R&D in the EU and Beyond*, Publications Office of the European Union, Luxembourg, *https://doi.org/10.2760/06479*.

Mazzucato, M. and C. Penna (2016), *Brazilian Innovation System: A Mission-oriented Policy Proposal*, Centro de Gestão e Estudos Estratégicos, Brasilia, *https://www.cgee.org.br/documents/10195/1774546/The_Brazilian_Innovation_System-CGEE-MazzucatoandPenna-FullReport.pdf*.

MCTIC (2019a), *Indicadores Nacionais de Ciência, Tecnologia e Inovação 2018* [National Indicators of Science, Technology and Innovation 2018], Ministério da Ciência, Tecnologia, Inovações e Comunicações, Brasilia, *https://www.mctic.gov.br/mctic/opencms/indicadores/indicadores_cti.html*.

MCTIC (2019b), *Guia Prático da Lei do Bem: Lei 11.196/2005, Versão 2019, Lei 11.196/2005* [Practical Guide of the Good Law: Law 11.196/2005], Ministério da Ciência, Tecnologia, Inovações e Comunicações, Brasilia, *https://www.mctic.gov.br/mctic/export/sites/institucional/publicacao/arquivos/GUIA_PRATICO_DA_LEI_DO_BEM_2019_MCTIC.pdf*.

MCTIC (2019c), *Estudo de Projetos de Alta Complexidade: Indicadores de Parques Tecnológicos* [Study of High Complexity Projects: Indicators of Technology Parks], Ministério da Ciência, Tecnologia, Inovações e Comunicações, Brasilia, *https://www.mctic.gov.br/mctic/export/sites/institucional/arquivos/MCTIC-UnB-ParquesTecnologicos-Portugues-final.pdf*.

MCTIC (2018), *Brazilian Digital Transformation Strategy: E-Digital*, Ministério da Ciência, Tecnologia, Inovações e Comunicações, Brasilia, *www.mctic.gov.br/mctic/export/sites/institucional/sessaoPublica/arquivos/digitalstrategy.pdf*.

MCTIC (2017), *Relatório de Resultados da Lei de Informática – Lei nº 8.248/91: Dados dos Relatórios Demonstrativos do Ano Base 2016 – Versão 1* [Report on the Results of the Informatics Law: Data from 2016 Annual Reports – Version 1], Ministério da Ciência, Tecnologia, Inovações e Comunicações, Brasilia.

MCTIC (2016), *Estratégia Nacional de Ciência, Tecnologia e Inovação 2016-2022* [National Strategy of Science, Technology and Innovation 2016-2022], Ministério da Ciência, Tecnologia, Inovações e Comunicações, Brasilia.

MCTIC/FINEP (2019), *Relatório de Gestão 2018* [Management Report 2018], Ministério da Ciência, Tecnologia, Inovações e Comunicações and Financiadora de Estudos e Projetos, Brasilia and Rio de Janeiro, *www.finep.gov.br/images/a-finep/FNDCT/05_06_2019-Relatorio_de_Gestao_Finep_2018.pdf*.

MCTIC/SETEC (2016), *Relatório Anual de Atividades de P&D (retificado) 2014. Lei do Bem - Utilização dos Incentivos Fiscais à Inovação Tecnológica – Ano Base 2014: Capítulo III* [Yearly report on R&D activities 2014 (rectified). Good Law – Use of tax incentives for Technological Innovation - Base Year 2014: Chapter III], Ministério da Ciência, Tecnologia, Inovações e Comunicações, Brasilia.

MEC (2018), *Censo da Educação Superior 2018* [Higher Education Census 2018], Ministério da Educação, Brasilia, *http://portal.mec.gov.br*.

Microsoft (2018), *Closing the STEM Gap: Why STEM Classes and Careers Still Lack Girls and What We Can Do About It*, Microsoft Philanthropies, *https://query.prod.cms.rt.microsoft.com/cms/api/am/binary/RE1UMWz*.

Ministère de l'Économie et des Finances (2020), *Innovation: Quels Sont les Aides et Crédits d'Impôt Existants?* (webpage), *www.economie.gouv.fr/entreprises/aides-financement-innovation* (accessed in March 2020).

Ministry of Economy (2019), "Boletim mensal sobre os Subsídios da União: Lei da Informática" [Monthly bulletin in the Union's Subsidies: Informatics Law], 6th Edition, March, Ministério da Economia, Secretaria de Avaliação de Políticas Públicas, Planejamento, Energia e Loteria, Brasilia, *www.gov.br/fazenda/pt-br/centrais-de-conteudos/publicacoes/orcamento-de-subsidios-da-uniao/arquivos/boletim-mensal-sobre-os-subsidios-da-uniao-lei-de-informatica/view*.

Ministry of Science and Technology (India) (2017), *Research and Development Statistics 2017-18*.

OECD (forthcoming), *OECD Economic Surveys: Brazil 2020*, OECD Publishing, Paris.

OECD (2020a), *OECD Economic Outlook, Volume 2020 Issue 1: Preliminary version*, OECD Publishing, Paris, *https://doi.org/10.1787/0d1d1e2e-en*.

OECD (2020b), *Main Science and Technology Indicators* (database), OECD, Paris, *http://oe.cd/msti* (accessed in March 2020).

OECD (2020c), *OECD Compendium of Information on R&D tax incentives, 2019*, *http://oe.cd/rdtax* (accessed in March 2020).

OECD (2020d), *The Digitalisation of Science, Technology and Innovation: Key Developments and Policies*, OECD Publishing, Paris, *https://doi.org/10.1787/b9e4a2c0-en*.

OECD (2020e), "Venture capital investments", *Structural and Demographic Business Statistics* (database), OECD Publishing, Paris, *https://doi.org/10.1787/60395228-en* (accessed in March 2020).

OECD (2020f), *SME and Entrepreneurship Policy in Brazil 2020*, OECD Studies on SMEs and Entrepreneurship, OECD Publishing, Paris, *https://doi.org/10.1787/cc5feb81-en*.

OECD (2019a), *Measuring the Digital Transformation: A Roadmap for the Future*, OECD Publishing, Paris, *https://doi.org/10.1787/9789264311992-en*.

OECD (2019b), "Productivity growth in the digital age", OECD Going Digital Policy Note, OECD, Paris, *https://www.oecd.org/going-digital/productivity-growth-in-the-digital-age.pdf*.

OECD (2019c), "Brazil", in *Education at a Glance 2019: OECD Indicators*, OECD Publishing, Paris, *https://doi.org/10.1787/246ea76d-en*.

OECD (2019d), *STI Micro-data Lab: Intellectual Property Database*, OECD, Paris, *http://oe.cd/ipstats* (accessed in September 2019).

OECD (2019e), "Using digital technologies to improve the design and enforcement of public policies", *OECD Digital Economy Papers*, No. 274, OECD Publishing, Paris, *https://doi.org/10.1787/99b9ba70-en*.

OECD (2019f), *OECD Investment Policy Reviews: Southeast Asia*, OECD, Paris, *www.oecd.org/investment/oecd-investment-policy-review-southeast-asia.htm*.

OECD (2019g), *Going Digital: Shaping Policies, Improving Lives*, OECD Publishing, Paris, *https://doi.org/10.1787/9789264312012-en*.

OECD (2018a), *OECD Economic Surveys: Brazil 2018*, OECD Publishing, Paris, *https://doi.org/10.1787/eco_surveys-bra-2018-en*.

OECD (2018b), *Rethinking Quality Assurance for Higher Education in Brazil*, Reviews of National Policies for Education, OECD Publishing, Paris, *https://doi.org/10.1787/9789264309050-en*.

OECD (2016), "Brazil", in *OECD Science, Technology and Innovation Outlook 2016*, OECD Publishing, Paris, *https://doi.org/10.1787/sti_in_outlook-2016-49-en*.

OECD/EC (2020), *STIP Compass*, OECD, Paris, *https://stip.oecd.org/stip.html*.

Ognyanova, D. (2017), "R&D tax incentives: How to make them most effective?", Working Paper Series, Publications Office of the European Union, Luxembourg, *https://rio.jrc.ec.europa.eu/sites/default/files/report/Tax_incentives_KI-04-17-666-EN-N.pdf*.

Planes-Satorra, S. and C. Paunov (2019), "The digital innovation policy landscape in 2019", *OECD Science Technology and Industry Policy Papers*, No. 71, OECD Publishing, Paris, *https://doi.org/10.1787/6171f649-en*.

Pojo, S. et al. (2016), "Management of intellectual property in Brazilian universities", *European Journal of Economics, Finance and Administrative Sciences*, Vol. 1/92, p.5.

Prochnik, V. et al. (2015), "A política da política industrial: O caso da Lei de Informática" [The politics of industrial policy: The case of the Informatics Law], *Revista Brasileira de Inovação*, Vol. 14, pp. 133-152, *http://dx.doi.org/10.20396/rbi.v14i0.8649103*.

PwC and ABFintech (2019), *Pesquisa Fintech: Deep Dive 2019* [Fintech Survey: Deep Dive 2019], PricewaterhouseCoopers Brasil Ltda, *https://www.pwc.com.br/pt/estudos/setores-atividades/financeiro/2020/fintech_deep_dive_pwc_fintechs_2019.pdf*.

Rapini, M., T. Chiarini and P. Bittencourt (2016), "Obstacles to innovation in Brazil: The lack of qualified individuals to implement innovation and establish university-firm interactions", *Industry and Higher Education*, Vol. 31/3, pp. 168-183, *https://doi.org/10.1177/0950422217698524*.

Rauen, C. (2016), "O novo marco legal da inovação no Brasil: O que muda na relação ICT – empresa?" [The new legal framework for innovation in Brazil: What does it change in the relationship between science and technology institutions and enterprises?], *Radar*, No. 43, *www.ipea.gov.br/portal/images/stories/PDFs/radar/160309_radar43_cap_3.pdf*.

Reynolds, E.B. and F. De Negri (2019), "Universities as engines of innovation: The context for tech transfer in case studies from Brazil and the US", in Reynolds, E.B., B.R. Schneider and E. Zylberberg (eds.), *Innovation in Brazil, Advancing Development in the 21st Century*, Routledge, London, pp. 227-275.

Ribeiro, E., V. Prochnik and J. De Negri (2011), *Productivity in the Brazilian Informatics Industry and Public Subsidies: A Quantitative Assessment*, 39o Encontro Nacional de Economia, Foz do Iguaçu-Paraná, *https://goo.gl/raH1zn*.

SBPC (2019), *A Política Brasileira de CT&I e as Manifestações da Comunidade Científica* [The Brazilian Science Technology and Innovation Policy and the Declarations of the Scientific Community], Sociedade Brasileira para o Progresso da Ciência, São Paulo, *http://portal.sbpcnet.org.br/wp-content/uploads/2019/12/cartilha_manifestos_SBPC_online.pdf*.

ShanghaiRanking Consultancy (2020), *Shanghai Ranking of World Universities*, *www.shanghairanking.com/ARWU2019.html* (accessed in February 2020).

Tortato Rauen, A. (2019), *Atualização do Mapeamento das Encomendas Tecnológicas no Brasil* [Update on Mapping of Technology Orders in Brazil], *Nota Técnica*, No. 53, Institute for Applied Economic Research, Brasilia, *www.ipea.gov.br/portal/images/stories/PDFs/nota_tecnica/191105_nt_53_diset.pdf*.

US National Science Foundation (2019), *Publication Output: U.S. Trends and International Comparisons. Science and Engineering Indicators 2020*, Alexandria, Virginia, *https://ncses.nsf.gov/pubs/nsb20206/*.

WIPO (2013), "IPC - Technology Concordance Table", World Intellectual Property Organization – Economics and Statistics Division.

World Economic Forum (2018), *Brazil Competitiveness and Inclusive Growth Lab Report: Insight Report*, World Economic Forum, Geneva, *www3.weforum.org/docs/WEF_43923_Brazil_COMP_Lab_report_2018.pdf*.

Zuniga, P. et al. (2016), "Conditions for innovation in Brazil: A review of key issues and policy challenges", *IPEA Discussion Papers*, No. 218, Institute for Applied Economic Research, Brasilia, *https://www.ipea.gov.br/portal/index.php?option=com_content&view=article&id=28969:dp-0218-conditions-for-innovation-in-brazil-a-review-of-key-issues-and-policy-challenges&catid=395:2016&directory=1*.

Zylberberg, E. and T. Sturgeon (2019), "Accelerating innovation in Brazil in the age of global value chains", in Reynolds, E.B., B.R. Schneider and E. Zylberberg (eds.), *Innovation in Brazil, Advancing Development in the 21st Century*, Routledge, London, pp. 93-132.

Note

Israel

The statistical data for Israel are supplied by and under the responsibility of the relevant Israeli authorities. The use of such data by the OECD is without prejudice to the status of the Golan Heights, East Jerusalem and Israeli settlements in the West Bank under the terms of international law.

Chapter 6

FOSTERING THE DIGITAL TRANSFORMATION OF THE BRAZILIAN ECONOMY

Digital transformation is reshaping established markets and creating new ones. Successful business models make innovative use of data and data analytics to create value, enhancing the efficiency of production processes, transforming data into new services or establishing entirely new markets (OECD, 2015a). Emerging technologies that enhance the availability and usability of data, including smart sensors and the Internet of Things (IoT), are significantly expanding the scope for data-driven business models (OECD, 2017a). In many cases, data services are integrated into existing products and value chains, creating new economies of scope (OECD, 2019a).

The digital environment has significantly increased transaction efficiency and reduced marginal costs, e.g. close to zero for some digital products, for many firms. New business models, even if small by standard measures, e.g. number of employees, have often been able to scale up quickly and overcome large geographical distances (scale without mass) (OECD, 2019a). These developments can create significant challenges and uncertainties for both firms and policy makers, for example due to regulations that are unfit for new business models.

In Brazil, the transformation of business models and blurring sector boundaries are clearly visible in many areas. Digital start-ups, some valued at over USD 1 billion (unicorns), are threatening to disrupt consolidated markets like transport (e.g. Loggi, 99) or banking (e.g. Nubank, Creditas). Mercado Libre, an Argentinian online marketplace with major stakes in Brazil, recently reported that its payment service Mercado Pago Point in the country by far surpassed its merchant service business in terms of volume. MercadoCredito, the platform's credit branch, provides sellers with access to finance (MercadoLibre, 2020). The business-to-consumer (B2C) food delivery app iFood has recently increased the scope of products, offering food supplies and market analysis to restaurant owners (B2B) (Natanson, 2019). The Chinese e-commerce giant Alibaba, as Amazon's AWS, is now offering Alibaba Cloud services to business customers in Brazil (Bnamericas, 2019).

With its E-Digital Strategy, Brazil has developed an encompassing strategy for digital transformation, highlighting some of the core enablers of this transformation as well as providing thematic explorations into the digital transformation of both government and the economy. The strategy acknowledges the changing market environment and puts an emphasis on the emergence of a data-driven economy and new business models, including for agriculture, industry and services.

As discussed in the remainder of this chapter, promising initiatives are already under way in some of these areas. However, an effective response to the overarching challenges mentioned above will require more than sectoral policies. In particular, it will rely on predictable and co-ordinated efforts by several government entities in close co-ordination with the private sector. Policy makers need to focus on rules that are flexible enough to accommodate changing business models and sectoral boundaries. By acknowledging the need for a whole-of-government approach, Brazil's digital strategy offers a way to tackle some of the challenges that are stifling the digital transformation of the economy.

Agribusiness

Precision agriculture and the Internet of Things are key drivers of productivity in agribusiness

Agribusiness is one of the most important sectors of the Brazilian economy, accounting for about 21% of gross domestic product (GDP) in 2018. Besides agricultural activities (5.1%), the sector aggregate encompasses agro-industry (6.3%), agro-services (8.7%) and the input (e.g. fertiliser) producing sector (1%) (CEPEA, 2019a). The sector employs over 18 million people, or close to 20% of total employment, of which almost half (46%) are engaged in agricultural activities, followed by agro-services (32%), agro-industry (21%) and the input-producing sector (1%) (CEPEA, 2019b).

The agricultural sub-sector has registered significant increases in productivity over the last three decades. Between 1975 and 2016, multifactor productivity more than tripled, with an annual average growth rate of approximately 3.1% (Figure 6.1). As a consequence, the price that Brazilian consumers had to pay for a basic consumption bundle diminished in real terms by about 50% between 1975 and 2013 (Embrapa, 2014). Consequently, after having been a food importer for a long time, by 2016 Brazil had become the world's third-largest agricultural exporter, behind the European Union (EU) and the

United States and ahead of the People's Republic of China (hereafter "China"). Brazil's share in total world export value increased from 3.2% in 2000 to 5.7% in 2016 (FAO, 2018).

Figure 6.1. Multifactor productivity growth in the agricultural sector, Brazil, 1975-2015

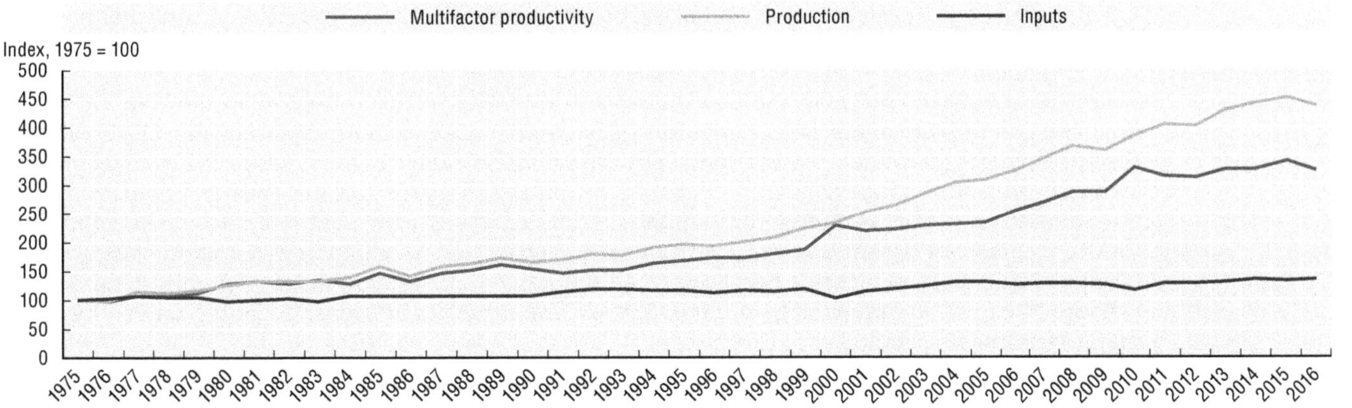

Source: Gasques, Piedade Bacchi and Teles Bastos (2018), "Nota técnica IV: Crescimento e produtividade da agricultura Brasileira de 1975 a 2016", *http://repositorio.ipea.gov.br/bitstream/11058/8326/1/cc38_nt_crescimento_e_producao_da_agricultura_brasileira_1975_a_2016.pdf*.

Much of the success of Brazil's agricultural sector over the past decades has been driven by a robust innovation ecosystem, led by the public Brazilian Agricultural Research Corporation (Empresa Brasileira de Pesquisa Agropecuária, Embrapa). Increasingly, the ecosystem also involves scientific and technological co-operation with other countries (e.g. through Embrapa's virtual laboratory programme, LABEX), high-quality academic institutions (e.g. the Luiz de Queiroz College of Agriculture [Escola Superior de Agricultura Luiz de Queiroz, ESALQ] in Piraciacaba, São Paulo) and private sector participation. Private sector participation includes an increasingly vibrant start-up scene, fostered by several incubators and accelerators (e.g. ESALQTec, Pulse, ScaleUp Endeavour, Wayra), many of which have been emerging in close proximity to research hubs such as ESALQ in Piraciacaba.

Advancements in precision agriculture, i.e. the application of technology to enhance the management of agricultural systems, is promising further large gains in terms of productivity and cost reductions (OECD, 2016a). According to some estimates (Brasscom, 2019), investments in IoT solutions, considered a key enabling technology in precision agriculture, totalled USD 57.5 million (BRL 210 million) in 2018 for the Brazilian agricultural sector. For the years 2019-21, IoT applications in agribusiness are expected to further grow with an average rate of 40% per year, involving additional investments of USD 330.8 million (BRL 1.3 billion).

Grupo SLC Agricola (SLC), one of the largest cotton, soybean and maize producers in Brazil, provides an example for the use of IoT applications among agricultural producers. Engaging with precision agriculture since the 1990s, SLC is now applying satellite images, sensors and drones to monitor the fields. Big data and machine learning are applied to enhance the efficient use of inputs, including fertilisers, chemicals, water or seeds and to monitor crop performance. According to the firm, the use of these technologies has reduced the use of fertilisers by up to 10% and the use of chemicals for plant protection by up to 3%. Other advantages include gasoline savings, efficiency gains in the management of processes, a better tracking of machines and the collection of vast amounts of data (MAPA, 2019a).

The government is fostering precision agriculture, but innovation would benefit from enhanced public-private co-operation

Despite the strong dynamism in Brazilian agribusiness and the increasing role of the private sector in agricultural innovation, there still remains a lot of untapped potential. In particular, the highly complex business environment and tax regulation create substantial bottlenecks for start-ups and firm innovation (see Chapter 5). This is aggravated by a lack of investment capital, management flexibility and a qualified workforce (OECD, 2015b). The poor infrastructure is further diminishing the profit margins of agricultural producers, limiting financial flexibility for innovations. For example, the cost of soybean transport in Brazil is estimated to be seven times higher than in the United States (Arias et al., 2017).

Furthermore, there is significant potential to enhance innovation synergies from better co-operation between the public, academic and private actors (OECD, 2015b). Embrapaand the different state agricultural research organisations, together with other research institutions, have been part of the National Agricultural Research System (Sistema Nacional de Pesquisa Agropecuária, SNPA) since 1992. Embrapa alone entails a network of over 40 different offices and research centres in different parts of Brazil. However, the private sector, and in particular the growing start-up scene, is currently not well integrated into the existing research system.

An important step to promote the precision agriculture ecosystem in Brazil was the creation of the Brazilian Commission of Precision Agriculture (Comissão Brasileiro de Aquapaisagismo, CBAP) through the Ministry of Agriculture, Livestock and Supply (Ministério da Agricultura, Pecuária e Abastecimento, MAPA) in 2012 (Ordinance 852). CBAP is based within the ministry and has mostly a consulting and co-ordinating function, including through the identification and articulation of relevant stakeholders. CBAP encompasses representatives from several ministries, the Brazilian Confederation of Agriculture (Confederação da Agricultura e Pecuária, CNA), Embrapa, the National Rural Apprenticeship Service (Serviço Nacional de Aprendizagem Rural, SENAR) and other institutions, including universities and major business associations.

Based on the discussions in CBAP, in 2014 MAPA published the Strategic Agenda for Precision Agriculture (2014-30), proposing several directions to promote precision agriculture in areas such as value chain governance, R&D, and sector diagnostics or regulation (MAPA, 2014). Among the proposed actions was the establishment of a permanent representation of the sector, allowing for continuous stakeholder discussions, and of a R&D network, integrating both public and private stakeholders. However, the document established neither specific timelines nor any organisational or budgetary responsibilities. It was rather considered a basis for future discussions.

The launch of Brazil's National IoT Plan in June 2019 recently provided the ground for the establishment of a new multi-stakeholder forum. The National IoT Plan is the result of a joint initiative between the Ministry of Science, Technology, Innovations and Communications (Ministério da Ciência, Tecnologia, Inovações e Comunicações, MCTIC) and the Brazilian Development Bank (Banco Nacional de Desenvolvimento Econômico e Social, BNDES) from 2014 and features agriculture as one of four core sectors (Box 6.1). In particular, the National IoT Plan considers the application of IoT solutions in agribusiness crucial for both the efficient use of inputs and sanitary security, for example with regard to animal health or the use of antibiotics. Following the launch of the plan, a technical co-operation agreement between MAPA and the MCTIC formally established the Agro 4.0 Chamber in August 2019. In line with the strategy documents, the chamber aims at strengthening stakeholder dialogue and has a stronger focus on private sector participation than CBAP. CBAP has taken an active role in informing the work of the Agro 4.0 Chamber. However, with regard to objectives such as stakeholder co-ordination or strategy setting, a clearer distinction of responsibilities between the two bodies in the future seems warranted.

The National IoT Plan also iterates the call for an innovation network that better accounts for private sector activities (BNDES, 2019a). In particular, the plan details that the envisaged innovation ecosystem should involve technology-based start-ups, large firms willing to invest in innovation as well as academic research centres. It also proposes adequately equipped competence centres as a means to provide technical and financial support for research projects with high market potential. Research projects could be clustered around particular topics and should involve all three types of actors. The innovation ecosystem should further improve matchmaking between IoT suppliers and potential customers and offer a forum for stakeholders to discuss common problems, such as a lack of a skilled workforce or a lack of interoperability between devices.

An interesting example of how such a network is already emerging at the regional level is AgriHub, a regional initiative of the Federation of Agriculture and Livestock of Mato Grosso (FAMATO), the Institute of Applied Economics in Mato Grosso (Instituto Mato-Grossense de Economia Agropecuária, IMEA) and SENAR-MT). AgriHub is an innovation network connecting agricultural producers with specific needs to start-ups, mentors, researchers or investors. Interested producers can register to the AgriHub's ALFA network, which also facilitates the testing and validation of new technologies and encourages investments in start-ups (Netto, 2017).

Box 6.1. Brazil's National Internet of Things Plan

The emergence of the Internet of Things (IoT), connecting devices to the Internet and among each other, is bringing radical changes to all economic sectors. Because modern sensors generate vast amounts of data, which can be transformed into information by smart devices and fed into production decisions, the IoT carries significant potential for process innovation and energy efficiency. The resulting big data sets create further benefits, including an integration of new services and service providers into the value chain (OECD, 2017a).

To promote the deployment of the IoT in Brazil, the government created the IoT Chamber (Decree 8.234) in 2014, a multi-stakeholder forum encompassing participants from government, the private sector and academia. The IoT Chamber was tasked to elaborate a National IoT Plan, aiming to "foster the implementation of IoT as a sustainable development instrument for the Brazilian society, capable of increasing competitiveness, strengthen national production chains and promote higher quality of life" (MCTIC, 2018). The plan was initiated by the Ministry of Science, Technology, Innovations and Communications in co-operation with the Brazilian Development Bank (BNDES) and involved a public call (01/2016, BNDES/FEP) for a series of studies, including on Brazil's IoT environment, the identification of key sectors and the formulation of policy proposals. Work on the plan began in December 2016 and entered its final stage (Phase 4) in 2018, encompassing the design of measures to support the implementation and establishment of a monitoring framework. The National IoT Plan, which builds upon several rounds of stakeholder interactions, was formalised in June 2019 through Decree 9.854. The plan now encompasses close to 30 documents that are openly accessible via a special website (BNDES, 2019a).

Four verticals (sectors) have been selected as priorities for IoT in Brazil, namely agribusiness, manufacturing, health and smart cities. The selection followed a multi-stage process involving over 160 specialists and more than 3 500 contributions obtained through different fora. Selection criteria encompassed demand factors, such as the potential impact on productivity and competitiveness or socio-environmental effects; supply factors, such as the potential to strengthen the existing IoT supply chain; and capacities, including institutional efficiency (e.g. governance structure), facilitators (e.g. ICT infrastructure) or the prospect for effective government interventions (incentivising supply or demand). The result of this process is shown as a prioritisation matrix in Figure 6.2.

Figure 6.2. National Internet of Things Plan: Prioritisation of sectors (verticals)

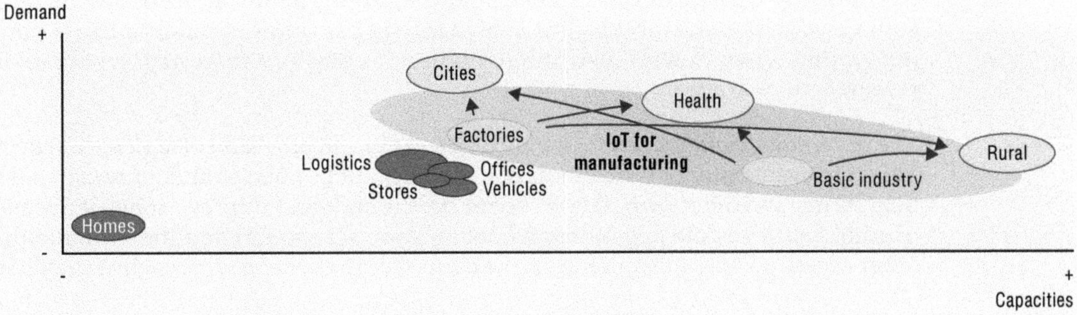

Notes: IoT = Internet of Things. Demand factors are depicted on the y-axis. Capacities are depicted on the x-axis. The size of the circle represents supply factors. Basic industry, including, for example, petroleum and minerals, and factories, including textiles or the automotive sector, form part of the manufacturing vertical. Health incorporates the use of the Internet of Things in hospitals and remote monitoring of patients.

Source: OECD adaptation and translation from BNDES (2017a), *5a: Apresentação do Resultado de Priorização de Verticais*, *www.bndes.gov.br/wps/wcm/connect/site/24590dd0-4e92-4053-a63d-4c3b3f5a316a/Apresenta%C3%A7%C3%A3o+do+resultado+de+prioriza%C3%A7%C3%A3o+de+verticais_050717.pdf?MOD=AJPERES&CVID=lQIPFoq*.

The National IoT Plan foresees 75 initiatives, organised along 4 transversal thematic axes, namely: 1) infrastructure for connectivity and interoperability; 2) innovation and international market integration; 3) human capital; and 4) regulatory environment, security and privacy.

Box 6.1. Brazil's National Internet of Things Plan *(cont.)*

Within these axes, the initiatives are distinguished by their envisaged time horizon, namely short-term actions (to be executed within one year), medium-term actions (two to three years) and long-term actions (four to five years). With this level of detail, the National IoT Plan is probably the most advanced and concrete initiative towards the digital transformation of the economy. Because of its focus on a specific technology (the IoT), the plan might seem narrow compared to advanced manufacturing plans in other countries, e.g. the People's Republic of China, Germany or the United States. However, the increasing availability of low-cost sensors implies that the use of most production technologies, including artificial intelligence, additive manufacturing or big data analytics, will be increasingly embedded in an IoT environment (OECD, 2017a).

However, as with the E-Digital Strategy, the National IoT Plan lacks clear funding mechanisms and mostly relies on the willingness of actors in a particular resort to reassign the existing budget to new areas. This includes expenditures of particular ministries, as well as the funding instruments of institutions like BNDES or the Brazilian Agency for Innovation and Research. There is also no clearly established hierarchy between different government strategies, which in some areas can be overlapping. For example, while the recently established Brazilian Chamber for Industry 4.0 is clearly linked to the National IoT Plan and its manufacturing vertical (MCTIC, 2019), other strategies (e.g. MCTIC's ProFuturo [MCTIC, 2017] or the Ministry of Economy's Brazilian Agenda for Industry 4.0) are also referred to as core guiding documents.

For the National IoT Plan to be successful, it will be crucial that different national, sectoral but also regional transformation strategies are well aligned and co-ordinated. Optimally, this would involve a strong overarching governance structure, predictable budget, and a clear allocation of funds and responsibilities among the different stakeholders involved. In the short term, it will also be important to implement the monitoring framework, foreseen in the National IoT Plan but currently not realised, as soon as possible.

Brazil should not only build upon these successful regional initiatives, but also leverage existing networks such as the National Agricultural Research System and Embrapa. Embrapa itself consists of a large research network and with strong capabilities in terms of innovation, training and technical assistance. It is already actively engaged in start-up acceleration, e.g. through a recent co-operation with Venture Hub (TechStart Agro Digital), and, jointly with private sector stakeholders, has recently carried out a detailed mapping of agricultural start-ups in Brazil).[1] While closely connected to MAPA, Embrapa has been a strong promoter of public-private partnerships and open innovation – two crucial instruments when it comes to fostering synergies from private-public research co-operation.

The government should also foster public access to and provision of agricultural data where appropriate. This is relevant both for the formulation of better public policies and for research purposes, but can also help farmers without own data to better benchmark and improve their performance. Both the reuse of administrative data (e.g. through pooling and aggregation) and the formulation of "open data" and other access policies (depending on the context) can be viable approaches in this regard (OECD, 2019b).

Embrapa is currently developing an API platform (AgroAPI) that opens its own agricultural data to third parties in order to foster the development of new services and applications. The platform could be leveraged for additional data, including for complementary open and administrative data.

A lack of connectivity, the high cost of sensors and regulatory uncertainty have limited the uptake of digital technologies

The first meeting of the Agro 4.0 Chamber in October 2019 focused on rural connectivity. The lack or high cost of connectivity in remote areas is explicitly discussed and acknowledged in the National IoT Plan (BNDES, 2017b). While in principle a connection via satellite is viable in most rural areas, the costs of this type of connection can be prohibitive, especially for small and medium-sized farmers.

Though supply-side data (e.g. broadband subscriptions) are mostly not available by rural and urban areas, household level surveys confirm a persistent digital divide between urban and rural areas (see also Chapters 2 and 3). In particular, in 2018, the percentage of households indicating they had access to the Internet was 70% for urban areas, compared to 44% in rural areas. While the relatively high cost of Internet access is the main reason for a lack of access in both areas, cited by 27% (urban) and 28% (rural) of individuals in households without Internet access, a lack of supply remained a significant impediment in rural areas, affecting 13% of households without Internet access. The corresponding percentage was only 3% in urban areas (CGI.br, 2018a).

MAPA also recognises that access remains one of the main challenges for the uptake of precision agriculture in Brazil and, through CBAP and the Agro 4.0 Chamber, has initiated a discussion on how to address this challenge in co-operation with the MCTIC and other public and private stakeholders (MAPA, 2019b). To map out priority areas for future investments, the government commissioned ESALQ/USP to prepare a report on the distribution of rural connectivity and clusters of productivity. Preliminary results of the study, which had not yet been published at the time of writing, indicate that less than 5% of the country's agricultural area is currently connected to the Internet. According to the study, at least 5 600 new antennas would be required to expand access to 3G and 4G to 90% of the country. Realising only a quarter of the required investments, involving estimated expenditures of around USD 1.5 billion (BRL 6 billion), could lead to an annual gain of around USD 15.3 billion (BRL 60 billion) according to the study. The final results, which are currently being revised by the National Telecommunications Agency (Agência Nacional de Telecomunicações, Anatel), will inform the National Connectivity Policy for Brazilian Agriculture, which the Ministry of Agriculture currently is developing in partnership with the Ministry of Science and Technology (MAPA, 2019c).

More widespread application of digital technologies in agriculture, including IoT, is further limited by the high cost of IoT deployment and sensors. The cost of sensors and the lack of connectivity are considered major barriers even by the largest and most advanced agricultural producers (MAPA, 2019a). Estimates suggest that in 2015, only 10% of the 45 000 tractors and harvesters in Brazil were connected, implying significant growth potential (Febratel, 2016).

Partly responsible for the high deployment cost of IoT is taxation (BNDES, 2017c). In particular, under the FISTEL tax regime, two different taxes are currently applied to the installation (TFI) and operation (TFF, applicable yearly) of telecommunication equipment, including machine-to-machine (M2M) SIM cards, sensors or base stations. Taxes imposed on M2M SIM cards have been reduced over time, but currently remain as high as USD 2.40 (TFI) and USD 0.80 (TFF) per M2M device (OECD, 2020d). In September 2019, the Constitution, Justice and Citizenship Commission of the House of Representatives approved Bill 7656 of 2017, reducing the TFI and TFF imposed on M2M SIM cards to zero. The bill is currently awaiting approval by the Senate and once approved is likely to foster IoT adoption.

The National IoT Plan further highlights two areas in the regulatory environment that might have contributed to limited uptake of digital technologies in agriculture, namely drone regulation and data governance. Until recently, drone regulation in Brazil involved three different agencies (the National Telecommunications Agency, the National Brazilian Agency for Civil Aviation and the Department of Airspace Control) and to comply with regulations was therefore relatively cumbersome (BNDES, 2017c). In particular, there was no clear distinction between professional use and use for leisure purposes. New regulation introduced in 2017 by the National Brazilian Agency for Civil Aviation, now explicitly allows the use of drones in the agricultural sector for production purposes (Regulation RBAC-E 94). This has brought more legal certainty to drone operators and established a first regulatory environment for professional use cases. It also clarified that previous regulation, developed in the context of urban use scenarios and limiting the autonomous operation of drones in agriculture, did not apply when the pilot can remotely intervene at any time.

As the use of drones in agriculture is constantly evolving, it will be important to ensure that drone regulation keeps up with emerging applications. This requires continuous and close interaction with the private sector, including representatives of at least two dozen Brazilian start-ups currently working to advance the technology (Jardim, 2018). The National Brazilian Agency for Civil Aviation has already signalled that it considered regulation RBAC-E 94 to be dynamic, in the sense that amendments and exceptions according to need are to be expected (BNDES, 2017c). Existing examples of co-operation between the public and the private sector, including the Drone Technology Development Program for

Precision Agriculture (Embrapa and Qualcomm) initiated in 2016, could provide important insights to regulators. While the National IoT Plan proposed CBAP as a forum for co-ordination between the government and the private sector in this area, the Agro 4.0 Chamber seems preferable if it implies a better integration of the private sector. The government further should expand training programmes on the use of drones, incorporating discussions of the relevant regulation. The regional branch of SENAR in Mato Grosso, for example, has been offering free courses on the use of drones in agriculture since September 2016, including on regulations (SENAR, 2016).

Precision agriculture is also raising issues about access and control rights for the vast amount of data generated by IoT sensors and other digital applications. As in OECD countries, a lack of clarity with regard to data governance has contributed to distrust among Brazilian farmers with regard to technology providers. A major concern for Brazilian farmers is, for example, that strategic data (e.g. on harvest) could be used by other parties to influence commodity prices (BNDES, 2017c). The Brazilian Association of Agriculture and Livestock therefore calls for an efficient normative environment for Brazil that establishes transparency and fosters confidence among rural producers interested in engaging with new technologies.

OECD countries are increasingly recognising the potentially stifling effects that mistrust and market failures arising from asymmetric information, a misalignment of incentives or a lack of clarity about control rights for agricultural data are creating for the uptake of digital technologies in agriculture. To inform the debate in OECD countries, the OECD is currently mapping out different regulatory approaches to data governance in the agricultural sector, with a detailed discussion of concepts like data ownership and practical approaches to data governance in agriculture. Brazil should closely follow these ongoing discussions, identifying concerns of particular relevance for Brazil and actively fostering stakeholder discussions that ensure the proper representation of all interests (OECD, forthcoming b).

Brazil should leverage multi-stakeholder fora, such as CBAP or the Agro 4.0 Chamber, to foster the development of a Brazilian framework for agricultural data governance. In the light of the large number of Brazilian smallholders, it will be particularly important to ensure that emerging regulation prevents the creation of new divides and inequalities. Recent discussions at the OECD in this regard highlight the need to foster digital literacy and transparent language in contracts for digital services (OECD, forthcoming b).

A discussion on data regulation in the context of agribusiness should also consider topics like liabilities, data standards and lock-in effects, cross-border data flow regulation, or access and use of data by public entities. The Brazilian Seed and Seedling Association (Associação Brasileira de Sementes e Mudas, ABRASEM) has further highlighted a possible interaction of data usage in precision agriculture with the regulation on personal data protection, which is particularly relevant in the context of combined or combinable data sets.

In Brazil, the lack of shared data standards is already creating difficulties for large agricultural producers that are trying integrate different technological solutions and combine equipment from different providers (Netto, 2018). With an increasing use of connected machines, the issue of data portability and open data standards is likely to become more important, including from a competition perspective (e.g. locked-in effects). As a regulator, the government can set or play an important role in the development of interoperability standards.

Mobile applications can improve technical assistance for small agriculture producers

Small family farmers still account for a significant share of Brazil's agricultural landscape. According to the latest Agriculture Census, in 2017, about 77% of all rural properties in Brazil were owned by family farmers, who account for 67% of Brazilians employed in the sector but only 23% of all Brazilian agricultural production. About 50% of agricultural holdings are smaller than 10 hectares, jointly accounting for only 2.3% of the total farming area (IGBE, 2019).

Technical assistance, including through public or private extension services, is a crucial element to promote technology adoption among small producers and to increase their productivity (OECD, 2015b; Ribeiro Vieira Filho, 2017). Agricultural extension and advisory services facilitate the access to knowledge, information and technologies for farmers, their organisations and other market actors; facilitate their interaction with partners in research, education, agribusiness and other relevant institutions; and assist them to develop their own technical, organisational, and management skills and practices (Christoplos,

2010). In 2017, about 20% of all farmers received technical assistance, slightly down from 22% in 2006. However, among smallholders with less than 2 hectares, only 2% are receiving technical assistance on a regular basis (Buainain and Garcia, 2018).

Currently a large number of institutions are involved in the provision of extension services, including Embrapa (WebAgritec), state-level extension agencies and a variety of agricultural research institutions. This has sometimes led to a duplication of efforts and an inefficient distribution of funds between research activities and extension services (Arias et al., 2017). To strengthen co-ordination on extension services, in 2014, the federal government created the Agency for Technical Assistance and Rural Extension (Agência Nacional de Assistência Técnica e Extensão Rural, ANATER). However, according to stakeholders, it is too early to assess how far the agency has been effective in reducing the heterogeneity of approaches in a still highly decentralised system of state-level extension services. A clarification of roles and enhanced co-operation mechanisms will therefore remain highly relevant to ensure greater efficiency in the provision of technical assistance and extension services.

The coverage and effectiveness of extension services could be greatly improved through better use of mobile applications. Smartphones can be a game changer in terms of adoption capacity, especially among smallholders and farmers in remote areas (Trendov, Varas and Zeng, 2019). Smartphones not only provide access to digital extension services, including from abroad (Jouanjean, 2019), but also to a large variety of additional information (e.g. on plant diseases), digital tools or services (e.g. accounting and planning software) that can be important enablers of higher productivity, sustainability and resilience. Embrapa has been using WhatsApp to reach farmers in remote areas and has developed apps that provide information on particular grains as well as training on the organisation of financial information.

However, especially for many small holders, the lack of digital skills and the limited use of digital tools will remain an important obstacle for uptake and needs to be addressed. Recent survey evidence from the Brazilian Micro and Small Business Support Services (Serviço Brasileiro de Apoio às Micro e Pequenas Empresas, SEBRAE) confirms that the use of even the most basic digital tools among Brazilian farmers remains low. While the percentage of rural producers using a cell phone reached almost 96% across different states, only 46% used their cell phone to access the Internet. A majority of rural producers does not engage in basic accounting activities (e.g. revenues, expenses or inventory) at all or only with pencil and paper (between 54% in Minas Gerais and 93% in Acre). Most farmers, however, reported that they would use digital technologies to manage their rural business if they had better access to digital tools (between 50% in Acre and 74% in Santa Catarina) (SEBRAE, 2017a). Providing access to affordable digital devices and local Internet access points, e.g. in partnership with co-operatives, potentially combined with local training on the use of basic digital tools, could be an effective strategy to increase productivity among poor Brazilian farmers. Examples from other countries also show that a lack of Internet access does not necessarily inhibit the use of digital extension services. For example, the mobile app "Kurima Mari" provides farmers in Zimbabwe with a self-help toolkit and library that can be used offline. The app has been adopted by the federal government and is scaled up to the national level (Welthungerhilfe, 2018).

Digital technologies also provide opportunities for new forms of communication and co-operation among agricultural producers (Trendov, Varas and Zeng, 2019). The small size of agricultural holdings can be an important impediment to adoption of digital technologies because it limits the cost-reducing benefits of many scale-dependent tools in precision agriculture (Buainain and Garcia, 2018). Social media and online networks, facilitating the creation of producer networks and other co-ordination mechanisms, can effectively help to overcome these impediments. The online platform "Uller", a Brazilian peer-sharing solution for agricultural machinery, is an interesting example in this regard and the government should foster the creation and use of similar solutions (Be Brasil, 2018).

Digital technologies could be fostered to enhance sustainability of livestock production

Agriculture, forestry and land use are responsible for close to a quarter of total greenhouse gas (GHG) emissions worldwide. By reducing the rate of deforestation, Brazil has managed to reduce overall emissions from agriculture, forestry and land use over the past years, achieving more environmentally friendly production along with significant productivity growth (OECD/FAO, 2019). However, recent data from Brazil's National Institute for Space Research suggest that deforestation in Brazil's portion of the Amazon rainforest is on the rise again. In particular, deforestation between August 2018 and July 2019 was around 30% higher than in the previous period (INPE, 2019).

Fostering the development of a competitive, sustainable and resilient agro-food sector is a high priority for OECD countries. As emissions have recently been rising rather than declining, Brazil will have to step up policy efforts to meet the pledges made in the Paris Agreement for 2025, cutting GHG emissions by around a third of 2018 emissions (OECD, forthcoming b). While countering illegal deforestation remains a priority in this regard, digital technologies can also be a powerful instrument, making farming more efficient (e.g. by combining data analysis with precision agricultural machinery) and helping policy makers to raise efficiency and expand the choice of policy options (OECD, 2019b).

One of the areas where Brazil has the most potential to reduce GHGs, apart from rainforest deforestation, is beef production, one of the main sources of emissions in Latin America and the Caribbean. In Brazil, direct emissions from agriculture have been increasing almost exclusively due to an expansion of beef herds (OECD/FAO, 2019). Brazil should therefore consider stronger incentives to move resources from livestock and cattle production towards crops or other forms of agriculture with lower emissions, for example by invoking corrective taxes that account for the external effects of cattle on global climate (OECD, forthcoming b). However, for the remaining livestock production, it will be crucial to focus on reducing the emission footprint.

Integrated Crop-Livestock-Forest (ICLF) systems have been proposed as a promising way for Brazil to reduce GHG emissions and overcome the outcome of decades of monoculture, including soil erosion, loss of fertility, watercourse silting, and soil and water pollution (Embrapa, 2018). These systems integrate different forms of agricultural activity, including cattle farming, within one geographic location (through combination, rotation or succession) and can thus optimise the biological cycles of plants and animals, inputs and residues, reducing environmental pressure and GHGs, and allowing for a year-round land use and higher productivity. ICLF systems are therefore a core component of the Brazilian ABC Plan, a low-carbon agriculture plan co-ordinated by the Ministry of Agriculture, Livestock and Food Supply, that has been providing low-interest credit since 2010 for farmers that adopt climate-smart agriculture techniques. ICLF was also enshrined in Law 12.805 in 2013 as a national policy (Embrapa, 2019; Arias et al., 2017). According to the latest available data from MAPA, over a period of five years, over 34 000 contracts were signed under the ABC Plan, representing a value of over USD 4.3 billion (BRL 17 billion) and covering over 9 million hectares of land (MAPA, 2018).

However, some studies have found that adoption rates of climate-smart agriculture practices have been moderate to low in many Latin American countries, in particular among small family farmers. Among the barriers to adoption are a lack of understanding of the technologies promoted, a lack of farm management skills, insufficient training and technical assistance for farmers, as well as high upfront costs for technology adoption (Arias et al., 2017). Additionally, the workload in mixed farming systems tends to be significantly higher, and livestock management in particular requires demanding management and observation skills, including with regard to the location and well-being of individual animals (Moraine et al., 2014).

The digital transformation can significantly ease many of these constraints, potentially providing a significant boost to ICLF and other climate-smart agriculture techniques. ICLF information management systems, based on IoT, autonomous data processing and intelligent automation, are therefore currently being developed and assessed in several countries (see, for example, EC [2015]). In Brazil, a related project has recently been selected as one of 15 pilot projects supported by BNDES with USD 7.6 million (BRL 30 million) in the wake of the National IoT Plan (BNDES, 2019b). The pilot focuses on the management of pests and machinery, monitoring of animal welfare in milk cattle, and use of IoT systems for crop-livestock-forest integration and will be realised and co-financed by the informatics arm of Embrapa. Other selected pilots for the rural sector involve complementary areas such as precision cattle breeding techniques, integrated data platforms for better monitoring and management of natural resources, inputs, and machinery and solutions aimed at smallholder farmers.

The Brazilian government should further support the development and testing of digital technologies for ICLF, for example by extending and upscaling the IoT pilot programme. Targeted policies to foster the uptake of new technologies could be used to scale up successful pilot projects, leveraging previous investments. This could involve, for example, the provision of technical assistance services to smaller producers or tax incentives for large producers. Additionally, credit extended by public banks to rural producers could be conditioned on compliance with sustainability goals and environmental laws (OECD, forthcoming b). In the absence of commercial credits for sustainable solutions, specific credit lines, e.g. for family farmers, can also provide fruitful ways forward (Buainain and Garcia, 2018; OECD/FAO, 2019). While earmarked credits have been a major channel to provide subsidies in Brazil, including for the agricultural sector, sustainability-related credits represent only a very small fraction of available rural credits (The World Bank, 2018a).

Brazil could also consider more targeted support for innovation in precision livestock technology, as this area of agricultural activities has high growth potential and is already attracting a lot of international attention (Hyland, 2017). For example, the German manufacturer Siemens recently opened its first technology innovation centre focused entirely on livestock in São Paulo. According to Siemens, this "Meat Competence Centre" is intended to become a global hub for new technology services aimed at improving meat production processes with innovative uses of tracking and automation (ZDNet, 2018). Another German manufacturer, Bosch, is also highly active in Brazil, and has recently turned a large Brazilian farm in Goiás into the first connected agriculture project relying on Bosch's Precision Livestock Farming system, which uses radio-frequency identification and IoT to help farmers manage large herds and keep track of animal weight gains.

The success of BovControl, a Brazilian start-up founded in São Paulo in 2013, illustrates that Brazilian innovators do not need to hide behind these large internationals. The firm's technology is now applied in farms across the globe, creating an "Internet of cows" through its cloud-based livestock managing system, which helps farmers keep track of their herds. Farmers start with feeding basic data on each cow into the app (including birth data, medication, vaccinations and weight). Further data collection can then be automated through integration with other technologies, including smart collars, collecting data on temperature or location, or Bluetooth-connected weight scales. The app then uses the available data to help farmers manage their herds, including through push notifications for pending vaccination, birthdate predictions, or by enhancing inventory and tracking capabilities. In 2017, the company was listed among Forbes list of the 25 Most Innovative Ag-Tech Startups (Sorvino, 2017).

Box 6.2. Policy recommendations for the digital transformation in agriculture

- Enhance synergies between public and private sector research activities by fostering a national innovation network and testbed environment for agribusiness. Leverage existing networks, e.g. the National Agricultural Research System and ALFA network, and promote the participation of start-ups.
- Use national innovation networks, e.g. competence centres, to create matchmaking opportunities for technology providers and agricultural businesses as well as a forum for stakeholders to discuss solutions to shared challenges.
- Enhance rural connectivity by finalising and implementing the National Connectivity Policy for Brazilian Agriculture. Prioritise regions with high productivity or where investments are likely to have high social returns.
- Ensure that drone regulation remains up to date by fostering a continuous and close co-ordination between the regulator and the private sector, e.g. through the Agro 4.0 Chamber. Expand training programmes on the use of drones and their regulation.
- Follow international discussions on best practices in agricultural data governance. Leverage multi-stakeholder institutions, like the Brazilian Commission of Precision Agriculture or the Agro 4.0 Chamber, to develop an inclusive framework for agricultural data governance in Brazil.
- Enhance data portability among different technologies and equipment, by promoting shared or open data standards. Foster public access to and provision of agricultural data where appropriate, e.g. through the reuse of administrative data or open data policies.
- Promote technical assistance and extension services, e.g. through mobile applications, with a focus on smallholders and farmers in remote areas. Enhance the effectiveness of extension services by improving co-ordination between different providers.
- Foster the use of basic digital technologies among poor farmers and smallholders, by enhancing access to affordable digital devices and providing tailored consultation and trainings, e.g. through telecentres and co-operation with local co-operatives.
- Raise awareness about the potential for peer-sharing and other digital solutions for the agricultural sector, for example through extension services and information campaigns.

Box 6.2. Policy recommendations for the digital transformation in agriculture *(cont.)*

- Further support the development of digital solutions for climate-smart agriculture, by scaling-up initiatives like the IoT pilot programme.
- Foster digital uptake through technical assistance, tax incentives for larger producers or earmarked credit lines for smallholders.
- Ensure alignment between the National IoT Plan and the Strategic Agenda for Precision Agriculture. Ensure clarity about the different roles and responsibilities of the National IoT Chamber, the Agro 4.0 Chamber and the Brazilian Commission of Precision Agriculture.
- Implement the monitoring framework as foreseen in the National IoT Plan.

Manufacturing

Industry 4.0 is a government priority, but the sector is far from the technological frontier

Unlike the agricultural sector, Brazil's manufacturing sector has contributed negatively to growth in recent years. In terms of size, the share of the sector in GDP diminished from 12.7% in 2010 to 10.8% in 2015. The sector's contribution to total manufacturing output from developing and emerging industrial economies has further continuously declined, from 14.9% in 1990 to 4.1% in 2016 (UNIDO, 2017).

Over the same period, Brazil lost ground in UNIDO's Competitive Industrial Performance ranking (falling from 26th to 35th), an index that captures countries' capacity to produce and export manufactured goods, the extent of technological deepening and upgrading, and their impact on world markets. In contrast, Brazil's regional peer Mexico climbed up the ranking from 31st to 20th. Moreover, the share of medium-high and high-tech value added in total manufacturing decreased from 36.6% to 35.2% (UNIDO, 2019).

As in several OECD countries, concerns about the sluggish performance of the manufacturing sector have put policies for Industry 4.0 high on the agenda of Brazilian policy makers (Planes-Satorra and Paunov, 2019). E-Digital calls for measures to raise readiness for IoT and increase digital adoption to regain competitiveness in the industrial sector. The manufacturing sector also features prominently as one of the four core verticals of the National IoT Plan and has been the at the centre of previous government initiatives, including the MCTIC's ProFuturo plan (MCTIC, 2017) and the Ministry of Economy's Agenda Brasileira para a Indústria 4.0.

The sector, however, is still far from the technological frontier. According to the World Economic Forum's Readiness for the Future of Production Index, which considers both the structure of production (e.g. complexity and scale) and drivers of production (e.g. technology, human capital or investment), Brazil displays one of the lowest levels of readiness among all G20 countries, together with Argentina and South Africa (WEF, 2018).

According to a recent survey (CNI, 2018), 73% of manufacturing firms in Brazil with 250 employees and more have used at least one digital technology, including digital automation process control sensors (46%), digital automation without sensors (30%), or integrated engineering systems for product development and product manufacturing (37%). However, more advanced manufacturing technologies have only been used by a small minority, including additive manufacturing and collaborative robots (cobots; 13%), or intelligent management systems (9%), e.g. M2M, Digital Twin or artificial intelligence (AI).[2] Additionally, while 81% of large companies foresaw investments of some kind in 2018, only 48% planned to invest in technology.

While comparable data on the use of these technologies in manufacturing are rare, available estimates of the dissemination of robots and M2M SIM card subscriptions seem to confirm the relatively low use of advanced technologies in Brazilian manufacturing. For example, the number of M2M SIM card connections per 100 inhabitants, a proxy for IoT deployment, was 10.6 in Brazil in 2019, less than half the OECD average of 22. While M2M deployment was higher than in regional peers like Mexico (2) or Chile (2.8), industrial leaders including France (29.6) or the United States (37.3) had significantly higher subscription rates (see Chapter 2).

Furthermore, the percentage of Brazilian manufacturing firms using industrial robots remained lower than in any European country with available data. In particular, in 2019, only around 4.5% of Brazilian manufacturers were using industrial robots. The corresponding percentage was 16% on average in EU countries (2018) (Figure 6.3). And while in 2014 Brazil had only 6 114 industrial robots in use, leading economies like Germany, Korea, Japan and the United States employed over 100 000 operational industrial robots each (OECD, 2017b).

Figure 6.3. Use of industrial robots in manufacturing in Brazil and the European Union

Firms with ten or more employees

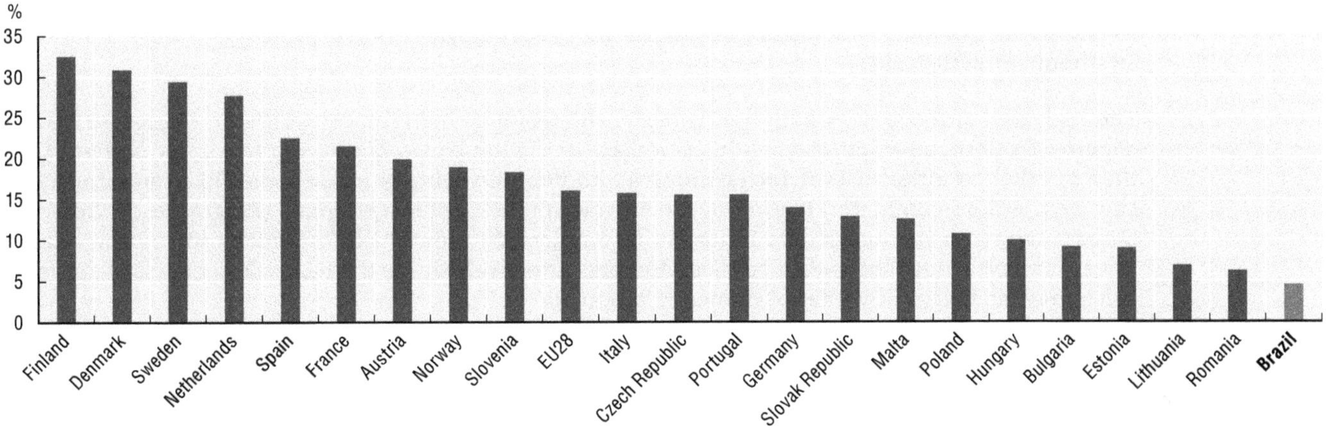

Notes: Data for Brazil are for 2019; data for EU28 are for 2018.

Sources: CGI.br (2020), *ICT Enterprises 2019: Survey on the Use of Information and Communication Technologies in Brazilian Enterprises* (database), *https://cetic.br/en/pesquisa/empresas/indicadores/* (accessed in July 2020); Eurostat (2020), *Digital Economy and Society* (database), *https://ec.europa.eu/eurostat/web/digital-economy-and-society/data/database* (accessed in February 2020).

A different proxy for digital intensity and specialisation of Brazilian industry is the share of ICT value added embedded in manufacturing exports.[3] ICTs may enter the production of manufacturing output in the form of installed computers and software for example, or as IT services that are required to manage and control digitised processes at the firm or plant level. This share is low in Brazil (2.2%), compared not only to major industrialised economies, such as Germany (5.3%) or the United States (9.4%), but also to other emerging economies, in particular Mexico (12.2%) and China (12.7%) (Figure 6.4).

Figure 6.4. ICT value-added content in manufacturing exports from Brazil and the OECD, 2015

Share of ICT value added in total manufacturing exports

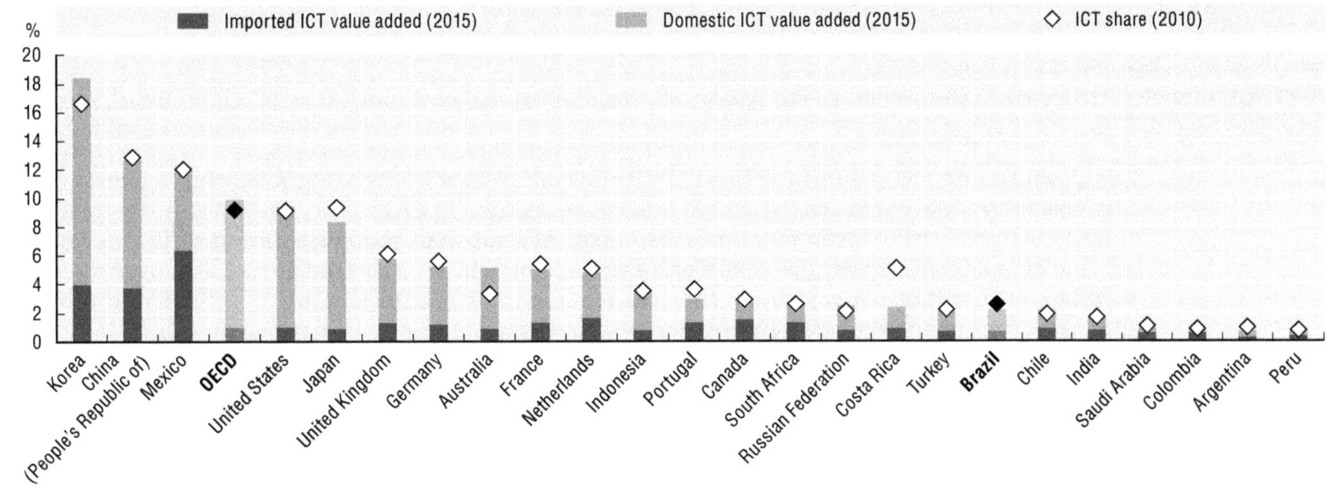

Notes: ICT = information and communication technology. ICT value-added content includes Computer, electronic and optical products (D26), Telecommunications services (D61), and IT and other information services (D62T63).

Source: OECD (2020a), "Trade in value added", *https://doi.org/10.1787/data-00648-en* (accessed on 10 March 2020).

Over the same period, the share of imported ICT value added in total ICT value added significantly increased, from 18.3% to 29.6%, comparable to China (29.7%) but significantly above the United States (10.4%). Manufacturing firms in Brazil therefore seem to be increasingly reliant on foreign ICT value added, illustrating the crucial importance of affordable access to foreign technology.

Enhancing access to foreign intermediates is crucial to boost industrial transformation

High adoption costs are one of the main barriers to technology adoption for Brazil's manufacturing sector (see Chapter 3). According to a survey by the Brazilian National Confederation of Industry among SMEs and large manufacturing firms, high costs are the most frequent barrier to technological adoption (reported by two-thirds of firms). Other barriers, like a lack of skilled workers (30%), inadequate infrastructure (26%) or difficulties to integrate new technologies and software (20%) were mentioned less frequently (CNI, 2016).

The high cost of technology adoption is partly the result of high import tariffs on foreign ICT goods (Figure 6.5). Companies purchasing intermediate or capital goods are paying markedly higher prices than in other countries (OECD, forthcoming a). Additionally, innovation schemes like the Informatics Law or the Semiconductor Technological Development Support Program (Programa de Apoio ao Desenvolvimento Tecnológico da Indústria de Semicondutores, PADIS) indirectly raised the relative price of imported technology (e.g. semiconductors), effectively tilting the technology choice of domestic firms towards potentially inferior domestic products.

Figure 6.5. Effectively applied tariffs on ICT goods in Brazil, the OECD and selected countries, 2017

Simple average as a percentage of import value

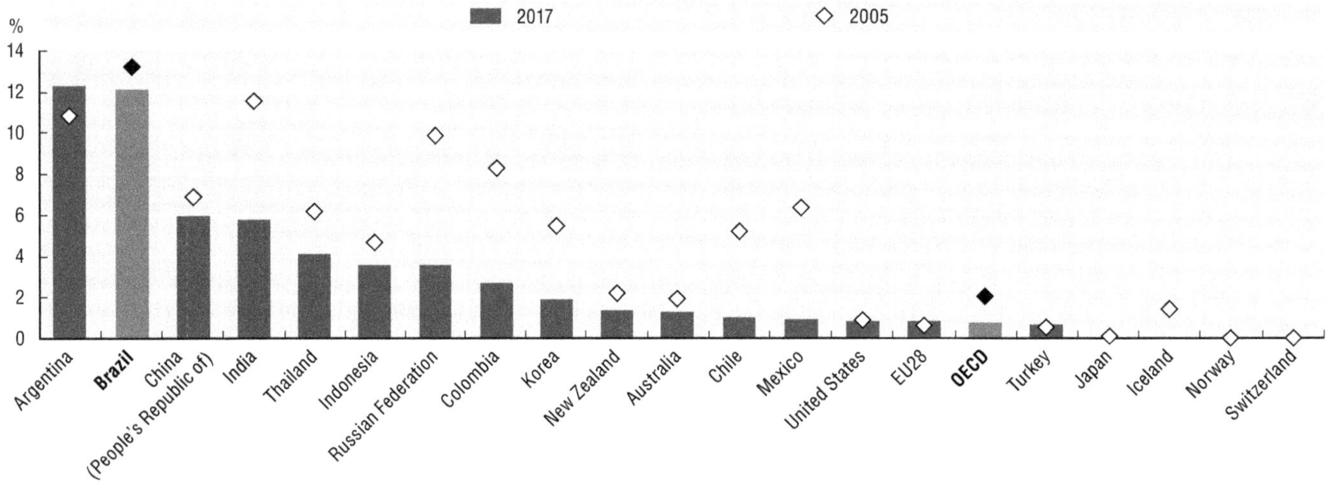

Note: Data for Thailand refer to 2015 instead of 2017.

Source: OECD (2019c), "Effectively applied tariffs on ICT goods, 2017: Simple average as a percentage of import value", *https://doi.org/10.1787/888933931504*.

The government has recently revised the Informatics Law and PADIS, following a World Trade Organization ruling that found the schemes to cause taxation in excess and a less favourable treatment of imported goods (see Chapter 5). It has also taken several steps to reduce import tariffs on selected ICT and capital goods under the *ex-tarifario* mechanism, which allows individual Mercosur members to reduce such duties temporarily in the absence of domestic equivalents. In particular, in February 2018, the government extended a temporary exemption from import duties on capital goods and ICT equipment until the end of 2019 (Camex Resolutions 14/2018 and 15/2018). On 12 September 2019, the government issued two ordinances (No. 2.023 and 2.024) lifting any import duty on 532 goods. These include 498 capital goods (e.g. machines for the production of medicines, medical equipment for exams and surgeries, cranes, tractors, or industrial robots) and 34 ICT goods (e.g. LED and photolithographic printing systems or data-processing machines for radar surveillance and airspace control).

The basket of goods exempted from import tariffs, however, is still limited. With only 34 ICT goods falling under the new regime, tariffs still apply to other, potentially crucial components. Brazil should therefore actively promote the entry of Mercosur countries into the WTO Information Technology Agreement, which would create a credible schedule for the reduction of tariffs on an increasing number of ICT goods. One estimate suggests that access to the ITA could increase GDP growth in Brazil by 0.08 percentage points in the first year alone. The increase in tax revenues from higher growth, including in the ICT sector, would exceed the loss in import tariffs from the fourth year onwards (Ezell and Foote, 2019).

Beyond ICT and capital goods, access to services at a competitive price has become crucial. Evidence from other BRIICS countries (Brazil, Russian Federation, India, Indonesia, China and South Africa), and in particular India, suggests that services reforms in markets such as banking, telecommunications, insurance or transport can have significant effects on the productivity of manufacturing firms (Arnold et al., 2015). These effects are likely to be significantly larger in the digital age, where the services content of manufacturing is steadily increasing (De Backer, Desnoyers-James and Moussiegt, 2015).

For example, digital transformation allows for the outsourcing of services previously performed in-house. In some cases, it also fosters the replacement of capital goods with services, e.g. when physical servers are replaced with cloud services. Additionally, manufacturing goods are increasingly bundled with services and emerging technologies, including additive manufacturing, are increasingly blurring the line between manufactured goods and services. Indeed, business services accounted for 36% of the valued added in all manufacturing goods exported by Brazil in 2015. About 19% of these services were imported, up from 14.4% in 2010.[4] Access to competitively priced services, therefore, is becoming increasingly important for manufacturing firms in Brazil. In this context, it would be important to reduce the cost burden currently associated with the import of services, for instance by reducing the special tax CIDE (Contribuição de Intervenção no Domínio Econômico), which is levied on several services imports, including administrative and technical assistance services provided by non-residents.

The increasing importance of "servitised" business models in manufacturing has been explicitly recognised in the National IoT Plan as well as in the National Industry Federation's (Confederação Nacional da Indústria, CNI) Industry 2027 initiative (IEL, 2018; BNDES, 2017d). The National IoT Plan, in particular, also highlights the additional challenges that arise with regard to emerging business models and bundles of goods and services. The Brazilian tax code treats goods and services taxation in two separate systems, namely the federal IPI for industrialised goods and the municipality level ISS on services (see Chapters 2 and 3). This can lead to ambiguities and uncertainties in cases where the boundaries between goods and services are blurring. To avoid these ambiguities from becoming a barrier to emerging business models, the government should consider harmonising the consumption tax schemes for goods and services, e.g. by consolidating consumption taxes at the state and federal levels into one value-added tax.

To promote innovation, the government should foster competition and support small and medium-sized enterprises

The relatively high level of tariff protection is one of the reasons for competition from abroad being relatively low in the manufacturing sector (OECD, 2015c). Another is the low level of domestic competition, which limits the redistribution of resources from large incumbents to potentially innovative market entrants (OECD, forthcoming b). In particular, the complex business environment and tax system, as well as limited access to credit, keep the relatively large number of small firms in the sector from growing into mid-sized competitors. For example, despite significant progress over recent years, the time required to comply with taxes for a benchmark company in Brazil was about 1 501 hours in 2018, longer than anywhere else in the world (PwC, 2019). Simplified procedures (Simples Nacional) are available for small firms, but growing larger implies that tax requirements can turn into additional compliance costs that may slow down growth. Additionally, the highly concentrated financial market structure implies that SMEs were facing average interest rates around 25% in 2017, about 16 percentage points higher than large firms (see below).

The limited growth potential for smaller firms, including innovative ones, has led to a rigid industry structure with a "missing middle" in the firm size distribution, involving a large number of small firms and a limited number of large incumbents with low investment incentives (OECD, 2017c; forthcoming b). The phenomenon is more severe in Brazil than in many other countries and particularly pronounced for the manufacturing sector, implying that resources remain trapped in low-productivity firms with limited incentives to invest in innovation and technological upgrading (OECD, 2018a). The fact that in 2016 over one in four manufacturing firms, close to 30% for large firms, had difficulties defining the return on adopting digital technologies (CNI, 2016) is a likely reflection of this environment.

Enhancing market openness would raise competitive pressure and could foster innovation, including among large incumbents. Experience from trade liberalisations in the 1990s suggests that Brazilian regions more exposed to liberalisation have seen a higher rate of resource reallocations from incumbents to new market entrants than other regions (Grundke et al., forthcoming). Additionally, easing access to finance for SMEs and simplifying the complex tax structure could help innovative firms to grow and transform the structure of the sector. Importantly, and as explained above, Brazil's manufacturing sector would also benefit from more competition in upstream services sectors, whose meagre long-term performance has been suggested as one of the reasons for low productivity in the manufacturing sector (Arbache, 2018; OECD, 2018a).

SEBRAE is running a programme that specifically aims to support productivity in upstream SMEs to foster innovation in large firms: the National Productive Chain programme (Programa Nacional de Encadeamento Productivo). In particular, the programme connects technological demand in large firms with solutions from innovative SMEs and provides consultation and training to help SMEs close potential performance gaps. According to SEBRAE, more than 65 000 SMEs had benefited from the programme by 2017, providing solutions to large firms in sectors like automobile, aviation or ICTs (SEBRAE, 2017b). SEBRAE has also created the programme Nexos, which offers fiscal incentives to large companies (e.g. Informatics Law or the Good Law) when they innovate with the help of innovative start-ups (see Chapter 5).

A more recent project with a clear focus on the role of start-ups for industry innovation is the National Connection Start-up Industry Program operated by the Brazilian Industrial Development Agency (Agência para o Desenvolvimento da Indústria, ABDI). The programme was launched in 2017 and aims at connecting start-up solutions to industry needs. In its first edition, ten industry leaders (BRF, Embraer, Natura, 3M, Embraco, Ericsson, Libbs, Botorantim Cimentos, Caterpillar and Dow) established relationships with 27 start-ups to co-develop 32 innovative solutions. The project has already led to ten implementations and is currently in its second edition.

The government is actively fostering Industry 4.0, but a multitude of initiatives require stronger co-ordination

In 2015, the Ministry of Economics, Foreign Trade and Services (MDIC, now part of the the Ministry of Economy) and the MCTIC initiated a first structured dialogue about advanced manufacturing in Brazil. Several workshops were organised, involving hundreds of experts from the private sector and large stakeholder organisations, such as the ABDI, BNDES and the CNI, among many others. The effort was seen as the potential kick-off for a National Strategy for Advanced Manufacturing that would provide the basis for multi-stakeholder co-operation in the coming years (MDIC-MCTIC, 2016). In 2017, the MDIC established a working group (GTI 4.0) to advance the national agenda while the MCTIC focused on an R&D plan for the industry (MCTIC, 2017).

Since then, an increasing number of initiatives specifically geared to promote advanced manufacturing in Brazil has emerged. This includes programmes focused on uptake of technologies, such as the BNDES and FINEP programmes discussed in Chapter 3 (e.g. FINAME Industry 4.0, Inovacred 4.0), as well as initiatives with a focus on innovation, such as the aforementioned ABDI National Connection Start-up Industry Program, research grants for advanced manufacturing from the National Council for Scientific and Technological Development (Conselho Nacional de Desenvolvimento Científico e Tecnológico, CNPq), or the Industry 4.0 IoT pilots implemented within the CNI/SENAI and EMBRAPII network.[5] Additionally, the Ministry of the Economy, together with the ABDI, has recently launched an Industry 4.0 testbed programme. Testbeds for Industry 4.0, signed in May 2019, is a USD 2.5 million (BRL 10 million) technical co-operation agreement, which scales-up a previous testbed programme by the ABDI from around 100 beneficiary companies to 1 000 companies. Several of EMBRAPII's units, distributed across 14 states and the Federal District, will be made available to validate Industry 4.0 technologies in a controlled environment. Both technology users as well as suppliers, including start-ups, will be able to benefit from the programme.

With this increasing number of sometimes rather small initiatives, and the multitude of actors involved, co-ordination across government agencies and industry stakeholders is becoming increasingly important. Recognising the need for better co-ordination, in April 2019 the Brazilian government (ME and MCTIC) launched the Industry 4.0 Chamber (Câmara Brasileira da Indústria 4.0). The chamber is the first formal platform to co-ordinate the development and implementation of an industrial transformation roadmap and involves over 30 private, public and academic entities. The creation of an industry-specific chamber fulfils one of the core actions foreseen in the National IoT Plan for the industry vertical (Box 6.1). The chamber consists of a Superior Council, an Executive Secretariat and four working groups, focused on research, technology and innovation, human capital, production chains as well as regulation, technical normalisation and infrastructure. The Superior Council, consisting of the MCTIC, the Ministry of Economy, CNI, the Brazilian Agency for Innovation and Research, the National Council for Scientific and Technological Development, BNDES, the ABDI, SEBRAE and EMBRAPII, met for the first time in May 2019 to initiate the work of the chamber.

In September 2019, the MCTIC and the Ministry of Economy published the Industry 4.0 Chamber Action Plan 2019-2022 which draws on previous documents and strategies from public and private actors to propose strategic actions in each of the four focus areas. The proposed actions partly build upon existing initiatives, such as the dissemination of Industry 4.0 online learning tools via SENAI in the area of human resources or the integration of Industry 4.0 into the Brasil Mais Produtivo programme (see Chapter 3). Among other things, the action plan also highlights the need to support micro, small and medium-sized enterprises in the adoption of advanced manufacturing technologies, proposes the use of test beds and multi-stakeholder open laboratories, and pledges to promote regulatory changes in areas such as data protection, labour legislation or the taxation of IoT devices. Responsible for the implementation are all stakeholders pertaining to a particular working group, which according to the plan will meet on a regular basis.

With regard to the multitude of available programmes, Action 2.3 of the innovation pillar explicitly foresees the collection and classification of existing funding instruments with focus on innovation in Industry 4.0 (e.g. from the Brazilian Agency for Innovation and Research, BNDES, the National Council for Scientific and Technological Development, EMBRAPII, SENAI or the State Research Foundation [Fundações de Amparo à Pesquisa, FAP]), by type of activity or maturity of the target company for example. These instruments will be considered to become part of the so-called "Basket 4.0" of instruments. A second step (Action 2.4) would then ensure that the selected instruments are adequate for the targeted firms in terms of cost, duration and financing conditions. With regard to technology adoption, the action plan foresees the further strengthening of the available funds (e.g. Inovacred 4.0 or FINEP IoT), and the creation of new financial sources (Action 2.2).

However, the absence of an overall budget plan, and the reliance on existing funding mechanisms in many cases, implies that a successful implementation of the envisaged actions stands and falls with the political will and financial capacities of the different institutions, and their disposition to co-operate. A strengthening of the overarching governance mechanism for digital transformation will be crucial in this regard.

The Industry 4.0 strategy should include energy efficiency among its objectives

The design of the Industry 4.0 Chamber as a forum for strategic planning follows similar initiatives in countries like Austria and Germany. However, it currently does not involve a focus on particular industries or technologies like the Made in China 2025 initiative or Japan's Robot Strategy (Planes-Satorra and Paunov, 2019) do. Nevertheless, the plan does highlight a need to identify industry segments and technologies with a high potential for Brazil. This can be of crucial importance to avoid the different initiatives from being spread out too thinly and to concentrate on certain crucial areas. The AMP 2.0 report, elaborated in the context of the US Advanced Manufacturing Partnership, can provide some guidance on the selection of relevant technology areas. The four criteria relate to: 1) industry or market pull, i.e. strong demand by industry or consumers; 2) cross-cutting impact across multiple industry sectors; 3) importance to national security and competitiveness; and 4) leveraging strength and competencies, including with regard to the available workforce and infrastructure (PCAST, 2014).

One area that might benefit from closer attention in Brazil's Industry 4.0 strategy is energy efficiency. Brazil is the only major industrial economy that registered a substantial increase in energy intensity, defined as energy consumption per unit of manufacturing value added, over the period 1997 to 2017 (Figure 6.6).

Figure 6.6. Manufacturing energy intensity in Brazil and selected countries, 1997-2017

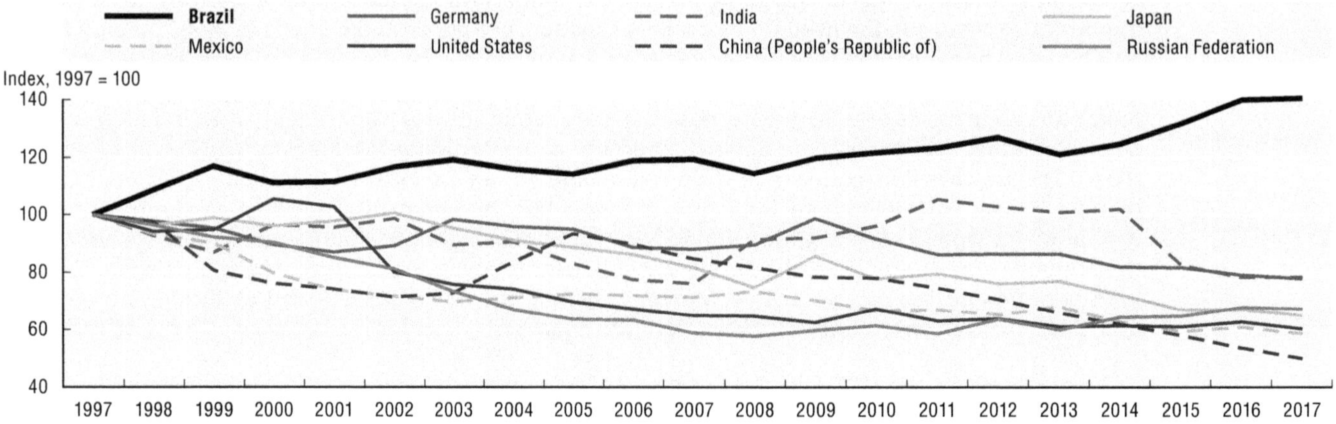

Note: Manufacturing energy intensity is measured in tonnes of oil equivalent per USD 100 manufacturing value added (constant 2010 USD). For China and the Russian Federation, data on both energy use and value added refer to industry rather than manufacturing.

Sources: OECD calculations based on IEA (2020), "Extended world energy balances", *https://dx.doi.org/10.1787/data-00513-en* and The World Bank (2020), *World Development Indicators*, *https://databank.worldbank.org/source/world-development-indicators*.

The use of digital technologies and energy management systems, for example in the context of motor-driven systems, could help Brazil boost energy efficiency and increase productivity in manufacturing (IEA, 2018). However, while the E-Digital Strategy (MCTIC, 2018) explicitly acknowledges the potential of Industry 4.0 and IoT to increase energy efficiency, associated with energy savings of 10-20% (MGI, 2015), neither the National IoT Plan nor the Industry 4.0 Action Plan establish concrete goals or actions in this regard.

Some initiatives with a focus on energy efficiency already underway would, however, likely benefit from an explicit incorporation into the advanced manufacturing strategy. Energy efficiency practices are part of the SME training programmes offered through Brasil Mais Produtivo (see Chapter 3). Awareness-raising and training programmes can also play an important role. In the study "Industry 2027", the CNI proposes that entrepreneurial training and business assistance services for small enterprises should cover environmental sustainability and energy efficiency. Corresponding activities could be executed within the SENAI network of technology and innovation institutes in partnership with SEBRAE (IEL, 2018).

Box 6.3. Policy recommendations for the digital transformation in manufacturing

- Enhance access to foreign technology with a long-term commitment to reduce tariffs on ICT and capital goods.
- Enhance access to imported services by reducing the special tax CIDE.
- Reduce uncertainty about taxation of goods and services arising from new business models enabled by digitalisation, e.g. by introducing a single tax scheme for both products (GST).
- Foster competition through market openness and improve the business environment, e.g. by simplifying the tax system and increasing SMEs' access to finance, to promote innovation.
- Scale-up programmes connecting manufacturing firms to innovative start-ups, SMEs and service providers.
- Strengthen governance and co-ordination mechanisms to ensure that Industry 4.0 policies, including those that promote digital uptake in SMEs, are well aligned and have sufficient scale.
- Include energy efficiency among the objectives of the Industry 4.0 strategy.

Fintech

Concentration in the financial market is limiting access to credit for small and medium-sized enterprises

Beginning with the privatisation of state banks in the 1990s, the Brazilian banking system went through a period of consolidation and increasing market concentration, with larger banks acquiring smaller ones or competing them out of the market

Around 85% of financial assets are held by financial conglomerates, often headed by large banks with subsidiaries in investment banking, securities brokerage, asset management and the insurance market. The three state-owned banks account for about 40% of the total banking sector's assets, providing 55% of bank credits. About half of all credits are earmarked by regulation for specific purposes, mainly for mortgages, investments or agriculture. Earmarked credits usually involve subsidised interest rates and longer maturities compared to the free market and are contributing to the segmentation of the credit market. In particular, the credit market for SMEs is dominated by large banks, providing mostly short-term financing, while long-term credits are almost exclusively provided by public-commercial banks (Banco do Brasil and Caixa Econômica Federal) and BNDES (IMF, 2018).

Market concentration in the banking sector, as well as restrictive monetary policies to curtail inflation, have led to some of the highest interest rates in the world. Borrowing costs are particularly high for SMEs, which were facing an average interest rate of 25.1% in 2017, about 16 percentage points higher than large firms (Figure 6.7). The interest rate spread has increased over time, implying tightening credit conditions for SMEs in relative terms (OECD, 2019d).

Figure 6.7. Interest rate spread between SMEs and large firms in Brazil, the OECD and selected countries, 2017

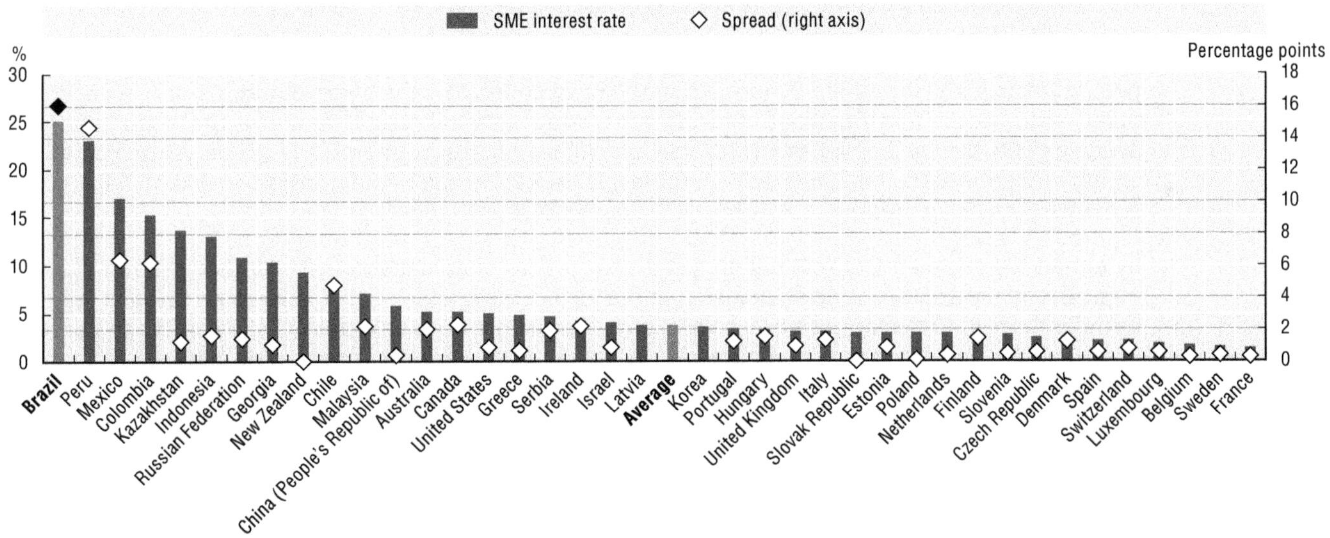

Note: SMEs = small and medium-sized enterprises.

Source: OECD (2019d), *Financing SMEs and Entrepreneurs 2019: An OECD Scoreboard, https://dx.doi.org/10.1787/fin_sme_ent-2019-en.*

The government has put in place several programmes to enhance access to credit for SMEs, including a micro-credit programme, quotas to finance loans to low-income individuals and micro-entrepreneurs, and an increase in the number of access points for financial services. New regulation in 2016 has further improved legal protection for angel investors in the case of company closure (OECD, 2018b). The government's focus is increasingly turning towards the emerging Fintech sector, which could significantly enhance competition in the market.

Brazilian Fintech is on the rise, but small compared to the traditional banking sector

Digitalisation is transforming the way in which the financial sector operates. While there is no precise definition of the term "Fintech", it broadly captures this development, enabled by emerging digital technologies and new business models (OECD, 2018c). Importantly, the characteristics of firms in the sector have been changing over time. Early start-ups have turned into professionally managed companies and several traditional incumbents have entered the market (EY, 2019a). Besides established banks, insurers and stockbrokers, this includes an increasing number of non-classical financial service providers (e.g. retailers, online platforms), which have begun to complement their portfolio with financial solutions (e.g. eWallets). In line with this horizontal expansion, adoption of Fintech solutions among consumers is constantly increasing.

Survey data from Australia, Canada, Hong Kong (China), Singapore, the United Kingdom and the United States, for which time series data are available, illustrate the dynamics in the sector, suggesting that Fintech adoption by consumers, defined as the use of two or more different Fintech services to capture regular users, rose from 16% in 2015 to 60% in 2019. The variety of instruments used is also growing, with significant increases in areas such as insurance products (EY, 2019a). The most recent data, covering 27 000 consumers in 27 economies, suggest that money transfers and payments remain the most frequently used instruments, with uptake reaching 75% in 2019. Across all 27 economies, Fintech adoption averaged 64% in 2019, reaching 87% in China and India. For Brazil, use among consumers currently matches the global average (64%), and was on par or above the uptake in many advanced countries, such as Germany (64%), the United States (46%) and France (35%). However, the uptake remained below other Latin American countries, such as Colombia (76%), Peru (75%), Mexico (72%) and Argentina (67%), implying substantial growth potential.

With regard to the supply of financial innovations, in particular mobile payment solutions, Brazil is currently ahead of other Latin American countries (AMI, 2019). In June 2019, 604 Fintechs and related companies were active in Brazil, up from 454 in August 2018 (Fintechlab, 2019). In 2018, Brazil accounted for about 33% of all Fintechs in Latin America (IDB, IDB Invest and Finnovista, 2018). Three of these companies are currently valued at over USD 1 billion: Nubank and Stone, both founded in 2013, and PagSegure, founded in 2006. The payment segment is the largest among Fintechs in Brazil (29% of Fintechs), followed by lending (18%) and financial management services (17%).

In areas like payments or banking, where Fintechs have been particularly active, the sizeable unbanked population is likely to sustain dynamism in the market. In 2017, the share of individuals (aged 15 and older) with access to a financial institution account in Brazil was 70%, above the Latin American average (55%), but well below the OECD average (95%). Among young people (15-24 years old), where digital affinity, and thus the potential for Fintech solutions, is the highest, access to a financial account remained at 47%, compared to 84% in OECD countries (Demirgüç-Kunt et al., 2018).

By enhancing competition and enabling digital access to financial accounts, Fintech solutions have a high potential to foster financial inclusion in the forthcoming years. Indeed, the main reasons reported by individuals in Brazil for not having a financial account are insufficient money to justify the use of an account (58%) and too expensive financial services (57%). Importantly, geographic distance to financial institutions in 2017 remained an obstacle for almost every third of the unbanked (32%) (Demirgüç-Kunt et al., 2018).

Recent regulatory changes are fostering the growth of new financial services

While financial regulation in Brazil is considered rather conservative by some stakeholders (Capgemini and BNP Paribas, 2018), regulators have undertaken several important changes over recent years, which have fostered the growth of Fintech companies and are slowly beginning to increase competition in the market.

New payment institutions are reshuffling the credit card market

A major step forward for the payments market was Law 12.865 of 2013 ("Payments Act"), which defined "payment institutions" and introduced a new regulatory framework, encompassing interoperability between different payment schemes, freedom of choice for consumers, and the provision of non-discriminatory access to infrastructure and services. The new framework, which aimed to level the playing field for new business models and increase innovation in the market, followed a previous ruling by Brazil's anti-trust regulator (CADE) in 2010 that opened access for competitors to the major credit card systems Visa and Mastercard (OECD, 2019e).

Since then, new payment institutions have begun issuing post-paid payment instruments (e.g. credit cards) and are reshuffling the cards in the concentrated market. Nubank, currently valued at over USD 4 billion and considered the largest digital bank outside of Asia in number of customers, is a good example of this dynamism. Founded in 2013, the branchless retail bank Nubank launched NuCard in 2014, a credit card with zero commissions, and has since attracted over 8 million customers in Brazil. The Fintech company is now among the five largest credit card issuers in Brazil and has received significant international investments, including from Tencent. It has added a debit card to its portfolio and in 2018 acquired a finance license, allowing it to offer a mixed current, savings and payment account (NuConta) and loans to private customers.

However, there is a need to further level the playing field between the new payment institutions and traditional banks. For example, in most cases, the new payment accounts cannot be used for automated, recurring payments initiated by the receiving entity, such as a utility provider or a tax authority (direct debit). The use of direct debit transactions in Brazil is mostly limited to intrabank transactions and requires the utility provider to establish a bank account with the customers' bank. Because this process is cumbersome, utility service providers typically offer direct debit transactions only to the customers of major banks. To establish a more level playing field between Fintechs and traditional banks, the Central Bank of Brazil (Banco Central do Brasil, BCB) should leverage the recent Instant Payment initiative to facilitate access to direct debit transactions for Fintechs.

On the acquirer side of the credit card network, Fintechs like Stone Pagamentos SA or PagSeguro have successfully entered the market, lowering prices for payment solutions directed at merchants (e.g. payment terminals) (Mandl, 2018). There are now over 20 authorised institutions providing solutions to merchants. This has put substantial pressure on the incumbents Cielo and Rede, which are owned by the major banks in Brazil and, until CADE's ruling in 2010, divided the acquirers' side of the market among them (OECD, 2019e). The introduction of new products, including the mobile terminal Lio by the incumbent Cielo, is one manifestation of the increasing competition. However, due to the high degree of vertical integration, i.e. the close links between acquirers and major banks, market concentration remains significant. In particular, Cielo and Rede still control close to 67% of the acquirer side of the credit card market and Fintech claims about anti-competitive behaviour by larger banks have spurred new investigations by CADE (Samor, 2019).

Mobile banking could receive a further boost from Brazil's Instant Payments initiative

New regulations accompanying the development of Fintechs are also transforming other areas of the retail banking sector. While digital-only bank accounts have existed in Brazil since 2011, clients were still required to visit a physical bank branch to open the account. This requirement was dropped with Resolution 4.480 of 2016, paving the way for pure online bank accounts, which can be opened remotely. Besides Fintech companies, this has also benefited some of the incumbents. For example, around the same time as Nubank, Bradesco, one of the largest incumbent banks in Brazil, opened its own digital subsidiary "Next", collaborating with tech companies such as Apple, Microsoft and Uber and specifically targeting young adults. Some smaller incumbents, including Banco Inter SA, have further completely reinvented themselves successfully as digital-only banks.

According to stakeholders, Brazil's regulators have been quite responsive to challenges arising during the transformation of the market. For example, BCB recently simplified the process through which employees can reassign their salary account from the employer's bank, which is the default option, to their own bank of choice.

The rise of online bank accounts is closely linked to the increasing availability of mobile devices with Internet access, which between 2015 and 2017, became the main channel for banking transactions (Figure 6.8). In 2018 alone, 2.5 million new online accounts were opened via mobile channels, an increase of 56% compared to the 1.6 million opened one year earlier. The total number of accounts using mobile banking reached 70 million in 2018, up from 25 million in 2014, exceeding for the first time the number of accounts using Internet banking (53 million in 2018) (FEBRABAN/Deloitte, 2019).

Additional momentum for mobile banking is likely to arise from BCB's recent push towards an instant payment ecosystem for Brazil. The initiative is part of the competitiveness dimension of BCB's strategic planning Agenda BC#. The criteria and modalities of participation in the Brazilian Instant Payment

Scheme (PIX), including a centralised settlement infrastructure (Instant Payments System, SPI) and the Proxy Identifier Database (DICT), have recently been published in Circular 3 985 of 2020. The scheme is expected to be operational as of November 2020 and participation will be mandatory for all licensed financial and payment institutions with more than 500 000 active customer accounts. In February 2020, BCB further signed an agreement with the National Treasury Secretariat to integrate federal tax payments into the system.

Figure 6.8. Financial service transactions in Brazil, by access channel

As a share of all financial service transactions

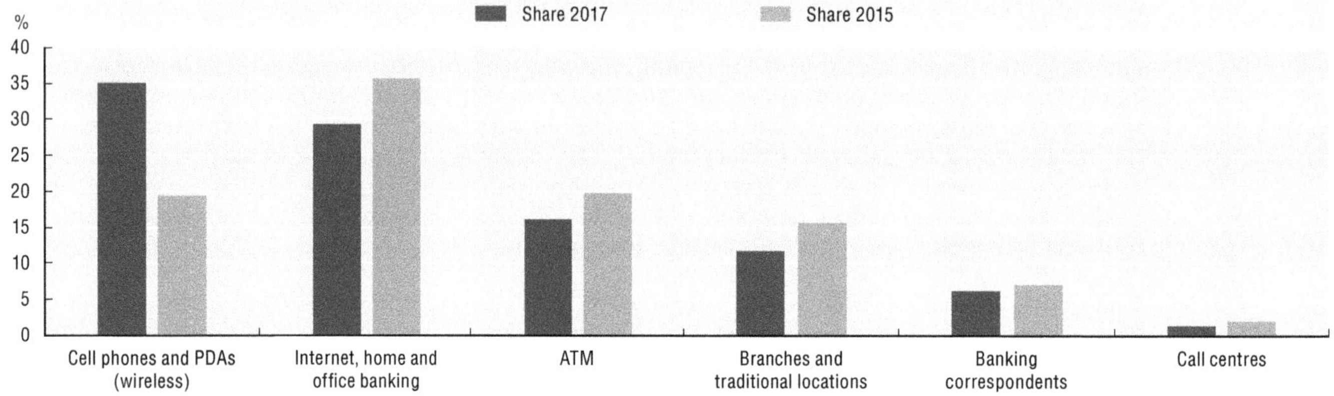

Note: PDA = personal digital assistant; ATM = automated teller machine.

Source: OECD calculations based on BCB (2018), *Report on Financial Citizenship 2018, www.bcb.gov.br/content/publications/report_fincit/Report%20on%20 Financial%20Citizenship%20-%202018.pdf.*

Importantly, PIX will simplify transactions via QR Code or proxy identifiers such as cell phone numbers. This will, in particular, benefit the emerging online payment services of business models like Google, Facebook, Uber or WhatsApp, which have a strong focus on mobile technologies. For example, WhatsApp Payments has already been successfully tested in India since 2018 and Facebook has recently announced it might soon launch the service in Brazil, the second largest market for WhatsApp (FT, 2019). This could have a significant impact on digital inclusion. In particular, only 46% of Internet users in the lowest income classes (strata D and E) currently use a credit card to pay for online purchases, compared to 64% to 77% in strata C to A. With 53%, *boletos bancarios* were the most frequently used payment method in the low-income strata (see Chapter 3) and still 29% paid goods and services upon delivery, compared to only 18% overall (CGI.br, 2018a).

Strengthening consumer trust in the credit market is key to success

Ongoing changes in regulation have also brought new dynamism to the credit market. In 2018, BCB introduced two new types of credit institutions with the aim to enhance competition in the credit market and to reduce high interest rates. A direct credit company, allowed to provide loans out of equity capital, and a peer-to-peer (P2P) loan company, serving as a platform to connect individual lenders and borrowers (Resolution 4 656/2018). Both entities are subject to a permanent minimum requirement of USD 254 000 (BRL 1 million) for corporate capital and net worth. Presidential Decree 9.544/2018 allows foreign capital participation of up to 100% in both types of financial institutions.

While online lending and P2P solutions existed before the new regulation, Fintechs usually had to collaborate with traditional financial institutions that were formally authorised to grant credits. Creditas, a São Paulo-based secured lending platform founded in 2012 (under the name BankFacil) and currently valued at about USD 750 million, is a good example of a Fintech that for a long time provided loans with collateral through the relatively complicated banking-partner model. At the beginning of 2019, the Fintech received the authorisation to operate as a direct credit company.

The number of new credit institutions, however, remains small and credits provided tend to be mostly short term and for a small amount. This is partly due to registration requirements being stricter for a credit institution than for payment services. Additionally, loans through the P2P are explicitly limited to USD 3 817 (BRL 15 000). Another major challenge is that many Brazilians, especially among the unbanked, lack a credit history. This makes it difficult for both banks and Fintechs to assess their credit risks, thus limiting lending. Several Fintechs, including Rebel or Nubli, are therefore focusing on alternative means of credit risk assessment, based on data analytics.

To promote access to credit and access to information, in particular for small and medium-sized financial institutions, BCB and the National Monetary Council (Conselho Monetário Nacional, CMN) have recently changed Brazil's credit scoring system (Positive Credit Report) to an opt-out model (BCB Circular 3.955 and CMN Resolution 4.737 of 2019). This implies that all consumers will be automatically included in the system until they decide to opt-out. The credit information is managed by credit bureaus (e.g. the Fintech Quod), which collect information on the payment history of citizens and companies from financial institutions, retailers, public utility providers, Fintechs and other lenders (BCB, 2019).

Credit Fintechs like Rebel or Nubli stand to benefit significantly from the increase in available data. This is particularly true in the light of the BCB's recent Open Banking initiative, another core pillar of Agenda BC#. The BCB defines open banking as the "*sharing of data, products and services by financial institutions and other licensed institutions, at the customers' discretion as far as their own data is concerned, through the opening and integration of platforms and infrastructures of information systems, in a safe, agile and convenient manner*". The scope and the fundamental requirements for the implementation of open banking in Brazil were disclosed by means of Communique 33 455 of April 2019. At a minimum, the Brazilian model would include the sharing of data on: products and services offered by participating institutions; customers' personal data; customers' transactional data; payment services. The latter three would be subject to customers' prior consent. The proposal, which requires the largest financial institutions (segments 1 and 2) to implement the measures as of the second half of 2020, was open for public consultation until 31 January 2020.

However, the successful implementation of Open Banking and the effective use of positive credit reports for financial inclusion critically hinge on enhancing consumer trust. According to EY, around 31% of surveyed consumers were worried about cyber risks associated with open banking and 36% said they intended to keep their banking data as private as possible. In particular, a majority of consumers explained that stronger assurances of data protection and clear liabilities with regard to potential damages resulting from open banking would be most effective in increasing participation (53% and 55%, respectively). Accordingly, to ensure the success of these recent initiatives, the government must focus on strengthening the regulatory system in areas such as data protection, data security and banking liabilities. Leaving these areas to auto-regulation by the sector is likely to the disadvantage of the Fintech sector, because consumer trust has been found to be significantly higher for traditional banks than for Fintech companies (EY, 2019b).

The government should clarify and enhance the conditions for co-operation between public banks and Fintech companies

The regulatory framework for co-operation between Fintech companies and public financial institutions currently remains highly fragmented and incomplete. A first assessment of the relevant legal basis, commissioned by the Laboratory of Financial Innovations (LAB) (Box 6.4), highlights in particular a need to adjust existing legal routes to public innovation contracting to better account for the start-up character of most Fintech companies, e.g. with regard to financial sustainability, scale or business model validation. Additionally, the analysis emphasises a lack of practical evaluations at scale and in some cases clearer provisions through the relevant control instances (BFBM, 2019).

To further enhance competition in credit markets, in particular for long-term credits, Fintech solutions should also be integrated into the lending reform currently underway in the national development bank BNDES. Unlike development banks in other countries, BNDES has mostly been providing direct loans to companies (e.g. for infrastructure projects) at an interest rate often significantly below the Central Bank's basic lending rate and with mixed results on firm performance (IMF, 2018). In January 2018, BNDES began replacing this interest rate, which is subsidised through loans from the Treasury and regulated by the CMN, with a market-based interest, linked to five-year government bonds. Linking the interest rate for BNDES credits to the higher market rates can incentivise private investors to co-finance and thus leverage public credits with commercial loans (Frischtak et al., 2017). The government should ensure that Fintechs, which are currently excluded from an immediate involvement in lending activities, are able participate in this process. In the context of the Covid-19 pandemic, Brazil's monetary council in March 2020 not only announced that Fintechs from now on will be able to obtain funding from BNDES, but also highlighted the role that Fintechs could play in reaching small entrepreneurs and unbanked individuals. However, it did not specify which services Fintechs may provide in partnership with the government (Mandl, 2020).

Box 6.4. The Laboratory of Financial Innovations

The Laboratory of Financial Innovations (LAB) is a multi-stakeholder initiative of the Brazilian Development Association (Associação Brasileira de Desenvolvimento, ABDE), the Inter-American Development Bank, and the Securities and Exchange Commission (Comissão de Valores Mobiliários, CVM). It was launched in August 2017 to foster the creation of financial mechanisms for sustainable development. Since then, more than 100 institutions, including government agencies, research institutions and representatives of the private sector, have participated in LAB's four working groups dealing with green bonds, green finance, financial instruments and impact investment, and Fintech.

The LAB not only fosters institutional learning, but also proposes concrete goals in each of the covered areas. Besides the implementation of a sandbox environment, this includes, for example, the implementation of a crowdfunding platform, a listing segment for green bonds in the Brazilian stock exchange or an Energy Efficiency Fund. In the context of Fintech, LAB also aims at expanding the interactions between Fintech and the traditional financial system, optimally including partnerships with state-owned companies (Vasco, 2019).

Additionally, BNDES could make more use of Fintech solutions to foster the use of credit guarantee schemes. For example, Fintech firms could help to (pre)assess the risk profile and performance of such schemes. Such schemes can compensate for imperfections in the collateral market and thus be an important tool to support funding for younger firms and SMEs with high growth potential, often avoided by private investors due to their risk profile. Credit guarantee schemes are currently underutilised in Brazil (The World Bank, 2018a). However, better evaluation of these schemes is crucial because, while the empirical literature has confirmed the positive effects they can have with regard to firm access to debt finance (financial additionally), evidence for improvements in firm performance (economic additionally) is mixed (OECD, 2018d).

BNDES is currently running some test programmes in this area. For example, with the MSME Developer Channel (Canal do Desenvolvedor MPME), BNDES has developed a digital platform to provide micro, small and medium-sized enterprises with better information and easier access to available financial products. BNDES is aiming to integrate Fintech solutions into this channel, including with regard to the analysis of credit ratings, financial education, linking of applicants and financial institutions, and reverse auctions. The project is supported by a USD 750 million credit line by the Inter-American Development Bank and USD 150 million of BNDES's own resources (IDB, 2018).

BNDES has recently also been engaged in the development of a so-called BNDES Token, a distributed ledger technology that is envisaged to enhance the transparency of the lending process and the monitoring of credit performance, with potential applications in combating corruption (OECD, 2019f). According to media reports, the token, which is based on token standard ERC-20 and the Brazilian real, is currently being tested in the funding of a documentary film in collaboration with a local producer (Partz, 2019). Similar pilots with a clear focus on social investments are currently also underway in the private sector, highlighting further opportunities for co-operation (Box 6.5).

The Fintech sector could benefit from better co-ordination among sectoral regulations

According to several industry representatives, the shortage of talent is currently one of the biggest challenges for Brazilian Fintech companies, which are increasingly trying to attract talent from abroad or have opened offices in other countries (e.g. Nubank in Berlin, Mexico City and Buenos Aires). However, further enhancing regulatory co-ordination will also remain crucial for the development of the Fintech sector. There are currently four regulators responsible for different segments of the financial system:

1) the BCB for banking, payment or lending; 2) the CVM for capital markets; 3) the Private Insurance Regulator (Superintendência de Seguros Privados, SUSEP); and 4) the Complementary Pension Regulator (Superintendência Nacional de Previdência Complementar, PREVIC). While the CMN, a policy committee composed of the governor of the BCB and representatives of the government, provides overall guidance on regulation of the financial system, arrangements among the regulatory agencies remain largely informal, which may be challenging in the context of the growing complexity and interconnectedness of the financial system (IMF, 2018). Recent developments in the regulation of cryptocurrencies provide an illustration of the potential challenges (Box 6.6).

Box 6.5. Moeda seed projects: Using blockchain for social investments

Moeda was launched in 2017 at a United Nations "hackathon" in order to address the 17 Sustainable Development Goals. Through selected seed projects, Moeda facilitates access to finance for impact projects involving entrepreneurs with difficulties accessing credit in the traditional banking system. The selected projects also receive support in technical areas, business planning and sustainability through the Moeda Seed Program. In early 2018, Moeda began a first pilot, involving the selection and support of 18 projects involving family farming co-operatives in Brazil.

For example, the Craft Beer project provides support to the Cooperval Cooperative in Formosa, Goiás. The first phase of the seed project in 2018 focused on the elaboration of a business plan for craft beer made from baru, a native chestnut found in the region. This phase involved the creation, testing and refinement of the product as well as an economic and financial analysis and the establishment of a loan plan. Phase 2 of the project established a customised credit contract and an action plan, including a production partnership with Dádiva Brewery for 1 500 bottles of the co-branded "Dona Divina Baru Beer". The revenues will be used to pay for initial contributions of USD 8 000, including fees, and to enhance the production of baru seedlings, spreading the cultivation to additional families.

Moeda uses blockchain technology and proprietary digital tokens (MDA, MDABRL) to enable instant end-to-end payments with enhanced transparency for investors. Investors directly invest in particular seed projects and can track investments and progress in the projects through the Moeda platform, which soon will be accessible through a dedicated currency seeds app. The Moeda platform further allows entrepreneurs to establish a financial track record, which linked to an immutable blockchain ID and, depending on performance, can simplify future access to funding.

Moeda receives support through the Securities and Exchange Commission and MDA tokens are currently traded in several exchanges, including Binance, LBank, BKex, EtherDelta, Allcoin and Coinbene. The company is now planning to open the programme to several hundred seed projects and begin with an expansion to other Latin American countries.

Source: Moeda Seeds (2020), *Moeda Seeds*, *www.moedaseeds.com* (accessed on 25 May 2020).

It is therefore promising that four different financial authorities and government institutions, namely the Secretariat for Financial Affairs of the Ministry of Economy (Secretariat Especial de Fazenda), the Central Bank of Brazil, the CVM and SUSEP, recently announced their intention to better co-ordinate sector-specific approaches and to issue joint regulations on Fintech and cryptocurrencies (CVM, 2019). Better co-ordination in these areas is likely to enhance legal security and foster innovation, even if some relevant stakeholders, such as the Financial Activities Control Council (Conselho de Controle de Atividades Financeiras, COAF) or the federal taxation authority in the context of cryptocurrencies, are currently not participants.

Importantly, the initiative also foresees co-ordination with regard to the establishment of regulatory sandbox environments in each of the four regulated markets. The establishment of regulatory sandboxes is one of the proposed actions of the E-Digital Strategy (Decree 9.319, 2018), aiming at providing a better enabling environment for emerging digital business models, while at the same time enhancing regulatory capabilities.

Box 6.6. The regulatory challenges related to cryptocurrencies in Brazil

With up to 1 million crypto-investors according to some estimates, compared to 800 000 investors currently in the stock exchange, the Brazilian market for crypto assets is large and, so far, largely unregulated. Lack of regulation is likely to have contributed to recent tensions between firms dealing with crypto assets (including cryptocurrencies), and several major incumbents in the formal banking sector. The Brazilian Administrative Council for Economic Defence (Conselho Administrativo de Defesa Econômica, CADE), for example, is currently investigating a case where major banks have allegedly frozen the bank accounts of companies dealing with cryptocurrencies (e.g. brokers) (Takar, 2019), effectively limiting competition from new market players. Fintech representatives, including the Bitcoin Bank Group (GBB), therefore in general tend to welcome new regulations to the extent that they foster the legal framework for crypto assets and facilitate the participation of institutional investors, including investment funds, in cryptocurrency trading (Cointelegraph, 2019).

Besides a number of informal discussions between financial regulators and industry representatives, such as the industry association ABCB, several official statements have also arisen more recently. For instance, in May 2019, the Chamber of Deputies established a commission on cryptocurrency regulation, tasked to elaborate an opinion on law proposal 2 203 from 2015. The proposal amends earlier laws on payment arrangements and payment institutions to include virtual currencies and air mileage programmes within the definition of "payment arrangements". The proposal would also require individuals and companies engaged in related investment projects to monitor deals for crimes of money laundering or concealment of assets (Alexandre, 2019).

Because the legal status of cryptocurrencies as financial assets had not been agreed upon, the technical division of the Brazilian Securities and Exchange Commission (CVM) issued a statement (Circular 1/2018) in January 2018 to inform investment fund managers that a direct acquisition of crypto assets by regulated investment funds would be illegal. A second statement from September of the same year (Circular 11/2018) later clarified that the prohibition does not apply to indirect investments, for example through foreign funds, as long as concerns such as money laundering, unfair practices or fraudulent operations are adequately addressed. Investments through exchanges that are subject to regulatory oversight with regard to illegal operations, for example, would be one way for investors to address these concerns (CVM, 2018).

In a confirmation of Circular 1/2018, in January 2018,the CVM also decided that the digital currency Niobium Coin was to be treated as a "utility token" rather than a financial asset or security, because there was no compensation for purchasers in terms of interest. This ruling implies that Niobium Coin is not subject to CVM oversight and has set a legal precedent at the global level (De Gobbi, 2018). In this regard, it is important to highlight that such decisions on the nature of initial offerings for cryptocurrencies remain subject to heated discussions in many countries, as illustrated by a recent court case on the initial offering of Kik Interactive Inc. in the United States (Levine, 2019).

Enhanced co-ordination is required to avoid recent regulatory initiatives from being contradictory or overlapping. For instance, the new tax regulation requires domestic cryptocurrency exchanges to report all domestic transactions within a month to the tax authorities. The regulation also applies to individuals and legal entities engaged in international transactions worth over USD 7 634 (BRL 30 000) if they are not intermediated through a domestic exchange (Normative Instruction 1.888/2019). Importantly, while the Brazilian tax authorities' current approach tends to align transactions involving cryptocurrencies with other financial transactions, the CVM's "utility token" interpretation seems to deviate from this approach (Chandler, 2018).

The CVM was the first regulator to take formal steps towards the creation of a sandbox environment within its own regulatory sphere, proposing an experimental regulatory framework for the securities market. The public note, which contains and accompanies the regulatory proposal and explicitly highlights alignment with the E-Digital Strategy, was open for public consultation until September 2019 (Edital da Audiência Pública SDM 05/19). The CVM's sandbox proposal has benefited substantially from the discussions on international best practices organised in the context of LAB (Box 6.4).

The proposed sandbox environment would establish temporary authorisations (up to one year, with one possible extension) to test innovative business models in the securities market. According to the note, innovative business models are those that make innovative use of technology or use new technologies, introduce new products or services, or promote efficiency gains or enhanced access to financial products and services. A "Sandbox Committee", consisting of CVM personnel, controls the environment and monitors participating firms, who may face restrictions on certain business activities to guarantee the safety, healthiness and efficiency of financial and capital markets. Importantly, participating business models may engage in contracts with official financial institutions and public entities. Innovative business models would also be able to apply for testing in international markets, i.e. in comparable sandboxes of foreign jurisdictions, and the sandbox environment is open for foreign entities.

Importantly, the proposal explicitly recognises the need to accommodate business models that enter the spheres of several regulatory bodies, including the Central Bank, SUSEP and the Complementary Pension Regulator. For these cases, the CVM's Sandbox Committee may create additional co-ordination procedures.

SUSEP and the Central Bank have recently followed suit and published notes with their own sandbox proposals. In particular, SUSEP's proposal was open for public consultation during October 2019 and the Central Bank's proposal, which has been experimenting with sandbox environments since 2018 (e.g. the Laboratory of Financial and Technological Innovation, LIFT), was open for public consultation between November 2019 and January 2020.

However, despite the previously stated intention of regulators to co-ordinate on aspects such as selection criteria, limits and periods, the current proposals partly differ in aspects such as eligibility criteria, admission procedures or duration of the experimental cycle. Because these procedural differences could complicate co-ordination, in particular in light of the cross-sectoral nature of some innovative business models, it will be important for regulators to further align the different sandbox environments (Ministry of Economy, 2019).

The establishment of a single contact point for firms unsure which regulator to address is also useful. The CVM is currently considering the establishment of such a one-stop shop as an entry point to the sandbox environment.

Box 6.7. Policy recommendations for the digital transformation in Fintech

- Leverage the Instant Payment initiative to create a level playing field for new payment institutions, including by facilitating the participation of Fintech firms in direct debit transactions.
- Foster competition in the payment card market by investigating and sanctioning anticompetitive behaviour.
- Enhance competition in the credit market by implementing the Open Banking initiative and strengthening regulations about data protection, data security and banking liabilities.
- Consider enhancing the use of credit guarantee schemes to foster financial access for SMEs and start-ups, using Fintech technologies to evaluate their performance in terms financial and economic outcomes.
- Enhance co-ordination among different financial regulators and better align regulation with regard to the emerging sandbox environments or cryptocurrencies.
- Establish a regulatory one-stop shop for Fintech companies to reduce uncertainty for Fintech companies crossing traditional market boundaries.

Health

E-health has the potential to enhance access to healthcare services

Brazil has made significant progress in terms of healthcare provision over the past decades. While still below the OECD average (80.3 years), life expectancy at birth increased significantly between 1988 and 2017, from 64.5 to 75.7 years, catching up to the average for Latin American and upper middle-income countries. Infant mortality declined dramatically from 56.6 per 1 000 live births to 14.6, slightly below the Latin American average, yet still significantly higher than in OECD countries (5.7) (The World Bank, 2020).

This is largely the result of the expansion of the Sistema Único de Saúde (SUS), a universal healthcare system based on a constitutional right to healthcare access introduced in 1988. Currently, close to three-quarters of Brazilians rely on services provided by the SUS while the remaining share of the population has some form of supplemental private insurance, mainly through their employer. Private health insurance plans are encouraged through tax incentives and mostly benefit individuals with formal employment, a higher education and in urban areas (Malta et al., 2017). In general, while total health expenditure as a proportion of GDP is in line with OECD levels, the public system is underfunded. Health expenditures as a share of GDP in Brazil are above the OECD average (9.2 versus 8.8, respectively). However, 57% of total health spending in Brazil is privately financed, compared to an average of 25% in the OECD. While innovation and investments in primary healthcare have contributed to the expansion of services and improved health outcomes in Brazil over the last decades (Guanais, 2013), many public family clinics still tend to be underfunded, lacking basic equipment and providing low-quality services. In Brazil, 47% of adults reported having access to primary healthcare on the same or next day as needed, compared to an average of 54% across 11 OECD countries, but 40% reported having high-quality primary healthcare, compared to 68% in the OECD, a much greater difference (Guanais et al., 2018).

Furthermore, the averages may hide important variations in the distribution of care. Access to the full range of health services is distributed unequally between urban and rural areas and among different states, leading to an acute shortage of healthcare services in many places. For instance, the number of doctors per 1 000 inhabitants ranges from 2.81 in the Southeast region (including the states of Rio de Janeiro and São Paulo) to only 0.87 in Maranhão and 0.97 in Pará. As most doctors are concentrated in the state capitals, this average hides a lower supply in many rural and remote areas (Scheffer et al., 2018). Fiscal austerity measures enacted after the economic crisis are likely to put additional strain on the public healthcare system in the coming years (Watts, 2016).

Fostering the uptake of digital technologies in the healthcare sector can help Brazil boost the provision of healthcare services in numerous ways. For example, the introduction of electronic health records can facilitate the evaluation of healthcare interventions, improve public health planning and raise the efficiency of the services provided. Telemedicine services can allow for a more timely access to healthcare services and facilitate healthcare provision in remote areas with limited resources. E-prescriptions can help prevent medication errors and enhance patient safety. The use of ICTs can also enhance the management and co-ordination of health services, thus enhancing the quality of care, for example for chronical diseases such as diabetes (OECD/IDB, 2016). Importantly, digital applications can also facilitate a move towards more people-centred healthcare, offering an opportunity to align health systems with what matters most to the people who use them (OECD, 2019g).

Investors and service providers, both private and public, increasingly recognise the growing market potential for digital health solutions in Brazil. In the first semester of 2018, an estimated total of 288 active Brazilian start-ups were applying proprietary technology for health applications such as marketplaces, wearables and IoT, telemedicine, medical devices, health education, or healthcare management (Distrito, 2018). Together with several incubators, accelerators and associations, they now form one of the most dynamic technology ecosystems in Latin America according to some investors (Lemos, 2018).

Many of these start-ups are directly involved in the amplification of access to healthcare for Brazilians. Dr. Consulta, for example, applies a data-driven business model to its chain of medical centres. The enhanced efficiency, focused on lowering prices and increasing customer satisfaction, has created a niche for the company between often less efficient public healthcare providers and expensive private competitors. Since its foundation in 2011, the company, which provides primary and secondary care to patients in predominantly poorer areas, has received substantial international investments, expanded to 51 branches, and is establishing one of the country's largest clinical data sets (FT, 2018). A similar business model is also applied by other companies, including Clínica Sim, Dr. Sem Filas, Docway or GlobalMed.

The Brazilian market is also seeing increasing dynamism in the area of telehealth solutions, which, due to their independence of geographical presence, can be crucial enablers for the provision of medical services in remote areas. Brasil Telemedicina, for example, is a private company offering online access to medical services since 2010, including medical reports, monitoring and, more recently, around-the-clock access to live medical and psychological orientations. The platform recently started employing artificial intelligence to help users find the right specialist after entering information on symptoms in an online form. In 2013, the digital development arm of Telefonica acquired AxisMed to provide B2B health monitoring services for chronic conditions via mobile apps, SMS and video streams. According to AxisMed, the service has served roughly 19 million patients since its launch, reducing the cost of private health insurers by an estimated 30% and the length of hospital stays by 50% (GSMA, 2017).

E-health requires significant public investments and enhanced data governance

In 2005, the World Health Organization endorsed the e-Health Resolution, recommending member states to integrate e-health into the national health systems. Since then, the Brazilian government has engaged in several related initiatives, culminating in a first national digital strategy ("digiSUS") in June 2017. The strategy, which, focuses on the public healthcare system, aims at digitally integrating all health service information available in SUS by 2020 (Resolution CIT 19/2017). It specifically highlights the advantages of technological solutions such as electronic health records, telemedicine or mobile health service applications. It also calls for an alignment of public and private sector initiatives to better integrate services and reduce the fragmentation of information (Ministry of Health, 2017).

In 2017, a majority of Brazilian healthcare facilities used computers (94%) and the Internet (87%), up from 83% and 77% respectively in 2013. However, these averages hide significant differences with regard to geographic regions and type of facility. In particular, while almost all healthcare facilities in state capitals, as well as private facilities, made use of computers (100%) and the Internet (99%), the availability of basic ICT infrastructure is significantly lower in the primary health units of the SUS (*unidades básicas de saúde*), the major access points to healthcare for most Brazilians. Among these primary healthcare facilities, about 12% did not have a computer and 28% lacked Internet access, an estimated total of 10 700 facilities (CGI.br, 2018b).

A significant challenge for public healthcare facilities is the lack of funds for ICT equipment. Thus, while a majority of healthcare facilities reported allocating resources for expenditure and investments in IT (63%), only 13% of managers in public facilities considered financial resources for investing in electronic systems to be in accordance with the need. This proportion was significantly higher in private institutions, where 61% of managers considered funds sufficient. A lack of funds is also reflected in the quality of available technology. In particular, IT equipment was not considered up to date by 68% of public facility managers, compared to 44% of managers in private facilities. Private facilities also used laptops and tablets significantly more often than public facilities (CGI.br, 2018b).

Available Internet speeds also remain a concern for public facilities, which are located more frequently in rural areas. Thus, while close to 98% of public health facilities with Internet access had a fixed broadband connection, only 25% of managers in public facilities considered the connection sufficient for the facility's need. This compares to 78% of managers in private facilities.

In 2017, the government launched a public tender, the Primary Health Unit Computerisation Program (PIUBS), to set up a digital infrastructure in public healthcare facilities. The goal was to foster the use of electronic patient records in primary health clinics by enhancing connectivity, IT equipment, technical support and training of health professionals. The original tender foresaw an investment of USD 381.7 million (BRL 1.5 billion) per year, envisaged to increase to USD 865.1 million (BRL 3.4 billion) by 2019, to equip 100% of primary health clinics in the SUS with the required IT equipment (DATASUS, 2017). However, because the Federal Court of Accounts had concerns with regard to the viability of a national rollout, PIUBS was recently replaced by Connect SUS.

The new programme, which was launched in November 2019 by the Ministry of Health, has two pillars: the establishment of the National Health Data Network (Rede Nacional de Dados em Saúde, RNDS) and a refreshed health unit computerisation programme. The health unit computerisation programme has started with a pilot in Brazil's second smallest state Alagoas. Besides hardware and software, the programme will also provide funds for basic infrastructure (e.g. electricity) or trainings and capacitation. Federal funds for the pilot will amount to USD 5.4 million (BRL 21.1 million), to be distributed mostly in 2020. The investments will involve a fixed instalment of USD 2 163 (BRL 8 500) to USD 2 799 (BRL 11 000) per health unit, followed by monthly support of USD 432.6 (BRL 1 700) to USD 585.2 (BRL 2 300). Trainings for medical staff on how to use the new system will be provided in addition to these funds. The aim of the National Health Data Network is to ensure that a patient's health information is available across different health units and remotely accessible by the patient. At a minimum, the health data in the system would provide information on the course of treatments, discharge certificates, medication, laboratory results and vaccinations. Overall, Connect SUS is likely to involve total investments of USD 1-1.5 billion (BRL 4-6 billion) over the next five years (Ministry of Health, 2019).

Given the potential of digital technologies to increase both technical and allocative efficiency in primary healthcare (HealthIT.gov, 2019; OECD, 2020b), it will be of utmost importance for the government to quickly validate and scale up the programme to other regions. Enhancing interoperability within the public health system (for example, between primary care, specialised care and hospitals), as well as with private sector systems early on is thereby crucial. Both branches of the health system are highly separate, making it harder for patients to benefit from the best treatment available. To provide a forum for better co-ordination among the different stakeholders, including at the state and municipality level, the Ministry of Health together with the MCTIC established the Health 4.0 Chamber in January 2020, in line with the National IoT Plan. However, the current focus of the chamber seems to remain the public healthcare system and it remains to be seen how efficient the chamber will be in bringing public and private stakeholders closer together.

With the increasing use and storage of patient information in digital form, it will also be important for the Brazilian government to ensure a sufficient level of health data protection, both in terms of privacy and security (see Chapter 4). In 2017, only 29% of health facilities in Brazil that used the Internet had an information security policy in place, 36% among private healthcare providers and 20% among public ones (CGI, 2018b). In January 2017, the Ministry of Health reinforced the regulatory framework for data protection and information security within the SUS and the Ministry of Health information system (Ordinance 271). However, data governance should be strengthened for the entire healthcare system, including for the private branch. The establishment of a data protection authority would be an important step in the right direction.

The government is also considering the application of distributed ledger technologies to enhance security in the National Health Data Network. The application of distributed ledger technologies for enhanced data integrity across healthcare providers, and secured access, is also being tested by the private sector. For example, the Instituto Latino Americano de Gestão de Saúde (INLAGS) and the blockchain company Unification are assigning unique digital identities to patients, which can connect to participating electronic health record systems via API. The patient, via a mobile app, controls access to the stored health information and can provide temporary access to hospitals and other healthcare associations. Depending on the access right granted, each user can then access and add data to the blockchain. The semi-private-public blockchain is hosted by participating healthcare facilities which serve as nodes in the system and validate the blockchain (Pollock, 2019).

As data-sharing activities are likely to increase, including between public and private facilities, systems interoperability remains a major challenge according to several stakeholders (BNDES, 2017c). Health information standards to enhance interoperability are formally regulated by the Ministry of Health's Ordinance 2 073 of 2011. New technological developments, including IoT and the rising importance of smartphones as an entry point to the Internet for most Brazilians, call for a reassessment of this ordinance, to ensure that technical standards are still up to date. According to the Ministry of Health, a major revision of the ordinance is currently underway and could be published soon. Importantly, an update to the regulation needs to enable better integration of healthcare providers along the highly fragmented healthcare value chain, a challenge that has stifled the efficiency of Brazil's healthcare system for several years (Tavener, 2014).

Enabling interoperability and access to electronic health records for the entire health system is key for efficient services and should be high on the agenda of Brazilian policy makers (Auraaen, Slawomirski and Klazinga, 2018). This implies not only the need to better integrate public and private health information systems, but also to ensure that patients can access, understand and interact with their own medical information. As outlined in the OECD *Recommendation of the Council on Health Data Governance* (OECD, 2016b), robust identity verification and authentication of individuals accessing personal health data is thereby key.

Countries like Estonia, for example, are using the national ID, a unique multi-purpose identifier, as access key to health data in a unified electronic health records system. The system not only gives patients access to all their medical data, it also provides for interactions, such as the possibility to update information or obtain certain medical certification, e.g. for a driver's license, without an appointment (The World Bank, 2018b). If Brazil realises its proposal of a National Civil Identification, an extension of use to the health sector could be highly beneficial.

Well-designed telehealth regulation would help enhance healthcare access in remote areas

Telemedicine in now being used to deliver healthcare in virtually all OECD countries (Oliveira Hashiguchi, 2020). The Brazilian government has put a strong emphasis on advancing the use of telehealth solutions in the public healthcare system. Three initiatives, launched between 2006 and 2009 among the Ministry of Health, the MCTIC, the Ministry of Education and other stakeholders, are particularly noteworthy. The University Telemedicine Network (Rute) focuses on the infrastructure connecting Brazil's university hospitals with so-called health education units or telehealth centres. UNA-SUS provides about 800 000 (mostly SUS) health professionals in 5 524 Brazilian cities with remote training and education opportunities, working like a virtual university. And the Brazil Telehealth Network (TBR) consists of 44 telehealth centres, supporting over 6 000 primary health units predominantly in remote areas through teleconsultations and training (Haddad, Figueiredo de Oliveira and Oliveira Serra, 2018).

Despite these initiatives, in 2017, only 22% of public healthcare facilities using the Internet participated in the national University Telemedicine Network Rute and only 26% in the Brazil Telehealth Network for primary care. Just above one-third of all public facilities using the Internet participated in a state-run telehealth network (36%). Overall, about 49% of all public health facilities did not participate in any telehealth network. As many of the current networks in Brazil focus almost exclusively on the public sector, the participation of private sector facilities was even more limited, with 88% of facilities not participating in any network.

Additionally, telehealth activities are mostly limited to applications that do not require real-time interactions (asynchronous), such as email consultations or remote access to learning material. Thus, while a significant share of public health facilities using the Internet had asynchronous telehealth solutions available (71%), synchronous solutions, such as teleconferencing (38%) but also remote patient monitoring systems (7%), were used only by a minority of facilities. For private facilities, the availability of most telehealth solutions was even lower, namely 56% for asynchronous interactions, 12% for real-time teleconferencing and 8% for remote patient monitoring (CGI, 2018b).

Lack of equipment is a major obstacle for an extended use of real-time telehealth in public facilities. For private facilities, regulatory uncertainty and constraints have likely been relatively more important impediments in past years. Telemedicine has been regulated since 2002, when the Federal Medical Council (Conselho Federal de Medicina) CFM) adopted Resolution 1642, formally establishing telemedicine as the use of interactive audio-visual communication and data for the purpose of medical exercise, including health assistance, education and research. However, the regulation fell short in terms of explicitly allowing the doctor-patient relationship through technology (Silva, Garcia and Terra, 2015). This implies that doctors in principle need to be present on both sides of the consultation, which is rather limiting compared to other countries (Oliveira Hashiguchi, 2020). Legal uncertainty with regard to telehealth services has also been highlighted as an issue by stakeholders, including in the context of TelesaúdeRS, a regional project conducted by the School of Medicine of the Federal University of Rio Grande do Sul (OECD/IDB, 2016).

Further to new technological opportunities in the field of telehealth, in February 2019 the CFM published new rules for telehealth applications (Resolution 2227/2018). The resolution enlarged the range of activities officially recognised as telehealth services (Article 1) and established new requirements with regard to the proper treatment of patient data (Article 3). The regulation also confirmed that a face-to-face relationship between doctor and patient is required prior to engaging in remote medical consultations (Article 4). However, a possibility for purely virtual consultations was opened for remote areas, provided required technical and physical conditions are met (Article 4, §3). The proposal provoked significant critique from several doctors, medical unions and regional medical councils, who did not feel sufficiently represented in the discussions leading up to the resolution. Responding to this criticism, the CFM revoked the resolution in March 2019 (Resolution 2228/2019) and has since received over 1 444 proposals for amendments.

The discussion about the potential benefits of telehealth solutions in Brazil has seen new dynamism in the context of the Covid-19 crisis, where avoiding a further spread of the disease has become vital. Several countries have therefore already begun to loosen regulations related to telemedicine, for example with regard to possible reimbursements or the need to consult a doctor face-to-face before initiating remote consultations (OECD, 2020c). In Brazil, for example, a recent partnership between the Ministry and Health and the Albert Einstein Hospital is fostering the use of virtual consultations for primary care within the TeleSUS framework. The government should support these measures through new telehealth regulation, ensuring that all relevant stakeholders participate in the process, e.g. through the Health 4.0 Chamber. Retaining the possibility of telehealth consultations for patients in remote areas, in particular for specialisations without local representation, could help to close persisting gaps in healthcare coverage. Additionally, the government should consider a better integration of private healthcare providers into existing telehealth networks.

Beyond telehealth, other limitations of current regulations have been identified in stakeholder discussions in the context of the National IoT Plan, which features the health sector as a core vertical (BNDES, 2017c). Critical areas include regulation for software as a medical device as well as regulation on drug-device combinations or nanotechnology-based drugs. The government has initiated discussions on several of these topics, including recent resolutions on advanced therapy medicinal products (e.g. Resolution 214/2018) or innovative drug products (RDC 200/2017), but other areas, including nanotechnology-based drugs or software as a medical device remain challenging and require further attention (Moreira Marina Araujo, 2018).

Box 6.8. Policy recommendations for the digital transformation of the health sector

- Validate and scale up Brazil's e-Health programme – Connect SUS – across all regions.
- Enhance interoperability and co-ordination between public and private health systems, leveraging the Health 4.0 Chamber.
- Update the regulatory framework for healthcare data protection and information security in both public and private facilities. Provide medical staff and hospitals with guidance on how to develop and implement effective information security policies.
- Foster the creation and use of digital health identities in line with the OECD *Recommendation of the Council on Health Data Governance.*
- Engage all stakeholders in regulatory reform that enables the use telemedicine as a substitute for face-to-face consultations in underserved areas.
- Promote new regulation in emerging areas, e.g. nanotechnology-based drugs and software as a medical device.

References

Alexandre, A. (2019), *Brazil Establishes Committee for Cryptocurrency Regulation*, Cointelegraph, *https://cointelegraph.com/news/brazil-establishes-committee-for-cryptocurrency-regulation* (accessed on 8 July 2019).

AMI (2019), *The State of Innovation in Latin America: Lessons from Innovative Companies Across the Region*, Americas Market Intelligence/VISA, *www.visa.com.bs/dam/VCOM/regional/lac/ENG/Default/The%20Visa%20Difference/Innovation/visa-innovation-14pages.pdf*.

Arbache, J. (2018), "Manufacturing, services, and the productivity gap", in Amann, E., C. Azzoni and W. Baer (eds.), *The Oxford Handbook of the Brazilian Economy*, Oxford University Press, pp. 338-357, *http://dx.doi.org/10.1093/oxfordhb/9780190499983.013.16*.

Arias, D. et al. (2017), *Agriculture Productivity Growth in Brazil: Recent Trends and Future Prospects*, World Bank Group, Washington, DC, *http://documents.worldbank.org/curated/en/268351520343354377/pdf/123948-WP-6-3-2018-8-39-22-AriasetalAgriculturalgrowthinBrazil.pdf*.

Arnold, J. et al. (2015), "Services reform and manufacturing performance: Evidence from India", *The Economic Journal*, Vol. 126/590, pp. 1-39, *http://dx.doi.org/10.1111/ecoj.12206*.

Auraaen, A., L. Slawomirski and N. Klazinga (2018), "The economics of patient safety in primary and ambulatory care: Flying blind", *OECD Health Working Papers*, No. 106, OECD Publishing, Paris, *https://dx.doi.org/10.1787/baf425ad-en*.

BCB (2019), *The Revitalized Positive Credit Report Has Become Fully Operational*, press release, Banco Central do Brasil, Rio de Janeiro, *www.bcb.gov.br/en/pressdetail/2279/nota*.

BCB (2018), *Report on Financial Citizenship 2018*, Banco Central do Brasil, Rio de Janeiro, *www.bcb.gov.br/content/publications/report_fincit/Report%20on%20Financial%20Citizenship%20-%202018.pdf*.

Be Brasil (2018), *Meet the Brazilian Apps Transforming Agribusiness*, ApexBrasil, *www.bebrasil.com.br/en/news/meet-the-brazilian-apps-transforming-agribusiness* (accessed on 8 July 2019).

BFBM (2019), *Memorandum*, 22 March, Barroso Fontelles, Barcellos, Mendonça Advogados, Rio de Janeiro, *www.bfbm.com.br*.

Bnamericas (2019), *Navigating the Maze of Cloud Service Rates*, Bnamericas, *www.bnamericas.com/en/features/navigating-the-maze-of-cloud-service-rates* (accessed on 3 September 2019).

BNDES (2019a), *Internet das Coisas: Um Plano de Ação para o Brasil* [Internet of Things: An Action Plan for Brazil], Brazilian Development Bank, Rio de Janeiro, *www.bndes.gov.br/wps/portal/site/home/conhecimento/pesquisaedados/estudos/estudo-internet-das-coisas-iot/estudo-internet-das-coisas-um-plano-de-acao-para-o-brasil/!ut/p/z1/zZNNc9owEIb_Si4-CgnLX_TmEMcQ7HGAJoAvGdkWWCmWjCVD019fmdIZGhJm2lN9Wkmrd999tIY* (accessed on 18 June 2019).

BNDES (2019b), *Internet of Things: BNDES Doubles Public Call Budget and Will Support 15 Pilot Projects*, Brazilian Development Bank, Rio de Janeiro, *www.bndes.gov.br/wps/portal/site/home/imprensa/noticias/conteudo/internet-das-coisas-bndes-dobra-orcamento-de-chamada-publica-e-apoiara-15-projetos-piloto* (accessed on 5 July 2019).

BNDES (2017a), *5a: Apresentação do Resultado de Priorização de Verticais* [Presentation of the Vertical Prioritisation Result], Brazilian Development Bank, Rio de Janeiro, *www.bndes.gov.br/wps/wcm/connect/site/24590dd0-4e92-4053-a63d-4c3b3f5a316a/Apresenta%C3%A7%C3%A3o+do+resultado+de+prioriza%C3%A7%C3%A3o+de+verticais_050717.pdf?MOD=AJPERES&CVID=lQIPFoq*.

BNDES (2017b), *Producto 8: Relatório do Plano de Ação – Iniciativas e Projetos Mobilizadoras* [Commodity 8: Action Plan Report – Mobilising Initiatives and Projects], Brazilian Development Bank, Rio de Janeiro, *www.bndes.gov.br/wps/wcm/connect/site/269bc780-8cdb-4b9b-a297-53955103d4c5/relatorio-final-plano-de-acao-produto-8-alterado.pdf?MOD=AJPERES&CVID=m0jDUok*.

BNDES (2017c), *Produto 8B: Relatório do Plano de Ação – Capítulo Regulatório* [Output 8B: Action Plan Report – Regulatory Chapter], Brazilian Development Bank, Rio de Janeiro, *www.bndes.gov.br/wps/wcm/connect/site/f9582d36-4355-4638-b931-e2e53af5e456/8B-relatorio-final-plano-de-acao-produto-ambiente-regulatorio.pdf?MOD=AJPERES&CVID=m7tyLs1*.

BNDES (2017d), *Producto 7D: Aprofundamento de Verticais – Indústrias* [Output 7D: Deepening of Verticals – Industries], Brazilian Development Bank, Rio de Janeiro, *www.bndes.gov.br/wps/wcm/connect/site/cfbd69ff-56d7-43f4-82df-f05b40459ec7/relatorio-aprofundamento-das-verticais-industria-produto-7D.pdf?MOD=AJPERES&CVID=m3xwf3m*.

Brasscom (2019), *Por uma Agricultura Digital, Conectada e Inovadora no Brasil* [For a Digital, Connected and Innovative Agriculture in Brazil], Brasscom – Associação Brasileira das Empresas de Tecnologia da Informação e Comunicação, São Paulo, *www.convergenciadigital.com.br/inf/brasscom-doc-2019-011.pdf* (accessed on 5 July 2019).

Buainain, A. and J. Garcia (2018), "Roles and challenges of Brazilian small holding agriculture", *Agroalimentaría*, Vol. 24/46, pp. 71-87, *www.researchgate.net/publication/330117534_Roles_and_challenges_of_Brazilian_small_holding_agriculture*.

Capgemini and BNP Paribas (2018), *World Payments Report 2018*, Capgemini and BNP Paribas, *https://worldpaymentsreport.com/wp-content/uploads/sites/5/2018/10/World-Payments-Report-2018.pdf*.

CEPEA (2019a), "Planilha PIB Cepea Portugues Site atualizado" [PIB spreadsheet Cepea Portuguese site updated], Centro de Estudos Avançados em Economia Aplicada ESALQ/USP, São Paulo, *www.cepea.esalq.usp.br/upload/kceditor/files/Planilha_PIB_Cepea_Portugues_Site_atualizada(1).xlsx* (accessed on 28 June 2019).

CEPEA (2019b), "Mercado de trabalho do agronegócio brasileiro 2018" [Brazilian agri-business labour market 2018], *Boletim CEPEA do Mercado de Trabalho*, Vol. 1/4, Centro de Estudos Avançados em Economia Aplicada – ESALQ/USP, São Paulo, *https://www.cepea.esalq.usp.br/upload/kceditor/files/2018_Relatorio%20MERCADODETRABALHO_CEPEA(1).pdf*.

CGI.br (2020), *ICT Enterprises 2019: Survey on the Use of Information and Communication Technologies in Brazilian Enterprises* (database), Comitê Gestor da Internet no Brasil, São Paulo, *https://cetic.br/en/pesquisa/empresas/indicadores/* (accessed in July 2020).

CGI.br. (2018a), *ICT Households 2018: Survey on the Use of Information and Communication Technologies in Brazilian Households* (database), Comitê Gestor da Internet no Brasil, São Paulo, *www.cetic.br/tics/domicilios/2018/individuos/H4*.

CGI.br (2018b), *ICT in Health 2017: Survey on the Use of Information and Communication Technologies in Brazilian Healthcare Facilities*, Comitê Gestor da Internet no Brasil, São Paulo, *www.cetic.br/media/docs/publicacoes/2/tic_saude_2017_livro_eletronico.pdf*.

Chandler, S. (2018), *Money or Assets? How World Governments Define Cryptocurrencies*, Cointelegraph, *https://cointelegraph.com/news/money-or-assets-how-world-governments-define-cryptocurrencies* (accessed on 9 July 2019).

Christoplos, I. (2010), *Mobilizing the Potential of Rural and Agricultural Extension*, Food and Agriculture Organization, Rome, *www.fao.org/3/i1444e/i1444e.pdf*.

CNI (2018), *Investments in Industry 4.0*, Confederação Nacional da Indústria, Brasilia, *https://bucket-gw-cni-static-cms-si.s3.amazonaws.com/media/filer_public/d4/c4/d4c48b24-0674-44a5-8799-b0fd5d0f8d11/investimentsinindustry40_2018.pdf*.

CNI (2016), "Industry 4.0: A new challenge for Brazilian industry", *Special Survey*, Vol. 2/66, Confederação Nacional da Indústria, Brasilia, *https://bucket-gw-cni-static-cms-si.s3.amazonaws.com/media/filer_public/f4/e8/f4e81f50-b13f-4339-89e1-8fd1b1d1a470/special_survey_industry40.pdf*.

Cointelegraph (2019), *Bitcoin Banco: "Novas normas da Receita Federal sobre criptomoedas são positivas"* [Bitcoin Banco: "The new rules of the Department of Federal Revenue on cryptocurrencies are positive"], Cointelegraph, *https://br.cointelegraph.com/news/bitcoin-bank-new-rules-of-the-internal-revenue-on-cryptos-are-positive* (accessed on 8 July 2019).

CVM (2019), *Comunicado Conjunto, de 13 de Junho de 2019* [Joint Communiqué of 13 June 2019], Securities and Exchange Commission, Rio de Janeiro, *www.cvm.gov.br/noticias/arquivos/2019/20190613-1.html* (accessed on 8 July 2019).

CVM (2018), *Guidelines for Investment Fund Managers*, Securities and Exchange Commission, Rio de Janeiro, *www.cvm.gov.br/noticias/arquivos/2018/20180919-1.html* (accessed on 9 July 2019).

DATASUS (2017), *Saúde Lança Edital para Informatizar 100% das Unidades Básicas do SUS*, Ministério da Saúde [Health Launched Notice to Digitalise 100% of SUS Basic Units], Brasilia, *https://www.saude.gov.br/noticias/agencia-saude/41783-saude-lanca-edital-para-informatizar-100-das-unidades-basicas-do-sus*.

De Backer, K., I. Desnoyers-James and L. Moussiegt (2015), "'Manufacturing or services – that is (not) the question': The role of manufacturing and services in OECD economies", *OECD Science, Technology and Industry Policy Papers*, No. 19, OECD Publishing Paris, *http://dx.doi.org/10.1787/5js64ks09dmn-en*.

De Gobbi, T. (2018), *CVM Board Confirms Decision on Niobium Coin*, Machado Meyer Advogados, *https://www.machadomeyer.com.br/index.php?option=com_content&catid=212&id=8907&view=article&Itemid=614&nosef=1&lang=en* (accessed on 9 July 2019).

Demirgüç-Kunt, A. et al. (2018), *The Global Findex Database 2017: Measuring Financial Inclusion and the Fintech Revolution*, The World Bank, Washington, DC, *http://documents.worldbank.org/curated/en/332881525873182837/The-Global-Findex-Database-2017-Measuring-Financial-Inclusion-and-the-Fintech-Revolution*.

Distrito (2018), *Healthtech Mining Report*, Distrito, *https://assets.kpmg/content/dam/kpmg/br/pdf/2018/06/br-healthtech-mining-report-2018.pdf*.

EC (2015), *CLAFIS: Crop, Livestock and Forests Integrated System for Intelligent Automation*, Processing and Control, European Commission, *https://cordis.europa.eu/project/rcn/110866/factsheet/en* (accessed on 5 July 2019).

Embrapa (2019), *Integrated Crop-Livestock-Forest Systems – ICLFS*, Brazilian Agricultural Research Corporation, Brasilia, *www.embrapa.br/en/tema-integracao-lavoura-pecuaria-floresta-ilpf/nota-tecnica* (accessed on 4 July 2019).

Embrapa (2018), *VISÃO 2030: O Futuro da Agricultura Brasileira* [VISION 2030: The Future of Brazilian Agriculture], Brazilian Agricultural Research Corporation, Brasilia, *www.embrapa.br/documents/10180/9543845/Vis%C3%A3o+2030+-+o+futuro+da+agricultura+brasileira/2a9a0f27-0ead-991a-8cbf-af8e89d62829*.

Embrapa (2014), *O Futuro do Desenvolvimento Tecnológico da Agricultura Brasileira* [The Future of Technological Development in Brazilian Agriculture], Brazilian Agricultural Research Corporation, Brasilia, *https://www.embrapa.br/documents/1024963/1658076/Documento+Vis%C3%A3o+-+vers%C3%A3o+completa/7bf520f2-7329-42c0-8bf0-15b3353c3fdb*.

Eurostat (2020), *Digital Economy and Society* (database), *https://ec.europa.eu/eurostat/web/digital-economy-and-society* (accessed on 15 February 2020).

EY (2019a), *Global Fintech Adoption Index 2019*, EYGM Ltd., *https://assets.ey.com/content/dam/ey-sites/ey-com/en_gl/topics/banking-and-capital-markets/ey-global-fintech-adoption-index.pdf*.

EY (2019b), "Why building consumer trust is key to Brazil's open banking success", *Open Banking Opportunity Index*, *www.ey.com/en_lu/banking-capital-markets/why-building-consumer-trust-is-key-to-brazil-open-banking-success.*

Ezell, S. and C. Foote (2019), *Assessing How Brazil Would Benefit From Joining the ITA*, Information Technology & Innovation Foundation, *www2.itif.org/2019-brazil-ita.pdf.*

FAO (2018), *The State of Agricultural Commodity Markets 2018: Agricultural Trade, Climate Change and Food Security*, Food and Agriculture Organization, Rome, *www.fao.org/3/I9542EN/i9542en.pdf.*

Febratel (2016), *Relatório do Projeto IoT Brasil* [IoT Brazil Project Report], Teleco, *www.telebrasil.org.br/component/docman/doc_download/1569-apresentacao-do-projeto-lot-brasil?Itemid=.*

FEBRABAN/Deloitte (2019), *2019 FEBRABAN Banking Technology Survey*, Federação Brasileira de Bancos, São Paulo, *www2.deloitte.com/br/en/pages/financial-services/articles/pesquisa-deloitte-febraban-tecnologia-bancaria.html.*

Fintechlab (2019), *8a Edição do Radar Fintechlab Registra Mais de 600 Iniciativas* [8th Edition of Fintechlab Radar Records Over 600 Initiatives], Fintechlab, *https://fintechlab.com.br/index.php/2019/06/12/8a-edicao-do-radar-fintechlab-registra-mais-de-600-iniciativas* (accessed on 11 July 2019).

Frischtak, C. et al. (2017), *Towards a More Effective BNDES*, World Bank Group, Washington, DC, *http://documents.worldbank.org/curated/en/306511499659990217/Towards-a-more-effective-BNDES* (accessed on 14 August 2019).

FT (2019), "WhatsApp's push into mobile payments", *Financial Times*, 2 January, *www.ft.com/content/e045cdd2-0503-11e9-99df-6183d3002ee1* (accessed on 15 February, 2020)

FT (2018), "Brazilian start-ups defy economic gloom with record fundraisings", *Financial Times*, 4 July, *www.ft.com/content/8742a6b2-7b18-11e8-bc55-50daf11b720d* (accessed on 31 August 2019).

Gasques, J., M. Piedade Bacchi and E. Teles Bastos (2018), "Nota técnica IV: Crescimento e produtividade da agricultura Brasileira de 1975 a 2016" [Technical note IV: Growth and productivity of Brazilian agriculture from 1975 to 2016], *Carta de Conjuntura*, No. 38, Institute for Applied Economic Research, *http://repositorio.ipea.gov.br/bitstream/11058/8326/1/cc38_nt_crescimento_e_producao_da_agricultura_brasileira_1975_a_2016.pdf.*

Grundke, R. et al. (forthcoming), "Brazils' trade liberalisation of the 1990s revisited: How targeted training can reduce adjustment costs for workers", *OECD Economics Department Working Papers*, OECD Publishing, Paris.

GSMA (2017), *Scaling Digital Health in Developing Markets*, GSMA Intelligence, *www.gsmaintelligence.com/research/?file=c581aa43bdb7b7d236bb937698c2d6fd&download* (accessed on 2 September 2019).

Guanais, F. (2013), "The combined effects of the expansion of primary health care and conditional cash transfers on infant mortality in Brazil, 1998-2010", *American Journal of Public Health*, Vol. 103/11, pp. 2000-2006, *http://dx.doi.org/10.2105/AJPH.2013.301452.*

Guanais, F. et al. (2018), "Primary health care and determinants of the perception of the health system and quality of care in 17 countries in LAC and the OECD", in Guanais, F. et al. (eds.), *From the Patient's Perspective: Experiences with Primary Health Care in Latin America and the Caribbean*, Inter-American Development Bank, Washington, DC, pp. 151-170, *https://publications.iadb.org/publications/english/document/From-the-Patients-Perspective-Experiences-with-Primary-Health-Care-in-Latin-America-and-the-Caribbean.pdf.*

Haddad, A., A. Figueiredo de Oliveira and H. Oliveira Serra (2018), *Telehealth and Brazilian Public Health Policies and Integration of Programs in Maranhão*, Comitê Gestor da Internet no Brasil, São Paulo,*www.cetic.br/media/docs/publicacoes/2/tic_saude_2017_livro_eletronico.pdf.*

HealthIT.gov (2019), "What are the advantages of electronic health records?", FAQ, HealthIT.gov, *www.healthit.gov/faq/what-are-advantages-electronic-health-records* (accessed on 26 September 2019).

Hyland, J. (2017), *Special Contribution: A Record Year for AgTech in Latin America?*, LAVCA Venture Investors, *https://lavca.org/2017/05/03/record-year-agtech-latin-america* (accessed on 5 July 2019).

IDB (2018), "Brazil promotes productivity of micro, small and medium-size enterprises with IDB support", *IDB News Releases*, Inter-American Development Bank, Washington, DC, *www.iadb.org/en/news/brazil-promotes-productivity-micro-small-and-medium-size-enterprises-idb-support* (accessed on 14 July 2019).

IDB, IDB Invest and Finnovista (2018), *Fintech: Latin America 2018 – Growth and Consolidation*, Inter-American Development Bank, Washington DC.

IEA (2020), "Extended world energy balances", *IEA World Energy Statistics and Balances*, International Energy Agency, Paris, *https://dx.doi.org/10.1787/data-00513-en.*

IEA (2018), *Energy Efficiency 2018: Analysis and Outlooks to 2040*, International Energy Agency, Paris, *https://www.iea.org/reports/energy-efficiency-2018.*

IEL (2018), *Indústria 2027: Riscos e Oportunidades para o Brasil Diante de Inovações Disruptivas* [Industry 2027: Risks and Opportunities for Brazil Before Disruptive Innovations], Instituto Euvaldo Lodi, Rio de Jaineiro, *https://bucket-gw-cni-static-cms-si.s3.amazonaws.com/media/filer_public/36/85/3685e664-7029-49ab-86b4-9c6f5137c480/industria_2027_capa_01_-_university_of_cambridge.pdf.*

IGBE (2019), *Censo Agropecuário 2017: Resultados Definitivos* [Agricultural Census 2017: Definitive Results], Brazilian Institute of Geography and Statistics, Rio de Janeiro, *https://biblioteca.ibge.gov.br/visualizacao/periodicos/3096/agro_2017_resultados_definitivos.pdf*.

IMF (2018), "Brazil: Financial system stability assessment", *IMF Country Report*, No. 18/339, International Monetary Fund, Washington DC, *www.imf.org/en/Publications/CR/Issues/2018/11/30/Brazil-Financial-System-Stability-Assessment-46411*.

INPE (2019), "A estimativa da taxa de desmatamento por corte raso para a Amazônia Legal em 2019 é de 9.762 km^2" [The estimated deforestation rate by shallow cut for the Legal Amazon in 2019 is 9 762 km^2], National Institute for Space Research, São José dos Campos, *www.inpe.br/noticias/noticia.php?Cod_Noticia=5294* (last accessed on 17 January 2020).

Jardim, F. (2018), "Brazil agtech market map: 338 startups innovating in agricultural powerhouse", AgFunderNews, *https://agfundernews.com/brazil-agtech-market-map-338-startups-innovating-in-agricultural-powerhouse.html* (accessed on 20 August 2019).

Jouanjean, M.-A. (2019), "Digital opportunities for trade in the agriculture and food sectors", *OECD Food, Agriculture and Fisheries Papers*, No. 122, OECD Publishing, Paris, *https://dx.doi.org/10.1787/91c40e07-en*.

Lemos, M. (2018), *Brazil's Healthtech Sector is New Hot Spot*, TechCrunch, *https://techcrunch.com/2018/10/09/brazils-healthtech-sector-is-new-hot-spot* (accessed on 31 August 2019).

Levine, M. (2019), *Kik Gets in Trouble Over Tokens*, Bloomberg, *www.bloomberg.com/opinion/articles/2019-06-05/kik-gets-in-trouble-over-tokens* (accessed on 9 July 2019).

Malta, D. et al. (2017), "Cobertura de planos de saúde na população brasileira, segundo a Pesquisa Nacional de Saúde, 2013" [Coverage of health plans in the Brazilian population, according to the National Health Survey, 2013], *Ciência & Saúde Coletiva*, Vol. 22/1, pp. 179-190, *http://dx.doi.org/10.1590/1413-81232017221.16782015*.

Mandl, C. (2020), *UPDATE 1-Brazil Opens Funding for Fintechs through State Development Bank*, Thomson Reuters, *https://www.reuters.com/article/health-coronavirus-brazil-fintechs/update-1-brazil-opens-funding-for-fintechs-through-state-development-bank-idUSL1N2BJ3FQ* (accessed on 27 March 2020).

Mandl, C. (2018), *Brazil Payments Processor Cielo Struggles Against Upstarts*, Thomson Reuters, *https://www.reuters.com/article/cielo-strategy/corrected-brazil-payments-processor-cielo-struggles-against-upstarts-idUSL2N1VP0SA* (accessed on 13 August 2019).

MAPA (2019a), *Agricultura de Precisão é Mais Rentável e Reduz a Necessidade do Uso de Insumos* [Precision Agriculture is More Profitable and Reduces the Need for the Use of Inputs], Ministério da Agricultura, Pecuária e Abastecimento, Brasilia, *http://antigo.agricultura.gov.br/noticias/agricultura-de-precisao-e-mais-rentavel-e-diminui-necessidade-do-uso-insumos*(accessed on 24 June July 2020).

MAPA (2019b), *Acesso à Internet no Campo Deve ter Proposta para Ampliação neste Ano* [There needs to be a Proposal for Internet Access in Rural Areas this Year], Ministério da Agricultura, Pecuária e Abastecimento, Brasilia, *https://www.gov.br/agricultura/pt-br/assuntos/noticias/acesso-a-internet-no-campo-deve-ter-proposta-para-ampliacao-neste-ano* (accessed on 24 June 2020).

MAPA (2019c), "Câmara do Agro 4.0 apresenta as principais demandas para ampliar o uso de novas tecnologias no campo" [Agro 4.0 Chamber presents the main demands to expand the use of new technologies in the field], Ministério da Agricultura, Pecuária e Abastecimento, Brasilia, *https://www.gov.br/agricultura/pt-br/assuntos/noticias/camara-do-agro-4-0-apresenta-as-principais-demandas-para-ampliar-o-uso-de-novas-tecnologias-no-campo* (accessed on 24 June 2020).

MAPA (2018), *Financiamentos do Plano ABC Superam R$ 1 Bilhão* [ABC Financing Plan Exceeds BRL 1 billion], Ministério da Agricultura, Pecuária e Abastecimento, Brasilia, *www.brasil.gov.br/noticias/economia-e-financas/2018/12/financiamentos-do-plano-abc-superam-r-1-bilhao* (accessed on 4 July 2019).

MAPA (2014), *Agricultura de Precisão – Agenda Estratégica: 2014-2030* [Precision Agriculture – Strategic Agenda: 2014-2030], Ministério da Agricultura, Pecuária e Abastecimento, Brasilia, *https://www.gov.br/agricultura/pt-br/assuntos/sustentabilidade/tecnologia-agropecuaria/agricultura-de-precisao-1/arquivos-de-agricultura-de-precisao/agenda-estrategica-do-setor-de-agricultura-de-precisao.pdf*.

MCTIC (2019), *Lançamento da Câmara Brasileira da Indústria 4.0 Vai Integrar Indústrias Inteligentes* [Launch of the Brazilian Chamber of Industry 4.0 Will Integrate Smart Industries], Ministério da Ciência, Tecnologia, Inovações e Comunicações, Brasilia, *www.mctic.gov.br/mctic/opencms/salaImprensa/noticias/arquivos/2019/04/Lancamento_da_Camara_Brasileira_da_Industria_40_integra_industrias_inteligentes_.html* (accessed on 27 June 2019).

MCTIC (2018), *Brazilian Digital Transformation Strategy: E-Digital*, Ministério da Ciência, Tecnologia, Inovações e Comunicações, Brasilia, *www.mctic.gov.br/mctic/export/sites/institucional/sessaoPublica/arquivos/digitalstrategy.pdf*.

MCTIC (2017), *ProFuturo – Produção do Futuro: Plano de CT&I para Manufatura Avançada no Brasil* [ProFuturo - Production of the Future: Science, Technology and Innovation Plan for Advanced Manufacturing in Brazil], Ministério da Ciência, Tecnologia, Inovações e Comunicações, Brasilia, *www.mctic.gov.br/mctic/export/sites/institucional/tecnologia/tecnologias_convergentes/arquivos/Cartilha-Plano-de-CTI_WEB.pdf*.

MDIC-MCTIC (2016), *Perspectivas de Especialistas Brasileiros sobre a Manufatura Avançada no Brazil* [Perspectives of Brazilian Experts on Advanced Manufacturing in Brazil], Ministério da Indústria, Comércio Exterior e Serviços and Ministério da Ciência, Tecnologia, Inovações e Comunicações, Brasilia, *www.mdic.gov.br/images/REPOSITORIO/si/dfin/Perspectivas_de_especialistas_brasileiros_sobre_a_manufatura_avan%C3%A7ada_no_Brasil.pdf*.

MercadoLibre (2020), *Form 10-K: Annual Report Pursuant to Section 13 or 15(d) of the Securities Exchange Act for the Fiscal Year Ended December 31, 2019*, MercadoLibre, Inc., *http://investor.mercadolibre.com/static-files/5cfa8a5d-6208-4cf6-bc76-488daafb7101.*

MGI (2015), *The Internet of Things: Mapping the Value beyond the Hype*, McKinsey & Company, *https://www.mckinsey.com/~/media/McKinsey/Industries/Technology%20Media%20and%20Telecommunications/High%20Tech/Our%20Insights/The%20Internet%20of%20Things%20The%20value%20of%20digitizing%20the%20physical%20world/The-Internet-of-things-Mapping-the-value-beyond-the-hype.ashx.*

Ministry of Economy (2019), *Fintechs e Sandbox no Brasil* [Fintechs and Sandbox in Brazil], Ministério da Economia, Brasilia, *www.economia.gov.br/central-de-conteudos/publicacoes/relatorios-e-boletins/2019/publicacao-spe-fintech.pdf.*

Ministry of Health (2019), *Saúde Será Conectada em Todo Brasil* [Health will be Connected Throughout Brazil], Ministério da Saúde, Brasilia, *https://saude.gov.br/noticias/agencia-saude/45989-saude-sera-conectada-em-todo-brasil* (accessed 12 January 2020).

Ministry of Health (2017), *Estratégia e-Saúde para o Brasil* [E-Health Strategy for Brazil], Ministério da Saúde, Brasilia, *http://portalarquivos.saude.gov.br/images/pdf/2017/julho/12/Estrategia-e-saude-para-o-Brasil.pdf.*

Moeda Seeds (2020), *Moeda Seeds*, (website), *https://moedaseeds.com* (accessed on 25 May 2020).

Moraine, M. et al. (2014), "Farming system design for innovative crop-livestock integration in Europe", *Animal*, Vol. 8/8, pp. 1204-1217, *http://dx.doi.org/doi:10.1017/S1751731114001189.*

Moreira Marina Araujo, A. (2018), "Medicinal products regulation in Brazil", presentation at the 4th Brazil-Japan Seminar of Regulations on Pharmaceuticals and Medical Devices, *https://www.mhlw.go.jp/content/11123000/000451940.pdf* (accessed on 11 June 2019).

Natanson, E. (2019), "From food delivery to Fintech, the new app convergence in Brazil", Forbes, *www.forbes.com/sites/eladnatanson/2019/07/01/from-food-delivery-to-fintech-the-new-app-convergence-in-brazil/#286cda9757cc* (accessed on 3 September 2019).

Netto, M. (2018), "ConBAP 2018 highlights precision agriculture in Brazil", PrecisionAg, *www.precisionag.com/market-watch/conbap-2018-highlights-precision-agriculture-in-brazil* (accessed on 8 July 2019).

Netto, M. (2017), "AgriHub: Connecting Brazilian producers to technologies worldwide", PrecisionAg, *www.precisionag.com/market-watch/agrihub-connecting-brazilian-producers-to-technologies-worldwide* (accessed 22 February 2020).

OECD (forthcoming a), *Regulatory Aspects of Data Governance for the Digital Transformation of Agriculture*, OECD Publishing, Paris.

OECD (forthcoming b), *OECD Economic Surveys: Brazil 2020*, OECD Publishing, Paris.

OECD (2020a), "Trade in value added", *OECD Statistics on Trade in Value Added* (database), OECD, Paris, *https://doi.org/10.1787/data-00648-en* (accessed on 10 March 2020).

OECD (2020b), *Realising the Potential of Primary Health Care*, OECD Health Policy Studies, OECD Publishing, Paris, *https://doi.org/10.1787/a92adee4-en.*

OECD (2020c), "Beyond containment: Health systems responses to Covid-19 in the OECD", *ELS Policy Brief on the Policy Response to the COVID-19 Crisis*, OECD, Paris, *https://read.oecd-ilibrary.org/view/?ref=119_119689-ud5comtf84&Title=Beyond%20Containment:Health%20systems%20responses%20to%20COVID-19%20in%20the%20OECD* (accessed on 27 March 2020).

OECD (2020d), *OECD Telecommunication and Broadcasting Review of Brazil*, OECD Publishing, Paris.

OECD (2019a), "Vectors of digital transformation", *OECD Digital Economy Papers*, No. 273, OECD Publishing, Paris, *https://doi.org/10.1787/5ade2bba-en.*

OECD (2019b), *Digital Opportunities for Better Agricultural Policies*, OECD Publishing, Paris, *https://dx.doi.org/10.1787/571a0812-en.*

OECD (2019c), "Effectively applied tariffs on ICT goods, 2017: Simple average as a percentage of import value", in *Measuring the Digital Transformation: A Roadmap for the Future*, OECD Publishing, Paris, *https://doi.org/10.1787/888933931504.*

OECD (2019d), *Financing SMEs and Entrepreneurs 2019: An OECD Scoreboard*, OECD Publishing, Paris, *https://dx.doi.org/10.1787/fin_sme_ent-2019-en.*

OECD (2019e), "Digital disruption in financial markets: Note by Brazil", OECD, Paris, *www.oecd.org/daf/competition/digital-disruption-in-financial-markets.htm.*

OECD (2019f), "Leveraging fintech to enhance integrity in public finance", *OECD on the Level: Towards a Level Playing Field for Government and Business*, OECD, Paris, *https://oecdonthelevel.com/2019/02/26/fintecgrity-leveraging-fintech-to-enhance-integrity-in-public-finance* (accessed on 14 July 2019).

OECD (2019g), *Health at a Glance 2019: OECD Indicators*, OECD Publishing, Paris, *https://dx.doi.org/10.1787/4dd50c09-en.*

OECD (2018a), *OECD Economic Surveys: Brazil 2018*, OECD Publishing, Paris, *https://doi.org/10.1787/eco_surveys-bra-2018-en.*

OECD (2018b), *Financing SMEs and Entrepreneurs 2018*, OECD Publishing, Paris, *https://doi.org/10.1787/fin_sme_ent-2018-en.*

OECD (2018c), *Financial Markets, Insurance and Private Pensions: Digitalisation and Finance*, OECD, Paris, *www.oecd.org/finance/Financial-markets-insurance-pensions-digitalisation-and-finance.pdf.*

OECD (2018d), "Evaluating publicly supported credit guarantee programmes for SMEs: Selected results from an OECD/EC survey", in *Financing SMEs and Entrepreneurs 2018: An OECD Scoreboard*, OECD Publishing, Paris, pp. 89-104, *https://dx.doi.org/10.1787/fin_sme_ent-2018-6-en*.

OECD (2017a), *The Next Production Revolution: Implications for Governments and Business*, OECD Publishing, Paris, *https://doi.org/10.1787/9789264271036-en*.

OECD (2017b), *OECD Digital Economy Outlook 2017*, OECD Publishing, Paris, *https://dx.doi.org/10.1787/9789264276284-en*.

OECD (2017c), *Business Dynamics and Productivity*, OECD Publishing, Paris, *https://doi.org/10.1787/9789264269231-en*.

OECD (2016a), "Is precision agriculture the start of a new revolution?", in *Farm Management Practices to Foster Green Growth*, OECD Publishing, pp. 137-59, Paris, *https://doi.org/10.1787/9789264238657-8-en*.

OECD (2016b), *Recommendation of the Council on Health Data Governance*, OECD, Paris, *https://legalinstruments.oecd.org/en/instruments/OECD-LEGAL-0433*.

OECD (2015a), *Data-Driven Innovation: Big Data for Growth and Well-Being*, OECD Publishing, Paris, *https://dx.doi.org/10.1787/9789264229358-en*.

OECD (2015b), *Innovation, Agricultural Productivity and Sustainability in Brazil*, OECD Food and Agricultural Reviews, OECD Publishing, Paris, *https://dx.doi.org/10.1787/9789264237056-en*.

OECD (2015c), *OECD Economic Surveys: Brazil 2015*, OECD Publishing, Paris, *https://dx.doi.org/10.1787/eco_surveys-bra-2015-en*.

OECD/FAO (2019), *OECD-FAO Agricultural Outlook 2019-2028*, OECD Publishing, Paris, *https://doi.org/10.1787/agr_outlook-2019-en*.

OECD/IDB (2016), *Broadband Policies for Latin America and the Caribbean: A Digital Economy Toolkit*, OECD Publishing, Paris, *https://dx.doi.org/10.1787/9789264251823-en*.

Oliveira Hashiguchi, T. (2020), "Bringing health care to the patient: An overview of the use of telemedicine in OECD countries", *OECD Health Working Papers*, No. 116, OECD Publishing, Paris, *https://dx.doi.org/10.1787/8e56ede7-en*.

Partz, H. (2019), "Brazilian state-owned bank funds documentary via its own Ethereum-based token", Cointelegraph, *https://cointelegraph.com/news/brazilian-state-owned-bank-funds-documentary-via-its-own-ethereum-based-token* (accessed on 14 July 2019).

PCAST (2014), *Accelerating U.S. Advanced Manufacturing: AMP2.0 Steering Committee Report*, President's Council of Advisors on Science and Technology, *https://www.manufacturing.gov/sites/default/files/2018-01/amp20_report_final.pdf*.

Planes-Satorra, S. and C. Paunov (2019), "The digital innovation policy landscape in 2019", *OECD Science, Technology and Industry Policy Papers*, No. 71, OECD Publishing, Paris, *https://dx.doi.org/10.1787/6171f649-en*.

Pollock, D. (2019), "Brazilian medical records getting blockchain boost may be the route to digital identity adoption", Forbes, *www.forbes.com/sites/darrynpollock/2019/04/26/brazilian-medical-records-getting-blockchain-boost-may-be-the-route-to-digital-identity-adoption/#4a5c58ef7b86* (accessed on 26 September 2019).

PwC (2019), *Paying Taxes 2020: The Changing Landscape of Tax Policy and Administration Across 190 Economies*, PwC and World Bank Group, London and Washington DC, *https://www.pwc.com/gx/en/paying-taxes/pdf/pwc-paying-taxes-2020.pdf*.

Ribeiro Vieira Filho, J. (2017), "Technological clusters in Brazilian agriculture: Production and challenges", *IPEA Discussion Papers*, No. 224, *https://pdfs.semanticscholar.org/a002/10b168d4fc4901a90046406f1564537f2dce.pdf*.

Samor, G. (2019), "Itaú has just escalated the war against Stone and PagSeguro – and they plan to react", *Brazil Journal*, 18 April, *https://braziljournal.com/itau-has-just-escalated-the-war-against-stone-and-pagseguro-and-they-plan-to-react* (accessed on 10 July 2019).

Scheffer, M. et al. (2018), *Demografia Médica no Brasil 2018*,Departamento de Medicina Preventiva da Faculdade de Medicina da USP, Conselho Regional de Medicina do Estado de São Paulo and Conselho Federal de Medicina, São Paulo, *www.flip3d.com.br/web/pub/cfm/index10/?numero=15&edicao=4278*.

SEBRAE (2017a), *Produtor Rural: Tecnologia da Informação no* Agronegócio [Rural Producer: Information Technology in Agri-business], Serviço Brasileiro de Apoio às Micro e Pequenas Empresas, Brasilia, *www.sebrae.com.br/file_source/Sebrae/Portal%20Sebrae/Anexos/Pesquisa%20SEBRAE%20-%20TIC%20no%20Agro.pdf*.

SEBRAE (2017b), *Encadeamento Productivo: Bons Negócios Conectando Pequenas e Grandes Empresas* [Productive Chaining: Good Businesses Connecting Small and Large Companies], Serviço Brasileiro de Apoio às Micro e Pequenas Empresas, Brasilia,*www.sebrae.com.br/Sebrae/Portal%20Sebrae/Anexos/Folder%20EP%20atualizado%20-%20set.%202017.pdf*.

SENAR (2016), "SENAR-MT lança treinamento sobre operação de drones na agropecuária" [SENAR-MT launches training on drone use in agriculture], *Agro de Precisão*, *www.cnabrasil.org.br/noticias/senar-mt-lan%C3%A7a-treinamento-sobre-opera%C3%A7%C3%A3o-de-drones-na-agropecu%C3%A1ria* (accessed on 22 August 2019).

Silva, E., L. Garcia and J. Terra (2015), "A comparison of telehealth programs between the USA and Brazil: A legal perspective", *Smart Homecare Technology and TeleHealth*, p. 139, *http://dx.doi.org/10.2147/shtt.s64447*.

Sorvino, C. (2017), *The 25 Most Innovative Ag-Tech Startups*, Forbes, *www.forbes.com/sites/maggiemcgrath/2017/06/28/the-25-most-innovative-ag-tech-startups/#156fd33f4883* (accessed on 5 July 2019).

Takar, T. (2019), "Bancos limitam Bitcoin, e corretoras esperam decisão do Cade há quase 1 ano"[Banks limit Bitcoin, and brokers have been waiting for Cade's decision for almost a year], Universo Online, *https://economia.uol.com.br/noticias/redacao/2019/04/02/corretoras-criptomoedas-brigam-com-bancos-no-cade.htm* (accessed on 8 July 2019).

Tavener, B. (2014), "How Brazil can make healthcare more efficient", Weforum, *www.weforum.org/agenda/2014/11/how-brazil-can-make-healthcare-more-efficient* (accessed on 2 September 2019).

The World Bank (2020), *World Development Indicators*, *https://databank.worldbank.org/source/world-development-indicators*.

The World Bank (2018a), *Brazil: Improving the Efficiency of Credit Markets*, The World Bank/FCI GP, Washington, DC, *http://pubdocs.worldbank.org/en/252851536597936709/Policy-Note-Credit-Markets.pdf*.

The World Bank (2018b), *The Role of Digital Identification for Healthcare: The Emerging Use Cases*, The World Bank, Washington, DC, *http://documents.worldbank.org/curated/en/595741519657604541/The-Role-of-Digital-Identification-for-Healthcare-The-Emerging-Use-Cases.pdf*.

Trendov, N., S. Varas and M. Zeng (2019), *Digital Technologies in Agriculture and Rural Areas: Briefing Paper*, Food and Agriculture Organization, Rome, *www.fao.org/3/ca4887en/ca4887en.pdf*.

UNIDO (2019), *Competitive Industrial Performance Report 2018*, United Nations Industrial Development Organization, *www.unido.org/sites/default/files/files/2019-05/CIP.pdf*.

UNIDO (2017), *Industrial Development Report 2018*, United Nations Industrial Development Organization, *https://www.unido.org/news/industrial-development-report-2018-launched#:~:text=Although%20industrial%20development%20has%20typically,of%20new%20and%20improved%20goods*.

Vasco, J. (2019), *LAB: Financial Innovation Lab*, Securities and Exchange Commission, Rio de Janeiro.

Watts, J. (2016), "Brazil's health system woes worsen in economic crisis", *The Lancet*, Vol. 387/10028, pp. 1603-1604, *http://dx.doi.org/10.1016/s0140-6736(16)30249-5*.

WEF (2018), *Readiness for the Future of Production Report 2018*, World Economic Forum, Geneva, *www3.weforum.org/docs/FOP_Readiness_Report_2018.pdf*.

Welthungerhilfe (2018), "E-agriculture webinar on transformative digital extension delivery and smallholder farm marketing in Zimbabwe through the Kurima Mari mobile app", E-agriculture, *www.fao.org/e-agriculture/webinars/e-agriculture-webinar-transformative-digital-extension-delivery-and-smallholder-farm* (accessed on 23 August 2019).

ZDNet (2018), *Siemens Launches Innovation Centre for Livestock in Brazil*, ZDNet, *www.zdnet.com/article/siemens-launches-innovation-centre-for-livestock-in-brazil* (accessed on 5 July 2019).

Notes

Israel

The statistical data for Israel are supplied by and under the responsibility of the relevant Israeli authorities. The use of such data by the OECD is without prejudice to the status of the Golan Heights, East Jerusalem and Israeli settlements in the West Bank under the terms of international law.

1. Available at: *https://www.radaragtech.com.br/*.
2. The results of an earlier survey confirm that the uptake of digital technologies is considerably lower among small firms, where the percentage of firms using at least one out of (slightly different) list of 10 digital technologies was only 25%, compared to 63% for large firms (CNI, 2016).
3. In industries other than the ICT manufacturing industry, the measure excludes ICT value added that is generated internally, e.g. if manufacturing firms produce their own computers or software.
4. OECD calculations based on OECD (2020a).
5. See *www.editaldeinovacao.com.br* for more information.

Chapter 7

POLICIES FOR DIGITAL TRANSFORMATION: RECOMMENDATIONS FOR A WHOLE-OF-GOVERNMENT APPROACH

Going Digital in Brazil: An integrated policy framework

The previous chapters of this Review analysed recent developments in digital transformation in several policy fields in Brazil. The analysis resulted in an assessment and a set of policy recommendations for each field. These recommendations are discussed below and mapped against the OECD Going Digital Integrated Policy Framework presented in Chapter 1 and summarised in Figure 7.1.

The components of the framework under analysis were those expressed as priorities by the Brazilian authorities: access, use, trust and innovation.

Figure 7.1. OECD Going Digital Integrated Policy Framework

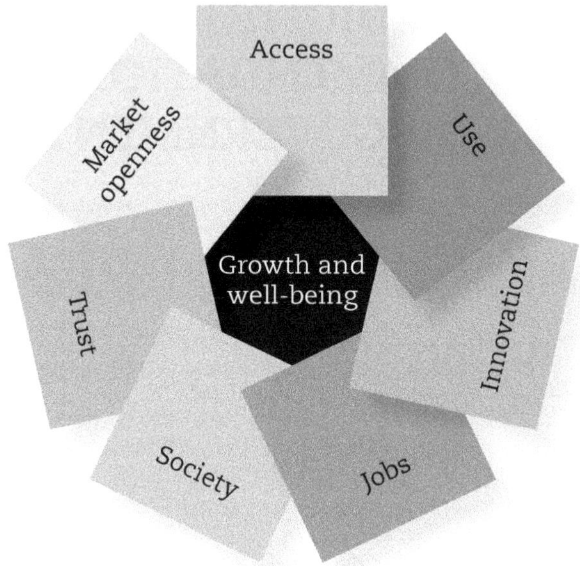

Source: OECD (2019a), *Going Digital: Shaping Policies, Improving Lives*, https://doi.org/10.1787/9789264312012-en.

Access

As noted in Chapter 2, the availability of high-quality fixed and mobile communication services at competitive prices are crucial for Brazil to go digital. One of Brazil's main challenges in this respect is expanding quality broadband to rural and remote areas. Fixed and mobile broadband penetration is similar to countries in the region, but well below the OECD average. Fixed broadband prices tend to be higher than in many OECD countries.

Brazil should take further action to promote access to broadband, increase the quality of communication services and promote competition in the market:

- Create a converged regulator for the communication and broadcasting sectors by merging the regulatory functions of the National Telecommunications Agency (Agência Nacional de Telecomunicações, Anatel); the National Film Agency (Agência Nacional do Cinema, Ancine); and the Ministry of Science, Technology, Innovations and Communications.
- Promote an independent decision-making process by the regulator while reforming personal liability regimes for public servants.
- Establish an independent oversight body to review the regulatory impact assessments of different institutions.
- Reform the legal framework to introduce a simple class-licensing regime for communication and broadcasting services.
- Enhance co-ordination among federal, state and municipal levels to promote broadband deployment, particularly in underserved areas.

- Upscale co-operation among the National Consumer Secretariat (Secretaria Nacional do Consumidor, Senacon), the consumer's protection and defence programmes (Procons) and Anatel on consumer protection regulations.
- Strengthen Anatel's enforcement framework based on quantitative evidence and targets.
- Merge sectoral funds into a single fund to support further development of the digital economy; consider abolishing all sectoral contributions in the long run.
- Further increase backhaul and backbone connectivity and promote open wholesale access models.
- Foster the Internet of Things (IoT) by abolishing fees (e.g. Telecommunications Oversight Fund) and establishing a separate IoT numbering plan.
- Consider removing the legal restrictions on foreign direct investment in broadcasting.
- Carefully design the upcoming 5G auction as to ensure competition in the market.
- Implement the recommendations of the OECD *Peer Review of Competition Law and Policy in Brazil* (OECD, 2019b), in relation to the assessment of market dominance.
- Design an integrated and overarching public policy vision for broadcasting, pay TV and emerging over-the-top services/video on demand.
- Improve the evidence base on broadcasting and communication services.

Use

Closing the digital divide

As explored in Chapter 3, Brazil has made significant progress in improving access to the Internet in recent years. In 2018, 72% of the population aged 16-74 was connected to the Internet, up from 50% in 2013. Despite rapid progress, 23% of the adult population has never used the Internet (CGI.br, 2019). Furthermore, the ability to use digital technologies effectively differs among individuals according to age, income and education.

While the digital transformation provides opportunities to foster inclusive growth, there is also a risk that the digital divide may add to the social divide, thus deepening social exclusion.

In Brazil, policies for digital inclusion have focused on bringing the Internet to remote areas and isolated communities. While Internet access should remain a priority, Brazil should put in place a wider set of policies to upgrade digital skills and address the digital divide:

- Raise awareness on the benefits of Internet use among all people.
- Develop content, services and applications that meet the needs of those with low digital uptake, e.g. low-educated, low-income and elderly people.
- Offer large-scale online courses on Internet safety and security, online banking, access to digital government services, e-commerce, content creation.
- Increase the role of telecentres as training providers, particularly in rural and remote areas, and ensure adequate funding and technical assistance from the federal government.
- Scale up the National Digital Inclusion Agent Training programme and the Computes for Inclusion programme, in co-operation with the private sector.
- Regularly monitor and evaluate the Connected Education programme.
- Implement the new Common Curriculum Guidelines across the country, by adapting textbooks, training teachers and aligning performance assessments in schools.

Fostering digital uptake in firms

Chapter 3 also showed that despite almost universal access to the Internet, Brazilian enterprises lag behind those in OECD countries in their use of digital technologies, the gap being particularly wide for micro-enterprises, which account for the large majority of firms. E-commerce is growing but some structural problems, such as low financial inclusion, poor transport infrastructures, low competition in the parcel delivery market and different tax regimes among states, hinder its development.

While advanced manufacturing and the IoT is a key strategic objective for the government, the share of Brazilian manufacturing firms using Industry 4.0 technologies remains lower than the OECD average. Lack of skills in the workforce hinders the digital transformation, with ICT professionals being the occupational category with the second most largest shortage in Brazil in 2018 (OECD, 2018a).

Brazil is stepping up support for the diffusion of digital technologies across the economy. The Brazilian Economic Development Bank (Banco Nacional de Desenvolvimento Econômico e Social, BNDES) and the Brazilian Agency for Innovation and Research (Financiadora de Estudos e Projetos, FINEP) are increasingly supporting investments in digital technologies. The Brazil More programme aims at fostering productivity in firms, including through digital technologies. The National Service for Industrial Apprenticeship provides training and consulting activities for Industry 4.0.

While continuing these programmes, Brazil should also:

- Run awareness-raising campaigns on the benefits of the Internet and digital technologies, targeting in particular micro-enterprises.
- Introduce incentives for firms to use online services, such as e-procurement.
- Take measures to foster greater competition in the parcel delivery market.
- Remove regulatory barriers to the development of e-commerce business models, such as multichannel models.
- Harmonise the rate of the tax on goods and services (ICMS) across states as a first step towards a federal value-added tax system.
- Improve co-ordination among programmes supporting digital uptake by firms; create a single portal where firms can access all information about these programmes.
- Introduce tax incentives for technological upgrade, training and ICT investments for all firms, irrespective of their sector and size.
- Facilitate the formal recognition of skills acquired in online courses and vocational training, through partnerships with vocational education institutions, companies or other entities.
- Increase funding for scholarships for students in science, technology, engineering, and mathematics (STEM) as well as PhD candidates in engineering, natural sciences and ICTs, in co-operation with businesses.

Pushing ahead with the digital transformation of the government

Chapter 3 also demonstrated that the digital transformation of government is a priority for Brazil, which is striving to make the administration more efficient and citizen-friendly. In 2016, the former Ministry of Planning (currently the Ministry of Economy) established the Digital Governance Strategy.

Brazil should push forward with the recommendations of the *OECD Digital Government Review of Brazil: Towards the Digital Transformation of the Public Sector* (OECD, 2018b). In particular:

- Continue reinforcing the responsibilities and resources of the Secretariat of Digital Government.
- Increase co-ordination and build synergies between the Digital Governance Strategy and E-Digital.
- Continue prioritising digital skills development in any policy or framework for the public sector.
- Continue enhancing interoperability among the public administration's systems.
- Advance the new legislation on the sharing of personal data among government bodies, initiated by the Data Sharing Decree (Decree 10.046/2019).
- Reinforce public efforts for the development of a digital identity framework.
- Speed up the establishment of the National System of National Digital Signature and Identification System.
- Reinforce efforts to develop a data-driven digital government.
- Update the digital government legal and regulatory framework so as to seize the opportunities of emerging technologies.

Trust

Fostering digital security

As discussed in Chapter 4, digital security incidents are on the rise in Brazil, but many firms lack contingency plans or budgets to deal with them (Marsh, 2019). To address this issue, Brazil is developing a broad digital security framework, starting with the adoption of its first National Cybersecurity Strategy. The strategy puts forward a vision for Brazil "to become a country of excellence in cybersecurity". Its objectives are to make Brazil more prosperous and reliable in the digital environment; increase Brazilian resilience to digital security threats; and strengthen Brazilian performance in cybersecurity in the international sphere.

The National Cybersecurity Strategy is clearly a step in the right direction. However, in order to achieve its objectives, a broader set of economic and social initiatives are necessary. In particular, Brazil should:

- Create a wide community of digital security leaders in the public and private sectors, academia, and civil society to implement the National Cybersecurity Strategy.
- Develop tools to evaluate the implementation of the strategy, assess progress and revise objectives accordingly.
- Significantly increase the budget for the implementation of the National Cybersecurity Strategy, setting clear and measurable milestones.
- Foster a decentralised approach to digital security governance, with ministries and agencies leading in their area of competence and the GSI/PR as a co-ordinator, by strengthening digital security expertise in government.
- Undertake awareness-raising campaigns among businesses, individuals and within government.
- Strengthen digital security training and education programmes at all levels; establish a national register of digital security trainers; encourage students to pursue carriers in digital security.
- Strengthen multi-stakeholder dialogue about digital security, building on the Brazilian Internet governance (CGI) model.

Enhancing trust through greater privacy

Chapter 4 also noted that Brazil passed the General Data Protection Law (LGDP) on 14 August 2018. The law creates a normative framework seeking to harmonise and expand the right to personal data protection. The law is largely aligned with the 2013 update of the OECD *Recommendation of the Council concerning Guidelines Governing the Protection of Privacy and Transborder Flows of Personal Data* (OECD, 2013), although some important differences remain, notably in relation to the governance and oversight structures. In particular, the guidelines call on OECD countries to establish and maintain privacy enforcement authorities with the governance, resources and technical expertise necessary to exercise their powers effectively and to take decisions on an "objective, impartial and consistent basis".

In order to enhance privacy, Brazil should:

- Re-evaluate and amend the conditions establishing the National Data Protection Authority (ANPD) in Article 55-A of Law 13.709 to ensure that the Authority operates with full independence from the date of its establishment.
- Ensure that the rules for appointing the ANPD's Board of Directors and the National Council for the Protection of Personal Data (CNPDP) are transparent, fair and based on technical expertise.
- Clarify the responsibilities and tasks of the CNPDP.
- Set clear rules for decision making within the ANPD and for their implementation by the Board of Directors.
- Guarantee an adequate and predictable budget to the ANPD through a transparent process.
- Align the National Strategy on Artificial Intelligence to the General Data Protection Law and other relevant legal frameworks, in co-operation with all stakeholders.

Protecting digital consumers

Chapter 4 also showed that while business-to-consumer (B2C) e-commerce sales are relatively small, Brazil's e-commerce market seems to offer outstanding opportunities for online retailers at local, regional and global levels. Available data show that 23% of Brazilian consumers shop on US-based websites compared to 9% of European consumers. Half of the Brazilian population, or about 100 million people, has purchased through international websites at least once (Société Générale, 2019).

Brazil has taken significant steps over the last decade to strengthen consumer trust in e-commerce. In 2014, the Civil Rights Framework for the Internet (Marco Civil da Internet) provided the foundational principles, guarantees, rights and obligations for Internet users in Brazil. In 2017, Law 13.543/2017 strengthened the rules of online advertising of goods and services sold through e-commerce.

To continue strengthening the protection of digital consumers, Brazil should further the implementation of the OECD *Recommendation of the Council on Consumer Protection in E-Commerce* (OECD, 2016a). In particular:

- Establish a framework for analysing consumer complaints data and identifying issues that require policy and enforcement responses.
- Collect and analyse consumer complaints specific to cross-border transactions in order to better understand the nature and scale of consumer issues associated with these transactions.
- Provide relevant domestic authorities, such as Senacon, with adequate powers, tools and resources to enhance their participation in cross-border co-operation for consumer protection, including the International Consumer Protection and Enforcement Network.
- Improve the effectiveness of the government's dispute resolution and redress platform, Consumidor.gov.br, by evaluating consumer usage and satisfaction and looking into unresolved cases.

Innovation

Unleashing digital innovation

As explored in Chapter 5, Brazil has made significant progress over the past decades in modernising its policies and institutions to support research and development (R&D) and innovation. R&D expenditures relative to gross domestic product are above Latin American and Caribbean countries, but still behind OECD countries. Furthermore, Brazil's R&D business expenditures account for a smaller share of total R&D, particularly in the ICT sector.

Low human capital, particularly in science, engineering and ICTs, is a major bottleneck in the innovation system. There is also a gap between basic and applied research, while collaboration between enterprises and academia remains limited. Although public support to business R&D has increased in recent years, young and small firms have limited access to it.

The main support to R&D in the ICT sector – the Informatics Law – has contributed to increase manufacturing production and employment. However, the policy does not seem to have achieved its objective to spur innovation and productivity.

Following the adoption of the E-digital Strategy and the National IoT plan, Brazil has been experimenting with new instruments and institutions to support key digital technologies. These include the "Technology Bonus and Grants in Advanced Manufacture" by the National Council for Scientific and Technological Development (Conselho Nacional de Desenvolvimento Científico e Tecnológico, CNPq), as well as several programmes for IoT or advanced manufacturing by BNDES, FINEP and the Brazilian Company for Research and Industrial Innovation (Empresa Brasileira de Pesquisa e Inovação Industrial, EMBRAPII). The National AI Strategy is also set to promote high public-private co-operation around key national challenges. While extremely useful, these initiatives remain limited in number and volume of funding.

Brazil hosts one of the most active high-tech entrepreneurial communities in Latin America, mostly active in professional services, ICTs and finance. The proposal for a legal framework for start-ups and innovative enterprises aims to overcome some obstacles for start-ups arising from administrative procedures, rigid labour regulations and a complex web of state and federal level taxes.

To strengthen digital innovation, Brazil should:

- Orient public support to digital innovation towards mission-oriented research, building on the model of the National IoT Plan.
- Ensure adequate, stable and predictable public resources for research in ICTs.
- Develop clear roadmaps for advancement in key digital technologies, such as artificial intelligence and data analytics, in co-ordination with sectoral ministries and private stakeholders.
- Build capacity in the public sector to procure high-tech innovative solutions, borrowing expertise from businesses and institutions, such as BNDES.
- Increase legal guarantees for public servants contracting procurement for innovation.
- Open e-procurement to innovative solutions from start-ups.
- Increase knowledge transfer from business to academia, for example through higher business participation in technology transfer offices and in teaching.
- Consider introducing cash-refund or carry-forward provisions to make the Good Law more suitable for young innovative firms.
- Reform the Informatics Law so as to strengthen its support to innovation.
- Increase co-ordination among FINEP, BNDES and EMBRAPII on innovation projects.
- Increase funding to EMBRAPII, for example by increasing compulsory funding from the Informatics Law to priority projects for innovation.
- Strengthen innovation hubs for experimentation and technological transfer to small and medium-sized enterprises (SMEs), e.g. EMBRAPII units as testbeds for digital technologies.
- Strengthen public-private partnerships for the advancement of artificial intelligence in a trustworthy way, ensuring participation by SMEs and start-ups.
- Strengthen programmes for start-ups targeting female entrepreneurship.

Fostering the digital transformation of the economy

As discussed in Chapter 6, digital transformation is reshaping established markets and creating new ones. With E-Digital, Brazil has developed an encompassing strategy for digital transformation, highlighting its core enablers and the emergence of new, data-driven business models in agriculture, industry and services.

While promising initiatives are under way in some of these areas, Brazil's capability to seize the opportunities and face the challenges arising from the digital transformation will require predictable and co-ordinated efforts by all government entities in close co-ordination with the private sector. Furthermore, policy makers need to focus on rules that are flexible enough to accommodate changing business models and sectoral boundaries.

Brazil should take specific policy actions in the following sectors, which are a priority in its policy agenda.

Agribusiness

- Foster a national innovation network and testbed environment for agribusiness through stronger synergies between public and private sector research.
- Develop an inclusive framework for agricultural data governance through multi-stakeholder institutions, like the Brazilian Commission of Precision Agriculture (CBAP) or the Agro 4.0 Chamber.
- Promote technical assistance and extension services, e.g. through mobile applications, with a focus on smallholders and farmers in remote areas.
- Ensure that drone regulation remains up to date through continuous co-ordination between the regulator and the private sector, e.g. through the Agro 4.0 Chamber.
- Further support the development of digital solutions for climate-smart agriculture, by scaling-up initiatives like the IoT pilot programme.
- Align the National IoT Plan and the Strategic Agenda for Precision Agriculture. Clarify the roles and responsibilities of the National IoT Chamber, the Agro 4.0 Chamber and the CBAP.

Manufacturing

- Enhance adoption of foreign technology with a long-term commitment to reduce tariffs on ICTs and capital goods.
- Enhance access to imported services by reducing the special tax on royalties and administrative and technical services provided by non-residents (CIDE).
- Reduce uncertainty about taxation of goods and services arising from new business models enabled by digitalisation, e.g. by introducing a single tax scheme on both goods and services (GST).
- Scale-up programmes connecting manufacturing firms to innovative start-ups, SMEs and service providers.
- Strengthen governance and co-ordination mechanisms to ensure that Industry 4.0 policies are well aligned and have sufficient scale.
- Include energy efficiency among the objectives of the Industry 4.0 Strategy.

Fintech

- Create a level playing field for new payment institutions by leveraging the Instant Payment initiative.
- Foster competition in the payment card market by investigating and sanctioning anticompetitive behaviour.
- Enhance competition in the credit market by implementing the Open Banking initiative and strengthening regulations about data protection, data security and banking liabilities.
- Consider enhancing the use of credit guarantee schemes to foster financial access for SMEs and start-ups.
- Enhance co-ordination among different financial regulators and better align regulation with regard to the emerging sandbox environments or cryptocurrencies.
- Establish a regulatory one-stop shop for Fintech companies to reduce uncertainty for Fintech companies crossing traditional market boundaries.

e-Health

- Validate and scale up Brazil's e-Health programme – Connect SUS – across all regions.
- Enhance interoperability and co-ordination between public and private health systems, leveraging the Health 4.0 Chamber.
- Update the regulatory framework for healthcare data protection and information security in both public and private facilities. Provide medical staff and hospitals with guidance on how to develop and implement information security policies.
- Foster the creation and use of digital health identities in line with the OECD *Recommendation of the Council on Health Data Governance*.
- Engage all stakeholders in regulatory reform that enables the use of telemedicine as a substitute for face-to-face consultations.
- Promote new regulation in emerging areas, such as nanotechnology-based drugs and software as a medical device.

Building a whole-of-government approach

The digital transformation affects different parts of the economy and society in complex and interrelated ways, making trade-offs between public policy objectives difficult to navigate. Leveraging the benefits and addressing the challenges of digital transformation requires co-ordination across all of the policy domains identified in the OECD Going Digital Integrated Policy Framework (Figure 7.1). It also requires consideration of transversal policy issues – e.g. skills, digital government and data governance – that cut across several of the framework's policy dimensions (OECD, 2019a). Therefore, the policy recommendations made in Section 7.1 do not stand in isolation, but need to be co-ordinated in a whole-of-government approach.

Co-ordination implies involving a wide range of actors in multiple parts and at different levels of government, as well as non-governmental stakeholders and international partners. A whole-of-government approach, however, may prove challenging. For example, high transaction costs, power and information asymmetries, and different governance approaches across levels of government can make co-ordination and negotiations cumbersome.

While well-designed governance is fundamental for effective co-ordination, there is no one-size-fits-all approach. Different approaches can reflect, for example, variations in countries' institutions, government organisation, or administrative culture and capacity. In addition, governance arrangements are likely to evolve over time, for example with changes in government, technological progress and shifts in the constellation of actors driving the digital transformation.

This section examines the current co-ordination mechanism of Brazil's digital strategy and makes recommendations to help ensure a coherent and cohesive whole-of-government approach to policies for digital transformation.

Strengthening the role of CITDigital

In March 2018, with the same decree issuing the Brazilian Digital Transformation Strategy: E-Digital (Decree 9.319/2018), Brazil established an Inter-ministerial Committee for Digital Transformation (CITDigital). CITDigital is mandated to:

- Support with evidence the policies undertaken by different bodies and public entities in relation to digitalisation.
- Promote synergies among these policies and their coherence with E-Digital.
- Promote information sharing and undertake impact analyses on sectoral initiatives related to digitalisation.
- Monitor and evaluate periodically the results of E-Digital based on a set of pre-defined targets and indicators.
- Co-operate with similar bodies in other countries, the states, the Federal District and the municipalities.
- Propose to the competent bodies the adoption of measures and norms to implement the strategic actions defined by E-Digital.

CITDigital is chaired by the Government Secretariat of the Presidency of the Republic and is composed of representatives (up to three) from: the Ministry of Foreign Affairs; the Ministry of the Economy; the Ministry of Education; the Ministry of Science, Technology, Innovations and Communications; and the Institutional Security Office of the Presidency of the Republic (Decree 9.804/2019).

Other public or private entities, as well as representatives of the legislature and the judiciary, may be invited to participate in meetings and activities of CITDigital, in accordance with its bylaws.

CITDigital's meetings are convened by its chair. Decisions are taken by simple majority of its members, with the chair having a casting vote.

The establishment of CITDigial has been a key step towards a whole-of-government approach to the digital transformation. The committee has helped to articulate and co-ordinate policy programmes across government institutions under the strategic actions set by E-Digital.

The chairmanship by the Government Secretariat of the Presidency of the Republic provides the committee with strong political leverage. The participation of the Ministry of Economy, which has taken up the portfolios of several former ministries, enhances the committee's capability to take decisions and to improve co-ordination with the government.

The legal effects of the decisions taken by CITDigital, however, remain unclear. Approved by a simple majority of the institutions sitting on the committee, they do not seem binding for those having voted against them. The effects on ministries not represented in the committee is even more problematic.

More fundamentally, there does not seem to be any predefined path through which a decision by CITDigital feeds into the regular policy-making process. As the committee is chaired by the Government

Secretariat of the Presidency of the Republic, there may be an expectation that its decisions would lead to some policy initiative by the government. However, there is not any formal or implicit mechanism for this outcome.

It would be useful to define such a mechanism, for instance by providing that decisions by CITDigital should lead to a law proposal by the Presidency of the Republic. The Government Secretariat of the Presidency of the Republic may be given the responsibility to draft the law proposal within a set period. Similarly, it would be useful to link CITDigital's proposals to the legislative process in the National Congress, in particular to the work of its standing committees.

In order to ensure sufficient support for the above process, a qualified majority for decision taking by CITDigital may also be required.

Increasing resources for the digital strategy

The aim of E-Digital is to harmonise the federal government's initiatives related to the digital transformation in order to harness the potential of digital technologies to promote sustainable and inclusive growth and increase competitiveness, productivity and employment.

E-Digital has made it possible to bring existing policy programmes under a common umbrella, e.g. the IoT Chamber, and has provided a forum where governmental and private stakeholders can develop together new initiatives, for example the proposal for a Legal Framework of Innovative Start-ups and Entrepreneurship currently open for public consultation. Most policy initiatives developed under the E-Digital umbrella have been of a regulatory nature, e.g. the regulatory sandbox established by the Securities and Exchange Commission, or have relied on resources that were already allocated for that purpose, e.g. Connected Education Program (Programa Educação Conectada).

Indeed, the budgetary law does not provide for any specific appropriation for the digital strategy. The strategic actions are projects under the responsibility of different ministries and government agencies, which already have specific budget allocations. So far, the digital strategy does not seem to have been able to shift policy priorities and resources to new programmes.

In 2019, ICT expenditures (USD 1.86 billion) accounted for as little as 0.23% of the federal fiscal and social security budget (Law 13.808/2019). This figure includes all expenditures on ICTs for the functioning of the public administration as well as for the implementation of policy programmes. It does not include expenditures for complementary policies, e.g. ICT-related education and training, nor ICT expenditures by the states and municipalities.[1]

The share of the federal and social security budget *planned* for ICT expenditures in 2019 is in line with the average of the period 2013-18 (0.22%). However, the share of *committed* expenditures on ICTs decreased from 0.40% in 2013 to 0.34% in 2018 (Figure 7.2).

Figure 7.2. ICT expenditures in the federal and social security budget in Brazil, 2013-19

As a percentage of the total budget

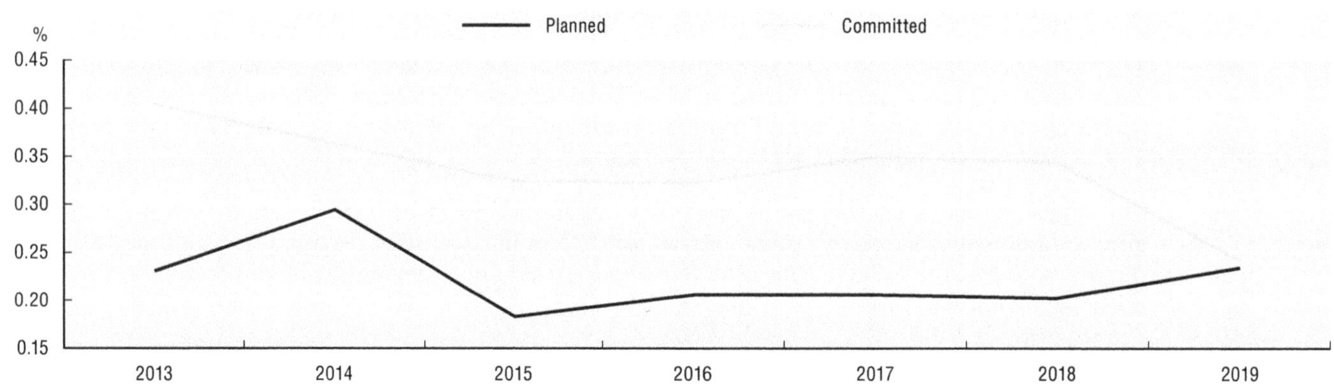

Source: OECD, based on SIOP (2020), *Sistema Integrado de Planejamento e Orçamento* (database), *https://www.siop.planejamento.gov.br/siop* (accessed on 4 May 2020).

Expenditures for the own functioning of the federal government and social security (*programas de gestão e manutenção*) account for 73% of all planned ICT expenditures in the 2019 budget, while only the remaining 27% is allocated to policy programmes (*programas temáticos*) (Figure 7.3).

Figure 7.3. Planned ICT expenditures in Brazil by type of programme, 2019

As a percentage of all planned ICT expenditures

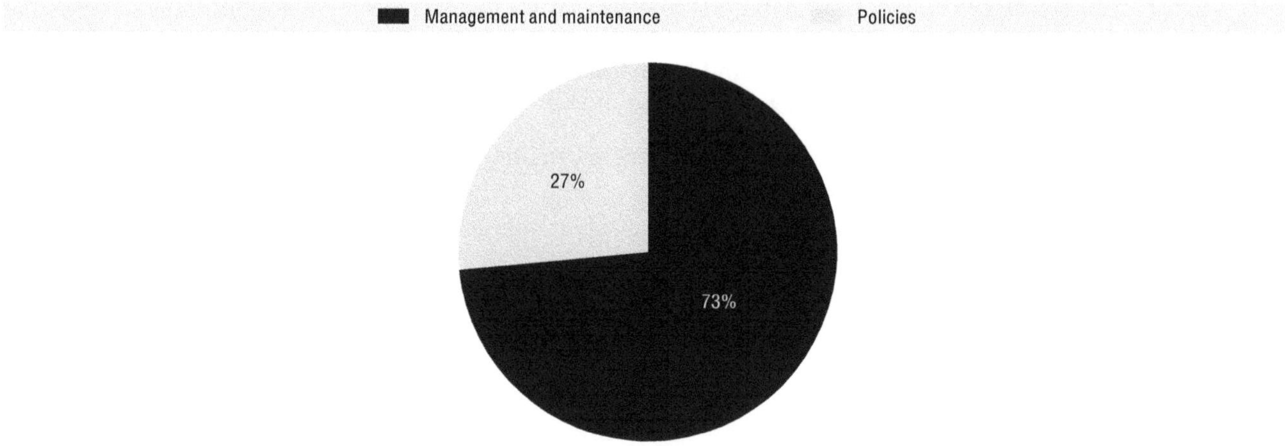

Source: OECD, based on Congresso National (2018), "Exercício financeiro de 2019, projeto de Lei N° 27, de 2018, Volume I, Quadro 13, Despesas com tecnologia da informação", *https://www.camara.leg.br/internet/comissao/index/mista/orca/orcamento/OR2019/red_final/Volume_I.pdf* (accessed on 26 September 2019).

ICT expenditures are allocated to 71 of the 125 programmes set in the federal budget. Five programmes account for 52% of all ICT expenditures planned in 2019: 1) management of the Ministry of Economy (24%); 2) social security (8%); 3) management of the Ministry of Health (8%); 4) management of the electoral process (7%); and 5) economic and financial policies (4%) (Figure 7.4).

Figure 7.4. Planned ICT expenditures in Brazil by programme, 2019

As a percentage of all planned ICT expenditures

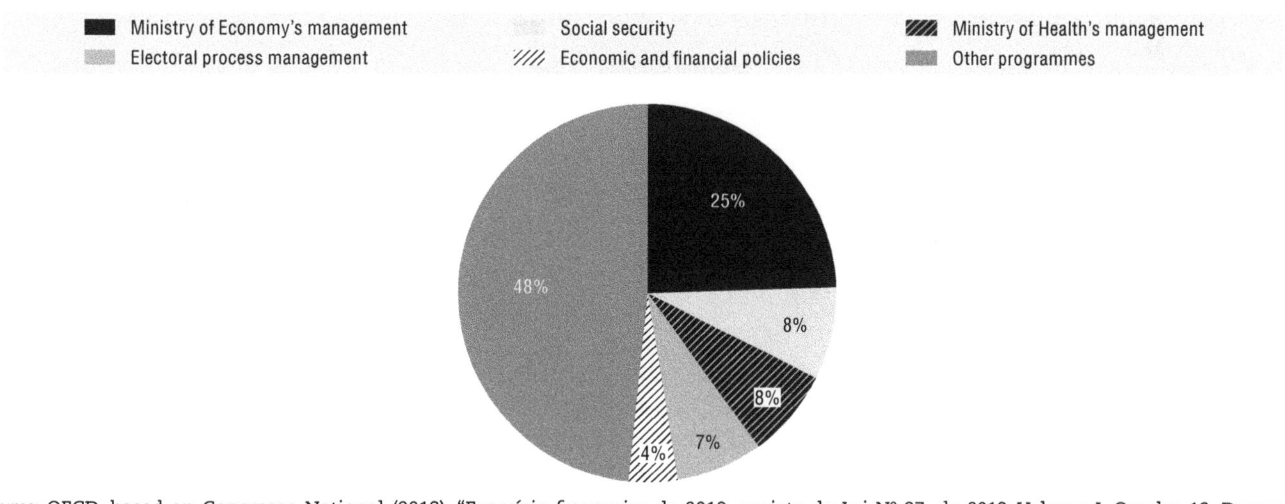

Source: OECD, based on Congresso National (2018), "Exercício financeiro de 2019, projeto de Lei N° 27, de 2018, Volume I, Quadro 13, Despesas com tecnologia da informação", *https://www.camara.leg.br/internet/comissao/index/mista/orca/orcamento/OR2019/red_final/Volume_I.pdf* (accessed on 26 September 2019).

The remaining 48% of ICT expenditures is scattered among 66 small-scale programmes. For instance, the Quality Education for All programme (Educação de Qualidade para Todos) accounts for only 2.5% of all ICT expenditures; urban mobility for 1.2%; administrative simplification for businesses and citizens (Bem Mais Simple Brazil), risk and disaster management as well as development of industry, trade and services for 0.1% each.

Overall, the level of resources allocated to ICTs seems low and largely focused on the back-office of the federal government and social security. Increasing the efficiency of the public administration and improving the quality of its services is, indeed, a very relevant objective, particularly because 40-50% of public employees are foreseen to retire in the forthcoming 4-5 years (Guedes, 2019). In addition, ICT expenditures in the government tend to have positive spillovers on digital adoption by businesses and individuals (OECD, 2016b).

Nonetheless, as argued throughout this report, other policies are equally important for the digital transformation. These include, among others, policies to improve access to broadband, support the adoption and use by individuals and businesses, foster digital skills, promote innovation as well as enhance security and trust in a digital environment.

For Brazil to engage further in the digital transformation, its digital strategy should be supported by an adequate level of resources.

References

CGI.br (2019), *ICT Households 2018: Survey on the Use of Information and Communication Technologies in Brazilian Households*, Comitê Gestor da Internet no Brasil, São Paulo,*https://cetic.br/en/publicacao/pesquisa-sobre-o-uso-das-tecnologias-de-informacao-e-comunicacao-nos-domicilios-brasileiros-tic-domicilios-2018/.*

Congresso National (2018), "Exercício financeiro de 2019, projeto de Lei N° 27, de 2018, Volume I, Quadro 13, Despesas com tecnologia da informação" [Financial year 2019, Bill No. 27, 2018, Volume I, Table 13, Expenses with information technology], *https://www.camara.leg.br/internet/comissao/index/mista/orca/orcamento/OR2019/red_final/Volume_I.pdf* (accessed on 26 September 2019).

Guedes, P. (2019), *The Latest on Brazil's Economic Reforms: A Conversation With Economy Minister Paulo Guedes*, The Brookings Institution, Washington, DC, *https://www.brookings.edu/wp-content/uploads/2019/04/es_20190411_brazil_guedes_transcript.pdf* (accessed on 27 September 2019).

Marsh (2019), *Global Cyber Risk Perception Survey Report 2019*, Marsh & McLennan Companies, *https://www.marsh.com/us/insights/research/marsh-microsoft-cyber-survey-report-2019.html.*

OECD (2019a), *Going Digital: Shaping Policies, Improving Lives*, OECD Publishing, Paris, *https://doi.org/10.1787/9789264312012-en.*

OECD (2019b), *Peer Review of Competition Law and Policy: Brazil 2019*, OECD, Paris, *https://www.oecd.org/competition/oecd-peer-reviews-of-competition-law-and-policy-brazil-2019.htm.*

OECD (2018a), *Getting Skills Right: Brazil*, Getting Skills Right, OECD Publishing, Paris, *https://doi.org/10.1787/9789264309838-en.*

OECD (2018b), *Digital Government Review of Brazil: Towards the Digital Transformation of the Public Sector*, OECD Digital Government Studies, OECD Publishing, Paris, *https://doi.org/10.1787/9789264307636-en.*

OECD (2016a), *Recommendation of the Council on Consumer Protection in E-commerce*, OECD, Paris, *https://legalinstruments.oecd.org/en/instruments/OECD-LEGAL-0422* (accessed on 14 August 2017).

OECD (2016b), "Stimulating digital innovation for growth and inclusiveness: The role of policies for the successful diffusion of ICT", *OECD Digital Economy Papers*, No. 256, OECD Publishing, Paris, *https://doi.org/10.1787/5jlwqvhg3l31-en.*

OECD (2013), *Recommendation of the Council concerning Guidelines Governing the Protection of Privacy and Transborder Flows of Personal Data*, OECD, Paris, *https://legalinstruments.oecd.org/en/instruments/OECD-LEGAL-0188.*

SIOP (2020), *Sistema Integrado de Planejamento e Orçamento* [Integrated Planning and Budgeting System] (database), *https://www.siop.planejamento.gov.br/siop* (accessed on 4 May 2020).

Société Générale (2019), *Brazilian Market: E-commerce*, Société Générale, *https://import-export.societegenerale.fr/en/country/brazil/ecommerce?accepter_cookies=oui* (accessed on 27 January 2020).

Note

1. Some ICT-related expenditures may not be reported as such in the federal fiscal and social security accounting system. The figures, nonetheless, provide a proxy of the resources allocated to ICT and their evolution over time.

List of Figures

List of Tables

List of Boxes

www.ingramcontent.com/pod-product-compliance
Ingram Content Group UK Ltd.
Pitfield, Milton Keynes, MK11 3LW, UK
UKHW051500290926
15471UKWH00008B/1309

9 789264 710788